Trade Liberalization, Competition and the WTO

Trade Liberalization, Competition and the WTO

Edited by

Chris Milner

Professor of International Economics, University of Nottingham, UK

and

Robert Read

Lecturer in International Economics, University of Lancaster, UK

Published in Association with the International Economics Study Group (IESG)

Edward Elgar
Cheltenham, UK • Northampton, MA, USA

Published by
Edward Elgar Publishing Limited
Glensanda House
Montpellier Parade
Cheltenham
Glos GL50 1UA
UK

Edward Elgar Publishing, Inc.
136 West Street
Suite 202
Northampton
Massachusetts 01060
USA

A catalogue record for this book
is available from the British Library

Library of Congress Cataloguing in Publication Data
Trade Liberalization, competition, and the WTO / edited by Chris Milner and Robert Read.
    p. cm.
'Published in association with the International Economics Study Group (IESG).'
Includes bibliographical references and index.
1. Free trade. 2. Foreign trade regulation. 3. Competition, International. 4. World Trade Organization. 5. General Agreement on Tariffs and Trade (Organization) I. Milner, Chris. II. Read, Robert, 1958–   III. International Economics Study Group.

HF1713 .T6948 2002
382'.92—dc21

2002023625

ISBN 1 84064 716 7

Printed and bound in Great Britain by MPG Books Ltd, Bodmin, Cornwall

Contents

List of figures

List of tables

Acknowledgements

The editors would like to express their thanks to John Black for his patient scrutiny and copy-editing of the manuscripts of this book at various stages of its production, and for compiling the index. Any remaining errors, of course, remain the responsibility of the editors.

List of contributors

Derek Bosworth is Professor of Economics at the Manchester School of Management, UMIST, UK.

David Collie is a Research Fellow at Cardiff Business School, UK.

David Evans is Reader in Economics at the Institute of Development Studies, University of Sussex, UK.

Peter Holmes is Jean Monnet Reader in Economics at the University of Sussex, UK.

Sam Laird is in the UNCTAD Secretariat and was formerly a Counsellor in the Trade and Development Division of the WTO, Geneva.

Steve McCorriston is Reader in Economics at the University of Exeter, UK.

Donald MacLaren is an Associate Professor in the Department of Economics, University of Melbourne, Australia.

Chris Milner is Professor of International Economics at the University of Nottingham, UK.

Victor Murinde is Professor of Finance at the University of Birmingham, UK.

Robert Read is Lecturer in International Economics at the University of Lancaster, UK.

Alan M. Rugman is Thames Water Professor of Management at Templeton College, University of Oxford, UK and Professor of International Business, University of Indiana.

Cillian Ryan is Jean Monnet Fellow in Economics at the University of Birmingham, UK.

Rod Tyers is Professor of Economics at the Australian National University.

Deli Yang is Lecturer in Economics at the University of Bradford, UK.

Yongzheng Yang is with the International Monetary Fund, Washington, DC.

List of abbreviations

ACP	African, Caribbean and Pacific Group States (Lomé Convention countries)
AFTA	ASEAN Free Trade Area (Association of South East Asian Nations)
AMS	Aggregate measure of support
ANZCERTA	Australia–New Zealand Trade Area
AoA	Uruguay Round Agreement on Agriculture
APEC	Asia Pacific Economic Cooperation
ATC	WTO Agreement on Textiles and Clothing
AWB	Australian Wheat Board
CACM	Central American Common Market
CAP	Common Agricultural Policy (of the EU)
CARICOM	Caribbean Common Market
CCT	Common Commercial Tariff (of the EU)
CEE	Central and East European (countries)
CES	Constant elasticity of supply
CFA	Communauté Financière Africaine (franc zone)
CGE	Computable general equilibrium (economic model)
CIETAC	China International Economic and Trade Arbitration Commission
CIF	Cost, insurance and freight
CITES	Convention on International Trade in Endangered Species
COMESA	Common Market of East and Southern Africa
CSE	Consumer subsidy equivalent
CTE	WTO Committee on Trade and Environment
CUSTA	Canada–US Free Trade Agreement
CWB	Canadian Wheat Board
DIAC	Draft International Anti-Trust Code
DOM	Département d'Outre Mer (overseas department)
DSB	WTO Dispute Settlement Body
DSM	Dispute settlement mechanism
DSP	WTO dispute settlement procedures
EU	European Union
FDI	Foreign direct investment

FOB	Free-on-board
FTA	Free trade area
FTAA	Free Trade Area of the Americas (proposed)
GAO	US General Accounting Office
GATS	General Agreement on Trade in Services
GATT	General Agreement on Tariffs and Trade
GATT 1947	The original 1947 GATT text
GATT 1994	The revised version of GATT 1947 ratified at Marrakesh, 1994
GCC	Gulf Cooperation Council
GE	General Electric
GPA	WTO Government Procurement Agreement
GSP	Generalized System of Preferences
GTAP	Global trade assistance and protection (economic model)
ICPAC	US International Competition Policy Advisory Committee
ILO	International Labour Organization
IMF	International Monetary Fund
IPRs	Intellectual property rights
ISI	Import-substituting industrialization
ITC	International Trade Centre (UNCTAD and WTO)
ITO	International Trade Organization (proposed)
MAI	Multilateral agreement on investment (proposed)
MDD	McDonnell-Douglas
MFA	Multi-Fibre Arrangement
MFN	Most favoured nation
MITI	Japan's Ministry of International Trade and Industry
MLAT	Multilateral Legal Assistance Treaty
MNE	Multinational enterprise
MRAs	Mutual recognition agreements
NAFTA	North American Free Trade Association
NGOs	Non-governmental organizations
NIC	Newly industrializing country
NTB	Non-tariff barriers
NTMs	Non-tariff measures
OECD	Organization for Economic Cooperation and Development
PREB	Chinese Patent Re-Examination Board
PSE	Producer subsidy equivalent
QRs	Quantitative restrictions
R&D	Research and development
RTA	Regional trade agreement

S&D	Special and Differential Treatment
SACU	Southern African Customs Union
SADC	Southern African Development Community
SADCC	Southern African Development Coordination Conference
SCM	WTO Agreement on Subsidies and Countervailing Measures
SII	US Structural Impediments Initiative
SMEs	Small- and medium-sized enterprises
SPS	WTO Agreement on Sanitary and Phytosanitary Measures
STE	State trading enterprise
TBT	WTO Agreement on Technical Barriers to Trade
TMB	Textiles Monitoring Body
TOM	Territoire d'Outre Mer (overseas territory)
TRIMs	Trade-Related Investment Measures
TRIPs	Trade-Related Intellectual Property Rights
TPRM	WTO Trade Policy Review Mechanism
TRQ	Tariff-rate quota
UAE	United Arab Emirates
UNCTAD	UN Commission for Trade and Development
UNDP	UN Development Programme
USITC	US International Trade Commission
USTR	US Trade Representative
VEPRs	Voluntary export price restraints
VERs	Voluntary export restraints
WIPO	World Intellectual Property Organization
WTO	World Trade Organization

1. Introduction: the GATT Uruguay Round, trade liberalization and the WTO

Chris Milner and Robert Read

The WTO Meeting in Seattle in November 1999 was intended to mark the start of the new Millennium Round of trade negotiations, the first since the completion of the GATT Uruguay Round and the creation of the WTO at Marrakesh in 1994. The primary purpose of the Seattle Ministerial Meeting was to agree upon the agenda for the new trade round over and above the 'built-in' agenda, the agenda for negotiations already agreed in the various Uruguay Round Agreements. The breakdown of the Seattle Meeting was the result of the failure of WTO member countries to agree upon a negotiated agenda for the next round of trade talks within the time available rather than anything to do with the high-profile anti-globalization protests outside. This failure was caused by a number of factors, notably the perception that the leading industrialized countries, particularly the USA and the EU, were setting the negotiation agenda to address their own particular concerns, including competition, foreign direct investment (FDI) and labour standards. Further, many developing-country members were effectively disenfranchised in that they were virtually excluded from the crucial 'Green Room process' in negotiating the agenda and were neither canvassed on their views concerning many issues of critical importance to them nor informed about the decisions taken on their behalf. In spite of the failure of the Seattle Meeting, negotiations based upon the built-in agenda began in 2000. The remaining agenda for the Millennium Round was due to be determined at the next Ministerial Meeting in Doha in November 2001.

The Uruguay Round Agreements concluded in Marrakesh in 1994 had, for the most part, been implemented by 2000. The only exceptions to this were the completion of the planned phasing in of the liberalization of textiles trade, the implementation of some of the developing-country commitments and some unfinished parts of the negotiations that led to commitments in 1997 by some WTO members on services (telecommunications and financial services). It was inevitable therefore that both academic and policy debate should, at the start of the new millennium, turn to international trade policy and WTO agendas. Nevertheless, the ambition and complexity of the Uruguay Round negotiations, as well as the substantial liberalizing potential of its associated Agreements, need to be borne in mind. This applies particularly in terms of their sectoral coverage (agriculture, services, textiles and other manufactures), policy areas (intellectual property rights, government procurement and traditional border measures such as tariffs) and countries, with much greater developing-country involvement than in previous rounds.

This introductory chapter sets the scene for the remainder of the book by providing a brief contextual overview of the multilateral trade liberalization process under GATT, the Uruguay Round and its associated Agreements, the creation of the WTO and the prospects and issues for the forthcoming Millennium Round. This provides a useful background for the analytical approach adopted in the remaining chapters. The nature and implications of the Uruguay Round Agreements as well as the advent and functions of the WTO, however, are well documented and analysed in greater depth elsewhere (see, for example, Schott, 1994; Baldwin, 1995; Martin and Winters, 1996; Trebilcock and Howse, 1999; Hoekman and Kostecki, 2001).

1. THE GATT AND THE MULTILATERAL TRADE LIBERALIZATION PROCESS

The General Agreement on Tariffs and Trade (GATT) was signed on 30 October 1947 and was, in effect, the residual outcome of the more ambitious attempt to create an International Trade Organization (ITO) under the 1947 Havana Charter which was never ratified. The GATT was an intergovernmental agreement rather than an international organization, and therefore not a legal entity in its own right such that member states were referred to as Contracting Parties of the Agreement. The initial GATT was agreed between 23 countries, including 11 developing countries, although three subsequently withdrew. By the end of the Uruguay Round negotiations, the number of GATT Contracting Parties had risen to 117 and membership of the WTO has since climbed steadily to over 140 countries, most recently with China's accession in November 2001.

The objectives of GATT, outlined in the Preamble to the 1947 text, include the conduct of trade to raise living standards, expand the production and exchange of goods by means of the substantial reduction of tariffs and other trade barriers and the elimination of discriminatory treatment (WTO, 1999). At no point does the text mention the attainment of free trade as the overall objective of the GATT (Hoekman and Kostecki, 2001); instead, the emphasis is upon the creation of rules for the fair conduct of trade between countries and the liberalization of international trade.

Key Principles of the GATT

The GATT is founded upon three key principles by means of which it seeks to achieve the objectives outlined above. These are non-discrimination, reciprocity and transparency.

Non-discrimination and the principle of most favoured nation (MFN)

This refers to the equality of treatment in trade matters of all member states under Article I such that all concessions offered by one member apply unconditionally (unilaterally) to all other members – the most favoured nation (MFN) clause. A second element of non-discrimination relates to the concept of national treatment under Article III whereby goods that have been imported and already subjected to border measures, such as tariffs and quotas, are treated in the same manner as domestic goods, for example in respect of liability to excise duties and taxes.

The MFN principle ensures that the beneficiary of a particular tariff negotiation is not disadvantaged by greater concessions subsequently being made to third countries which are also GATT members. This ensures the long-term value of trade concessions obtained in bilateral or multilateral negotiations and extends the process of tariff reduction and trade liberalization to all members through the multilateralization of these concessions. This multilateral approach to the reduction in trade barriers means that non-discrimination under MFN allows comparative advantage to be the principal determinant of trade flows. National treatment ensures that members cannot use discriminatory domestic measures to counteract the impact of the liberalization of border measures.

There are three major exceptions to the principle of MFN and non-discrimination. The first is the provisions under Part IV of the GATT for the more favourable treatment of developing countries on the grounds of their development, trade and financial needs, generally referred to as Special and Differential (S&D) Treatment. S&D was incorporated into the GATT as part of the Tokyo Round (1973–79), building upon the introduction of the Generalized System of Preferences (GSP) in the Kennedy Round (1963–67), under which the industrialized countries granted non-reciprocal tariff preferences to developing countries. The second exception relates to the formation of regional trade agreements (RTAs) which, under Article XXIV, are permitted to discriminate between partners and third countries so long as external protection does not increase. GATT 1994 incorporates a number of important revisions relating to the interpretation of Article XXIV and the measurement of external protection. The final exception to the MFN principle is balance of payment difficulties when emergency (temporary) intervention is permitted. Again, this condition was revised in GATT 1994.

Reciprocity

Reciprocity is a fundamental element of trade negotiations and refers to the application of *quid pro quo* liberalization so as to avoid free-riding by members that are unwilling to make trade concessions. Depending upon the type of negotiations being undertaken, reciprocity may apply specifically to certain product sectors or be more general across-the-board concessions. Reciprocity is also important because any concessions made are applicable to all members on the principle of non-discrimination through the application of MFN.

Transparency

The transparency of members' trade schedules, as required under Article X of the GATT on the Publication and Administration of Trade Regulations, is important for several reasons. In the first place, the publication of tariff schedules and other trade regulations by the customs authorities of member states provides crucial information concerning the structure and magnitude of national trade barriers. Further, under Article XI on the General Elimination of Quantitative Restrictions, tariffs are the only generally permitted method of trade protection leading to the tariffication of most non-tariff barriers. The publication of members' customs schedules therefore facilitates the calculation of tariff equivalents to reveal the extent of *ad valorem* protection. Finally, transparency is also necessary to assess and enforce undertakings by members to liberalize their trade barriers.

The Multilateral Trade Liberalization Process

The importance of the multilateral trade liberalization process needs to be understood in the context of its alternatives and also its implications for achieving global trade liberalization. The general case for trade liberalization is fairly unambiguous in terms of its positive effects upon economic growth, international allocative efficiency, incomes and consumer welfare. The critical issue is therefore not whether trade liberalization should take place but rather how it can be achieved in a fair manner.

The GATT rules for the conduct of trade provide the framework for trade liberalization on a multilateral basis by means of the principles of non-discrimination and reciprocity. Trade liberalization has progressed on the basis of successive rounds of multilateral trade negotiations, the most recent being the Uruguay Round (1986–94), in which *quid pro quo* trade concessions by each member are multilateralized to all members under the MFN principle. Concessions made as a result of bilateral negotiations between the major industrialized countries (the EU, Japan and the USA), usually but not always the leading proponents of liberalization, therefore apply to all other members, regardless of their own bargaining power. The multilateral trade liberalization process is thus of particular benefit to smaller and weaker countries, notably the developing countries, in that it delivers enhanced market access to the major global markets which would otherwise have been virtually impossible to obtain on the basis of bilateral negotiations outside a GATT-type framework.

The alternative, that is bilateral trade liberalization, would mean trade concessions being determined primarily by relative economic and political bargaining power, which would favour the leading industrialized countries above all others. This would result in the virtual exclusion from the international trading system of many small and weaker countries, particularly the developing countries, leading to significant international asymmetries in trade patterns, growth, incomes and consumer welfare. The GATT regulations for the conduct of trade therefore provide a legal basis for the multilateral implementation of trade concessions and so greatly reduce the reliance of developing countries in particular on the bilateral altruism of the major industrialized economies. It is for this reason that many developing countries are already members of the WTO or are keen to accede.

The GATT rules and the current multilateral trade liberalization process are by no means perfect since they suffer from a number of significant shortcomings. Some of these issues were addressed in the Uruguay Round; hence the creation of the WTO, the GATT 1994, the improved dispute settlement procedures and the incorporation of several new agreements. Nevertheless, progress is still necessary in some areas, notably the participation of members in setting the agenda for future multilateral trade negotiations, exemplified by the breakdown of the 1999 Seattle Meeting, and a focus on broader issues such as competition rather than pure trade matters (discussed by Peter Holmes in Chapter 6). In this respect, it is to be hoped that the new WTO Millennium Round will be able to sustain the progress made during the previous Uruguay Round.

2. THE GATT URUGUAY ROUND

The GATT Uruguay Round was the eighth round of multilateral trade negotiations and the third, after the Kennedy and Tokyo Rounds (1963–67 and 1973–79 respectively) which immediately preceded it, to make substantial progress in the liberalization of international trade. The Round began at Punte del Este in Uruguay in 1986 and was finally completed, after some delay, with the signing of the Marrakesh Declaration in April 1994. The Uruguay Round negotiations resulted in a fall in the average tariff on manufactures in industrialized countries from 6.4 to 4.0 per cent, a reduction of 40 per cent compared with an objective of one-third (Hoekman and Kostecki, 2001). The Uruguay Round was the largest trade round to date both in terms of the breadth of its coverage and the number of countries involved, 117 countries at the time of its completion. The Uruguay Round continued the trend begun in the previous Tokyo Round in addressing a broader trade agenda rather than the issues covered specifically by GATT disciplines. The discussions were aimed at improving existing trade measures relating to agriculture (Agreement on Agriculture), textiles (Agreement on Textiles and Clothing) and disputes settlement as well as being extended to include trade in services (General Agreement on Trade in Services – GATS), Trade-Related Intellectual Property Rights (TRIPs) and Trade-Related Investment Measures (TRIMs). The key Agreements of the Uruguay Round are summarized briefly below.

GATT 1994

The GATT 1994 refers to the revised version of the original 1947 GATT text agreed in Marrakesh. GATT 1994 incorporates several important amendments to the original 1947 text, reflecting the outcome of negotiations on issues relating to the interpretation of specific articles. As such, GATT 1994 embodies: the provisions of the original GATT 1947; the provisions which entered into force under GATT 1947 before the date of entry into force of the WTO Agreement (1 January 1995); specific Understandings with respect to several GATT Articles, Obligations and Provisions; and the Marrakesh Protocol to GATT 1994. The principal changes were to Article II (tariff schedules), Article XVII (State Trading Enterprises – STEs), Article XXIV (regional trade agreements – RTAs), Article XXVIII (modification of tariff schedules) and the balance of payments provisions (Articles XII and XVIII).

GATT 1994 was designed to enable the GATT Contracting Parties (member countries) to bypass the need formally to amend the original GATT 1947 and so agree a Single Undertaking applying to all. This means that all new WTO members are only required to sign GATT 1994 as opposed to GATT 1947 together with all of its subsequent amendments. The signing of GATT 1994 and the creation of the WTO separated the institution (WTO) from the set of rules for the conduct of international trade (the GATT).

The Agreement on Agriculture (AoA)

Agriculture has traditionally been a highly protected sector in many industrialized countries, notably in Europe, Japan and the USA, as well as developing countries for reasons of policy and as a strategy for ensuring
domestic food security. Until the advent of the Uruguay Round, little
progress had been made in the liberalization of trade in agricultural products during successive rounds of multilateral trade negotiations. Progress
in the Uruguay Round was the result of pressure from the USA supported
by the Cairns Group, a strong coalition of several large agricultural exporting countries – including Argentina, Australia, Brazil, Canada, Indonesia,
New Zealand, Thailand and Uruguay. The great length of the Uruguay
Round negotiations was partly the result of the slow progress of the agriculture discussions and the reluctance of the EU to agree to substantial cuts
in the Common Agricultural Policy (CAP) budget in particular. Deadlock
was broken by the 1992 Blair House Accord between the EU and the Cairns
Group after the latter cross-linked progress on agriculture to that of other
negotiations of interest to the EU, such as those on services.

The Agreement on Agriculture has 13 parts, of which four are of particular importance: Market Access (Part III); Domestic Support Commitments (Part IV); Export Competition Commitments (Part V); and Sanitary
and Phytosanitary Measures (Part VIII). Article 4 on market access
required tariffication by all countries of their agricultural trade barriers
and reducing them relative to a 1986–88 reference period by an average of
36 per cent for the industrialized countries and 24 per cent for developing
countries by 2000 (Hoekman and Kostecki, 2001). The commitments on
domestic support required a 20 per cent reduction in Aggregate Measures
of Support (AMS) by 2000 relative to the same base period. The commitments on export subsidies required their reduction by between 21 and 36
per cent (14 to 24 per cent for developing countries) by 2000 relative to a
1986–90 base period (Article 9:2). Article 14 of Part VIII is purely agreement to effect the Agreement on the Application of Sanitary and
Phytosanitary Measures, a separate Uruguay Round Agreement.

The Agreement on Textiles and Clothing (ATC)

Before the Uruguay Round, trade negotiations on textiles and clothing were
independent of GATT disciplines and, from 1973, were covered by a separate international agreement, the Multi-Fibre Arrangement (MFA). The
underlying reason for the exclusion of textiles and clothing from GATT and
the creation of the MFA was the susceptibility of the sector in the industrialized countries to import penetration by low-cost labour-intensive exports

from developing countries. The inclusion of negotiations on textiles and clothing in the Uruguay Round was therefore at the behest of many newly industrializing and developing countries and the cross-linking of negotiations with progress on TRIPs and services (see below).

The Agreement on Textiles and Clothing made trade in these goods subject to GATT disciplines, requiring the removal of long-standing quantitative restrictions in the form of quotas and voluntary export restraints (VERs). The phasing-out of the MFA was made a three-stage process starting with the immediate integration into GATT 1994 of some 16 per cent of trade by volume, a further 17 per cent after three years (1997), another 18 per cent after seven years (2001) and complete integration after ten years (2004) (Articles 6 and 8). In addition, Article 14 required import quotas to be increased over and above the 6 per cent per annum under the MFA; by 16 per cent in Stage 1, 1995–97 (that is, by 7 per cent), 25 per cent in Stage 2, 1998–2001 (8.7 per cent) and 27 per cent in Stage 3, 2002–04 (11.05 per cent) (Articles 13 and 14).

The Agreement on Trade-Related Investment Measures (TRIMs)

TRIMs have been a common feature of the domestic regulatory framework affecting inflows of FDI in many countries, particularly developing ones, and encompass a wide variety of incentives and rules for the activities of foreign-owned firms – multinational enterprises (MNEs). They include investment incentives, tax holidays and subsidies as well as limits on foreign equity participation and requirements for the employment of local nationals, local content, exports and foreign exchange generation. Most of these measures are designed to maximize the potential domestic benefits of FDI so as to promote development.

TRIMs were included in the Uruguay Round negotiations because they may have a distortionary impact on trade flows but were subject to some resistance by developing countries because of the perceived threat to their national regulatory control over FDI. Discussions of a separate multilateral agreement on investment (MAI), discussed in Chapter 7 by Alan Rugman, was felt to be a more appropriate forum for TRIMs negotiations. The final TRIMs Agreement is relatively short and simple, primarily emphasizing its consistency with GATT disciplines, particularly Articles III (National Treatment) and XI (Elimination of Quantitative Restrictions), and imposing a timetable for the phasing out of prohibited measures (Article 5:2).

Other Multilateral Agreements on Trade in Goods

The Uruguay Round Agreement incorporates several other multilateral agreements on trade in goods in addition to those already outlined above. The Agreement on the Application of Sanitary and Phytosanitary Measures covers safety requirements for products for human or animal consumption. The Agreement on Technical Barriers to Trade covers technical regulations, standards, testing and certification. The Agreements on the Implementation of GATT 1994 Articles VI and VII cover subsidies/countervailing duties and customs valuation respectively. The Agreement on Preshipment Inspection covers the verification of quality, price and customs classification of goods. The Agreements on Rules of Origin, Import Licensing Procedures, Subsidies and Countervailing Measures and Safeguards are self-explanatory.

The General Agreement on Trade in Services (GATS)

The General Agreement on Trade in Services (GATS) was the most ambitious feature of the Uruguay Round negotiations, and certainly one of its most important outcomes, in creating a multilateral framework covering the regulation of trade in services equivalent to that of the GATT for trade in goods. Trade in services applies to a wide range of economic activities not covered by the GATT, including insurance, finance and banking, advertising, telecommunications, construction, transport and computer and data-processing services. The Uruguay Round discussions of GATS were initiated by the USA but their objective of a 'hard' agreement fell foul of domestic lobbying. The EU and Japan sustained the pressure for a 'soft' agreement in spite of significant resistance from developing countries. The primary reason for this opposition is that the industrialized countries have a strong comparative advantage in many services, because they are intensive in the use of technology and human capital, and dominate global trade. Nevertheless, many developing countries can be expected to gain significantly from trade liberalization in services under the GATS. This is because some are labour-intensive, notably data-processing, but also because they are intermediate inputs in the production of other goods and services and so have positive multiplier effects on the competitiveness of other sectors.

Services are distinct from goods in that they are very often intangible and impossible to store such that their production and consumption is often simultaneous. This affects their physical delivery and has important implications for trade and associated factor movements. In addition, these characteristics mean that trade in services is difficult to measure, monitor and tax and also subject to a wide range of non-tariff restrictions. The key elements of the GATS are Scope and Definition (Part I), General Obligations and Disciplines (Part II) and Specific Commitments (Part III). The scope and definition of the GATS are outlined in Article I and adopt the modality approach to the supply of services according to the necessary mobility of producers and consumers.

- Mode 1: Cross-border trade, that is, physical proximity is inessential and so does not require the physical movement of supplier or consumer.
- Mode 2: An immobile service provider and a mobile consumer, that is, physical proximity is necessary in the location of the supplier (for example specialist hospital medical treatment).
- Mode 3: A mobile service provider and an immobile consumer, that is, physical proximity is necessary and requires the commercial presence of the supplier (for example construction).
- Mode 4: A mobile service provider and a mobile consumer, that is, physical proximity is necessary and requires the temporary movement of natural persons.

The general obligations and disciplines in Part II provide a core framework for the GATS similar to that of the GATT, most importantly MFN treatment (Article II), although an annexe allows members to list any exemptions. The key specific commitments under Part III are Market Access (Article XVI) and National Treatment (Article XVII); the former identifies six types of restrictions on the right of establishment which are prohibited in principle (XVI:2), while the latter ensures no less favourable treatment than national service suppliers as revealed by its effects on the competitiveness of foreign suppliers (XVII:3). Several service sectors were specifically excluded from the GATS, and included in the annexes, where agreement had not been reached by the end of the Uruguay Round negotiations – the movement of people, air transport, financial services, maritime transport and telecommunications. With the exception of air transport, these negotiations were restarted after Marrakesh although only financial services and basic telecommunications have been concluded successfully.

The Agreement on Trade-Related Intellectual Property Rights (TRIPs)

Intellectual property rights (IPRs) were included in the Uruguay Round negotiations at the instigation of the industrialized countries and, like services, were opposed by many developing countries. The intention of TRIPs was to protect international trade in IPRs, so complementing the role of the World Intellectual Property Organization (WIPO) in enforcing IPRs within countries. The primary justification for TRIPs is therefore the legal protection of the international income streams accruing to R&D and the creation of knowledge rather than the liberalization of trade. The TRIPs Agreement was therefore designed to tackle both counterfeiting and increasing trade in IPRs, much of it associated with the growth of FDI and the accompanying flows of technology and information. Many developing countries feared larger outflows of fees and royalties to the industrialized countries coupled with higher IPR prices (monopoly rents) for products such as pharmaceuticals. The success of the TRIPs negotiations in setting minimum IPR standards owed much to the cross-linking of the issue with developing-country demands for progress on the Agreement on Textiles and Clothing (discussed above).

The TRIPs Agreement applies the basic GATT principles to IPRs, with allowances for existing international conventions (Part I), and outlines the standards concerning the availability, scope and use of IPRs (Part II). These standards are applied to Copyright (Section 1), Trademarks (Section 2), Geographical Indications (Section 3), Industrial Designs (Section 4), Patents (Section 5), Lay-Out Designs of Integrated Circuits (Section 6), Undisclosed Information (Section 7) and Anti-Competitive Practices in Contractual Licences (Section 8).

Understanding on Rules and Procedures Governing the Settlement of Disputes

The enforcement of the GATT 1947 relied upon a consensus approach to dispute settlement that required the disputing parties to accept and adopt the findings of GATT panels. The consensus approach was subject to extensive criticism, particularly in cases where parties vetoed the findings of a GATT panel, for example the EU regarding bananas, although the system had a success rate above 90 per cent (Hudec, 1993). Pressure for reform of the disputes procedures, however, grew during the 1980s, as non-adoption increased significantly primarily because of the lack of clarity of the GATT rules in certain areas (Hoekman and Kostecki, 2001).

The new WTO dispute settlement procedures (DSP), contained in a separate Understanding (Annex 2), are viewed as being one of the major achievements of the Uruguay Round in that it was made applicable to all of the associated Agreements (Appendix 1). The new DSP dropped the unanimity requirement and introduced new rules concerning the panels (Articles 6, 7, 8, 11 and 12), a strict timetable for consultations, panel reports and responses (Articles 4, 5, 12, 16 and 20) as well as creating a new Appellate Body (Article 17), clear rules on compensation and suspension of concessions (Article 22) and arbitration (Article 25). Differences in the enforceability of the GATT and WTO DSPs are highlighted by the banana case (see Chapter 11). The performance of the new DSP is reviewed by Hudec (1999).

Other Agreements and Understandings

The Uruguay Round Agreement also included a new Trade Policy Review Mechanism (TPRM) (Annex 3), four Plurilateral Trade Agreements (Annex 4), several Ministerial Decisions and Declarations and an Understanding on Commitments in Financial Services. The TPRM is the means by which the WTO aims to ensure the compliance of member states with its rules and disciplines through periodic review of their trade policies and practices. Plurilateral agreements are those in which the signatories are free to discriminate against non-members, in this case even if they are WTO members. The plurilateral Uruguay Round Agreements apply to civil aircraft, government procurement, dairy and bovine meat, although the latter two were terminated at the end of 1997 and incorporated into the WTO's multilateral disciplines.

3. THE WORLD TRADE ORGANIZATION (WTO)

The World Trade Organization (WTO) was created as part of the Uruguay Round negotiations as the successor organization to the GATT Secretariat with the responsibility of overseeing all of the Uruguay Round Agreements outlined above. The creation of a new multilateral trade organization in the Marrakesh Declaration was necessitated by the superseding of GATT 1947 by GATT 1994 and the need for an institution to oversee the additional Agreements covering trade in services and IPRs as well as goods. The WTO came into being on 1 January 1995 at the same time as the Uruguay Round Agreements came into effect. Membership is open to any state or separate customs territory with full autonomy over its external trade subject to terms agreed with the WTO (Article XII:1 of the Marrakesh Agreement).

The functions of the WTO, outlined in Article III of the Marrakesh Agreement, are:

- To facilitate the implementation, administration and operation of the Uruguay Round Agreements (III:1).
- To provide a forum for negotiations between its members (III:2).
- To administer the dispute settlement procedures (DSP) (III:3).
- To administer the Trade Policy Review Mechanism (III:4).
- To cooperate with the IMF and World Bank to achieve greater coherence in global economic policy-making (III:5).

These functions are performed by the WTO Secretariat in Geneva in collaboration with the national delegations of member states. It is the member states, however, through their delegations, that are the primary movers in the WTO since they are responsible for determining the multilateral rules for trade, the agenda for multilateral trade negotiations, policy initiatives, decision-making, interpreting the WTO rules and initiating complaints against other members. The operation of the WTO is therefore very much in the hands of its member states with the Secretariat at its centre playing the supporting role of institutional facilitator.

Decision-making is covered under Article IX and amendments to the provisions of the WTO Agreement or any other of the Uruguay Round Agreements are covered in Article X of the Marrakesh Agreement. The general principle follows that of GATT 1947 in that each member state has one vote and decisions are taken on the basis of consensus or, if this is not possible, by majority voting (IX:1). Unanimity is required for the amendment of general principles (X:2), a three-quarters majority for the interpretation of the WTO provisions (IX:2) and waivers (IX:3), and a two-thirds majority for other amendments (X:3, 4 and 5) and accession (XII:2).

4. TRADE LIBERALIZATION, COMPETITION AND THE WTO: THE FOLLOWING CHAPTERS

The concern of this book is not with the past agenda of the Uruguay Round *per se* but with its implications for the future. The Uruguay Round Agreements outlined above established both a built-in agenda for future negotiations and a set of major new challenges and responsibilities for the WTO Secretariat and its member states. The built-in agenda has already been referred to above in the case of services and the commitment there to negotiate under the GATS. Further negotiations in agriculture and intellectual property were also anticipated at the time of the Uruguay Round Agreement. At the same time, the WTO has had an expanded role in terms of monitoring, for example the Trade Policy Review Mechanism, and adjudicating compliance, for example in the area of dispute settlement resolution, while members are now subject to new disciplines and compliance burdens, for example on subsidies, standards and intellectual property.

Given the scale of the built-in agenda and the policy burden, it is perhaps not too surprising that it has so far proved difficult to move beyond this agenda. Many commentators on global trade policy issues and some WTO member states certainly want to go beyond the built-in agenda and, in particular, to extend or strengthen the WTO rules in policy areas beyond border trade measures. This would cover the conditions affecting FDI and the support provided for investment by domestic firms. It would also cover the regulatory framework for the conduct of industrial and competition policies and of trade-related environmental regulations. There are, however, analytical complexities and political economy issues to be resolved around whether and how these issues – investment, competition and the environment – should be introduced into the multilateral trade policy agenda. These issues helped, in combination with their sensitivity for different groups of WTO members, to stall progress in establishing a research agenda for the new Millennium Round at the Ministerial Meeting in Seattle in November 1999. Even more problematic and divisive at Seattle was the issue of the possible introduction of a linkage between trade sanctions and labour standards and, with it, the corresponding danger of promoting protectionism as well as or instead of humanitarianism.

The contents of this book remain timely since the debate about how to put the post-Uruguay Round and WTO agendas back on the rails and what to include on the agenda for the new Millennium Round remains central among WTO member states. They offer a series of stand-alone but linked discussions on most of the general and specific issues that relate to the current debate surrounding the setting of the WTO agenda and the coverage of a future round of multilateral trade negotiations. The essays have been loosely grouped together around the themes of trade liberalization, competition and the WTO.

Trade Liberalization

The first group of chapters is concerned with market access in manufactures and agricultural goods on a multilateral or regional basis arising out of the liberalization of traditional border tariff or non-tariff measures. In addition, it is concerned with the widening of the market access agenda associated with the extension, following the Uruguay Round, of WTO disciplines to trade in services.

In Chapter 2, Sam Laird investigates the state of market access in goods and services. This review of the post-Uruguay Round level and pattern of tariff and non-tariff measures of protection clearly establishes that there is a remaining agenda for conventional multilateral market access negotiations. Significant tariff peaks still remain, especially following the tariffication of non-tariff measures in agriculture and textiles. These and the remaining tariff escalation in some sectors mean that there are substantial potential welfare gains to be reaped in both developed and developing countries from further traditional trade liberalization. Laird, however, also shows that there is a much wider range of opportunities for welfare-enhancing liberalization in any future negotiations, which includes improving market access for services and FDI and the tightening of disciplines on the rules governing, *inter alia*, anti-dumping, safeguards, technical barriers and government procurement.

In Chapter 3, the focus on the potential gains from further multilateral liberalization shifts to a potential source of resistance to the negotiation and implementation of further liberalization, namely farmers in the industrialized countries. Rod Tyers and Yongzheng Yang investigate the global resource allocation implications of the 1997 Asian crisis. They show that the Asian recession has reduced global demand for agricultural commodities and pushed down their world prices. 'Northern' farmers, where they have not been effectively insulated by their governments, have been the main losers outside Asia from this recession. Further agricultural trade reform in a new Millennium Round would therefore have to follow on from a period of costly adjustment in 'northern' agriculture. Even greater protectionist sentiment among 'northern' farmers will be a considerable challenge to setting up, negotiating and implementing a further round of multilateral negotiations.

The implications of liberalization for a different sector and set of countries is investigated in Chapter 4 by Victor Murinde and Cillian Ryan on the potential impact of the liberalization of banking services in the Gulf Region as a result of the GATS. In the case of financial services, it has been anxiety about liberalization in the developing countries that has been widely expressed, with size, technology, experience or expertise disadvantages being seen as reasons for increased penetration of home markets by industrialized-country suppliers. The authors show, using data on efficiency levels, that liberalization is certainly likely to cause a major shake-up of the financial sector in the Gulf. They envisage much greater adjustment, however, for labour, and for lower-skilled foreign workers in particular, than for locally owned capital.

Finally in this section, attention shifts from multilateral to regional liberalization issues, specifically to the relative costs and benefits of alternative forms of regional integration in Southern Africa. In Chapter 5, David Evans considers the impact of a free trade area (FTA), customs union (CU) and open regionalism (OR) using a CGE model of 12 countries in the region. He shows that there may be trade-offs that need to be struck between the depth of regional integration and the costliness of diverting trade from outside the region. External tariffs, that is the tariffs applying on imports from outside the region, will need to be set with care.

Competition

The group of chapters forming Part II moves away from traditional trade policy issues to the 'new' or newer trade policy issues. Although the links between competition and other industrial policies or interventions and competitiveness and, in turn, international trade have long been discussed, they have received even more attention in academic and policy circles in recent years. It has certainly been recognized that there is a wider set of policy instruments than traditional border interventions that may have important cross-border implications. It has also been widely anticipated that the establishment of multilateral rules is a likely item for the WTO's future agenda.

In Chapter 6, Peter Holmes reviews the background to the 'trade and competition' debate and the case for an international agreement within or outside of the WTO machinery, as well as establishing the positions of the EU, USA and developing countries on these issues. Holmes identifies the existing international provisions within GATT, GATS and the large number of bilateral, in particular EU, agreements, and argues that there is a powerful case for some form of international regulation of competition and competition policy. The WTO is a natural vehicle for negotiating on this. However, Holmes also shows that there is much opposition to starting multilateral negotiations on this issue. The US position, for instance, is that there are serious international cartel problems but that voluntary and inter-government cooperation is more likely to deal with the problems than a WTO regime because it will be difficult to establish a multilateral agreement with clear core principles.

The case for a multilateral agreement on investment (MAI), and one within the WTO, is forcibly made by Alan Rugman in Chapter 7. Rugman recognizes the concerns of developing countries about the loss of sover-eignty and of NGOs about the possible lowering of environmental and labour standards. He argues, however, that there would be long-term efficiency and dynamic advantages for both industrialized and developing countries from liberalizing FDI. The blueprint for an agreement has already been provided by NAFTA and is based on the principles of *national treatment* and *transparency* and the provision of a dispute settlement mech-anism. This has been mirrored in the work at the OECD on trying to estab-lish an MAI. Indeed, the concentration of FDI by MNEs based within the OECD and the history of OECD work in this area make the OECD a possible vehicle for a plurilateral agreement that could precede a more ambitious multilateral agreement within the WTO.

Attention in the next two chapters turns from a discussion of general policy issues in the area of trade and competition and the influence of competition policy on the practices of firms to the specific issue of the role of the state in affecting the competitiveness and fairness of behaviour in domestic and international markets. In Chapter 8, David Collie investigates the incentive for countries to give state aid strategically in the presence of oligopolistic markets and the opportunity for rent-shifting interventions. He constructs a formal analytical framework to carry out the investigation and uses it to assess the rationale for prohibitions on the use of state aid. In this latter case, it specifically assesses the EU's regulation (prohibition in principle) on the use of subsidies or other forms of state aid by member states. In the context of his specific model of Cournot oligopolists in each EU state, a homogeneous product and import from foreign (non-EU) firms, he shows that trade liberalization, which increases the number of foreign firms supplying the EU, increases the incentive for EU members to use state aid to domestic firms strategically so as to improve their terms of trade. Further, the reduction of foreign competition, the number of foreign firms supplying the EU market, reduces the incentive of the EU to prohibit state aid if there are more foreign than EU firms, which is more likely with liberalized trade. This is an interesting analytical finding but does not, as is also pointed out by the author, provide a general and robust basis for the design of policy.

Rather than intervening in markets, the state may itself act in markets. The literature on trade and competition traditionally concentrates on the conduct of privately owned firms but a significant role may be played in some markets by state trading enterprises (STEs). In Chapter 9, Steve McCorriston and Donald MacLaren investigate the potentially anti-competitive practices of STEs in domestic and world markets in the context of agricultural trade. They focus in particular on how STEs may exercise their monopoly power to price discriminate across markets and to affect trade flows, illustrating their analysis with a review of the activities of the Australian and Canadian Wheat Boards. The possibility of both under- and over-exporting is identified, depending upon the market power and efficiency of the STEs and their scope for market segmentation. There are also, of course, price implications for domestic producers and consumers that may give rise to domestic public policy debate. This is evident in Australia but the potential international trade effects mean that there is also an international policy issue. The authors therefore believe that the issue will be an important one on the future WTO agenda.

The World Trade Organization (WTO)

The role and responsibilities of the world's multilateral trade organization as the successor of the GATT were substantially increased by the Uruguay

Round itself. In addition, there have also been changes in many national economies as well as in the global economy that have increased countries' interest in the WTO and the international trade policy agenda. For example, many developing countries have undertaken significant trade policy reforms, often initiated unilaterally and under the influence of agencies other than the WTO, for example the World Bank. The growing effects of the globalization processes, driven by forces beyond national policy influences, have also meant that countries are more concerned with supranational policies and regulations. This was evident in the increased role played by the developing countries in the Uruguay Round and has since been manifest in the growth in both applications and membership of the WTO. The recognition that international rules affect them and that appropriate ones are needed by them has led the developing countries to take an even more active role in the post-Uruguay Round agenda-setting process. The failure to set the agenda for a future round at Seattle is evidence of this involvement and of the importance that more countries and their citizens are attaching to the WTO.

In Chapter 10, Sam Laird examines the interests of the developing countries in the WTO agenda in detail. He first outlines what has been implemented as a result of the Uruguay Round Agreements, and their significance for the developing countries, building here upon the earlier discussion of the current international trade policy debate in chapter 2. The remainder of the chapter is concerned with the future WTO agenda and is best understood in the context of what has happened on trade liberalization and what the 'new' issues on competition and investment involve. Laird provides a very concise discussion of what is a potentially enormous future multilateral trade policy agenda. He helpfully distinguishes between the built-in agenda from the Uruguay Round and the potential traditional and 'new' policy issues that might be driven on to the agenda for a future trade round. He establishes a strong motive for a wide-ranging agenda and for developing-country involvement in agenda-setting in any future negotiations.

Given the increasing complexities of international exchanges and their regulation, the role of the WTO in 'policing' the system and arbitrating in disputes between member states is likely to increase. The dispute settlement role of the GATT and the WTO has thus far been limited and, where it has been implemented, it has tended to be rather cumbersome and slow. In order to understand how best to reform and strengthen the dispute settlement function of the WTO, an understanding of how it currently operates is needed. As a contribution to this, Robert Read in Chapter 11 investigates in detail the origins, development and resolution of the EU–US banana dispute at the WTO. He also very usefully and topically highlights the relationship between dispute settlement and regulation/competition issues. Although the WTO's dispute settlement procedures (DSP) have worked better in this case than under the GATT, the pre-eminence of WTO rules over bargaining power in the resolution of trade disputes cannot yet be viewed as being established.

The final chapter of the book (Chapter 12) turns to the issue of the protection of intellectual property rights (IPRs) and to the role that the WTO has played in the development of a patent system in China. Derek Bosworth and Deli Yang trace the development of China's current IPR system and identify the specific role the TRIPs Agreement of the Uruguay Round played in bringing about amendments to Chinese patent law. These amendments increased the protective scope of the law, followed by a clear jump in patent applications and flows, including from non-residents. These policy reforms are consistent with China's Open Door policy, its promotion of development through FDI inflows and inward technology transfer and preparation for WTO accession. Although this case illustrates how international discipline can have benefits for development, it must be also recognized that many developing countries are concerned that TRIPs may also impose higher prices and transfer rents abroad in areas such as pharmaceutical products. These tensions, however, only emphasize the need for multilateral disciplines and dispute settlement mechanisms to defuse trade-related IPR frictions and to deter unilateral actions by the large trading nations.

REFERENCES

Baldwin, R. (1995), 'An economic evaluation of the Uruguay Round Agreements', in S. Arndt and C. Milner (eds), *The World Economy: Global Trade Policy 1995*, Oxford: Blackwell, pp. 153–72.

Hoekman, B.M. and M.M. Kostecki (2001), *The Political Economy of the World Trading System*, Oxford: Oxford University Press, 2nd edn.

Hudec, R. (1993), *Enforcing International Trade Law: the Evolution of the Modern GATT Legal System*, New York: Butterworth.

Hudec, R. (1999), 'The new WTO Dispute Settlement Procedure: an overview of the first three years', *Minnesota Journal of Global Trade*, **8** (1), 1–53.

Martin, W. and L.A. Winters (eds) (1996), *The Uruguay Round and the Developing Countries*, Cambridge: Cambridge University Press.

Schott, J. (1994), *The Uruguay Round: an Assessment*, Washington, DC: Institute for International Economics.

Trebilcock, M.J. and R. Howse (1999), *The Regulation of International Trade*, London: Routledge.

WTO (1999), *The Legal Texts: the Results of the Uruguay Round of Multilateral Trade Negotiations*, Cambridge: Cambridge University Press.

PART I

Trade Liberalization

2. Multilateral market access negotiations in goods and services

Sam Laird*

Protection in goods and services has changed markedly in recent years but, in spite of the free trade hype by some opponents of globalization, there is still substantial protection in developed and developing countries and this is loaded against developing countries (section 1). Under the WTO Agreements, many non-tariff measures in agriculture were converted to tariffs (tariffied) and quantitative restrictions on trade in textiles and clothing are being eliminated, making tariffs the binding constraint in key goods sectors. Tariff peaks and escalation will need to be addressed in conventional market access negotiations. These negotiations will also be the principal means for addressing other barriers in the agricultural sector as well as in services. Much intervention in trade or production in goods and services is regulated by WTO rules and any further negotiated reductions in the incidence of such measures would come under negotiations on such rules. While it is difficult to quantify the effects of existing protection and other forms of sectoral intervention, particularly in the services sector, it is possible to draw some conclusions about a welfare-enhancing liberalization strategy for the new negotiations (sections 4, 5 and 6).

1. LEVELS AND PATTERNS OF TARIFF PROTECTION

Overall, most favoured nation (MFN) bound tariffs at the end of the implementation of the Uruguay Round will be some 6.5 per cent across all countries and products (Table 2.1), while applied rates will be some 4.3 per cent. In general, developing countries' bound rates are higher than those of the developed countries and, for some regions, there is a large gap between their applied and bound rates. The binding coverage, which increased substantially for all regions in the Uruguay Round, is also lower for developing regions outside Latin America. To a large degree, the higher rates and the lower binding coverage for developing countries are a remnant of earlier

Table 2.1   Post-Uruguay Round import-weighted applied and bound tariff rates (%)

Country group or region	Applied	Bound
World	4.3	6.5
High-income economies	2.5	3.5
Latin America	11.7	32.7
East Asia and Pacific	11.9	21.0
South Asia	30.4	50.8
Eastern Europe	6.7	13.3
Rest of Europe	24.2	16.3
North Africa	24.8	48.7
Sub-Saharan Africa	9.0	19.4

Note:
Weighted averages, excluding trade within FTAs. The applied rates are those for the base period while the bound rates are those applying after the implementation. The data on developing countries were based on 26 out of 93 developing-country participants in the Round, representing 80 per cent of merchandise trade and 30 per cent of tariff lines.

Source: Finger et al. (1996).

import-substituting industrialization (ISI) strategies. The application of Special and Differential (S&D) treatment meant that no serious demands had been made on them to lower tariff rates. The reduction of developing countries' applied rates, especially in the last decade, and the increase in binding coverage reflect their shift towards more open economies and the growing belief that it is necessary to participate more fully in negotiations in order to obtain improved access for their exports.

Nevertheless, protection is still quite high in sensitive product areas such as textiles and clothing and transport equipment (Table 2.2) where trade is large and imports are relatively responsive to price changes. In addition, most developed and developing countries show substantial tariff escalation: uniform tariffs are rare, applied, with minor exceptions, in Chile, Peru, Hong Kong China and Singapore; in the latter two cases at zero. An analysis of tariff escalation by industrial countries in the post-Uruguay Round era shows a substantial loading against imports from developing countries, making it more difficult for them to develop downstream processing (Table 2.3). Based on WTO Trade Policy Reviews of some 42 developing countries, marked escalation is also a feature of most of their tariff structures (Michalopoulos, 1999). Thus, how to eliminate or reduce tariff peaks and escalation is one of the key questions to be addressed in future negotiations.

To some degree, the problem of high trade barriers may be overstated

Table 2.2   Post-Uruguay Round applied and bound rates of developed and developing countries, by major product group (%)

Product group	Developed		Developing	
	Applied	Bound	Applied	Bound
Agriculture, exc. fish	5.2	7.2	18.6	19.9
Fish & fish products	4.2	4.9	8.6	25.9
Petroleum	0.7	0.9	7.9	8.4
Wood, pulp, paper & furniture	0.5	0.9	8.9	10.3
Textiles & clothing	8.4	11.0	21.2	25.5
Leather, rubber, footwear	5.5	6.5	14.9	15.4
Metals	0.9	1.6	10.8	10.4
Chemical & photo. supplies	2.2	3.6	12.4	16.8
Transport equipment	4.2	5.6	19.9	13.2
Non-electric machinery	1.1	1.9	13.5	14.5
Electric machinery	2.3	3.7	14.6	17.2
Mineral prods, precious stones & metals	0.7	1.0	7.8	8.1
Manufactures, n.e.s.	1.4	2.0	12.1	9.2
Industrial goods (rows 4–13)	2.5	3.5	13.3	13.3
All merchandise trade	**2.6**	**3.7**	**13.3**	**13.0**

Note:
Weighted averages, excluding trade within FTAs. The applied rates are those for the base period while the bound rates are those applying after the implementation; in some instances this means that the applied rates are higher than the bound rates.

Source: Finger et al. (1996).

because of the growing importance of regional trade agreements (RTAs) and preferences, including between developing countries as well as between developed countries and countries at different stages of development. Examples are AFTA, APEC, CACM, the Canada–Chile FTA, CARICOM, COMESA, the Europe Agreements, Mercosur, NAFTA, SADC, and so on. These agreements seem to have given a stimulus to intra-regional trade, raising fears of trade diversion. In some of the smaller, faster-growing RTAs however, trade with third countries is growing faster than world trade in general and the EU's trade with members and non-members is growing at an equivalent rate (Crawford and Laird, 2000). Nevertheless, there must be some concern about the widely varying preferential rules of origin, which are not subject to WTO disciplines. Even the Pan-European System of Cumulation of Origin, now being applied in the Europe Agreements of the EU and EFTA with the other European countries, has over 100 pages of detailed rules. The overlapping of RTAs, with

Table 2.3   Tariff escalation on products imported by developed economies from developing economies (%)

Product	Post-UR bound tariff
All industrial products (exc. petroleum)	4.3
Raw materials	0.8
Semi-manufactures	2.8
Finished products	6.2
All tropical products	1.9
Raw materials	0.0
Semi-manufactures	3.5
Finished products	2.6
Natural-resource-based products	2.7
Raw materials	2.0
Semi-manufactures	2.0
Finished products	5.9

Source: GATT (1994).

different product coverage and implementation periods, adds to the complexity of trade regimes.

Previous multilateral rounds have reduced the importance of the GSP. Other unilateral preference schemes, such as the Cotonou Agreement (and its predecessor, the Lomé Convention) and the Caribbean Basin Initiative, now offer better treatment than the GSP. While these schemes have facilitated market access for developing countries to developed-country markets, the benefits have been captured by relatively few exporters and there have also been important exclusions. To some extent, they diverted attention from the need to reduce or eliminate high MFN protection against developing countries' key exports, as discussed above, and to build supply capabilities in the developing countries. The Cotonou Agreement replaced Lomé's ACP preferences with a series of reciprocal RTAs centred on the EU. This requires some liberalization by developing-country partners but the hub-and-spoke nature of such arrangements reduces the potential benefits from intra-developing-country trade. These countries should also be looking at multilateral negotiations to gain wider benefits than are possible from regional schemes alone.

There are several additional features of tariff protection that might usefully be addressed in the market access negotiations. For example, as a result of tariffication in agriculture, there has now been a major expansion in the use of specific, mixed and compound tariff rates for which it is often difficult to estimate the *ad valorem* equivalence. Again, many countries use schemes for concessional entry of certain types of goods, for example related to investment, industrial promotion or regional development schemes. These can be used to favour imports from certain trading partners but there are no disciplines on the use of such schemes other than those under the Agreement on Trade-Related Investment Measures (TRIMs). There are also no disciplines on the use of the FOB or CIF value for duty purposes and, in at least one case, there is differential treatment of an RTA partner in the implementation period. Finally, in the Uruguay Round, other charges on imports were to be listed in schedule and included within a global binding commitment. The practical application of this provision, however, lacks clarity, mainly because some additional charges are for services, for example port fees, inspection fees, statistical taxes, and so on. In some instances, however, these are actually levied on an *ad valorem* basis, unrelated to the value of the service.

2. LEVELS AND PATTERNS OF NON-TARIFF MEASURES (NTMS) IN GOODS

The Uruguay Round had a major impact on reducing the incidence of NTMs. Further reductions are expected as commitments continue to be implemented over agreed phase-in periods. Under the Single Undertaking of the Uruguay Round, commitments in respect of NTMs affect both developed and developing countries, with the latter often having extended implementation periods. Previously, developing countries, invoking GATT provisions on S&D treatment, were able to avoid many of the commitments of the developed countries.

The Developed Countries

A representative picture of the pre- and post-Uruguay Round NTMs by broad type and sectoral coverage in OECD countries is given in Tables 2.4 and 2.5. The two outstanding features of these tables are the reduction in the use of NTMs in agriculture, principally through tariffication or elimination of prohibited measures, and the reduced application of export restraints in the area of textiles and clothing.

The major reduction in the use of export restraints is related to the prohibition of voluntary export restraints (VERs) under Article 11 of the WTO Agreement on Safeguards. Remaining VERs, including the EU–Japan consensus on automobiles, were to be eliminated by the end of 1999; other significant export restraints are those under the WTO Agreement on Textiles and Clothing, which replaced the Multi-Fibre Arrangement (MFA). There

Table 2.4 *Import coverage of major NTBs in OECD countries, 1989 and 1996*

(A) 1989

Indicator	Australia	EU	Iceland	Japan	New Zealand	Norway	Mexico	Turkey	Switzerland	USA
All NTBs	3.4	26.6	n.a.	13.1	14.1	26.6	2.0	0.1	12.9	25.5
Core NTBs	3.4	25.2	n.a.	12.5	14.1	25.2	2.0	0.0	3.3	25.5
Quantitative restrictions (QRs)	0.5	19.5	n.a.	11.7	13.9	19.5	1.9	0.0	1.7	20.4
Export restraints	0.0	15.5	n.a.	0.3	0.0	15.5	0.0	0.0	0.0	19.5
Non-auto licensing	0.5	4.4	n.a.	8.9	0.0	4.3	1.8	0.0	0.4	0.0
Other QRs	0.0	0.2	n.a.	2.8	13.9	0.2	0.2	0.0	1.4	6.6
Price controls (PCMs)	2.9	12.4	n.a.	0.8	0.3	12.4	0.1	0.0	1.6	17.8
Variable levies	0.0	6.3	n.a.	0.8	0.0	6.3	0.0	0.0	1.5	0.1
AD/CVs & VEPRs	2.9	2.6	n.a.	0.0	0.3	2.6	0.1	0.0	0.0	17.8
Other PCMs	0.0	4.3	n.a.	0.0	0.0	4.3	0.0	0.0	0.1	0.0

(B) 1996

Indicator	Australia	EU	Iceland	Japan	New Zealand	Norway	Mexico	Turkey	Switzerland	USA
All NTBs	0.7	19.1	3.6	10.7	0.8	4.3	14.1	0.4	7.6	16.8
Core NTBs	0.7	15.1	1.5	10.0	0.8	2.6	14.1	0.4	0.2	16.7
Quantitative restrictions (QRs)	0.0	13.1	1.5	9.2	0.0	2.6	1.0	0.2	0.2	10.9
Export restraints	0.0	11.4	0.0	0.0	0.0	1.2	0.0	0.0	0.0	10.8
Non-auto licensing	0.0	1.5	1.4	8.6	0.0	0.0	1.0	0.2	0.0	0.0
Other QRs	0.0	0.2	0.1	0.6	0.0	2.6	0.0	0.0	0.2	0.6
Price controls (PCMs)	0.7	3.2	0.0	0.7	0.8	0.0	13.1	0.3	0.0	7.6
Variable levies	0.0	1.4	0.0	0.6	0.0	0.0	0.0	0.0	0.0	0.1
AD/CVs & VEPRs	0.4	0.9	0.0	0.0	0.8	0.0	13.1	0.3	0.0	7.6
Other PCMs	0.3	1.0	0.0	0.0	0.0	0.0	0.0	0.0	0.0	0.1

Note:
Core NTBs are QRs and PCMs shown in the table, imposed 'with the specific intent of modifying or restricting international trade' (OECD, 1997).
Non-core NTBs include automatic licensing and monitoring measures. See OECD (1997) for further details of methodology.

Source: OECD (1997).

28

Table 2.5 Import coverage of core NTBs in OECD countries by major sector, 1989 and 1996

(A) 1989

ISIC	Description	Australia	EU	Iceland	Japan	New Zealand	Norway	Mexico	Turkey	Switzerland	USA
1	Agric., forestry & fishing	0.9	18.8	n.a.	11.3	0.6	14.2	6.7	0.0	12.7	5.5
2	Mining & quarrying	0.0	0.0	n.a.	3.5	0.0	0.0	35.4	0.0	0.0	0.3
21	Coal mining	n.a.	0.0	n.a.	n.a.	n.a.	0.0	0.0	n.a.	0.0	0.0
22	Crude petroleum	n.a.	n.a.	n.a.	n.a.	n.a.	0.0	66.7	n.a.	n.a.	0.0
23	Metal ores	n.a.	n.a.	n.a.	n.a.	n.a.	0.0	0.0	n.a.	0.0	0.0
29	Other	n.a.	0.0	n.a.	n.a.	n.a.	0.0	0.0	n.a.	3.0	3.4
3	Manufacturing	3.9	12.6	n.a.	3.9	3.6	4.4	6.6	0.0	3.0	16.0
31	Food, bevs, tobacco	2.1	48.5	n.a.	24.3	0.0	13.3	15.0	0.0	25.2	16.4
32	Textiles & apparel	0.5	74.9	n.a.	28.8	0.0	34.1	0.5	0.0	0.0	84.1
33	Wood & wood prods	0.0	0.0	n.a.	0.0	0.0	3.7	0.0	0.0	0.0	3.9
34	Paper & paper prods	0.2	1.2	n.a.	0.0	0.5	0.0	3.8	0.0	0.0	1.5
35	Chemical & petroleum prods	2.2	3.5	n.a.	1.4	20.4	3.8	1.7	0.0	0.0	8.6
36	Non-metallic mineral prods	4.3	4.4	n.a.	0.0	0.0	0.0	1.9	0.0	0.0	10.7
37	Basic metal industries	10.3	37.7	n.a.	2.5	0.0	0.0	0.0	0.0	0.0	53.2
38	Fabricated metals	6.3	4.6	n.a.	0.0	0.0	0.0	8.1	0.0	0.0	13.0
39	Other	5.5	1.3	n.a.	0.0	0.0	0.2	0.0	0.0	0.0	4.2
	Total	**3.4**	**12.7**	**n.a.**	**4.4**	**2.7**	**3.4**	**8.4**	**0.0**	**3.3**	**17.2**

Table 2.5 (cont.)

. (B) 1996

ISIC	Description	Australia	EU	Iceland	Japan	New Zealand	Norway	Mexico	Turkey	Switzerland	USA
1	Agric., forestry & fishing	0.5	7.2	0.2	7.0	0.0	0.0	5.2	0.0	0.6	2.8
2	Mining & quarrying	0.0	6.7	n.a.	0.4	0.0	0.0	24.5	0.0	0.0	0.4
21	Coal mining	n.a.	42.9	n.a.	n.a.	n.a.	0.0	0.0	n.a.	0.0	0.0
22	Crude petroleum	n.a.	0.0	n.a.	n.a.	n.a.	0.0	46.2	n.a.	n.a.	0.0
23	Metal ores	n.a.	4.4	n.a.	n.a.	n.a.	0.0	0.0	n.a.	n.a.	4.0
29	Other	n.a.	3.6	n.a.	n.a.	n.a.	0.0	0.0	n.a.	0.0	2.3
3	Manufacturing	1.7	5.4	0.1	2.5	0.0	0.9	12.9	0.3	0.1	8.1
31	Food, bevs., tobacco	8.3	11.1	0.0	8.6	0.0	0.0	1.9	0.0	0.8	1.2
32	Textiles & apparel	0.0	75.4	0.0	28.7	0.0	24.3	70.6	0.0	0.0	68.3
33	Wood & wood prods	0.0	0.0	0.0	0.0	0.0	0.0	0.0	0.0	0.0	0.8
34	Paper & paper prods	0.0	1.9	0.0	0.0	0.0	0.0	0.0	0.1	0.0	1.3
35	Chemical & petroleum prods	0.6	1.6	0.0	1.4	0.2	3.7	3.8	0.0	0.0	3.2
36	Non-metallic mineral prods	0.5	0.0	0.0	0.0	0.0	0.0	0.4	0.0	0.0	6.1
37	Basic metal industries	0.0	0.6	0.0	2.6	0.0	0.0	36.5	6.6	0.0	30.4
38	Fabricated metals	0.2	0.0	0.0	0.0	0.0	0.0	15.1	0.1	0.0	6.1
39	Other	0.0	0.0	1.3	0.0	0.0	0.2	31.9	0.0	0.0	1.7
	Total	**1.5**	**5.6**	**0.1**	**2.8**	**0.0**	**0.4**	**11.8**	**0.2**	**0.1**	**7.2**

Note:
See OECD (1997) for details of methodology. Sectoral production coverage refers to the value-added covered by NTBs.

Source: OECD (1997).

are two effects of this prohibition on VERs: first, in a number of cases, mainly in the iron and steel industry, the VERs were replaced by anti-dumping measures; and, second, some flexibility was introduced into the application of safeguards, allowing discrimination among suppliers in exceptional circumstances although their use continues to be rare. In anti-dumping cases, a common outcome is now negotiated price undertakings by suppliers, voluntary export price restraints (VEPRs), which are similar in effect to VERs.

Textiles and clothing
The phase-out of the MFA and the gradual integration of the textiles and clothing sector within the normal WTO rules is being effected over a ten-year period under the supervision of a Textiles Monitoring Body (TMB). Under the Agreement on Textiles and Clothing, which is intended to include products from four different groups (tops and yarn; fabrics; made-up textiles; and clothing), a minimum of 16 per cent of total 1990 volume of imports covered by the MFA was integrated into the WTO in 1995. At least another 17 per cent of the value of 1990 imports was due to be integrated following the third year of the phase-out period. An additional minimum of 18 per cent is to be integrated after the seventh year, while the remaining 41 per cent will be brought under WTO rules at the very end of the phase-out period (2002–4). Quota restrictions are being expanded by the amount of the prevailing quota growth rates plus 16 per cent annually for the first three years. A further expansion of 25 per cent will take place in the subsequent four years and an additional 27 per cent in the final three years. These annual growth rates may be adjusted if it is found that member countries are not complying with their obligations.

The integration of the sector into the GATT 1994 has not been without its problems. Thus, concerns have been raised about the back-loading of the integration process, the large number of safeguard measures in use, more restrictive use of Rules of Origin by the USA, tariff increases, the introduction of specific rates, minimum import-pricing regimes, labelling and certification requirements, the maintenance of balance of payments provisions affecting textiles and clothing, export visa requirements, as well as the double jeopardy arising from the application of anti-dumping measures to products covered by the Agreement.

Given that the textiles and clothing sector has been under restraint for more than 40 years, some developing countries are concerned about the effects of the integration of the sector into the GATT 1994. For example, constrained exporters expect to lose some of the quota rents afforded by the MFA. Moreover, countries such as Bangladesh, which had relatively large quotas, will now face stiffer competition from China. It can therefore be expected that there will be a major restructuring of the world textiles and clothing industry unless the special safeguard measures or anti-dumping actions take the place of existing restraints. One aspect of the special safeguards is that it may be unnecessary during the integration process to invoke the exceptional provisions of Article XIX of the GATT for textiles and clothing products, but this could change when the integration is complete.

Agriculture

In the area of agriculture, the WTO Agreement encompassed the elimination or tariffication of NTMs based on 1986–88 prices, the full binding of the new tariffs by developed and developing countries and phased tariff reductions, reductions in the level of domestic support measures (except for 'green box' and *de minimis* amounts) and reductions in outlays on export subsidies and the volume of subsidized exports. The main exceptions to tariffication were rice and, for developing countries, some staple foods, where minimum access commitments apply. In addition, import licensing is still widely used, ostensibly as a sanitary and phytosanitary measure. Many countries also chose to introduce tariff quotas for a number of products but these are not included as an NTM in Tables 2.5 and 2.6. In addition, some developing countries regard the prohibition of the use of variable levies not as an absolute ban but rather as an admonition not to exceed bound levels where a variable charge is imposed. These are also covered by the tables as price control measures.[1] Domestic support measures and export subsidies, however, are not covered in the tables; nor are special safeguards, triggered by increased import volumes or price reductions (by comparison with average 1986–88 prices expressed in domestic currency), which take the form of increased duties.

An indication of the importance of assistance in the area of agriculture can be obtained from the OECD (1998a, 1998b). As shown in Table 2.6, the overall level of support for the OECD countries, which now include some countries usually considered as developing or transitional economies, has shown a slow downward trend with percentage producer subsidy equivalents (PSEs) of intervention declining from 45 per cent in 1986–87 to 35 per cent in 1996. There are, however, still quite significant differences in the level of support between countries and also between commodities (see OECD, 1998a for details). Although 1996 was the first year of implementation of the Uruguay Round results, the OECD attributes much of the decline to reduced levels of market price support, caused by a rise in world prices, with little change in producer prices. While market price support has fallen, it remains the principal form of support, but direct payments have become relatively more important. As a result of this shift to direct support, the per-

Table 2.6   OECD producer subsidy equivalents by country, 1986–97 (%)

Country or group	1986–88	1992–94	1995	1996p	1997e
Australia	10	10	10	8	0
Canada	42	31	22	22	20
European Union[1]	48	48	49	43	42
Iceland	82	77	75	69	68
Japan	73	74	76	71	69
New Zealand	18	3	3	3	3
Norway	74	74	72	70	71
Switzerland	79	80	79	77	76
Turkey	26	32	30	25	38
United States	30	21	13	15	16
OECD[2,3]	45	42	40	35	35
Czech Republic	54	26	15	14	11
Hungary	24	25	21	15	16
Mexico	23	34	0	8	16
Poland	−3	19	19	23	22
OECD[2,4]	39	41	38	34	34

Notes:
e – estimate; p – provisional
[1] EU12 for 1986–94, EU15 from 1995. EU includes GDR from 1990.
[2] Austria, Finland and Sweden are included in the OECD total for the 1986–94 period and in the EU for 1995–97.
[3] Excludes Korea, the Czech Republic, Hungary, Mexico and Poland.
[4] Excludes Korea.

Source: OECD (1998a, 1998b).

centage consumer subsidy equivalents (CSEs), a measure of the implicit tax on consumers of agricultural policies, has also fallen from 37 per cent in 1986–87 to 24 per cent in 1996.

Overall, given the entrenched interests in agriculture, the WTO Agreement was undoubtedly one of the main achievements of the Uruguay Round. Although some commentators, focusing on large-volume temperate zone commodities, have suggested that the tariffication process led to little increase in market access, the Agreement brought the agricultural sector under more transparent rules and set the stage for future progressive liberalization of trade in the sector. It is also important, however, to draw attention to the substantial tariff cuts for a wide variety of fruits, vegetable and tropical products.

Some other important forms of trade measure are not reflected in either Table 2.4 or 2.5. These are technical barriers to trade – including sanitary and phytosanitary measures, state trading and Rules of Origin. As other forms of import protection have been reduced or eliminated, technical barriers to trade are becoming increasingly important, particularly as sanitary and phytosanitary measures affect agricultural products. Tensions concerning import controls related to the use of hormones are a prominent example of the testing of WTO rules in this area. In addition, there is now the negotiation of mutual recognition agreements (MRAs) under which testing is recognized only for goods originating in the participating countries (the EU and the USA), not for third countries. Article XVII of the GATT on state trading enterprises (STEs) has also begun to receive increasing attention (Davey, 1998). This is because of the important role that such enterprises play in agriculture (see Chapter 9). Now that the sector has been brought more fully under the WTO rules with the completion of the Uruguay Round Agreement on Agriculture (AoA), any measure or procedure that could circumvent the commitments on export subsidies, market access and domestic support is being closely scrutinized. Another reason is the role that such enterprises play in the transition economies which are in the process of accession to the WTO.

Another gap in the coverage of Tables 2.4 and 2.5 is the absence of production or export measures, which are still important in the agricultural sector for a number of OECD countries. If fixed producer prices, one of the main forms of support, are set higher than the world price plus the tariff, then importing is attractive and surpluses develop in the domestic market; export subsidies may then be used to dispose of these surpluses on the world market. Before the conclusion of the Uruguay Round, variable levies or quantitative restrictions were used to ensure that imports did not pose a serious threat to the supported domestic sector and these would have shown up as NTMs in Tables 2.5 and 2.6, and the existence of other forms of support and export subsidies could be inferred. In the post-Uruguay Round period, however, these measures have been replaced by tariffs and sometimes tariff quotas, neither of which is included as an NTM.

Other non-tariff measures (NTMs)

A feature of Table 2.4 is the relative importance of anti-dumping measures, particularly in the USA. As mentioned earlier, these became much more important when VERs started to be eliminated in 1992 and are now the principal form of contingency protection. It is expected that these will become even more important as other measures are phased out in the agriculture, textiles and clothing sectors. This is because many countries prefer anti-dumping actions over other forms of contingency protection: the injury test is lower, material injury versus serious injury for safeguards; they allow discrimination against specific firms; there is a lower burden of proof, versus countervailing measures; there is no adjustment requirement, versus safeguards; they can be applied for a longer period than can safeguards; and there is no compensation requirement (Laird, 1999a). Moreover, it has also been found that even the opening of an anti-dumping investigation has a chilling effect on imports.

In the past, export performance requirements and local content requirements were used extensively in developed and developing countries. These would have appeared as NTMs to the extent that they involved import restrictions. The WTO Agreement on Trade-Related Investment Measures (TRIMs), however, prohibits measures that: (i) require particular levels of local sourcing by an enterprise (local content requirements); (ii) restrict the volume or value of imports which an enterprise can buy or use to the volume or value of products it exports (trade balancing requirements); (iii) restrict the volume of imports to the amount of foreign exchange inflows attributable to an enterprise; and (iv) restrict the export by an enterprise of products, whether specified in terms of the particular type, volume or value of products or of a proportion of volume or value of local production. Thus, such measures have now disappeared among the developed countries.

Production subsidies still exist in the industrial sector of the developed countries but, under the WTO Agreement on Subsidies and Countervailing Measures (the SCM Agreement), specific subsidies under three different categories are classified as: prohibited (red); actionable (amber); and non-actionable (green) subsidies (the 'traffic lights approach') (Laird, 1999a). Export subsidies for manufactures are prohibited (red). Actionable (amber) subsidies, which include production subsidies, are those that cause adverse effects – injury, nullification or impairment of benefits or serious prejudice – to a member. Serious prejudice can be demonstrated on the basis of displacement of or impedance of exports into the subsidizing-country market or a third-country market, significant price undercutting, price suppression or depression, lost sales or an increase in the world market share of a primary commodity.[2] The class of non-actionable subsidies included all non-specific as well as certain specific subsidies that involve assistance to industrial research and pre-competitive development activity, assistance to disadvantaged regions and subsidies for environmental adaptation, so long as such subsidies meet certain criteria. These non-actionable subsidies could not be challenged multilaterally nor countervailed up to the end of 1999 but, since 2000, under the terms of Article 31 of the SCM Agreement, this class of subsidies has disappeared and is now subject to countervailing actions. No overall consistent quantitative estimates are readily available for OECD countries[3] but evidence from GATT/WTO Trade Policy Reviews of these countries indicate a wide variety of state aids for industry. Further work, however, is necessary to collect such information on a consistent basis compatible with WTO definitions.

On the whole, the developed countries do not use export taxes or export restrictions for commercial purposes, although the EU has, at times, restricted grain sales to ensure supplies for animal fodder.

The Developing Countries

A major reform in developing-country trade policies took place from the mid-1980s, with some variation in dates. This was often associated with IMF/World Bank stabilization and structural adjustment lending operations. As part of the unilateral trade reforms and commitments in the Uruguay Round, developing countries and transition economies have shifted the emphasis from NTMs to tariffs, establishing a clearer linkage to international price movements. In addition, there is much less use of foreign exchange controls and import restrictions for balance of payments purposes. These have largely been abandoned as greater emphasis has come to be placed on macroeconomic policies to solve what is essentially a macroeconomic problem.

The principal NTMs now used by developing countries are similar to those used by the developed countries (Tables 2.7 and 2.8). The agricultural sector has a number of import-licensing systems, mostly linked to the allocation of tariff quotas under the Uruguay Round tariffication. Also in agriculture, some countries still use variable levies and there are also some production and export subsidies. Other measures include: import/export quotas related to trade in textiles and clothing; local content and export balancing requirements (TRIMs), mostly in the automotive industry, due to be phased out by the end of 1999;[4] export subsidies to develop non-traditional manufactures, sometimes administered as tax breaks or subsidized finance but direct subsidies have almost disappeared under fiscal pressures; and state-trading operations.

Developing countries are now also starting to make greater use of other NTMs which are generally consistent with WTO rules. For example, technical barriers to trade, including sanitary and phytosanitary controls, are now being used more by developing countries and in this they are also starting to approximate the use of such measures by the developed countries. Other measures include prohibitions on the importation of pornography, arms and munitions, and so on.

Among the more worrying trends is the increasing adoption of anti-dumping measures by developing countries (Table 2.9). Thus Miranda et al. (1998) note that 'new users' – those that began conducting anti-dumping investigations in the 1980s – now conduct 54 per cent of all anti-dumping

*Table 2.7   Frequency of major NTBs in selected developing countries,
1995–98 (%)*

Country	Non-auto licensing	Prohibitions	Quotas	Tariff quotas	Import monitoring	Var. levies
Argentina	1	0	1	0	0	1
Brazil	11	11	1	0	0	1
Chile	0	1	0	0	0	4
Colombia	6	1	0	0	0	6
Costa Rica	6	0	0	6	0	0
Côte d'Ivoire	31	0	5	0	0	0
Dominican R.	5	1	0	0	1	0
El Salvador	5	1	1	0	0	0
Fiji	5	0	0	0	0	0
Hong Kong	2	0	0	0	0	0
India	94	1	0	0	0	0
Indonesia	31	0	0	0	0	0
Malaysia	20	14	2	7	0	0
Mauritius	9	7	0	0	0	0
Mexico	6	1	0	7	0	0
Morocco	13	0	0	1	0	0
Nigeria	2	9	0	0	0	0
Singapore	1	1	0	0	0	0
South Africa	5	0	3	0	0	0
Sri Lanka	23	0	0	0	0	0
Thailand	11	6	1	12	0	0
Uganda	3	0	0	0	0	0
Venezuela	2	3	0	0	0	13
Average	10	2	1	3	0	1

Note:
Frequencies in % of total HS 2-digit categories. See Michalopoulos (1999) for further details
of methodology.

Source: Michalopoulos (1999), based on WTO Trade Policy Reviews of the individual
countries.

investigations by WTO members, compared with 12–21 per cent in the
1987–92 period. Mexico is the most frequent user, followed by Argentina,
Brazil, South Africa, India and the Republic of Korea. It is sometimes
argued that the increased use of anti-dumping procedures is the price to pay
for the greater openness of developing countries' economies, but a number
of concerns have been expressed about the legitimacy of the use of anti-
dumping measures, including the conduct of investigations. In essence,
anti-dumping is not being used against predatory dumping or even 'unfair'

Table 2.8   Frequency of NTBs in major sector by developing countries, 1995–98 (%)

HS	Description	Non-auto licensing	Prohibitions	Quotas	Tariff quotas	Var. levies and admin. pricing
I	Animal products	14	3	0	9	3
II	Vegetables	19	3	2	9	3
III	Fats & oils	17	7	0	10	13
IV	Prepared foodstuffs	11	2	1	4	3
V	Minerals	24	6	0	2	0
VI	Chemicals	9	1	0	2	0
VII	Plastics	17	7	2	2	2
VIII	Leather	2	0	0	0	0
IX	Wood	6	2	0	2	0
X	Pulp and paper	4	1	0	2	0
XI	Textiles	7	1	2	2	0
XII	Footwear	3	0	0	1	0
XIII	Glass	6	1	0	1	0
XIV	Pearls	17	0	0	0	0
XV	Base metals	7	2	0	2	0
XVI	Mach. & elec. equip.	22	7	0	3	0
XVII	Vehicles	11	6	2	1	0
XVIII	Instruments	4	0	0	0	0
XIX	Arms	3	0	0	3	0
XX	Other manufs.	7	1	0	0	0
XXI	Works of art, antiques	3	0	0	0	0

Note:
Percentages of countries using the measures in each HS 2-digit category. See Michalopoulos (1999) for further details of methodology.

Source: Michalopoulos (1999), based on WTO Trade Policy Reviews of the individual countries

trading practices of foreign firms but rather to protect the entrenched position of oligopolistic firms in the iron and steel, chemicals industries, and so on. It has also been observed in several countries that there is a correlation between the level of economic activity and anti-dumping investigations.

Developing countries are more often targeted by developed countries' anti-dumping actions than other countries; moreover, they are often the target of such actions by other developing countries (Miranda et al., 1998). This trend in the use of NTMs against imports by developing countries also marks a trend towards a level of discrimination that did not exist in the

Table 2.9   Anti-dumping investigations by groups of reporting countries and countries investigated, 1987–97

Reporting country group	Affected country group			
	Developed	Developing	Economies in transition	Total
Developed	570	591	340	1501
Developing	249	216	205	670
Economies in transition	24	0	1	25
Total	843	807	546	2196

Source: Miranda et al. (1998).

past. For example, NTMs used by developing countries were on the whole non-discriminatory (UNCTAD, 1990). In a study of some 50 developing countries, UNCTAD conclude that most NTMs were of a general nature and not pointed at individual suppliers. The NTMs involved were import-licensing, advanced import deposits and central bank authorizations.

Some developing countries also apply export taxes on foodstuffs and other materials for use in domestic processing industries, for example oil seeds, tropical timbers, raw hides and skins, and so on. Quantitative restrictions on exports have mainly been replaced by export taxes. In general, quantitative restrictions are prohibited under Article XI of the GATT. Certain exceptions to this general prohibition, however, are allowed (Laird, 1999a). For example, under Article XI:2 of the GATT, temporary prohibitions or restrictions are allowed to relieve critical shortages of foodstuffs. Article XX on General Exceptions also allows the use of export restrictions in certain circumstances, including those applied under the Convention on International Trade in Endangered Species (CITES). Sub-paragraph (g) allows exceptions relating to the conservation of exhaustible natural resources, provided that such measures are made effective in conjunction with restrictions on domestic production or consumption. This provision has been used *inter alia* to justify restrictions on the export of tropical timbers. Moreover, sub-paragraph (h) may provide cover for export restrictions undertaken in pursuance of obligations under intergovernmental commodity agreements.

The WTO Agreement on Technical Barriers to Trade (TBT) also makes it clear that a member may take measures 'necessary to ensure the quality of its exports'. Under Article XX (i), a WTO member may restrict exports of domestic materials necessary to ensure essential quantities of such materials to a domestic processing industry during periods when the domestic

price of such materials is held below the world price as part of a governmental stabilization plan. Such restrictions are only allowed if they do not
result in an increase in the exports of or the protection afforded to the
domestic processing industry; hence the switch to the use of export taxes to
achieve such goals.

3.   LEVELS AND PATTERNS OF NON-TARIFF MEASURES (NTMS) IN SERVICES

Available data on trade in services are weak compared to those for merchandise trade and cross-country data on the magnitude of barriers to
trade in services do not exist. Tariffs are not applied to such trade although
conceptually some kind of tax on the consumption of foreign services
could work like a tariff. The main forms of intervention are prohibitions,
quantitative restrictions (QRs) and discriminatory practices affecting
cross-border supplies, foreign commercial presence and movements of individual suppliers. They may be accompanied by domestic regulatory barriers in individual markets. Private sector associations may also have a role
in defining 'sound' practices and so on. Thus foreign firms may be prohibited from the provision of certain services; QRs may apply to the value or
quantity of specific services or to the number of firms allowed to contest a
particular market. There may be licensing and qualification requirements
relating to consumer protection, prudential supervision, pricing and so on.
The reservation of certain segments of services markets to the state is quite
common although this has been much reduced in recent years.

Many governments set limits or conditions on FDI, perhaps the most
important mode of supply of services. For example, FDI may be limited to
less than a controlling interest, for example less than 50 per cent of total or
equity shares. In cases such as joint ventures or industrial collaboration
arrangements, special terms for FDI may be imposed by the host government. Controls may be imposed on the royalty payments or the repatriation
of profits, and there may be limits on sales of assets, perhaps to discourage
footloose industries (Laird, 1999b). Terms may also include local content
requirements, export performance requirements, a need to use local labour
or upgrade local management, technology requirements and the like. The
host government may set limits to patents on products and/or processes.

On the other hand, some governments promote FDI by offering a variety
of incentives, including tax holidays, tax exemptions, tax rebates and so on
as well as protection or industry assistance. Such incentives, which are not
currently the subject of GATS disciplines, can dissipate the benefits of FDI.
The costs and benefits of promotional policies may not be transparent and

this opacity makes it difficult for taxpayers and other countries to know how much protection is being afforded and what are its effects.

> It is doubtful that governments ever know the exact tax or subsidy on firms achieved by investment policies. But the great variety of policy instruments and the proliferation of investment-screening agencies with discretionary powers suggest a strong desire to intervene in a discriminating fashion rather than to remain passive providers of protection. (Guisinger, 1987)

The principal source of information about intervention in the services sector is the GATS schedules of WTO members plus China, which participated in the Uruguay Round although it was not yet a WTO member. Like tariff bindings, they represent a commitment and, in a number of cases, markets are more open in practice. In a positive list, the schedules contain specific commitments in respect of market access and national treatment, structured by one of the four modes of supply covered by the GATS: cross-border; movement of the consumer to the service supplier abroad; commercial presence; and temporary movement of natural persons. Concerning market access, the GATS prohibits limitations on the number of service suppliers allowed, the value of transactions or assets, the total quantity of service output, the number of natural persons that may be employed, the type of legal entity through which a service may be supplied and the level of participation of foreign capital. If a WTO member maintains any of these restrictions, they must be listed in its schedule of specific commitments. The coverage of MFN treatment accorded by WTO members is determined by a negative list of services which are exceptions to the application of the MFN rule, mostly invoked because of concerns about the adequacy of offers by other countries or to 'grandfather' pre-existing bilateral arrangements in individual sectors.[5] The sectors particularly affected by such exemptions are the various transport sectors and audio-visual services.

Although the sectoral commitment of the GATS members is essentially qualitative, Hoekman (1996) provides a number of quantitative estimates of the extent to which measures are bound and the share of such sectors where the binding relates to free trade. Some of this information is reproduced in Tables 2.10 and 2.11. The indicators, which are similar to frequency coverage ratios sometimes used to describe the prevalence of NTMs for goods, give some indication of the degree of openness in some cases, particularly in sectors where the members have made market access and national treatment commitments without limitation. Hoekman makes the point that most commitments undertaken in services in the Uruguay Round are of a standstill nature, that is, they amounted to promises not to become more restrictive than at the time of the negotiation. It is also

Table 2.10   Sectoral coverage of specific commitments in services (%)

	High-income countries	Low- and middle-income countries	Large developing countries
Market access			
Unweighted average count (sectors/modes as a share of maximum possible)	47.3	16.2	38.6
Average coverage (sectors/modes listed as a share of maximum possible, weighted by openness/binding factors)	35.9	10.3	22.9
Coverage/count (average coverage as a share of the average count)	75.9	63.6	59.3
'No restrictions' as a share of total offer (unweighted count)	57.3	45.5	38.7
'No restrictions' as a share of maximum possible	27.1	7.3	14.9
National treatment			
Unweighted average count (sectors/modes as a share of maximum possible)	47.3	16.2	38.8
Average coverage (sectors/modes listed as a share of maximum possible, weighted by openness/binding factors)	37.2	11.2	25.5
Coverage/count (average coverage as a share of the average count)	78.6	69.1	66.1
'No restrictions' as a share of total offer (unweighted count)	65.1	58.0	52.3
'No restrictions' as a share of maximum possible	30.8	9.4	20.2
Memo items:			
No restrictions on MA and NT as a share of maximum possible	24.8	6.9	14.3

Source: Hoekman (1996).

Table 2.11 Commitments by services sector

	No. of GATS sectors	Av. no. of commitments		Commitments/GATS items per sector	
		High-income countries	Low- and middle-income countries	High-income countries	Low- and middle-income countries
Construction	20	11.2	3.3	56.0	16.5
Motor vehicle repair	4	1.8	0.3	45.0	7.5
Wholesale trade	8	4.6	0.5	57.5	6.3
Retail trade	8	4.4	0.8	55.0	10.0
Hotels, restaurants	4	2.8	2.8	70.0	70.0
Land transport	40	9.4	2.3	23.5	5.8
Water transport	48	4.4	3.0	9.2	6.3
Air transport	20	3.7	1.5	18.5	7.5
Auxiliary transport	20	5.1	1.3	25.5	6.5
Postal services	4	1.3	0.6	32.5	15.0
Basic telecommunications	28	1.5	1.3	5.4	4.6
Value-added telecomms	28	18.7	5.0	66.8	7.8
Financial services	60	31.3	12.4	52.2	20.6
Real-estate services	8	3.5	0.3	43.8	3.8
Rental activities	20	9.5	1.3	47.5	6.5
Computer-related	20	15.5	4.2	77.5	21.0
R&D services	12	4.1	1.0	34.2	0.3
Business services	108	56.5	12.2	47.9	11.3
Refuse disposal	16	8.8	1.0	55.0	6.3
Education	20	4.7	1.3	23.5	6.5
Health & social	24	5.0	1.9	20.8	7.9
Recreation & culture	48	13.3	4.6	27.9	9.6

Source: Hoekman (1996).

recalled that some countries' sectors are already more open than the commitment in their schedules.

Table 2.10 gives an overview of the Uruguay Round commitments, that is, excluding the results of the extended negotiations on basic telecommunications and financial services, by three major country groupings: (i) the high-income countries, comprising OECD countries plus Hong Kong China, the Republic of Korea and Singapore; (ii) all other GATS members; and (iii) a subset of (ii), being a group of large developing countries – Argentina, Brazil, Chile, China, Colombia, India, Indonesia, Israel, Malaysia, Pakistan, the Philippines, Poland, South Africa, Thailand and Venezuela. Four indicators are reported: (i) the share of sectors where a commitment was made; (ii) the weighted average coverage of the commitments, adjusted for qualifications; (iii) the share of sectors where commitments include no exceptions or qualifications on national treatment or market access (no restrictions) relative to a member's total commitments; (iv) the share of 'no restrictions' relative to the 155 possible sectors of the GATS classification list. The higher the ratio, the more liberal the country. The indicators show that GATS members as a whole are still a long way from free trade in services, and developing countries have made substantially fewer commitments than high-income countries (Hoekman, 1996).

4. LIBERALIZATION STRATEGIES: MARKET ACCESS

The basic objectives of the WTO are freer, not necessarily free, trade and predictable international trading relationships. Intervention is allowed within the rules agreed by consensus. While average industrial tariffs have fallen, most NTMs eliminated and clearer rules now govern international trade, the preceding review of protection shows that there is still considerable scope for further liberalization and for greater transparency and predictability in the use of trade measures. On tariffs alone, it has been estimated that a 40 per cent reduction in tariff protection in manufactures would yield approximately $US70 billion in global income (welfare) gains in 2005, while the potential gains from similar cuts in agricultural tariffs would add $US60 billion and a further $US10 billion from similar cuts in subsidies (Hertel et al., 1999). It is also estimated, albeit more tentatively, that liberalization in the services sector would produce welfare gains of as much as $US332 billion in 2005 (ibid.). In absolute terms, developing countries would gain more from the industrial tariff cuts, but they would gain more in proportion to their production from the liberalization in the

agricultural sector. Thus tariff negotiations in agriculture and manufactures still have considerable potential for increasing welfare although, at
the time of writing, it has not yet been decided to conduct market access
negotiations in industrial tariffs. The built-in agenda, however, will tackle
NTMs in the agriculture and services negotiations on market access.

Market Access and the Interrelation between Tariff and NTM Liberalization

As a general proposition, trade liberalization increases economic welfare,
unless protection is associated with externalities, and government intervention, whether in the form of tariffs, subsidies or other means, is associated
with a national welfare loss. Whatever the initial gains associated with ISI,
as promoted by Prebisch and Singer, there is also clear evidence that it
caused considerable harm to the agricultural sectors and increased rural
poverty in many developing countries. Intervention in the rural sector has
also been mismanaged, badly targeted and costly. Thus, it is generally desirable to move towards less intervention in developed and developing countries alike. Strategically, however, some countries believe that reciprocal or
multilateral agreements have the advantage over unilateral liberalization in
terms of selling a reform to domestic lobbies and that a progressive reform,
while more costly, minimizes political risks in the short term.

Nevertheless, there are some important questions about the best approach
to liberalization, even on a multilateral basis. For example, it can be shown
from simple analysis of effective rates of protection that distortions and,
hence, welfare losses can be increased by liberalizing sectors with low levels
of protection.[6] Thus, effective protection can be increased by reducing protection on inputs while leaving the duty on finished goods unchanged. This
effect is exacerbated, the higher the materials/output ratio in production.
This is not merely a matter of theory. Dee et al. (1998), in an analysis of
APEC's proposals for Early Voluntary Sectoral Liberalization (EVSL),
show that partial liberalization can lead to economic welfare losses, particularly where relatively low-protected upstream sectors are liberalized and
more highly protected downstream processing sectors remain protected.
Concerning services, these are often inputs into the production, transport
and marketing of goods. Where protection or other forms of intervention
in services is lower than for the goods the services are used to produce,
reduction of such protection can increase protection for the production
process. Where the services protection is higher, liberalization of the services sector can help eliminate or compress negative effective protection for
the production process.

The problem is that it is very difficult to be precise about the overall level of trade intervention in goods and services. In any particular case, tariffs may be clear although, as explained above, it is sometimes difficult to be sure about tariff treatment. To estimate the combined effect of all barriers in all sectors, however, requires some heroic assumptions[7] but if both tariffs and NTMs across the goods and services sectors are not taken into consideration, estimates of the effects of protection and liberalization could be quite erroneous (Deardorff and Stern, 1985). Nevertheless, it is possible to state some stylized facts about the general tendencies and to establish some procedures for liberalization that would tend to be welfare increasing.

An approach which would resolve procedural issues would be to opt for complete trade liberalization as has been proposed by Bergsten (1998) and others. This would, however, cut deeply into sensitive sectors in the industrial countries while many developing countries still rely on tariffs for revenue purposes, although they are making determined efforts to shift the burden of revenue-raising on to domestic indirect taxes. In addition, this would also require equivalent efforts in domestic supports and export subsidies in agriculture, otherwise there would be a growth of surpluses to be dumped on world markets.

Short of agreeing on complete trade liberalization, the approach which would seem to best address the issues of tariff peaks and tariff escalation, and which would lead to a general reduction and compression of effective rates of protection, would be a formula approach, such as the Swiss formula used in the Tokyo Round. This would also be an advantage to smaller countries which have little negotiating power, so that their requests tend to be of little interest to the larger trading countries. Other methods include: request and offer; zero-for-zero; or a mixture of these various approaches.[8] The compression power of the Swiss formula can be seen from Figure 2.1, which compares a linear cut of 50 per cent with the Swiss formula with the coefficient value of 14.[9] While this would not necessarily exclude exceptions, the history of the Tokyo Round was that such exclusions tended to be concentrated in areas of export interest to the developing countries. The impact of such exceptions could be reduced by using a minimum cut for each tariff line but, if exceptions are to be allowed, it would be preferable to allow a backloading of the implementation to allow more time for sensitive sectors to adjust rather than allowing deviations from the formula. The formula could also be varied, for example, by increasing or reducing the coefficient to give shallower or deeper cuts if so desired. The danger of the zero-for-zero approach is that it tends to be focused on products which already have low protection, and such partial liberalization can lead to economic welfare losses, as noted earlier in Dee et al. (1998).

The usefulness of the harmonizing approach extends to, indeed is also

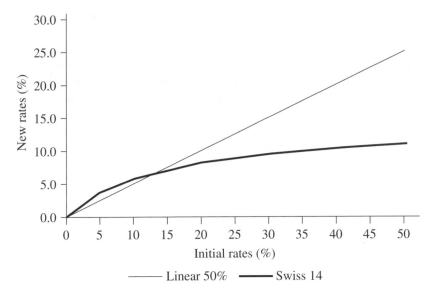

Figure 2.1   Comparison of 50 % linear cut with Swiss (14) formula

applicable to, a global analysis of protection in which other countries also use sectoral interventions and these are sufficient to affect world prices or the terms of trade. For example, if high levels of intervention in a sector in one country are matched by similar intervention abroad, then the combined effect will be to reduce world demand for the good and thus reduce its price both at home and abroad, that is, the terms of trade. So, if high levels of intervention are correlated internationally, then high intervention may be associated with low protection rather than high.[10] Empirically, this effect has been found to be most marked in the textiles, clothing and footwear industries (Deardorff and Stern, 1985). In such cases, liberalization by an important bloc of countries could affect the terms of trade and increase the protective effect of regimes in countries which do not liberalize.

On the other hand, for some goods, liberalization may lead to increased international prices, for example some subsidized agricultural commodities. Brown et al. (1996), in a global analysis of liberalization of trade in goods and services, note that positive welfare gains are not inevitable for all countries when trade is liberalized, because the terms of trade for any one country could deteriorate if its import prices rose and its export prices fell. They note, however, that these effects tend to be small. They also note that, under their simulation scenarios with equivalent liberalization in goods and services, services would expand in some countries and contract in others.

The effect of services liberalization on goods depends on whether the two are complements or substitutes.

These complex interactions tend to reinforce the point that, to sell a liberalization package, it is desirable to move multilaterally to remove intervention simultaneously across sectors so as to compress the spread of intervention. Theory and empirical research both point to the importance of taking a comprehensive approach, tackling tariffs and NTMs across all sectors and countries in a systematic manner. Thus, procedures for liberalization should be focused on a top-down approach, 'lopping the tall poppies'. All in all, a formula approach, adopted multilaterally without giving way to special pleading and carve-outs for highly protected sectors, allows governments to portray domestic liberalization as a *quid pro quo* for improved access to foreign markets. This should not prevent individual countries from pursuing their own reform programmes, but suggests that, strategically, the binding of such autonomous reforms should be the objective in multilateral negotiations rather than holding off making concessions (liberalization) that might not draw forth equivalent concessions from trading partners.

Apart from the general approach to liberalization, there are also a number of other technical questions to be addressed in relation to tariff negotiations; these also have a bearing on the level of market access. For example, one important decision relates to the selection of the base period or base rates for negotiated liberalization and the implementation period for the tariff cuts. One radical suggestion might be to work on the basis of current applied rates rather than bound rates to ensure that the tariff cuts will provide meaningful liberalization instead of merely reducing the gap between bound and applied rates. The averaging technique is also important. In industrial products, import-weighted averages are normally used, but this allows lower cuts on items with high protection (and, hence, lower trade weights) unless minimum cuts are agreed for each tariff item, as was done in the Uruguay Round, often for the more sensitive highly protected items. Simple averages were used in the agricultural sector in the Uruguay Round where there were insufficient data to allow the use of weighted averages.

Balanced market access negotiations would also need to tackle the use of NTMs in goods and services. NTMs, however, are difficult to quantify but studies point out that they are costly to administer, costly to consumers, costly to exporters (in terms of lost trade), inefficient ways of creating jobs, lack transparency, are inherently discriminatory and are most intensively used against developing countries and transition economies (Laird, 1998). Moreover, in isolating domestic industry from international competition, domestic firms are relatively unaffected by price trends on world markets and have little incentive to adopt new technologies or modern business practices.

Market Access in Manufactures

The brief discussion of theory above points clearly to the importance of including manufactures in the market access negotiations for a new round. As noted earlier, developing countries in particular have a major stake in liberalization of trade in manufactures since the larger share of the gains from global liberalization of trade in this sector would accrue to them (Hertel et al., 1999). This derives from the fact that their exports of manufactures have been increasing dramatically, from some 28.8 per cent as a share of total exports in 1980 to 66.6 per cent of the total in 1995 (UNCTAD, 1999). In addition, developing countries have now become important markets for one another's exports of manufactures: in 1990 developing countries' exports of manufactures to other developing countries was 37.2 per cent of their total exports of such products and this share rose to 43.1 per cent in 1995 (ibid.).

The importance of manufactures liberalization for developing countries is also evidenced by a joint UNCTAD–WTO study (UNCTAD–WTO, 1998) which shows that, in a number of sectors with a relatively high value-added and technological content, annual export growth of the developing countries in the period 1990–95 was 15 per cent compared with 9.6 per cent for their exports as a whole. This performance, however, is strongly influenced by the exports of a small number of major developing-country exporters of manufactures. The dynamic exports were those that faced the lowest tariff barriers, while much lower export growth was achieved where tariffs were higher. At the lower end of the development process, lower-income countries and the least-developed countries have a major interest in agricultural products and products with low value-added and technological content – textiles, clothing, footwear and leather products, and these are areas where market access barriers are highest.

Proposals for accelerated tariff liberalization in eight industrial sectors – chemicals, energy and energy equipment, environmental products, gems and jewellery, fish and fish products, medical and scientific equipment, and toys – have been proposed by APEC. The APEC Summit in July 1999 was unable to agree on liberalization within these sectors and referred the idea to the WTO in the hope of an early harvest before the Seattle Ministerial Meeting. The idea was developed out of an APEC proposal for Early Voluntary Sectoral Liberalization. The EU, however, rejected the notion of any tariff deal outside the context of a wider set of negotiations[11] and the opening of negotiations in industrial products remains a matter of uncertainty. On the other hand, a number of developed and developing countries have already announced improved market access for the least-developed countries, including tariff and quota-free access for *essentially all* products from these countries.

Market Access in Agriculture

In the built-in agenda, the market access aspect of NTMs will mainly be covered in the negotiations in agriculture and services, while other aspects will be covered in the review of the operation of the WTO agreements (discussed later).

In agriculture, the NTM aspect of the negotiations will encompass the elimination or the expansion of tariff quotas and, perhaps, a discussion on the manner of their allocation. The negotiations will also discuss the elimination or relaxation of remaining domestic supports, and negotiations are likely to focus on a further reduction in AMS which, in the Uruguay Round, is being reduced by 20 per cent *vis-à-vis* the 1986–88 base period, excluding green and blue box measures[12] which were exempt from the reductions. Since the Uruguay Round commitment was in terms of overall spending, it might also be expected that exporters too would want to see some limitations on intersectoral shifts in funding, comparable to the minimum cuts per tariff line in the tariff negotiations. There are also likely to be efforts to reduce further the scope for the use of market price supports to limit, or even eliminate, any linking of supports to production levels.

While a number of agricultural exporters, such as Argentina and Australia, would like to see the elimination of export subsidies, the main question to be resolved will be the extent of the reduction in their use. In principle, this could take place in the context of negotiations on rules leading to the alignment of rules on domestic supports for agriculture with those for manufactures. The more likely scenario, however, is for some further rolling back of support through extended volume and budget commitments, including limiting the scope for intersectoral shifts in subsidies. There may also be an attempt to ratchet down subsidies by limiting the scope for building up credits in unused subsidies when prices are high. It is also likely that there will be some further discussion of the scope of green box, blue box or S&D box exemptions, all of which are technically rules negotiations with implications for market access.

Market Access in Services

Market access negotiations in services, which started in February 2000, are part of the built-in agenda of the WTO (Article XIX of the GATS) and will address MFN exemptions which were, in principle, to last no longer than ten years. In relation to these renegotiations and any expansion of specific commitments, the absence of customs tariffs or easily quantifiable NTMs makes it difficult to negotiate on expanded market access through the progressive reduction of intervention in services trade. This is why, beyond discussion of how GATT concepts of MFN and national treatment could be applied to trade in services, the Uruguay Round and subsequent sectoral negotiations focused on achieving a degree of intrasectoral reciprocity (Hoekman and Kostecki, 1995). To the extent that it is possible to compute a price wedge associated with the supply of services, however, one option for future market access negotiations in services would be some form of tariffication (or indirect taxation on foreign providers) as in the Uruguay Round agricultural negotiations (Snape, 1994). This may prove possible in areas where standardized services are provided, for example basic telecommunications or banking services. Even in these areas some questions remain, such as how to control for the risk premia required in certain markets or for the additional costs associated with universal service obligations. It is also possible to think about other automatic or formula approaches or about a system of benchmarks to be applied across all members. One possibility would be to start with the generally more ambitious commitments undertaken by the countries that have become members since the establishment of the WTO although, no doubt, this would be resisted by certain developing countries.

In principle, the sectoral approach should encourage countries to make offers to liberalize in order to obtain the benefits of their own liberalization. Given the key role that services plays in the production, transport and marketing of their exports of goods, they could be expected to have been anxious to ensure that they could obtain services at world prices. In the Uruguay Round, however, a number of developed and developing countries placed great emphasis on ensuring that there was reciprocal liberalization in key markets, and finding such a balance in narrowly defined sectoral negotiations in services is difficult. Moreover, a number of developing countries, in particular, remained concerned about the perceived effects of opening up to FDI, estimated to be the principal mode of supply (Hoekman and Kostecki, 1995), and, initially, did not even want services to be included in the Uruguay Round. As a result, the specific commitments leave most of production and trade in services unbound even where it is already liberalized, as discussed above.

Market Access for Foreign Direct Investment (FDI)

The issue of the treatment of FDI (commercial presence) is much less emotive than some years ago. Many developing countries are now actively promoting FDI to capture associated technology gains and market access and thus accelerate their own development and integration into the world economy. A number of countries, however, still place great emphasis on being able to impose conditions on inward FDI and the provision of support for investment by domestic firms. This attitude continues to block efforts to adopt a comprehensive framework for international investment, such as the MAI (reviewed in Daly, 1998; see also Chapter 7). WTO negotiations may begin on this issue in 2003.

Nevertheless, given the structure of the GATS, with the scheduling of commitments on the basis of mode of supply and sectoral specific commitments, it seems likely that further negotiations in the services area will again be sectoral, driven by vested interests in member states (Hoekman and Kostecki, 1995). This implies attempting to achieve a balance of concessions in a situation where the weight of import-competing sectors greatly exceeds that of export interests. On the other hand, given the inclusion of commercial presence as a mode of supply, labour interests may see FDI as job-creating, or at least providing alternative employment opportunities, and be less opposed to liberalization than in the goods area. It has been suggested that regulatory agencies have a vested interest in maintaining their positions, which could be weakened by the presence in their markets of firms located in foreign jurisdictions; this would also lead governments to favour commercial presence.

The bulk of experience of recent years is that FDI brings important advantages through new technologies and enhanced access to overseas markets, stimulating production and trade. FDI, like domestic investment, increases income and employment in the process of capital formation and, in due course, increases capacity to reach even higher income levels after capital has been formed. The gains from trade liberalization can be enhanced by allowing investment to pursue the more efficient production capabilities from comparative advantage and hence also achieve the increased consumption possibilities associated with trade. If markets are functioning efficiently, FDI, like foreign trade, increases global economic welfare and can also eventually help to equalize the returns to the different factors. With appropriate pricing and regulatory policies, many of the fears about FDI are proving unjustified. It is therefore important to generate further information on these effects, to foster an atmosphere that will favour liberalization.

Market Access: Conclusions

There will still be the dilemma of course between the desire to gain the benefits of domestic liberalization and obtaining reciprocity. In this respect, one difficulty is that developing countries, which were interested in offering the supply of labour, found that in the Uruguay Round this mode of supply remained largely restricted except for human-capital-intensive segments and movements directly related to commercial presence. No doubt this issue would also re-emerge in a new round. Drawing the developing countries more fully into future negotiations is also complicated by the provision in Article XIX:2 of the GATS which grants 'appropriate flexibility for individual developing countries for opening fewer sectors, liberalizing fewer types of transactions, progressively extending market access in line with their development situation and, when making access to their markets available to foreign service suppliers, attaching to it conditions aimed at achieving the objectives referred to in Article IV' (of increasing participation of the developing countries in world trade). This would appear to give developing countries scope for limiting their offers, but the experience of the Uruguay Round in the goods areas and subsequent sectoral negotiations in telecommunications and financial services suggests that there will be considerable pressure on the developing countries to participate with substantive offers.

5. LIBERALIZATION STRATEGIES: TRANSPARENCY

As discussed in section 1, conditions of market access could be made more secure and transparent even in the tariff area, and this would have the advantage of clarifying the conditions for trade and investment. Increased transparency would also reduce the difficulties of making quantitative estimates of the levels of protection at the national and global levels. There is a need for greater simplification of tariff structures, transparency in or limitations on the use of different tariff types, such as tariff quotas, specific and mixed rates and so on. Consideration might also be given to setting conditions on the use of specific and compound rates as well as tariff quota administration although, if the use of such rates were prohibited, greater use might then be made of anti-dumping duties as a form of contingency protection. Information should be made public on preferential and concessional rates, together with the relevant trade flows as well as the application of other charges. Transparency would also be enhanced if an effort were made to simplify tariff structures to a uniform rate, for revenue purposes, or a few broad bands, where industrial policy dictates. Consideration might also be given to limiting tariffs to the six-digit level for statistical reporting of trade. It might also be agreed to establish value for duty only on an FOB (eliminating the option of a CIF) basis, which would also reduce the level of protection as well as improving the transparency of the *ad valorem* incidence on the good itself. The need for information, however, is greatest in the area of services, where consistent detailed reporting is necessary as a precursor to estimating the effects of intervention.

Simplification of rules of origin and accumulation would also increase transparency and reduce the risk of preferential rules being used for protection purposes. Tests such as change of tariff heading or a (varying) percentage of domestic value-added are intended to simplify the computation of value for duty, but most countries use a mixture of such rules and these vary even for the same product in different regional agreements. These could be simplified by a single approach, such as change of tariff heading. A more radical approach would be to charge duties according to the value-added in countries which enjoy different tariff treatment, but the complexity of the calculations and the scope for fraud make this an unlikely option. Certainly, there is a need for WTO disciplines in this area.

Finally, there is a need for greater transparency in the use of other charges on trade. An effort might be made to ensure that these are based on the cost of the service and are not simply an additional *ad valorem* charge for revenue purposes. Similarly, there is a need to tighten the application of national rules which allow indirect taxes to differentiate between domestic and imported goods by modifying descriptions of products that are close substitutes in consumption.

The services negotiations will also suffer from the lack of information on production and trade in the various sectors and sub-sectors, particularly those not covered by specific commitments. There is also a lack of information on the quantitative significance of the various forms of intervention in the sector and, hence, also on the direct and indirect effects of such intervention. This information is often useful in building lobbies in favour of liberalization when domestic firms can see clearly how they are penalized by the prices they pay for the inputs of services.

6.   LIBERALIZATION STRATEGIES: RULES ISSUES

In the built-in agenda, the review of the operation of the WTO Agreements offers the best possibility for any tightening of disciplines on the use of NTMs although the review *per se* does not absolutely guarantee negotiated changes in the rules. The rules discussions are expected to cover anti-dumping, countervailing and safeguard measures, technical barriers, TRIPs, rules of origin and government procurement, most of which have important implications for market access.

One of the key areas is the use of contingency protection. As mentioned earlier, the WTO Agreement on Safeguards allows for some discretion in the allocation of quotas but, so far, there has been no major surge in the use of safeguard measures under Article XIX. The main area of contingency protection has been anti-dumping, except in the textiles and clothing area, where special safeguards under the Agreement on Textiles and Clothing have also been widely used. When this sector is fully integrated into GATT 1994 in 2002, there may be an increase in the use of safeguards under these provisions of the Safeguards Agreement, but it is equally possible that the strain will be taken up by anti-dumping mechanisms. This could also arise from the progressive liberalization of the agricultural sector. So far, however, it is difficult to envisage a reopening of the Safeguards Agreement, which is largely untested. On the other hand, it is the Safeguards Agreement which prohibits the use of VERs and, from press reports, this is an area where it is evident that a number of measures are still being negotiated between governments, for example in the iron and steel and automotive sectors. Similarly, there are a number of product areas – such as petroleum and aluminium – where production quotas fulfil the role of export restraints. Again, price undertakings as a negotiated outcome of anti-dumping cases have similar effects to VERs; this seems inconsistent and may be worth examining. It might be useful to investigate whether a single set of rules on contingency protection, allowing legalized backsliding over an adjustment period, could be developed to encompass anti-dumping, countervailing measures, safeguards and the various special safeguards provisions. A linkage to competition policy ideas could also be beneficial.

Two other areas deserve special mention. First, government procurement is one of the few exceptions to the Single Undertaking of the Uruguay Round. In this area, efforts have focused mainly on increasing the transparency of procurement procedures rather than access negotiations as such. In addition, the issue of whether some rules on competition policy should be part of the WTO is currently being discussed. A number of countries remain opposed to negotiations on any binding code, but might accept further study that could lead to the establishment of some kind of rules at a later stage.

Rules negotiations will also form part of the forthcoming services negotiations. The GATS is a major achievement in bringing services trade under multilateral disciplines, but it is only the first step in this direction and there is much more to be done. Indeed, this is recognized in GATS Article VI, which calls for continued negotiations in order to fill the general disciplines on domestic regulation with actual content. Negotiations on safeguards, subsidies and procurement in services are still under way. At the broadest level, consideration might be given to re-establishing the GATS along the lines of the more general approach used in the EU, NAFTA and ANZCERTA, involving a negative list and making national treatment an obligation (Hoekman, 1996), although this is probably unrealistic. There is considerable weight being attached to the 'flexibility' of the GATS, meaning only taking on commitments when a country feels able, and this is even being held up as an example for other areas in the WTO. Nevertheless, there is a need for tightening disciplines in some areas; for example, in contrast with GATT rules on goods, the GATS imposes no disciplines on subsidies subject to the national treatment constraint with regard to alternative suppliers or services, and even this may be subject to limitations. In recent rounds of GATT negotiations, a concern was to ensure that the expected benefits of negotiated tariff reductions were not undermined by the use of NTMs. This explains the tightening of disciplines on the use of subsidies under the SCM Agreement and the AoA. In services, however, there are no similar constraints. Again, consistent treatment of safeguards and government procurement could usefully be addressed and, in general, the development of a consistent set of disciplines in goods and services should be agenda items for the new round.

In services, the need for rules on competition and regulatory policy is even more pressing than in the case of goods because the prevalence of state or private monopolies and oligopolies in services effectively debases the value of market access and national treatment commitments. This does not imply deregulation of state enterprises, for example in health and education as some have suggested, but establishment of consistent and transparent standards of behaviour.

NOTES

*   The views expressed here are those of the author and do not necessarily represent the views of UNCTAD, the WTO or its member states. Helpful comments on an earlier draft were received from Rolf Adlung and Costas Michalopoulos.
1. The prohibition on certain measures is included in Article 4.2 of the WTO Agreement on Agriculture and the list of specific measures, including variable levies, covered by the prohibition is in footnote 1 to the article.
2. A rebuttable presumption of serious prejudice arises in cases where the amount of the total *ad valorem* subsidy exceeds 5 per cent, when subsidies are used to cover operating losses, or when there is direct debt forgiveness.
3. World Development Indicators publish data on transfers, but these do not correspond to subsidies within the meaning of the WTO Agreement.
4. Some developing countries have obtained an extension of the right to use TRIMs.
5. This negative list approach contrasts with the NAFTA and proposals for a free trade area for the Americas in which a positive list approach is used, identifying sectors to be covered.
6. Effective protection is the protection afforded to value-added in production processes resulting from the combined effects of protection on materials inputs into the process and protection on the outputs. It can be given by the formula: $g = ((Df - X.Dm)/(1 - X))$ where g is the effective rate, Df is the tariff rate on outputs, Dm is the rate on material inputs, X the materials–output ratio at free trade prices, adjusted by the formula $X = X' * ((1 + Df)/(1 + Dm))$, where X' is the observed materials–output ratio under protection. Protection can be measured by tariffs or tariffs and NTBs.

7. Brown et al. (1996) estimate the redistribution effects of a 25 per cent reduction in the incidence of barriers to trade in services, using the 'guesstimates' (*sic*) computed by Hoekman (1996) which are reproduced in Tables 2.10 and 2.11.
8. For further details, see Laird (1998).
9. The Swiss formula is given by $T_1 = aT_0/(a + T_0)$. In the Tokyo Round, the coefficient a was generally set at the value of 14.
10. This analysis was originally for tariffs by Deardorff and Stern (1985).
11. EU negotiator, Peter Carl, reported in *Journal of Commerce* (1999).
12. 'Green box' measures are permitted general or non-specific trade interventions by governments. 'Blue box' measures are direct payments made to farmers by the USA and the EU which were exempted in the Uruguay Round agricultural negotiations under the Blair House Agreement.

REFERENCES

Bergsten, C.F. (1998), 'Fifty years of the GATT/WTO: lessons from the past for strategies for the future', paper presented to the Symposium on the World Trading System, *Fifty Years: Looking Back, Looking Forward*, Geneva, 30 April.

Brown, D., A. Deardorff and R.M. Stern (1996), 'The liberalization of services trade: potential impacts in the aftermath of the Uruguay Round', in W. Martin and L.A. Winters (eds), *The Uruguay Round and the Developing Countries*, Cambridge: Cambridge University Press, pp. 292–315.

Crawford, J.A. and S. Laird (2000), 'Regional trade agreements and the WTO', *Journal of the North American Economics Association*, **12**(2), 193–211.

Daly, M. (1998), 'Investment incentives and the Multilateral Agreement on Investment', *Journal of World Trade*, **32** (2).

Davey, W.J. (1998), 'Article XVII GATT: an overview', mimeo, Geneva: WTO.

Deardorff, A. and R.M. Stern (1985), 'The structure of tariff protection: effects of foreign tariffs and existing NTBs', *The Review of Economics and Statistics*, **LXVII** (4), 539–48.

Dee, P., A. Hardin and M. Schuele (1998), 'APEC Early Voluntary Sectoral Liberalisation', Productivity Commission Staff Research Paper, Ausinfo, Canberra.

Finger, J.M., M. Ingco and U. Reincke (1996), *The Uruguay Round: Statistics on Tariff Concessions Given and Received*, Washington, DC: The World Bank.

GATT (1994), 'News of the Uruguay Round of Multilateral Trade Negotiations', press release, 12 April, Geneva: WTO.

Guisinger, S. (1987), 'Investment related to trade', in J.M. Finger and A. Olechowski (eds), *The Uruguay Round: a Handbook for the Multilateral Trade Negotiations*, Washington, DC: The World Bank.

Hertel, T., K. Anderson, J.F. Francois, B. Hoekman and W. Martin (1999), 'Agriculture and non-agricultural liberalization in the Millennium Round', paper presented at the *Agriculture and the New Trade Agenda in the WTO 2000 Negotiations* Conference, Geneva, 1–2 October.

Hoekman, B. (1996), 'Assessing the General Agreement on Trade in Services', in W. Martin and L.A. Winters, *The Uruguay Round and the Developing Countries*, Cambridge: Cambridge University Press, pp. 88–124.

Hoekman, B. and M. Kostecki (1995), *The Political Economy of the World Trading System*, Oxford: Oxford University Press.

Journal of Commerce (1999), 29 July.

Laird, S. (1998), 'Multilateral Approaches to Market Access Negotiations', paper for the OAS, WTO and Georgetown University Conference 'Multilateral and Regional Trade Agreements: an Analysis of Current Trade Policy Issues', Washington, DC, 26–27 May.

Laird, S. (1999a), 'Export policy and the WTO', *Journal of International Trade and Economic Development*, **8** (1), 73–88.

Laird, S. (1999b), 'Transition economies, business and the WTO', *World Competition*, **22** (1), 171–87.

Michalopoulos, C. (1999), 'Trade policy and market Access issues for developing countries', Development Division, WTO, Geneva.

Miranda, J., R.A. Torres and M. Ruiz (1998), 'The international use of anti-dumping: 1987–1997', *Journal of World Trade*, **32** (5), 5–71.

OECD (1997), *Indicators of Tariff and Non-tariff Trade Barriers*, Paris: OECD.

OECD (1998a), *Agricultural Policies in OECD Countries – Monitoring and Evaluation*, Paris: OECD.

OECD (1998b), *Agricultural Policies in OECD Countries – Measurement of Support and Background Information*, Paris: OECD.

Snape, R. (1994), 'Principles in trade in services', in *The New World Trading System: Readings*, Paris: OECD, pp. 197–8.

UNCTAD (1990), *Trade Expansion Among Developing Countries: Constraints and Measures to Overcome Them*, TD/B/1260, Geneva: UNCTAD.

UNCTAD (1999), *Handbook of International Trade and Development Statistics 1996, 1997*, Geneva: United Nations.

UNCTAD–WTO (1998), 'Market access developments since the Uruguay Round: implications, opportunities and challenges, in particular for developing countries and least-developed countries, in the context of globalization and liberalization', Report by the UNCTAD Secretariat and the WTO Secretariat, Geneva.

3. Agricultural trade reform after the Asian recession: a bridge too far?

Rod Tyers and Yongzheng Yang*

Since 1997, Asian growth has stalled following a combined financial and currency crisis that brought on what is referred to here as the 'Asian recession'.[1] Several of the developing economies that had earlier been major contributors to both Asian growth and commodity imports experienced very substantial contractions associated with a surge of insolvencies following capital flight and unexpectedly large currency depreciations. This saw their capital accounts shift from surplus to deficit and necessitated dramatic contractions in imports. Accordingly, global demand for agricultural commodities contracted and international commodity prices fell.

In the North, that is, the older industrial economies of Europe, North America and Australasia, some governments did not pass these price declines through to farmers and so the level of agricultural protection rose. The bridge to reforms envisaged during the Uruguay Round has therefore grown longer. Even in countries whose governments have allowed the effects of the Asian recession to pass through to their farmers, further trade reform will have to come on top of already costly adjustment. Moreover, the effects of the Asian recession are unlikely to be fully reversed by the now ongoing recovery. Although output and asset prices in Asia have begun to recover, the crisis-induced reversals in Asian capital accounts remain. This redistribution of global investment could well extend well into the negotiation period of the Millennium Round (Krugman, 1999a).

This chapter first explores why the reallocation of global investment away from the affected Asian economies will be long-lasting. It then examines the magnitudes of the structural adjustments that liberalization would have imposed on protected agricultural sectors in 1995 and estimates the extent to which these have been magnified by the Asian recession. Although global general equilibrium analysis is used to simulate the recession,[2] no attempt is made to reproduce the short-run dynamics of the crisis.[3] Instead, the analysis is comparative static, taking as its starting-point the real shocks that emerged in the wake of the crisis. In the short run, these included a severe contraction of domestic investment, as home savings fled abroad and foreign savings in Asia were withdrawn, and the temporary unemployment of capital as many Asian firms foundered under the escalated cost of foreign borrowings and the credit crunch that followed.[4] Recent evidence suggests that a considerable number of firms in the most affected countries were rendered insolvent and a larger number illiquid (World Bank, 1999a) and that this explains the bulk of the initial contractions in output.

The emphasis here is on the medium-run effects of the recession.[5] Property rights issues are assumed to be resolved eventually, but there is a longer-lasting reallocation of world savings away from Asia. The effects of this reallocation on trade in agricultural products and, ultimately, on real returns to the assets of Northern farmers is estimated. The results are then compared with the corresponding effects of an indicative reduction of all agricultural distortions by 50 per cent. Where the effects of the Asian recession on Northern farmers have been muted by insulating trade policies, such policies have raised protection levels and therefore increased the scale of structural changes that would have to accompany further agricultural trade reform. Section 1 offers a brief review of the Asian recession and spells out the reasons for expecting the medium-run effects of the recession to be long-lasting. A preliminary assessment of the importance of the recession for agricultural markets is also offered. Section 2 then introduces the model and provides a summary of its structure and behaviour. The analysis of the Asian recession experiments is detailed in section 3 and its potential interaction with trade reforms is discussed in section 4. Section 5 then offers conclusions.

1.   THE ASIAN RECESSION AND AGRICULTURAL MARKETS

The Asian Recession

The events of 1997 are already well documented in a number of studies (see Corsetti et al., 1998; Goldstein, 1998; IMF, 1998, 1999; McLeod and Garnaut, 1998; Radelet and Sachs, 1998; and Wong, 1998). This study is concerned with the associated real shocks and their implications for agricultural commodity markets. Japan is included in the analysis in spite of important differences in the character of its recession from those elsewhere in developing Asia.[6] The bursting of the 1980s asset bubble there caused a decline in investment that accelerated in 1997 in spite of a macroeconomic policy that maintained very low short-term interest rates. Private consumption in Japan remained comparatively stable during the 1990s but declined in the crisis period. The associated decline in investment has further expanded Japan's capital account deficit and hence its current account surplus. In addition, a trend towards lower working hours, combined with the recent implementation of a standard 40-hour week, caused a decline in total labour hours and an associated reduction in output per worker (Bayoumi and Towe, 1998). Thus, Japan's trade surplus rose while its GDP fell (IMF, 1998).

In the most affected countries of developing Asia, the scale of the contractions was proportionally larger.[7] Worst hit have been Indonesia and Thailand, but the economies of Malaysia and Korea also contracted substantially. The crisis in these countries began in Thailand in mid-1997, following a period during which export performance had begun to falter and foreign-currency-denominated debt to accumulate. As doubts arose about the government's commitment to honour implicit guarantees to maintain the nominal exchange rate, capital flight ensued, eventually resulting in a very substantial currency depreciation. The sharp rise in domestic debt and debt service costs that followed precipitated the associated financial crisis.[8] Fear of similar developments appears then to have been self-fulfilling in near neighbours Indonesia and Malaysia. As savings were withdrawn from these economies and their currencies depreciated, asset prices fell and considerable wealth was lost. Private consumption fell and savings rose. Very large declines in domestic investment combined with the rise in savings to create substantial capital account deficits were counterbalanced on the current account side by collapses in imports.

One year after the onset of the crisis, export values had not fallen, but neither had they yet begun to rise (IMF, 1998, table 2.6). Considering the substantial currency depreciations these countries experienced, this does of course imply a rise in export volumes offset by a fall in US dollar export prices.[9] Moreover, the growth of competing exports from China began to decelerate as the Chinese and Hong Kong currencies appreciated against those of recession-hit developing Asia. Although the Chinese and Hong Kong governments held fast to their nominal exchange rates against the US dollar, the contractionary policies required to achieve this depressed domestic consumption and raised saving. Their domestic price levels fell and their real exchange rates depreciated against trading partners in the North even while they appreciated against competitors elsewhere in developing Asia (Huang and Song, 1999).

For the most affected Asian economies, the primary real shocks were of two types. First, as savings fled, domestic investment declined. In Japan, where the process was more gradual, investment fell by about 10 per cent in the two years from late 1997.[10] In the most affected economies of developing Asia, however, the initial panic of 1997 was so great that domestic investment declined by as much as half. Demand for domestic capital goods and construction collapsed and private consumption demand also fell, driven by the associated wealth effects of asset price declines. Imports therefore fell dramatically.

The second of the real shocks was a further short-run decline in domestic production in the affected economies. Because the credit squeeze was greatly exacerbated by an associated currency crisis and hence a blowing out of dollar-denominated debt service costs, there was a high incidence of illiquidity and insolvency.[11] This effect was greater in developing Asia because of the rapid expansion of private sector credit there during the early 1990s. In the decade to 1995, for example, private sector credit as a proportion of GDP tripled in Indonesia and doubled in Thailand (IMF, 1998, table 3.8). Equity markets were comparatively underdeveloped and investment during the period was financed primarily by debt. Debt–equity ratios of Korean domestic manufacturing firms in the mid-1990s, for example, were double those of manufacturing firms in the USA. It was therefore inevitable that the substantial rise in debt service costs would drive a higher than usual proportion of firms in the most affected economies into insolvency.[12] This was the principal cause of the contractions in output experienced in developing Asia in the first year following the onset of the crisis. These real shocks are examined and compared in Yang and Tyers (1999). This chapter takes the same approach but focuses on the longer-lasting 'medium-run' shock, the flight of savings from Asia or the reallocation of global investment away from Asia.

Why the 'Medium-run' Effects of the Recession Might be Long-lasting

In support of the conclusion that the medium-run effects of the Asian recession will last into the Millennium Round negotiation period, four points are offered. First, through the initial two years of the recession, the crisis-induced shifts in Asian balances of payments in favour of capital account deficits (current account surpluses) have abated only slowly in the affected Asian economies. Currencies and stock markets in many affected countries have recovered somewhat but, even where countries ran capital account surpluses (current account deficits) before 1997, the apparent trend is towards retention of deficits (*The Economist*, 1999).

Second, although political regimes have changed since the onset of the recession in most affected countries, financial reforms and the restructuring of the financial services sector have been very slow in all.

Third, much of the investment in the affected countries through the mid-1990s was financed by borrowing abroad, with private domestic assets as collateral. In the crisis, lenders were burned and a substantial part of the private wealth that facilitated the investment has been lost.[13] Moreover, the

changes of political regime that followed should combine with the anticipated financial reforms to make it more difficult than before for a select few
individuals to accumulate private wealth at the same rate as before.

Finally, there is the observation by Krugman (1994) and others that evidence of diminishing returns to capital had begun to appear in East Asia
during the early 1990s. The returns may simply not be there to justify the
share of the world's investment achieved in the pre-recession period. The
changed pattern of global savings and investment is therefore likely to
endure, at least through the early stages of the WTO's built-in agenda,
which began in 2000.

Asia and Agricultural Markets

The affected economies of Japan, China and Southeast Asia contributed a
quarter of global GDP in the mid-1990s. Even if retained within the region,
a recession in these countries must affect the rest of the world substantially.
The significance of the region for agricultural markets goes beyond this,
however. Over the two decades before the recession, as these economies
opened to trade, their poor endowments of land per capita saw them transit
from net exporters of commodities to net exporters of manufactures and
importers of agricultural products. For the economies most affected by the
Asian recession, by the mid-1990s two-thirds of these agricultural imports
were from the USA, the EU, Canada and Australasia. More importantly,
however, the combined imports of the recession-hit developing economies
of Asia, Japan and China made up about a third of US total exports, yet
their imports of agricultural products made up half of US total agricultural exports. The corresponding shares for the EU and Australasia were
20 and 57 per cent, respectively.[14] Any decline in Asian imports or realign-
ment of currencies between Asia and the Northern economies was therefore bound to have a substantial effect on Northern farmers.

Indeed, the Asian recession did affect Northern farmers directly through
trade in the commodities they produce. This is evident from the traded commodity prices plotted in Figure 3.1, including two cereals, a natural fibre and
sugar, all deflated by the US GDP deflator. Since 1980, there have been only
two occasions on which all the prices turned downward simultaneously. The
first was during the early 1980s when the high interest rate policy of the early
Reagan period caused a substantial real appreciation in the US dollar relative to the rest of the world. This was the period that precipitated the
Uruguay Round of trade negotiations and, in particular, the priority given
in that round to an agreement on agriculture (OECD, 1998). The second was
between 1997 and 1998, again associated with a real appreciation in the
North, this time relative to Asia and some other developing countries.

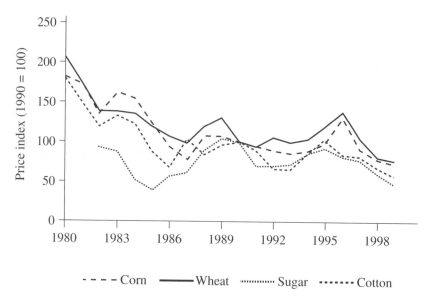

Note: Nominal prices are deflated by the US GDP deflator.

Source: World Bank (1999b).

Figure 3.1   Agricultural commodity prices, 1980–99 (1990 = 100)

The effect on Northern farmers did not take the form of commodity price changes and a wider real appreciation alone;[15] it also changed the composition of international trade in goods that compete with agriculture for resources. A clear view of both the direct and indirect effects requires an accurate representation of factor markets in the North and hence of the proportions in which primary factors and inputs are used across industries. In this, the EU is fairly typical. Its 1995 factor proportions are summarized in Table 3.1. Broadly, agriculture is land- and labour-intensive, mining is capital-intensive and manufacturing labour-intensive. Typical of all the Northern industrial economies, however, the dominant services sector is capital-intensive relative to manufacturing and it comprises two sub-sectors, one of which is intensive in unskilled labour while the other combines relatively balanced shares of the three mobile factors. The labour-intensity of agriculture proved important in affecting the position of farmers for, as it turned out, the Asian recession raised labour demand in the North. Thus, Northern farmers were hurt not only by declines in both Asian agricultural imports and traded commodity prices but also by a rise in the real cost of their most important mobile factor of production.

Table 3.1   Factor proportions in the EU, %[a]

Sector	Land	Labour	Skill	Capital	Nat. rescs	Total
Agriculture	10 (7)	58 (53)	4 (11)	24 (26)	4 (3)	100
Mining	0 (0)	17 (24)	9 (14)	38 (37)	36 (25)	100
Manufacturing:						
labour-intensive	0 (1)	57 (50)	20 (21)	23 (27)	0 (1)	100
skill-intensive	0 (0)	48 (45)	26 (26)	26 (29)	0 (0)	100
Services:						
labour-intensive	0 (0)	41 (41)	17 (20)	42 (39)	0 (0)	100
skill-intensive	0 (0)	34 (36)	36 (33)	30 (31)	0 (0)	100

Note:
[a] Listed are value-added shares with, in parentheses, *total* factor proportions (including the factor content of intermediate inputs).

Source: GTAP Database Version 4.1. See McDougall *et al.* (1998).

2.   THE MODEL OF THE ASIAN RECESSION

In quantifying the effects of the Asian crisis on Northern agriculture, the concern is with a medium run in which labour is mobile between sectors while physical capital is immobile. The model used must accommodate this in combination with an open capital account in each region and therefore an explicit treatment of savings and investment. An adapted global trade assistance and protection (GTAP) general equilibrium model is used.[16] Its analytics are summarized in Table 3.2. As a starting-point, it offers the following useful generalizations: (i) a capital goods sector in each region to service investment; (ii) explicit savings, albeit at an exogenous rate, in each region combined with open regional capital accounts that permit savings in one region to finance investment in others; (iii) multiple trading regions, goods and primary factors; (iv) non-traded goods and services; (v) product differentiation by country of origin; (vi) empirically based differences in tastes and technology across regions; (vii) non-homothetic preferences; and (ix) explicit allowance for transportation costs and policy distortions.

For the corresponding database, the GTAP Version 4 database for 1995 is used, aggregated into the regions listed in Table 3.3.[17] Note that the aggregate, Recessed Developing Asia, is used to represent the most seriously affected Asian region. Although it excludes less-affected China, there is considerable variance in the degree to which countries were affected by the recession within this region. The Asian recession shocks imposed are

Table 3.2   Model analytics

Single household in each region
Utility Cobb–Douglas in:
    private household expenditure
    government expenditure
    savings (share and marginal propensity can be modified exogenously)
Government consumption: Cobb–Douglas composite of all goods
Private household consumption: CDE[a] expenditure function
    CES decomposition between home goods and imports
    CES decomposition of imports by region of origin
Firms are perfectly competitive with constant returns to scale
Technology is a CES combination of intermediate inputs with a separate CES
    composite of primary factors
Intermediate demand is decomposed to home goods and imports as for household
    final consumption
Primary factor demand: nested CES system[b]
Factor specificity: Land specific to agriculture
    Natural resources specific to mining
    Physical capital is sector-specific
    Labour and skill intersectorally mobile
Primary factor supply: all factors are inelastic in supply
Capital returns are intraregional
Investment: worldwide sum across regions' savings
    Does not affect the current productive capital stock
    Does consume 'capital goods' and enter the capital account of each region's
    balance of payments
    Capital goods are a Cobb–Douglas composite of domestic goods and services
    The endogenous allocation of investment across 'non-Asia' equalizes 'expected
    returns' in each region. These are a decreasing function of regional investment[c]

Notes:
Households can transform labour between skilled and unskilled. However, this capability is reduced to negligibility in the applications discussed here.
[a] Constant difference of elasticities (see Hertel, 1997).
[b] For the primary factor demand structure, see Yang and Tyers (1999), figure 1.
[c] The formulation of expected returns, along with some alternative investment allocation rules, is discussed in Hertel and Tsigas (1997).

Table 3.3   Model structure

Regions	Share of world GDP[f]
1. Recessed developing Asia[a]	5.1
2. Japan	18.0
3. China[b]	2.5
4. European Union[c]	29.0
5. USA	25.2
6. Australasia	1.4
7. Rest of world	18.8

Primary factors
  1. Agricultural land
  2. Natural resources
  3. Skill[d]
  4. Labour[d]
  5. Physical capital

Sectors[e]
  1. Cereals (paddy and processed rice, wheat and other cereals)
  2. Other crops (vegetables, oil seeds, processed vegetable oils, sugar cane and sugar, crop based fibres and other crops)
  3. Livestock products (cattle, meat and meat products, raw milk and dairy products, animal fibres and other animal products)
  4. Other agricultural products (forest products, fish and other agricultural products)
  5. Mining and energy (coal, oil, gas and other minerals)
  6. Skill-intensive manufacturing (petroleum, paper, chemicals, processed minerals, metals, motor vehicles and other transport equipment, electronic equipment and other machinery and equipment)
  7. Labour-intensive manufacturing (textiles, apparel, leather and wood products, metal products, other manufactures)
  8. Skill-intensive services (electricity, gas, water, financial services and public administration)
  9. Labour-intensive services (construction, retail and wholesale trade, dwellings)

Notes:
[a] Korea (Rep.), Indonesia, Philippines, Malaysia, Singapore, Thailand, Vietnam.
[b] China includes Hong Kong and Taiwan.
[c] The EU15.
[d] The labour disaggregation is based on the ILO Classification of Occupations. Professional workers are defined as including managers and administrators, professionals and para-professionals. Production workers are plant and machine operators and drivers, tradespersons, clerks, labourers and related workers, salespersons and personal service workers.
[e] These are aggregates of the 50-sector GTAP Version 4 database (see McDougall et al., 1998).
[f] Share of 1995 GDP in US$ measured at market prices and exchange rates.

therefore averages across the region and do not reflect the severity of the effects in individual economies such as Indonesia.

Households and firms in the model consume a composite of goods and services that is a blend of home products and imports, the composition depending upon relative prices and an elasticity of substitution. In turn, imports are a blend of the products of all regions and the composition depends upon regional trading prices and a further elasticity of substitution. This structure facilitates the departures from the law of one price that tend to occur even in tradable goods sectors in the short and medium run.[18] For this reason, the common practice among GTAP users of choosing larger than the standard elasticities of substitution in all industries when doing long-run comparative static analysis is not adopted.[19] Larger than the standard elasticities, however, are used for the comparatively homogeneous agricultural products. The elasticities used are listed in Table 3.4.

Table 3.4   Elasticities of substitution in intermediate and primary factor demand[a]

Sector	In product demand, between domestic and imported	In import demand, between regions of origin	In factor demand, between primary factor groups[b]
Cereals	8.8	17.6	0.2
Other crops	6.0	12.0	0.6
Livestock products	5.2	10.5	0.4
Other agriculture	4.8	9.6	0.8
Mining	2.8	5.6	0.2
Manufacturing:			
labour-intensive	3.0	6.4	1.2
skill-intensive	2.8	6.0	1.2
Services:			
labour-intensive	1.9	3.8	1.5
skill-intensive	2.0	3.8	1.3

Notes:
[a] These are group-specific weighted averages across the 50 industries defined in the database. The structure of intermediate and primary factor demand is indicated in figure 1 in Yang and Tyers (1999). The CDE parameters governing substitution in final demand are discussed in McDougall et al. (1998). Substitution elasticities in intermediate product demand, and between intermediates and primary factors, are set to unity (Cobb–Douglas) in this analysis.
[b] The elasticity of substitution within the labour group, between skilled and unskilled labour, is set at unity. Households' corresponding elasticity of transformation between skilled and unskilled labour is set to negligibility for this analysis.

Source: GTAP Database Version 4.1 (see McDougall et al., 1998).

This adaptation of the model involves changes to its intermediate input and labour demand structures. In particular, output is made a CES composite of intermediate products and primary factors so as more accurately to represent substitution between inputs and primary factors. A further composite of skilled and unskilled labour is also introduced better to reflect factor market impacts of external shocks. This allows the two types of labour to be more substitutable for each other than each is substitutable for the other mobile factor, capital.[20] Finally, the short-run nature of the Asian crisis requires a closure in which capital is industry-specific in all regions.

3. MEDIUM-RUN EFFECTS OF THE ASIAN RECESSION

The Medium-run Asian Recession Experiment

The construction of the Asian recession shock follows Yang and Tyers (1999). Since further trade negotiations will take place in the more distant aftermath of the recession, for the present purpose the medium run is emphasized, in which property rights issues are resolved and capital is no longer made idle in developing Asia and Japan. The essential element of the medium-run story is the continued reallocation of global investment away from the affected countries. The exercise undertaken here differs from that in Yang and Tyers, however, not only because of the emphasis here on the medium run. In this analysis, both the country and commodity aggregates used also differ and the role of China is accounted for more explicitly.[21]

Although the focus is on the medium run, a version of the model that restricts intersectoral capital mobility in all regions is used throughout. Returns to capital therefore vary across industries. Some attention must be paid to the short run, however, because the model does not have intertemporal optimization by households or firms and short-run analysis is used to establish benchmark average savings rates in recession-hit developing Asia and Japan. Since some data are now available for the affected countries for 1998, levels of investment and output can be observed, as well as current account imbalances in the immediate aftermath of the crisis. Because these data are incomplete, they are used to formulate short-run shocks and the model is applied to calculate the implied average rates of saving. These are then held constant in the medium-run analysis.[22] Because the details of the short-run shocks are presented in Yang and Tyers (1999), they are not repeated here.

In the medium run, debt workouts have resolved property rights issues and capital is no longer unemployed in recession-hit developing Asia and Japan. Capital remains immobile between industries, however. As capital utilization rates return to benchmark levels, the short-run retreat of labour to agriculture is reversed and factor productivity in agriculture returns to its reference levels. GDP levels in recession-hit developing Asia and Japan therefore approach their pre-recession benchmarks. None the less, investment is set, relative to GDP, to remain at 1998 levels in these two regions. Their current account balances are restored to endogeneity to ensure consistency with the capital account. This allows the recovery in their national incomes to further raise total savings and hence widens the trade surplus as growth in exports underwrites their recoveries.[23]

China is added as a distinct region in this analysis and its behaviour is represented as 'in between' that of the recession-hit economies and those of the North. Recent data on China's domestic investment and its balance of payments are incomplete and, probably, highly inaccurate. The rise in declared official foreign reserves of $US5 billion during 1998 and evidence of substantial domestic deflation are guides to hypothesizing a rise in China's current account surplus by this amount (Huang and Song, 1999). Domestic investment is made endogenous to equalize regional average 'expected rates of return' (Hertel and Tsigas, 1997), but the average rate of saving is made endogenous to ensure consistency with the exogenous current account change. The full set of shocks and closures adopted in this medium-run scenario are detailed in Table 3.5.

Table 3.5   Medium-run Asian recession shocks and closure[a]

Recessed developing Asia:
   Regional investment is exogenous and reduced from 1995 to 1998 levels.
   The average regional saving rate is now made exogenous at the value achieved
       in the short-run solution.[b] The trade balance $(X - M)$ is endogenous.
   Sectoral production volumes are endogenous, while sectoral capital use is
       exogenous.
   Labour and land productivity in agriculture is restored to reference levels.
   Labour (skilled and unskilled) remains sectorally mobile and is fully employed.
   Agricultural and other policies maintain constant nominal protection
       coefficients.[c]
Japan:
   Regional investment is exogenous and reduced from 1995 to 1998 levels.
   The average regional saving rate is now made exogenous at the value achieved
       in the short-run solution.[b] The trade balance $(X - M)$ is endogenous.
   Sectoral production volumes are endogenous, while sectoral capital use is
       exogenous.
   Labour (skilled and unskilled) remains sectorally mobile and is fully employed.
   Agricultural and other policies maintain constant nominal protection
       coefficients.[c]

Table 3.5 (continued)

China:

Regional investment is endogenous, equalizing regional average 'expected returns' across China, EU, USA, Australasia and the rest of the world.[d]

The average saving rate is endogenous, while the current account surplus $(X - M)$ is made exogenous and shocked as per the observed 1998 change.

Sectoral production volumes are endogenous, while sectoral capital use is exogenous.

Labour (skilled and unskilled) remains sectorally mobile and is fully employed.

Agricultural and other policies maintain constant nominal protection coefficients.[c]

EU, Australasia:

Regional investment is endogenous to equalize regional average 'expected returns' across EU, USA, Australasia and the rest of the world.[d]

The trade balance is endogenous, while the average saving rate is retained exogenous.

Sectoral production volumes are endogenous, while sectoral capital use is exogenous.

Labour (skilled and unskilled) remains sectorally mobile and the real wage of raw labour is flexible upward only.[e]

Agricultural and other policies maintain constant nominal protection coefficients.[c]

USA, and rest of world:

Regional investment is endogenous to equalize regional average 'expected returns' across EU, USA, Australasia and the rest of the world.[d]

The trade balance is endogenous, while the average saving rate is retained exogenous.

Sectoral production volumes are endogenous, while sectoral capital use is exogenous.

Labour (skilled and unskilled) remains sectorally mobile and both real wages are flexible.

Agricultural and other policies maintain constant nominal protection coefficients.[c]

Notes:

[a] In both the short and medium run, capital is completely sector-specific in all regions, so that the rate of return differs across sectors.

[b] Since the capital account and current account must be equal in magnitude and opposite in sign, $I - S = M - X$. For both developing Asia (incl. China) and Japan, these changes impose explicit contractions in investment and rises in the average rate of saving, balanced by a now endogenous rise in exports relative to imports. Details of the short-run solution are available in Yang and Tyers (1999).

[c] Since home products are differentiated from imports, the ratio of home goods prices and import prices does vary. That between home goods prices and export prices remains fixed, however.

[d] See Table 3.2 for further explanation.

[e] In the end, this constraint does not bind since both real wages rise.

Source: IMF (1998, 1999), Statistics Indonesia and MITI, Japan websites, 1997–98 changes.

Effects with Full Pass-through in the North

The main simulation assumes that *ad valorem* tariff and export subsidy equivalents in the North remain unchanged. This implies that proportional changes in international prices are passed through to Northern farmers and consumers. That this might not have been the case is discussed in the next sub-section.

The simulated medium-run effects of the Asian recession on the balance of payments in each region are displayed in Table 3.6. As mentioned earlier, investment falls and savings rise in both recession-hit developing Asia and Japan, and these changes are balanced by substantial declines in imports and rises in exports. The allocation of investment across the recession-free regions is endogenous in the model.[24] Investment rises in China but, because its current account surplus is constrained to rise by $US5 billion, the average rate of saving adjusts to ensure that total savings increase by this much more than the change in investment. All the other regions experience increased investment and (fixed rate) savings rise slightly with national income in each case. In the Northern regions, substantial shifts in their capital accounts towards surplus are matched by shifts in their current accounts towards deficit. These take the form of very substantial rises in imports and smaller falls in exports.

Estimates of the associated real exchange rate and terms-of-trade changes are also shown in Table 3.6. All the other regions appreciate against the two recession-hit ones, referred hereafter in combination as 'recession-hit Asia'. Note, however, that China's real appreciation relative to the recession-hit regions is smaller than the others; hence it experiences a real depreciation against its Northern trading partners. As exports from recession-hit Asia become cheaper, China and all the Northern regions enjoy terms-of-trade gains, of which the USA experiences the largest. The associated changes in agricultural commodity prices are shown in Table 3.7. In recession-hit Asia, substantial real depreciations cause real increases in both import and domestic producer prices. Correspondingly, reduced exports to depressed Asia from the North combined with the Northern real appreciations cause its import and producer prices to fall. These declines are smaller than the rises in depressed Asia, however, because Asia has a smaller share of the North's trade than the North has of Asia's.

In the intermediate case of China, agricultural import prices rise relative to the local GDP deflator. This is because China mainly imports agricultural products from the North, against which it experiences a real depreciation of about four percentage points. Note also that, in the North, the magnitudes of changes in import prices are larger than the corresponding changes in producer prices. This is because home products are differentiated from imports,

Table 3.6   Medium-run changes in the balance of payments and the real exchange rate following the recession in developing Asia and Japan, 1995 $US billion[a]

Sector	Dev. Asia[b]	Japan	China	USA	EU	Australasia	Rest of world
Capital account surplus (I – S)	−184	−259	−5	127	198	10	113
Investment, I	−105	−202	11	140	217	10	125
Saving, S	79	57	16	13	19	1	11
Current account deficit (M − X)	−184	−259	−5	127	198	10	113
Imports, M	−90	−80	1	72	117	4	59
Exports, X	94	179	6	−55	−81	−6	−54
Real appreciation, %[c]							
relative to developing Asia[d]	0.0	−2.8	5.4	9.3	9.6	7.8	8.9
Terms of trade, %[d]	−2.3	−7.6	2.3	3.2	1.2	1.8	0.9

Notes:
[a] Medium-run closure details are indicated in Table 3.5.
[b] Recessed developing Asia, excluding China.
[c] Here the change in the real exchange rate is approximated by the per cent change in the ratio of the region's GDP deflator with that of developing Asia.
[d] Change in the value of exports at endogenous prices, weighted by fixed 1995 (base period) export volumes, divided by the value of imports, weighted by fixed 1995 import volumes.

Source: Model simulations described in the text.

Table 3.7 Medium-run changes in real import and producer commodity prices following the recession in developing Asia and Japan, %[a]

Sector		Dev. Asia	Japan	China	USA	EU	Australasia	Rest of world
Cereals	Import [b]	8.2	11.6	1.7	-2.1	-2.0	-1.2	-1.7
	Producer	2.6	2.4	-0.4	-1.4	-1.4	-0.7	-1.0
Other crops	Import [b]	7.6	10.2	1.2	-2.1	-2.2	-1.5	-2.0
	Producer	4.9	5.4	-0.6	-1.7	-1.3	-1.5	-1.0
Livestock	Import [b]	7.7	10.0	0.9	-1.3	-2.1	-1.5	-1.0
	Producer	1.9	2.0	-0.7	-1.0	-0.8	-0.8	-0.5
Other agriculture	Import [b]	6.7	9.4	0.1	-2.9	-2.3	-2.3	-1.1
	Producer	2.5	2.1	-0.9	-1.2	-0.8	-1.6	-1.0
Mfg. labour int.	Import	4.9	9.3	-2.4	-3.6	-3.3	-2.4	-1.9
	Producer	3.1	1.3	-0.3	-0.7	-0.5	-0.7	-0.5
Mfg. skill int.	Import	4.3	10.4	-1.6	-4.3	-3.9	-2.6	-1.8
	Producer	2.9	2.0	-0.2	-0.9	-0.7	-1.0	-0.6

Notes:
[a] Medium-run closure details are indicated in Table 3.5. All price changes listed are measured relative to region-specific GDP deflators.
[b] Import prices are here a CES index of source-specific prices excluding intraregional trade.

Source: Model simulations described in the text.

and so switching by consumers from home products to imports is incomplete. This affords Northern farmers a measure of 'natural' insulation. In the case of the EU, for example, the declines in farm prices are between one-half and two-thirds of the corresponding border price changes.

The effects on sectoral output are detailed in Table 3.8. The broad pattern is for the tradable goods sectors to be advantaged in recession-hit Asia and disadvantaged in China and the North. In association with the increased levels of investment in the North, demand for Northern capital goods, and hence indirect demand for relatively untraded services, rises substantially. The expanding services sectors absorb labour released by the tradable goods sectors. Most notable, however, is that the contractions across the North's tradable goods sectors are nowhere near as large as they are in agriculture. The dominant contractions are in cereals and other crops in the USA. In the EU they are in cereals and in Australasia they are in 'other crops' and 'other agriculture'.[25] Thus, although the real appreciations relative to recession-hit Asia accompany terms-of-trade gains for the Northern regions and overall expansions in GDP, farmers are the principal losers.

The distributional effects of these changes in the North are best illustrated by the associated changes in unit factor rewards there, presented in Table 3.9. Workers, who are intersectorally mobile in the analysis, are gainers because they move to the more prosperous and expanding services sectors. This is not a particularly costly adjustment in the industrialized North since the services sectors there are already very much larger than the contracting tradable goods sectors. The rise in real wages is a further cost to farmers, however, whose activities are relatively labour-intensive. With real product prices falling and the real price of the key input rising, the squeeze on farmers causes the real unit rewards of land and other natural resources to fall by relatively large margins. Turning to the real reward to capital, average real returns rise in the North, but this is driven by rises in the very large services sectors. There are falls in the real rates of return on capital specific to all the tradable goods sectors. Again, however, the declines are largest in the agricultural sector. In the EU, for example, the falls in capital returns are three times larger than those in other tradable goods sectors. Outside recession-hit Asia, Northern farmers are clearly the sectoral group most hurt by the Asian recession.

Why Farmers Lose Most in the North When Recession Effects are Passed Through

Superficially, Engel's law might be expected to ensure that the substantial contractions in income in Asia cause its consumption of agricultural products to fall by less than that of manufactures. This leads to the presumption

Table 3.8 Medium-run changes in gross sectoral output and GDP following the recession in developing Asia and Japan, %[a]

Sector	Dev. Asia	Japan	China	USA	EU	Australasia	Rest of world
Cereals	1.0	0.0	-0.4	-1.5	-1.8	-0.2	-0.9
Other crops	1.5	0.3	-0.7	-1.5	-1.5	-2.0	-0.6
Livestock	-0.1	-0.9	-1.3	-0.6	-0.7	-0.5	0.0
Other agriculture	0.3	-0.5	-1.2	-1.1	-1.1	-3.5	-1.0
Mining	1.4	5.2	0.5	-0.5	-0.9	-0.6	-0.6
Manufacturing:							
labour-intensive	7.3	2.0	1.0	-1.0	-0.4	-0.7	-0.8
skill-intensive	3.6	5.0	0.6	-1.1	-1.6	-1.1	-0.7
Services:							
labour-intensive	-5.8	-3.3	1.4	1.4	1.7	1.3	1.7
skill-intensive	-2.3	-1.4	0.2	0.2	0.2	0.2	0.1
GDP	-0.39	-0.04	0.72	0.07	0.12	0.26	0.31

Note:
[a] Medium-run closure details are indicated in Table 3.5.

Source: Model simulations described in the text.

Table 3.9 Medium-run changes in real unit factor rewards, %[a]

Primary factor	Dev. Asia	Japan	China	USA	EU	Australasia	Rest of world
Labour	-2.0	-0.9	1.0	0.6	0.4	0.7	0.8
Skill	-3.0	-1.1	1.1	0.3	0.3	0.6	0.6
Natural resources	3.5	5.9	-0.3	-2.1	-3.0	-2.8	-2.4
Land	3.7	2.9	-2.8	-3.8	-4.5	-3.2	-1.7
Capital (regional average return)	-1.8	-0.3	1.0	0.3	0.5	0.5	0.3
Capital specific to:							
Cereals	5.4	3.2	-1	-3.9	-6.0	-1.0	-2.8
Other crops	6.6	4.2	-3	-4.5	-5.0	-5.4	-2.5
Livestock	1.8	1.4	-5	-1.6	-2.1	-2.1	-0.4
Other agriculture	2.5	2.2	-2	-2.3	-2.1	-5.2	-2.4
Mining	8.8	13.6	1	-2.2	-3.1	-2.5	-2.5
Manufacturing:							
labour-intensive	9.2	2.8	1	-1.4	-0.7	-1.1	-1.0
skill-intensive	5.8	6.2	0	-1.6	-1.9	-1.8	-1.1
Services:							
labour-intensive	-5.7	-2.6	1	1.2	1.4	1.2	1.8
skill-intensive	-2.4	-1.7	0	0.1	0.0	0.1	0.2

Note:
[a] Medium-run closure details are indicated in Table 3.5. All entries are unit rewards relative to the region's consumer price index.

Source: Model simulations described in the text.

that the North's agricultural exports would decline by less than manufactured exports and hence that manufacturers would lose most. In fact, the North's agricultural exports to Asia decline by more than do its manufactured exports.

The reasons for this begin with the contractions in investment and consumption in recession-hit Asia. As seen in Table 3.8, medium-run aggregate real incomes in these regions are almost at their benchmark levels. Consumption contracts a little as savings rise, but the income effects on consumption, which should bolster relative demand for agricultural products, are slight. This is more than offset by the effect of the surge in manufactured exports from these regions at the onset of the recession, driven by the decline in private consumption. To feed these exports, as indicated by Table 3.8, manufacturing output rises above its pre-recession levels in the three affected Asian regions. This increased manufacturing production draws in imports of intermediate inputs, mainly comprising manufactures. The net decline in manufactured imports is therefore smaller than that in agricultural imports. That this should be true is clear from Table 3.10, which lists both the sectoral contribution to the exports of the affected Asian regions and the share of imported manufactures in input costs. In all three Asian regions, exports are dominated by manufactures and, in each case, manufacturing costs have the largest import intensity, with imported manufactures predominant amongst imported intermediate inputs.

The story, however, does not end with the North's agricultural exports to recession-hit Asia declining by more than its manufactured exports. As indicated in Table 3.7, agricultural import prices fall by less than the import prices of manufactures in the USA, EU and Australasia. This is because, as the elasticities of substitution in Table 3.4 attest, manufactures are more highly differentiated across regions than agricultural products. The surge in Asian exports therefore tends to push down traded Asian manufactures prices by more. Of course, this also means that changes in the prices of imported manufactures in the North are passed through with more natural insulation than similar changes in agricultural import prices. In the end, as shown in Table 3.7, the declines in Northern producer prices are larger for agriculture than for the other traded goods, particularly manufactures.

The Effects Without Full Pass-through in the EU and the USA

It has been assumed throughout this analysis that *ad valorem* tariff and export subsidy equivalents were held constant by Northern governments. That this is not the case is indicated by the OECD's annual estimates of agricultural producer subsidy equivalents (PSEs) for the EU and the USA (OECD, 1999) shown in Table 3.11. These rose between 1997 and 1998, just

Table 3.10 Manufactured imports in total cost, 1995, %[a]

Sector	Japan			Recessed dev. Asia			China		
	% of exports	% of imports in TC	% of mfg imports in TC	% of exports	% of imports in TC	% of mfg imports in TC	% of exports	% of imports in TC	% of mfg imports in TC
Agriculture	0.4	7.9	0.2	6.3	8.3	2.3	5.0	5.1	3.1
Mining	0.2	1.0	0.4	2.9	10.9	4.4	2.6	6.3	5.3
Mfg:									
labour-intensive	6.9	4.8	2.5	19.1	22.8	19.2	46.4	13.6	12.4
skill-intensive	77.6	5.9	2.9	49.2	29.8	25.1	36.1	11.6	10.5
Services:									
labour-intensive	11.4	2.4	0.5	18.4	12.2	7.5	6.1	5.7	4.8
skill-intensive	3.5	1.6	0.4	4.1	10.1	5.9	3.8	7.1	3.6

Note:
[a] Mfg is manufacturing and TC refers to total production cost.

Source: GTAP Database Version 4.1 (see McDougall et al., 1998).

Table 3.11   *Observed* ad valorem *nominal assistance rates, %*[a]

Primary factor		1986–88	1991–93	1997	1998
European Union					
Wheat	Producer	117	128	88	125
	Consumer	45	38	−3	11
Maize	Producer	111	119	54	79
	Consumer	8	6	−1	2
Other grains	Producer	160	172	124	208
	Consumer	13	13	2	8
Sugar (refined equiv.)	Producer	113	210	55	75
	Consumer	347	238	169	210
Milk	Producer	142	135	101	132
	Consumer	166	138	88	125
Beef and veal	Producer	96	124	124	161
	Consumer	95	113	75	105
All commodities	Producer	86	88	61	83
	Consumer	73	63	30	48
USA					
Wheat	Producer	106	75	34	61
	Consumer	−2	−1	−16	−20
Maize	Producer	64	23	17	33
	Consumer	−9	−11	−11	−14
Other grains	Producer	75	41	30	60
	Consumer	−2	−3	−11	−15
Sugar (refined equiv.)	Producer	146	112	67	70
	Consumer	196	133	76	76
Milk	Producer	168	106	81	155
	Consumer	140	74	50	115
Beef and veal	Producer	6	5	3	4
	Consumer	−4	−7	−10	−10
All commodities	Producer	35	24	17	28
	Consumer	9	1	−3	3

Note:
[a] Shown are values of the Nominal Assistance Coefficient (NAC) minus one, expressed in
%. The NAC is the ratio of the producer or consumer subsidy equivalent (in domestic
currency) and the value of total farm receipts at international prices and excluding any
budgetary support. It expresses the transfers to agriculture in relation to border prices.

Source: OECD (1999), part III, tables III.30, III.31, III.63 and III.64.

as international commodity prices took their Asian recession-driven dip. Indeed, the power of the overall average EU *ad valorem* PSE rose by 22 per cent in 1998 while that for the USA rose by 11 per cent. It is therefore likely that farmers in these and some other Northern regions were partially, if not completely, insulated from the shock of the Asian recession by the rise in trade distortions.

That *ad valorem* agricultural protection rates should have risen in spite of the Uruguay Round Agreement on Agriculture (AoA) is not surprising. The three main commitments to reform under the AoA required tariffica-tion, market access and a ceiling on an aggregate measure of support (AMS). For many Northern regions, tariffs were set at prohibitive levels. Moreover, at least in the case of the EU, these tariffs were specific, so that when international prices fell, the power of the tariff (and the *ad valorem* protection rate) rose.[26] Market access was ensured through the establish-ment of tariff-rate quotas (TRQs) that offered lower tariffs on a limited quantity of imports. Regions took a variety of approaches to the allocation of these TRQs, however, and they have often been unfulfilled. Finally, many Northern regions were able to have a substantial part of their support for farmers classified into the 'green' and 'blue' boxes which, under Article 13 of the AoA (the 'peace clause') will not be contestable until 2003.[27] This meant that the AMS constraint did not bind in the mid-1990s and scope remained for increased overall support.

To examine the effects of an insulating rise in Northern agricultural pro-tection, the experiment of the previous sub-section was re-run. This time it was assumed that the governments of the EU and the USA would hold real farm prices constant, relative to their respective GDP deflators, and allow agricultural trade distortions to rise. The power of US and EU agricultural import tariff and export subsidy equivalents then rises by between 3 and 5 per cent. The earlier declines in the real unit reward of land and capital in agriculture are largely arrested in these two regions. Because this change of policy reduces the share of adjustment borne by the USA and the EU, however, traded agricultural prices decline by more and the losses to farmers in non-insulating Australasia are increased by all measures. Indeed, measured in terms of real returns to land and agricultural capital, Australasian farmers' losses from the medium-run effects of the Asian recession double.[28]

The extent of such insulation might therefore have saved some Northern farmers from the direct effects of the Asian recession. However, it imposed on their economies the greater burden of increased trade distortion and hence it enlarged the gap to be spanned by the next WTO round of trade negotiations. In those regions where no such insulation took place, farmers have borne the substantial adjustment costs highlighted here. Those among

them who none the less enjoy government assistance might therefore be
expected to view with less favour any further adjustment costs associated
with the removal, or scaling back, of existing protection.

4. ASIAN RECESSION EFFECTS AND THE SCALE OF AGRICULTURAL TRADE REFORM

The pattern of agricultural trade distortions as of 1995 is built into the
GTAP Version IV database, derived for OECD countries from PSE and
CSE estimates of the type listed in Table 3.11. The resulting 1995 *ad
valorem* tariff and export subsidy equivalents are listed in Table 3.12. From
this pattern, it is evident that agricultural trade in developing Asia and
Japan remained quite distorted, with rates that were highest in the cereals
and livestock industries. The region is not homogeneous, however. In
Korea, where tariff and export subsidy equivalents had been extremely high
in the Uruguay Round benchmark period, rates had fallen by one-half in
the decade to 1995.

In Japan, on the other hand, no significant decline was apparent in this
period. Indeed, part of the home agricultural price rises associated with the
depreciation of the yen in 1997–98 appear to have been passed through to
farmers in rejection of an important opportunity for reform. In fact,
Japanese agricultural protection rates rose during this period (OECD,
1999, appendix III). Not least in Japan, but also elsewhere in recession-hit
Asia, the recession depreciated the domestic currency and raised home
agricultural prices relative to prices in less traded sectors. It therefore
offered an opportunity to reduce agricultural distortions permanently. At
the fixed *ad valorem* protection rates assumed in this analysis of the Asian
recession, the substantial real depreciations experienced by these economies appear to have greatly enhanced both the welfare and the international competitiveness of their farmers.

The main threat to further global agricultural trade reform, however, is
in the Northern regions and, most particularly, in the EU. There, *ad
valorem* rates of protection remained very high in 1995. In the face of the
real appreciation that came with the Asian recession, average EU rates of
protection rose, as indicated in Table 3.11. To compare the effects of a substantial future liberalization with those associated with the Asian recession,
a simple global liberalization of all agricultural distortions by 50 per cent
of the *ad valorem* rates indicated in Table 3.12 is implemented.[29] The same
model is used as for the Asian recession experiment in the previous section
and, for comparability, the assumption that capital is immobile between
industries is retained. Unlike the Asian recession experiments, however,

Table 3.12 Ad valorem import tariff and export subsidy equivalents, agricultural products, 1995, %[a]

Sector		Dev. Asia	Japan	China	USA	EU	Australasia	Rest of world
Cereals	Tariff	113	471	−9	1	54	0	5
	Subsidy	107	494	−7	1	29	0	−3
Other crops	Tariff	10	18	18	9	11	3	25
	Subsidy	−4	7	1	0	16	2	−3
Livestock	Tariff	28	68	7	7	52	11	25
	Subsidy	23	67	−20	5	74	5	2
Other agriculture	Tariff	14	5	19	2	7	4	13
	Subsidy	−2	0	6	−1	−1	0	−2

Note:
[a] For the OECD countries, these are based on PSE calculations. For regional aggregates, such as the EU, these are the rates applicable to interregional trade. Intraregional trade rates are excluded.

Source: GTAP Database Version 4.1 (see McDougall et al., 1998).

there are no associated shocks to the capital account. In this case, the question is how different would the world of 1995 have been had there been only half the agricultural protection in all regions. The average rate of saving in each region is therefore fixed at its 1995 level and the regional distribution of investment is endogenous. While the liberalization shock does cause substantial terms-of-trade changes, the associated real capital account changes, and hence changes to real exchange rates, are therefore minimal.

The resulting changes in real unit factor rewards are presented in Table 3.13. The regional pattern that emerges depends upon the extent of the domestic distortions removed and on any terms-of-trade gains or losses. Factors such as land and agricultural capital, which previously gained from protection, clearly lose from its removal. In the EU, they lose substantially. This is in spite of increases in traded agricultural commodity prices arising out of the collective nature of the liberalization in this experiment.[30] Disappointingly, virtually no primary factors enjoy real gains in the EU and the USA, the two regions that will be the principal protagonists in the Millennium Round.

Leaving aside its domestic political implications, this result appears more pessimistic than it really is. Both the USA and the EU do experience small real GDP gains from liberalization. These occur in spite of the declines in unit factor rewards because a substantial part of the agricultural distortions in the EU and the USA are either export subsidies or deficiency payments, both of which burden the tax-payer. When these distortions are reduced, there is a large increase in net government revenue, sufficient to convert a decline in GDP at factor cost into a rise in real GDP. In addition, the increases in GDP thus calculated tend to underestimate the gains from agricultural reform. This is because, in this model, government revenue is raised by lump sum taxes and so incurs no dead weight loss in the analysis. In reality, the recoupment of such losses would be a major part of any potential gains from liberalization that would be enjoyed in the EU and the USA.

In recession-hit Asia, a high average level of pre-existing agricultural protection ensures that factors other than land are significant gainers from liberalization. At the same time, because liberalization raises traded agricultural prices, China and Australasia enjoy relatively substantial terms-of-trade gains that ultimately favour both their farmers and workers. Many countries in recession-hit Asia, however, have strong farm lobbies born out of rapid overall economic growth and relative agricultural contraction. They have not been active in promoting the cause of agricultural liberalization. A prominent case in point is China, where there is widespread concern about declining agricultural self-sufficiency. This follows the East Asian pattern of commercial policy reform and infrastructural development, revealing the economy's comparative disadvantage in

Table 3.13 Changes in real factor rewards following the 50% liberalization of 1995 agricultural trade distortions, %[a]

Primary factor	Dev. Asia	Japan	China	USA	EU	Australasia	Rest of world
Labour	2.8	1.1	0.1	-0.4	-0.5	0.3	-0.2
Skill	2.8	1.2	-0.9	-0.4	-0.1	0.1	-0.2
Natural resources	2.7	1.1	-0.7	-0.6	0.1	-3.8	-0.3
Land	-2.8	-12.4	10.5	-1.2	-34.4	7.9	-0.7
Capital (regional average return)	3.0	0.9	-0.3	-0.4	-0.7	0.2	-0.2
Capital specific to[b]:							
Cereals	-18.4	-22.4	14.1	8.8	-75.0	-4.5	7.6
Other crops	22.2	-0.4	2.6	-6.4	-7.6	-2.5	-3.6
Livestock	0.2	-11.6	24.5	2.2	-16.7	26.8	2.4
Other agriculture	6.8	-1.4	0.6	-0.8	-2.8	-5.7	-0.6
Mining	0.3	0.8	-0.9	-0.2	1.0	-4.0	-0.1
Manufacturing:							
labour-intensive	0.3	0.7	-1.8	-0.2	0.7	-2.5	-0.1
skill-intensive	0.3	0.6	-0.8	-0.2	0.6	-2.5	-0.2
Services:							
labour-intensive	1.1	0.5	0.3	0.0	0.1	0.1	0.3
skill-intensive	0.9	0.5	0.1	-0.1	0.2	-0.1	0.2

Notes:
[a] Medium-run closure details are indicated in Table 3.5. All entries are unit rewards relative to the region's consumer price index.
[b] Capital is sector-specific and hence has returns that differ by sector.

Source: Model simulations described in the text.

agriculture. Meanwhile, as farmer numbers contract, their political cohesion increases and pressure on provincial and national governments for protection mount. In spite of the potential economy-wide gains the above results suggest that China might enjoy from a global liberalization, it is therefore unlikely to support a more liberal trade regime for agriculture.

In the important case of the EU, in spite of the very large diminution in farmer welfare that a 50 per cent liberalization would bring, the effects of the Asian recession shock are not insignificant by comparison. Had that shock been passed through to farmers, their real return on land would have fallen by 15 per cent of the hypothetical liberalization decline. The corresponding percentage for returns to capital specific to cereals is 8 per cent, other crops 63 per cent, livestock products 12 per cent and other agriculture 67 per cent. In effect, whether passed through or not, the Asian recession has raised the stakes for European farmers by these proportions.

5. CONCLUSION

By forcing a sudden enlargement of Asian current account surpluses, the Asian recession has reduced global demand for agricultural commodities and caused international trading prices to fall. While there have been associated declines in Asian demand for other tradable goods, that for agricultural commodities as a group is the largest. This is because the surge in Asian, mainly manufactured, exports that has been part of the recovery phase has drawn into the recessed Asian economies imported intermediate inputs that comprise mainly mineral, energy and manufactured products. Outside Asia, unless government policies have effectively insulated them, farmers have been the principal losers from the Asian recession. Had no Northern farmers been insulated by changes in their governments' policies, their losses, measured in terms of the real returns to land- and sector-specific capital, would have been substantial. In the case of the highly protected farmers of the EU, the losses range between 8 per cent and two-thirds of those that would be endured were there to be a reduction by half in the tariff and export subsidy equivalents of the instruments now protecting them.

Even if farmers in such regions have been insulated, and the evidence suggests that those in the EU and some other regions have been, the scale of the protection they receive has thereby been expanded, leaving a more daunting task for future rounds of trade negotiations. And it is likely that the effects of the Asian recession will be long-lasting. The global redistribution of investment that has occurred since 1997, and which is given emphasis in this analysis, will probably never be fully reversed. Effects of the type simulated here will quite probably be felt through the next round of negotiations. Yet, this is no reason not to pursue agricultural reform in the Millennium Round. It is true that more open Northern markets for all goods and services, and particularly Asia's mainly manufactured exports, will aid Asia's adjustment. This means that, since Northern farmers have been the principal Northern losers from the Asian recession, they have an interest in the extension of the 'built-in agenda' to incorporate trade in manufactured products.

The machinery for future reductions in agricultural protection was incorporated into the WTO during the Uruguay Round. The further discussions as part of the WTO's built-in agenda incorporate trade in agriculture, services and intellectual property. They will consolidate this machinery. The rise in protectionist sentiment amongst Northern farmers, as induced in part by the effects of the Asian recession, will be a challenge for its implementation, however. That challenge will be less insurmountable if a full round is undertaken and there is the opportunity for net gains to be made by all participating countries.

NOTES

*   Thanks are due Robert McDougall, Tom Hertel, Ron Duncan and Kym Anderson for useful discussions in the formative stages and to Shujuan Lin for providing access to the most recent OECD data on PSEs. Constructive comments on an early draft were provided by Sam Laird, Steve McCorriston, Robert Read and other participants at the 24th Annual Conference of the UK International Economics Study Group in Birmingham, September 1999. The views expressed in this chapter are those of the authors alone and are in no way representative of views held in the IMF or any of its policy positions.

1. Subsequent but associated 'crises' in Latin America, Eastern Europe and Russia have magnified the effects of the initial shocks in Asia. This chapter focuses on the effects of the Asian shocks only.
2. Earlier applications to the Asian recession include those by Adams (1998), Noland et al. (1998), Suryahadi (1998), Coyle et al. (1999) and Yang and Tyers (1999).
3. Although the events that precipitated the crisis are now fairly well understood (theoretical treatments of the underlying behaviour include those by Chang and Velasco, 1998 and Krugman, 1999a), the best dynamic global macroeconomic models to date still do not fully endogenize the capital flight of 1997 (McKibbin, 1998a, 1998b).
4. These related impacts are foreshadowed by Corbett and Vines (1999).
5. The short- and medium-run effects of the Asian recession are compared by Yang and Tyers (1999).
6. The financial origins of the Japanese recession are discussed in Horiuchi (1998).
7. Their contributions to global GDP are smaller in magnitude than that of Japan, however. The 1998 contraction of the Japanese economy by 2.8 per cent reduced global output by $US114 billion. This compares with a total of $US83 billion from the combined contractions in the affected developing Asian countries. Although PPP-based comparisons would enhance the latter figure, they would not nullify the point of the comparison.
8. A clear retrospective summary of these events is provided by Corbett and Vines (1999).

9.   Interestingly, however, since Japan has been an important destination for exports from developing Asia, holding the line on export values has meant a considerable redirection of exports towards the EU and the USA.
10. According to IMF (1998, table 3), gross fixed capital formation in Japan declined by 3.5 per cent in 1997 and was forecast to decline by 7.2 per cent in 1998.
11. See the discussion of this in Corbett and Vines (1999). This effect is also noted in Lane et al. (1999).
12. This is borne out in a recent World Bank survey of 3700 companies in the worst affected economies (World Bank, 1999a) as reported in *Asiaweek*, 16 April 1999.
13. Krugman (1999a) refers to this as the 'decapitation of the entrepreneurial class'. He offers a theoretical model of the process in which the denomination of debt is explicit (Krugman, 1999b).
14. These statistics stem originally from the UN *Commodity Trade Statistics*. The secondary source is, however, the GTAP Version IV Database (see McDougall et al., 1998).
15. The indirect effects of real exchange rate changes on agriculture were noted by Krueger et al. (1991) and, more recently, by Schiff and Valdes (1998).
16. For a detailed description of the standard version of this model, see Hertel (1997). The modifications to the structure of the model, detailed in Yang and Tyers (1999), are principally changes to the factor demand structure. For the present purpose, they include the sector-specificity of capital in all regions.
17. For a detailed description of the database, see McDougall et al. (1998).
18. The early literature on real exchange rate changes tends to focus on associated relative price changes where tradable goods prices retain parity with international trading prices. More recently it has become certain that short-run departures from the law of one price occur across all tradable goods sectors (see Engel, 1999).
19. See the discussion of long-run shocks in Gehlhar (1994), Gehlhar et al. (1994) and Hertel et al. (1996, appendix C, p. 212).
20. Further research by the authors experiments with two alternative nested CES structures that allow experiments with different mixes of substitutability and complementarity across primary factors and intermediate inputs.
21. The specific role of China during the crisis is addressed more explicitly using a similar model in Tyers and Yang (2000) and Yang and Tyers (2001).
22. It is assumed that, during the long process of recovery, these high savings rates will be maintained to enable the recessed economies eventually to pay off their crisis-enhanced foreign debt.
23. Although there is evidence that investment has begun to rise again in developing Asia, the effect this might have had in reducing the capital account deficit there is probably balanced by savings changes that support a rise in debt service flows on the current account. Since this model allows no interregional factor ownership, there are no interregional flows of capital returns. For this reason, the same investment levels and savings rates are maintained as in the short run.
24. Policy-induced differences in the accessibility of domestic capital markets across regions are not represented. As it turns out, the rise in investment is most substantial in Europe and, therefore, so also is the rise in European imports.
25. These results suggest more uniformly adverse impacts on US farmers than those of Coyle et al. (1999).
26. The authors are indebted to Sam Laird for this observation (see Laird, 1999).
27. For a thorough review of the implementation of the Uruguay Round Agreement on Agriculture, see Josling and Tangermann (1999). More detail about its implementation in the EU is provided by Swinbank (1999).
28. Details from this simulation are available on request from the authors.
29. More than a 50 per cent liberalization of agricultural distortions is extremely unlikely. More than that would, in any case, be difficult to justify as a first-best reform given the substantial size of services sectors and the as yet poorly measured barriers to trade therein.

30. Where protection is the more prevalent distortion, unilateral liberalization by any single region always imposes high losses on previously assisted factors in comparison with multilateral liberalization (see Tyers and Anderson, 1992).

REFERENCES

Adams, P.D. (1998), 'Computable general equilibrium analysis of the consequences for Australia of the Asian crisis', Centre of Policy Studies, Monash University.

Bayoumi, T. and C. Towe (1998), 'Macroeconomic developments and prospects', in *Japan – Selected Issues*, Staff Country Report, Washington, DC: IMF, July.

Chang, R. and A. Velasco (1998), 'Financial crises in emerging markets: a canonical model', NBER Working Paper, No. 6606, Cambridge, MA; http://www.nber.org/papers/w6606.

Commodity Markets and the Developing Countries, The World Bank, various issues.

Corbett, J. and D. Vines (1999), 'The Asian Crisis: lessons from the collapse of financial systems, exchange rates and macroeconomic policy', in R. Agenor, M. Miller, D. Vines and A. Weber (eds), *The Asian Financial Crisis: Causes, Contagion and Consequences*, Cambridge: Cambridge University Press, pp. 67–110.

Corsetti, G., P. Pesenti and N. Roubini (1998), 'What caused the Asian currency and financial crisis?', Department of Economics, New York University.

Coyle, W.T., W.J. McKibbin and Z. Wang (1999), 'The Asian financial crisis: effects on US agriculture', Market and Trade Economics Division, Staff Paper No. 9805, Economic Research Service, US Department of Agriculture, Washington, DC.

Economist, The (1999), 21–7 August, pp. 14–16.

Engel, C.M. (1999), 'Exchange rates and prices', *NBER Reporter*, Winter, pp. 13–17.

Gehlhar, M. (1994), 'Economic growth and trade in the Pacific rim: an analysis of trade patterns', doctoral dissertation, Purdue University.

Gehlhar, M.J., T.W. Hertel and W. Martin (1994), 'Economic growth and the changing structure of trade and production in the Pacific Rim', *American Journal of Agricultural Economics*, **76** (5), 1101–10.

Goldstein, M. (1998), *The Asian Financial Crisis: Causes, Cures and Systemic Implications*, Policy Analysis in International Economics, No. 55, Washington, DC: Institute for International Economics.

Hertel, T.W. (ed.) (1997), *Global Trade Analysis Using the GTAP Model*, New York: Cambridge University Press.

Hertel, T., W. Martin, Y. Yanagishma and B. Dimaranan (1996), 'Liberalising manufactures trade in a changing world economy', in W. Martin and L.A. Winters (eds), *The Uruguay Round and the Developing Countries*, Cambridge: Cambridge University Press, pp. 183–215.

Hertel, T.W. and M.E. Tsigas (1997), 'Structure of GTAP', in T.W. Hertel (ed.), *Global Trade Analysis Using the GTAP Model*, New York: Cambridge University Press, pp. 13–73.

Horiuchi, A. (1998), 'Japan', in R. McLeod and R. Garnaut (eds), *East Asia in Crisis: From Being a Miracle to Needing One*, London: Routledge, pp. 189–206.

Huang, Y. and L. Song (1999), 'China in the aftermath of the East Asian financial crisis', paper presented at the Conference on International Capital Mobility and

Domestic Economic Stability, hosted by the Reinventing Bretton Woods Committee and the World Bank, Australian National University, Canberra, July.

IMF (1998), *World Economic Outlook*, Washington, DC: IMF.

IMF (1999), *World Economic Outlook*, Washington, DC: IMF.

Josling, T. and S. Tangermann (1999), 'The WTO agreement on agriculture and the next negotiating round', *European Review of Agricultural Economics*, **26** (3), 271–88.

Krueger, A.O., M. Schiff and A. Valdes (1991), 'Measuring the effects of intervention in agricultural prices', in A.O. Krueger, M. Schiff and A. Valdes (eds), *The Political Economy of Agricultural Pricing Policy*, Baltimore: Johns Hopkins University Press for the World Bank, pp. 1–14.

Krugman, P. (1994), 'The myth of Asia's miracle', *Foreign Affairs*, **73** (6), 62–78.

Krugman, P. (1999a), 'Recovery? Don't bet on it', *Time Magazine Asia*, 21 June; www.pathfinder.com/time/asia/magazine/1999/990621/cover1.html.

Krugman, P. (1999b), 'Balance sheets, the transfer problem and financial crises', paper prepared for Festschrift in honour of Robert Flood; http://web.mit.edu/krugman/www/whatsnew.html.

Laird, S. (1999), 'Millennium Round negotiations on market access in goods and services', paper presented at the 24th Annual Conference of the UK International Economics Study Group, University of Birmingham, September.

Lane, T., A.R. Ghosh, J. Hamann, S. Phillips, M. Schulze-Ghattas and T. Tsikata (1999), *IMF-Supported Programs in Indonesia, Korea and Thailand: a Preliminary Assessment*, Washington, DC: IMF.

McDougall, R.A., A. Elbehri and T.P. Truong (eds) (1998), *Global Trade, Assistance and Protection: the GTAP 4 Database*, Center for Global Trade Analysis, Purdue University.

McKibbin, W.J. (1998a), 'The crisis in Asia: an empirical assessment', *Brookings Discussion Paper in International Economics, No. 136*, Washington, DC: The Brookings Institute.

McKibbin, W.J. (1998b), 'Internationally mobile capital and the global economy', in R. McLeod and R. Garnaut (eds), *East Asia in Crisis: From Being a Miracle to Needing One*, London: Routledge, pp. 227–44.

McLeod, R.H. and R. Garnaut (eds) (1998), *East Asia in Crisis: From Being a Miracle to Needing One*, London: Routledge.

Noland, M., L. Liu, S. Robinson and Z. Wang (1998), *Global Effects of the Asian Currency Devaluations*, Policy Analysis in International Economics, No. 56, Washington, DC: Institute for International Economics.

OECD (1998), 'Agricultural policy reform: stocktaking of achievements', Discussion Paper for Meeting of the Committee for Agriculture at Ministerial Level, Paris, 5–6 March.

OECD (1999), *Agricultural Policy in OECD Countries: Monitoring and Evaluations 1999*, Paris: OECD.

Radelet, S. and J. Sachs (1998), 'The onset of the East Asian financial crisis', Harvard Institute for International Development.

Schiff, M. and A. Valdes (1998), 'Agriculture and the macroeconomy', World Bank Working Paper No. 1967, Washington, DC: World Bank.

Suryahadi, A.Y. (1998), 'The effects of openness on developing country labour markets: the case of Indonesia', doctoral dissertation, Australian National University.

Swinbank, A. (1999), 'CAP reform and the WTO: compatibility and developments', *European Review of Agricultural Economics*, **26** (3), 389–408.

Tyers, R. and K. Anderson (1992), *Disarray in World Food Markets: a Quantitative Assessment*, Cambridge: Cambridge University Press.

Tyers, R. and Y. Yang (2000), 'Weathering the crisis: the role of China', Pacific Economic Papers, No. 308.

Wong, K.Y. (ed.) (1998), 'The Asian crisis: what has happened and why?', Department of Economics, University of Washington, Seattle.

World Bank (1999a), 'The crisis pictured', in *Asiaweek*, 16 April, as presented on the website: www.pathfinder.com/asiaweek/99/0416/cs3a_crisis.html.

World Bank (1999b), *Global Commodity Markets*, Washington, DC: World Bank.

Yang, Y. and R. Tyers (1999), 'The Asian recession and northern labour markets', Working Papers in Economics and Econometrics, No. 372, Australian National University, Canberra; http://ecocomm.anu.edu.au/departments/ecoh/staff/tyers.html.

Yang, Y. and R. Tyers (2001), 'The crisis and economic change in China', *Japanese Economic Review*, **52** (4), 491–510.

4. The implications of the General Agreement on Trade in Services (GATS) for the banking sector in the Gulf Region

Victor Murinde and Cillian Ryan

One main innovation of the WTO in supplanting the GATT was to take a much broader view of trade and, in particular, add to the trade negotiations issues such as Trade-Related Intellectual Property Rights (TRIPS), Trade-Related Investment Measures (TRIMS) and the General Agreement on Trade in Services (GATS).[1] The provisions regarding trade in financial services, which are an integral element of the GATS, have proved to be a source of considerable anxiety for the non-industrialized countries generally. This concern arises, in part, because the consequences of the GATS are not well understood and there is a sense among these countries that they are being pressurized into signing up for something which may yet turn out to be to their detriment.

The potential effects of the GATS on developing countries has been analysed (see, for example, Lensink et al., 1998) but the group of countries which are the subject of this chapter are somewhat special. The Gulf Cooperation Council (GCC) states, while not part of the mainstream industrialized world, have concerns which differ considerably from those of the bulk of emerging and developing nations. To a greater or lesser extent, these states are oil exporters which enjoy considerable surpluses and are largely open to the Western world. They are, however, acutely aware of the exhaustibility of their primary source of wealth and are seeking both to diversify their domestic economies and to build up a suitable portfolio of overseas interests as a safeguard against future diminishing oil revenues. For some, such as Bahrain and some of the smaller Emirate states, the relevant time horizon is relatively short, whereas Saudi Arabia and Qatar still have considerable oil reserves.

This issue has a number of financial sector implications, but four critical ones are analysed here. First, because of their comparative wealth, these countries tend to have clearly identifiable financial sectors. It is thus a matter of concern to government how their financial sectors will respond to the increased competition brought about by the GATS. Second, these countries also differ because their relative wealth, and the needs of the oil-exporting agencies, has typically led to a significant, if restricted, foreign presence. Third, in the drive to diversify their economic base, these countries face the dilemma between investing in projects overseas and 'newly engineered' domestic industries which often rely upon migrant labour from non-oil states in the region to provide a significant proportion of their inputs. At present, much of this investment is undertaken via local financial intermediaries which may be more disposed towards local investment than their international counterparts. Finally, these countries have a particularly strong desire to see their financial sectors survive and prosper. One of the difficulties of diversification facing Gulf governments is to identify sectors that will yield a standard of living comparable to that which their citizens, if not the imported labour, currently enjoy. The concern is not just with remuneration but also, and perhaps more importantly, in terms of standards of living and prestige. For this reason, the financial sector is sometimes identified by these countries as a potential source of future economic activity because of its appeal as a high-skill, high-income industry. For these reasons, the effects of trade liberalization in financial services under the GATS have a special significance for this group of countries.

This chapter assesses the implications of the GATS for the banking sector in the GCC states in the context of their membership benefits of the WTO as well as non-membership disadvantages. The idea is to review the relevant provisions of the GATS for banking services with emphasis on the free trade element and the implications for full liberalization of the banking sector. While the discussion is largely framed in the context of the GATS, the 1998 GCC Heads of State summit agreed in principle to allow the establishment of Gulf banks in each other's territories, although this has yet to be implemented. Nevertheless, much of the analysis relates to these liberalization policies and this regional initiative can be seen as an interim step towards the GATS. Section 1 briefly considers the pure theory of international trade as it applies to trade in financial services and identifies, in broad terms, the expected winners from trade liberalization in this sector. The main provisions of the GATS as they apply to the financial sector and the main exemptions currently enjoyed by the Gulf states are considered in section 2. Section 3 discusses the current state of the industry in the Gulf and considers the likely scenario (and the likely time-scale) as a consequence of the implementation of the GATS. Some conclusions are drawn in section 4.

1. TRADE THEORY AND TRADE IN FINANCIAL SERVICES

The pressure for including financial services within the Uruguay Round came predominantly from the developed countries and, in particular, from those currently with a major presence in the international banking market. The explanation for the dominance of these particular countries in international banking differs in each case, but a recurring theme is the distortionary historical impact of banking regulations. This resulted in the development or an enhancement of a comparative advantage in the provision of financial services in some countries.

Trade Theory and the Pattern of Trade in Financial Services

It is instructive to consider briefly the traditional models of international trade, although they are not particularly helpful in explaining patterns of such trade in banking and financial services. For example, technology may be a source of comparative advantage and differences in technology or method of production of financial services between countries can be identified, but there is nothing intrinsically fixed about this advantage. Thus, unlike food production or raw-materials-based industries, there is nothing about the physical environment that necessarily suggests that one country may have a technological advantage on the basis of its physical geography or infrastructure. There may, of course, be differences such as population density which affect branching costs or the cost and efficiency of telephone and other electronic communication systems, but there is no discernible international pattern which might suggest these factors are overwhelmingly important. Thus, if there is a difference in 'technology' it is invariably because there are differences in 'ways of doing things'. The question is, how do such differences in the level of 'know-how' arise and why are they not readily copied?

Factor intensity arguments lead to a similar conclusion. In the case of trade in goods, relative capital and labour intensity in production might be readily accepted as differing between countries. This is harder to discern in financial services. Capital infrastructure, in terms of branch networks and so on, may be superficially important but financial capital is equally, if not more, important in the case of financial services. Overall capital requirements for banks and financial institutions certainly differed in the past and, indeed, a low capital/asset requirement is often cited as one of the principal reasons for the rapid international expansion of Japanese banks in the 1980s and early 1990s. This possible source of difference, however, has systematically disappeared as a consequence of the Basle Agreement on the global capital/asset requirements and the increasing role of the Bank for International Settlements. While relative capital abundance might therefore still be an issue, once again differences in production methods do not depend upon differences in factor intensity *per se* but rather upon differences in 'ways of doing it' and the skills and know-how embodied in labour. Furthermore, the removal of barriers to capital flows, particularly over the last two decades, has diminished the issue of relative capital scarcity.

The main conventional explanations of specialization in financial services reduce to differences in know-how. This difference in skills and knowledge is usually attributed, in part, to investment in human capital but, even more importantly, to learning-by-doing (see Ryan, 1990).

The third major explanation is trade attributable to economies of scale. While recent research is more supportive of returns to scale and scope, these are notoriously difficult to establish in financial services. Differences in tastes do not appear particularly fruitful either since they require some element of production specialization to be relevant and there is no obvious conventional argument for this.

The Impact of Fiscal and Regulatory Distortions on Trade in Financial Services

An alternative explanation of trade in financial services relates to the impact of tax and regulatory distortions. For a wide variety of reasons, this turns out to be vital in the context of financial services. The case of Japanese international growth, allegedly encouraged by low capital/asset requirements, has already been mentioned. In contrast, the importance of US banks is often attributed to the restrictive regulatory regime they face domestically, which gave them an incentive to develop their international operations as a means of circumventing these restrictions. It is the very absence of restrictive regulations and an appropriate supervisory regime, however, that reinforced the strength of certain financial centres, such as London, and which enabled it to attract banks from the USA and elsewhere, attempting to circumvent their own restrictive domestic requirements. While comparative regulatory regimes may be important in explaining the performance of London as a centre in the twentieth century, its growth was initially determined by its location at the centre of the British Empire. London's early growth as a financial centre owes much to the fact that there were restrictions on trade in goods between colonies and third parties, forcing trade through the UK. Restrictions, this time on trade, therefore also provide part of the explanation as to why London became the focus for the finance of international trade between third parties.

The key, however, is not the restriction itself. If this were the only element in the story then the removal of the restriction or regulatory distortion would return the world to a level playing field. More importantly, the distortion not only allows a country to gain an advantage today, but also to capitalize on the learning-by-doing element of banking and thus to increase its 'know-how' and compound its comparative advantage.

These historical factors have therefore enabled the existing major players to developed specific banking skills and expertise over many years which are seen as the most important ingredients in the provision of banking services. The generalized implementation of the GATS in addition to the Basle Agreement on capital ratios would have the effect of removing the distortionary regulations that led to the development of comparative advantage in these countries. The new Agreement, when fully implemented, will remove the possibility of similar protection for new market entrants by eliminating distortionary regulatory factors and the taxes and subsidies that encouraged and enabled existing market participants to acquire their specialist skills.

The Impact of Liberalization on Trade in Financial Services

There is a general presumption that the GATS will therefore largely enshrine historic comparative advantage and favour the existing market leaders at the expense of other countries with a less well-developed presence in international financial markets. It would be wrong to imagine, however, that the gains from financial liberalization will accrue only to the suppliers of international financial services or, indeed, that domestic production will be wiped out.

It should be emphasized that a more efficient financial service sector is beneficial, not just because it yields static private-consumption benefits (which are typically quite low) but also because these services are important as an allocative intermediate input in production. An efficient financial service sector is therefore vital if a country is to enjoy the dynamic benefits of trade liberalization. Further, as argued below in more detail, domestic presence is likely to remain an important form of supply for a considerable period yet. While liberalization might therefore be expected to yield significant improvements, particularly in labour productivity and managerial and process efficiency, the sector is unlikely to decline to the extent that might be expected in the case of a goods sector at a similar comparative disadvantage. Although theory might suggest that the current world leaders in international finance may have the most to gain (as suppliers), the implications for the retail banking, insurance and other financial services need to be qualified considerably at a country level. Before this can be done, however, it is necessary to review the main provisions of the

GATS Agreement for the financial sector and to consider the current state of the financial services sector in the Gulf.

2. THE MAIN PROVISIONS OF THE GATS AND TRADE LIBERALIZATION

The Main Provisions of the GATS

In its most general form, the liberalization of financial trade under the GATS envisages that signatory states will: (i) remove capital account restrictions to permit cross-border supply and consumption abroad;[2] (ii) grant 'market access' to all; that is, grant everyone the right to establish in the national market or service it freely; and (iii) ensure 'national treatment'; that is, the authorities should seek to treat all banks, regardless of country of origin, on an equal basis and make them all subject to the same regulatory and tax regimes. The GATS also envisages that signatories will take steps to ensure that their regulatory and supervisory regime conforms with international best practice, although these requirements need not be specified in the Agreement.[3]

The GATS Agreement in the Uruguay Round, in contrast to the GATT, stopped short of requiring full reciprocity in access, opting instead for the less stringent market access and national treatment requirements. Full reciprocity would require that foreign financial institutions be allowed the same degree of market access in the domestic market as is permitted to domestic firms in foreign markets. This provision would have effectively forced countries to liberalize their financial markets to a common standard. Reaching consensus over this sector proved so difficult, however, that this traditional negotiating approach was abandoned.

The initial Agreement on financial services, as set out in 1995, instead required developed countries to implement the GATS within a year but allowed emerging and developing countries to take exemptions, initially for five years. From a practical viewpoint, the way these exemptions were established was very important. Instead of a general commitment to the Agreement, with exemptions claimed for non-conforming measures, as in the GATT (a so-called 'negative' list), the GATS followed what is called a 'hybrid' list. This required signatories to opt into specific sectors (and/or sub-sectors) and then to list a set of negative exemptions where appropriate. Many countries disaggregated their sectors in such detail, however, that their specific commitments amounted more to a positive list of 'opt-ins' for a particular mode rather than any kind of general commitment to freer trade in financial services. Furthermore, many countries chose to be 'unbound' in a particular sector, meaning that they were making no commitments, and then specified what they would nevertheless allow. This further reinforced the perspective that the GATS Agreement was essentially a 'positive' list of low-level commitments.

This bottom-up approach had the effect of making the GATS Agreement a piecemeal collection of opt-ins broadly corresponding with the *status quo ante* for many countries. Thus, for the most part, non-Eastern European emerging and developing countries only agreed to continue what they were already doing. Furthermore, and in contrast to the GATT, there was nothing in the Agreement to stop them putting in place further restrictive measures.[4] As a consequence, the original aspiration for an early move to eliminate exemptions in the Agreement was clearly infeasible and overly optimistic. In practice, emerging and developing countries had little idea what liberalization entailed and felt they were being rushed into a commitment they did not understand. They therefore had no clear vision of what the implications of the Agreement might be nor even what full compliance might entail and, privately at least, did not take the proposed time-schedule seriously. The subsequent Asian financial crisis compounded this problem and many developing countries now argue that the effect of the GATS would be to leave them susceptible to a similar sort of crash.

The WTO appears, as a consequence, to have conceded that progress will be slower than originally envisaged. Article XIX on Progressive Liberalization calls for a series of rounds to review exemptions to be held at five-year intervals. The article also contains a considerable number of escape clauses which may 'facilitate' those countries seeking further delays.

The Effects of Liberalization in Principle

What are the likely effects, in principle, of liberalizing trade in banking services in compliance with the long-term aspiration of the GATS, both on the use and availability of funds in the Gulf and on the banking sector within the countries themselves? In studying the effects of liberalization, there are two distinct concepts to keep in mind. The first is the effect of GATS on the flow of funds in and out of countries, and the second is the effect on financial service provision. The former relates to the issue of improved capital mobility while the latter addresses the issue of who intermediates between borrowers and lenders both inside and outside the country.

GATS and the flow of funds

GATS requires the removal of capital account restrictions in order to facilitate cross-border supplies and consumption abroad. Thus, in principle, by facilitating the international flow of capital, GATS ensures that investment flows internationally to those enterprises where it will be most productive in terms of risk and returns. In theory, therefore, freer capital flows are an opportunity for producers to attract the new investment necessary for development and an opportunity for domestic savers to invest in projects anywhere in the world.

In the Gulf region, Bahrain, Kuwait, Qatar and the United Arab Emirates (UAE) all have fairly liberal regimes regarding cross-border supply and consumption abroad, with no regulatory restrictions on capital flows. The absence of regulations limiting capital flows, however, does not necessarily mean that the market operates efficiently. The extent of capital flows in and out of a country depends, to a large extent, on the ease with which domestic residents can gain access to projects abroad and foreign investors in turn can gain access to domestic projects. In the case of domestic investors, this means the ease with which they can enter the international capital market. For wealthy individuals, this may be relatively easy but, for the vast majority, it depends upon domestic financial intermediaries and is therefore predicated on their level of efficiency and/or biases. Similarly, in practice, local entrepreneurs are restricted in their access to funds by the extent to which foreign banks can locate in the domestic economy or by the exposure and efficiency of their local intermediary in operating in the international market.

In spite of a lack of prohibitions on the flows of funds, distortions and lack of efficiency in the local market may therefore result in the misallocation of resources. Some measures of bank efficiency in the Gulf region are examined in section 3, but one important possible distortion needs to be noted here. At present, national and regional governments exert a significant influence over elements of the financial sector in some of these countries, and their desire to promote local development may be leading to an inappropriate level of regional investment. As mentioned earlier, a major preoccupation of the regional ruling institutions is the need to diversify their economic base. This could be by means of investing overseas but, more commonly, they are choosing to develop industries and enterprises in their home economies. This is in spite of the fact that these industries frequently require large immigrant communities to operate them. Their argument is that such development is less risky than similar investment abroad. An alternative strategy would be to invest in regional non-oil economies, but there is a perception that such investment is fraught with political risk. The West, with its history of European and world wars, is perceived as not much better. Of course, if the governments really reflect the tastes of the local population in relation to regional and political risk and the population is well informed, then they will choose to invest their monies in a bank which reflects this investment strategy without the need for political interference. It remains to be seen, however, whether a competitive local banking system, be it domestic or foreign in ownership, would choose a similar level of domestic investment or opt to diversify more internationally, either at a regional or global level. In response to a recent UNCTAD report, the UAE argued that the significant level of inward investment was an indication that their own preference for domestic investment was appropriate. Of course, appropriate diversification by foreign investors is neither evidence that domestic intermediaries are efficient nor a legitimate reason for a bias in domestic investment towards the domestic economy.

GATS and the provision of banking services
The second dimension of the GATS relates to the domestic provision of financial services and the possibility that foreign banks can enter domestic markets to compete with domestic banks. There are a number of ways this might happen. Banks could: (i) provide an arm's-length service directly to customers across borders without any domestic presence; (ii) invest directly, establishing a new financial firm within a country; (iii) purchase an existing financial services provider; or (iv) enter into a partnership with an established domestic bank.

In the arm's-length scenario, a foreign-based bank could bypass domestic banks and collect funds directly from domestic savers, provide them with payment instruments (credit cards and even cheques) and arrange loans using telephone and computer technology. In principle, all banking services could be provided in this manner although, in practice, consumers expect to have some direct contact, however occasional, with their financial service provider.

The other scenarios all envisage a direct presence in the domestic economy and are similar to FDI in that the foreign bank invests money directly in the domestic economy. Unlike other sectors, however, investment in substantial tangible assets, such as plant and machinery, is not necessary to conduct business and even their property requirements may be quite limited. Furthermore, the labour requirements of such an operation might, in principle, be quite modest and limited, in the extreme, to a handful of expatriate specialist advisers providing the occasional contact alluded to above. At the other end of the spectrum, an incoming bank may establish or purchase an entire branch network and all of its associated electronic payments systems and so on.

Evidence relating to the level of efficiency of Gulf-based banks is considered in section 3 but, given the presumption of the comparative advantage of the major existing players, there is a theoretical possibility that a market could be completely dominated by low-cost foreign banks, either providing cross-border financial services directly or with only a minimal domestic presence. There are two factors which tend to militate against this. In order to meet local demand for finance by domestic trading enterprises, banks will continue to maintain a sizeable staff with local knowledge to vet and monitor loans. Furthermore, in spite of the advances in arm's-length banking via telephone and computer, there is still a demand for personal contact with financial service providers. Indeed, deposit collection, traditionally the most costly element of banking services, is likely to remain branch-intensive for some time to come. Taken together, these factors imply that the scenario whereby the market is serviced at arm's-length by foreign banks is unlikely to develop in the foreseeable future.

A second piece of evidence regarding domestic versus foreign provision relates to the developments in the EU in the wake of the Single Market, an initiative which most closely resembles the effects of implementing the GATS Agreement in full. Before the implementation of the Single Market, measures of efficiency suggested widespread differences between member countries, even adjusting for differences in the levels and types of services (see Ryan, 1992). There was also considerable evidence of differences in efficiency levels within countries. The EU's Single Market, like GATS, was designed to ensure that banks would have reciprocal rights of entry into domestic markets at no less favourable terms than domestic providers, the so-called National Treatment Provision. Given the pre-liberalization measures of efficiency, there might have been a presumption of significant market entry by the more efficient providers, mainly in Belgium, Germany and, to a lesser extent, the UK and the Netherlands.

Significantly, this is not what happened. The advent of the Single Market provided an impetus for significant labour-shedding and internal bank reorganization in the less efficient markets rather than widespread take-overs or new entrants. There is some evidence of joint ventures and new entry but, interestingly, the level of intra-EU mergers and acquisitions has not been significantly greater than those with banks from outside the EU. Indeed, the level of activity between EU countries is probably lower than the level within countries, where smaller banks have frequently merged to compete more effectively with their larger competitors in terms of regional coverage and product range. While the levels of efficiency within the EU have converged in the wake of the Single Market, the impetus for rationalization and efficiency gains probably owed as much to the threat of mergers, acquisitions and new competition as it did to actual outside entrants (Murinde et al., 1999).

3. THE EFFICIENCY OF BANKING SYSTEMS IN THE GULF REGION

The standard measure of comparative advantage is usually the pre-liberalization prices prevailing in a country. While this measure can be an indicator of comparative advantage, this is not always certain, particularly in financial services where different regulations across countries can distort the true underlying prices. In the case of banking, the prices in question are such things as interest rate and foreign exchange margins as well as charges for specific services, letters of credit and the like.

The Structure of the GCC Banking Systems in the Context of the GATS

The banking systems of Bahrain, the UAE, Saudi Arabia, Kuwait, Oman and Qatar all exhibit individual peculiarities in terms of their structure, regulation, performance and implications for the GATS. Of the six Gulf states, Bahrain, Kuwait, Qatar and the UAE initially offered restricted commitments in the financial services sector. By the end of 1999, however, only Bahrain and Kuwait had registered their commitments and exemptions under the latest (Fifth) Protocol across the full range of financial services (insurance, banking, brokering and so on). These four countries take a fairly liberal view of cross-border supply and consumption abroad, which is perhaps unsurprising for oil-rich economies. As discussed below, however, Kuwait, the UAE and Qatar have chosen either to be unbound or to restrict market access as regards commercial presence. These restrictions and other exemptions, such as limitations on representative offices and branch networks for existing foreign financial institutions, effectively enshrine current practice in the GATS in these countries.

Bahrain

Bahrain, with its aspirations to being an international banking centre, is dominated by international banks. The offshore banking market has its origins in the period of recycling petro-dollars in the 1970s; it reached its peak in 1984 with 74 offshore banks; there were about 47 operating in off-shore banking services by the end of 1998. In terms of traditional commercial banking services, there are 13 international banks and five local banks, making a total of 18 commercial banks. Local assets are held predominantly with local banks; for example, the two largest local banks (by asset size) hold 60 per cent of local assets. In addition, there are 22 investment banks, of which six are locally incorporated. The offshore, commercial and investment banks are all regulated by the Bahrain Monetary Agency (BMA); thus, the BMA acts as a central bank.

In terms of the GATS provisions, Bahrain offers what is arguably the most open banking sector in the Gulf region, primarily because the financial system is based on offshore business. The only significant restriction imposed is an upper limit on foreign ownership of 49 per cent of locally incorporated banking enterprises conducting business 'onshore'. Of course, such a limitation is qualitatively different to a tariff restriction in its impact on foreign suppliers. The downside of this openness, however, is that the financial system is vulnerable to international financial changes; for example, the 1994 bond market crash adversely affected some Bahrain-based banks, notably the National Bank of Bahrain. In general, Bahrain out-performs Dubai and continues to be the lead banking centre in the GCC, especially in syndicated lending and advisory services.

Saudi Arabia

The banking system in Saudi Arabia comprises 12 commercial banks. Although foreign commercial banks were allowed to operate in Saudi Arabia before 1976, they were forced into partial or full nationalization after 1976. Hence, in terms of the GATS, the banking market is closed to foreign banks; for example, no new licences have been issued since 1988. Moreover, state development banks are supported by large subsidies and therefore operate on non-competitive terms. Saudi banks appear to be the most profitable in the GCC in terms of return on average equity (Table 4.1), but their published performance ratios do not take into account the subsidy element (see Murinde and Kariisa, 1997).

The regulatory framework is provided by the Central Bank, the Saudi Arabian Monetary Agency (SAMA), and there is considerable political interference in bank regulation. As yet, neither Saudi Arabia nor Oman are members of the WTO, although their applications for accession are pending and they currently hold observer status. The path to accession, however, is not smooth and there is considerable controversy concerning what they see as excessive WTO demands regarding compliance and so on. Notwithstanding these difficulties, these states are likely to accede in the near future with a set of exemptions similar to those enjoyed by the UAE and Qatar.

Kuwait

The Kuwaiti banking system is the third largest in the GCC in terms of asset size. It comprises seven commercial banks, 13 investment, development or other specialist banks plus an Islamic bank. However, the sector has been adversely affected by two shocks: the crash of the stock exchange in 1982, later followed by the Iraqi invasion. The Central Bank of Kuwait regulates all the banks except the Kuwait Finance House – the Islamic bank.

Table 4.1 Selected banking and liquidity indicators for the Gulf region (millions of local currency)

Indicator	Bahrain			Kuwait			Oman			Qatar			Saudi Arabia			UAE ('000)		
	1996	1997	1998	1996	1997	1998	1996	1997	1998	1996	1997	1998	1996	1997	1998	1996	1997	1998
Central Bank																		
Foreign assets	516	514	535	1112	1108	1228	780	822	712	264	304	369	n/a	n/a	n/a	30	31	32
Reserve money	166	234	105	474	426	n/a	326	354	344	226	248	255	43	46	47	20	20	21
Foreign liabilities	17	n/a	n/a	n/a	n/a	n/a	0.4	0.6	0.9	n/a	n/a	n/a	n/a	n/a	n/a	n/a	n/a	n/a
Liquidity indicators																		
Domestic credit	263	423	491	7475	8504	8792	1550	2025	2325	19	22	24	n/a	n/a	n/a	63	62	61
Money supply	283	290	310	1242	1247	1298	503	549	524	388	413	435	133	141	148	22	25	28
Deposits																		
Demand deposits	188	201	214	892	902	893	272	307	280	248	257	3041	81	90	101	15	18	20
T & S deposits	1146	1249	1384	6088	6385	6299	1130	1484	1484	1577	1746	1827	81	86	88	64	69	70

Source: IMF (1999).

In terms of the GATS provisions, as already noted, Kuwait has chosen to be unbound in the Fifth Protocol and it has the most severe form of protectionism for banking services in the GCC; all commercial banks are wholly owned by Kuwaiti interests, that is, the royal family or government. In 1994, however, foreign investors were allowed to hold up to 40 per cent of local banks.

The United Arab Emirates

The structure of the financial system in the UAE comprises depository institutions, representative offices, money exchange houses and financial brokers. The depository institutions consist of 19 locally incorporated banks and 28 foreign banks, with the former having the more extensive branch network (254 branches and cash offices). In addition, there are two dedicated investment banks and, owing to recent liberalization, 28 representative offices, 164 exchange houses and branches and 13 financial brokers. While the UAE has yet to make commitments under the GATS Fifth Protocol and chose to place severe restrictions on market entry in their previous submission, they have recently established an offshore banking centre and free zone at Saadiyat. Invitations have been issued to 50 major international banks to establish centres there.

Oman and Qatar

Oman and Qatar are the two smallest countries by total assets. Qatar has only five commercial banks and is dominated by the Qatar National Bank with assets in excess of $US5 billion, while three further banks have assets in excess of $US1 billion, including the Qatar Islamic Bank. Oman is slightly more competitive, with ten banks. Each of the top five, however, controls more than double the assets of any other and together they hold 66 per cent of the total.

Other banking restrictions in the Gulf Region

In addition to the exemptions detailed in their schedule of commitments, the member states often have other restrictions which are not immediately apparent, such as restrictions on the foreign ownership of property and limitations on the number and duration of stay of overseas managers and specialists. Furthermore, foreign banks often face discriminatory tax treatment, at the hands of either national or regional governments. For example, while the national government in the UAE treats all banks equally for tax purposes, individual emirates levy supplementary taxes on foreign banks, which contravenes the GATS.

Islamic banking also exists in the region. Again, Bahrain has the most extensive presence with four banks, Qatar and the UAE two, while Saudi

Arabia and Kuwait have one each. Ranked by asset size, however, the Kuwait Finance House ($US5 billion), the Islamic Development Bank from Saudi Arabia ($US4.5 billion) and the Dubai Islamic Bank ($US2.1 billion) are the largest. In overall terms, these banks are dwarfed by their Iranian counterparts, where the three largest banks have assets in excess of $US60 billion. Nevertheless, these three GCC banks are ranked as the next largest outside Iran. The *modus operandi* of these banks is via investment activities rather than the interest rate yardstick, as emphasized by Murinde et al. (1995).[5]

The Efficiency of the Gulf Region Banking Sector

The results of an assessment of the efficiency of the main banks, by asset size and some standard indicators, namely asset quality, capital strength, the return on equity and liquidity, in each of the Gulf states are shown in Table 4.1. A detailed assessment of efficiency for the UAE is shown in Table 4.2. These results provide some indication of the variance of efficiency measures within particular states.

Almost all of the banks reported in Table 4.1 compare favourably with those in other (particularly oil-rich) developing countries in terms of efficiency, although their ratings fall short of those scored by the main banks in the OECD countries. The most striking feature of the data on financial ratios, however, is the wide differential in levels of efficiency both within and across GCC states. This suggests that, as a whole, the sector is not sufficiently competitive at present. Increased market access, whether in the context of the liberalization of financial services within the GCC or the GATS, is therefore likely to have a significant impact on efficiency levels.[6]

As noted above, however, some countries in the GCC have, in the context of the Schedule of Specific Commitments and the List of Article II (MFN) Exemptions, effectively placed restrictions on market access, and such exemptions had to be justified in the context of the previous round of offers. The UAE, for example, argued that it was 'a small country and already saturated'. The notion that the market, with free entry and exit, is saturated is one which economists have difficulty comprehending. If the market truly is saturated, then prices for services and profits would be such that there would be no incentive for new domestic or foreign firms to enter. Firms will only seek to enter if they believe that they can provide a better service at a lower price and, given a lower cost of service provision, generate sufficient profits to warrant the investment. If the UAE market really was oversupplied, such opportunities would not exist and restrictions on entry would therefore be unnecessary.

Some other evidence would also appear to contradict the VAE viewpoint

Table 4.2   Efficiency indicators for the banking sector in the Gulf Region

Name of top five banks in each of the GCC countries	Strength $USm	Strength %Δ	Size $USm	Size %Δ	CAR %	Profits $USm	ROC %	ROA %	BIS %	NPL %
Bahrain										
Arab Banking Corporation	2071	7.9	26064	10.5	7.95	65	3.3	0.25	13.9	7.5
Gulf International Bank	731	5.3	10209	7.2	7.16	82	11.5	0.8	11.3	0.98
Investcorp	672	13.6	2234	17.4	30.1	114	18.1	5.12	n/a	n/a
Bank of Bahrain & Kuwait	265	1.2	2517	10.0	10.5	29	10.9	1.14	15.7	21.6
National Bank of Bahrain	264	7.2	2298	-11.1	11.5	41	15.9	1.76	23.1	4.1
Kuwait										
National Bank of Kuwait	1264	3.0	12716	-6.9	9.94	265	21.3	2.09	n/a	n/a
Gulf Investment Corp	1163	3.6	13494	11.2	8.62	97	8.5	0.72	13.0	10.04
Gulf Bank	592	6.5	6247	8.4	9.47	100	17.4	1.60	21.2	n/a
Kuwait Finance House*	534	15.3	5535	5.6	9.7	146	29.2	2.63	n/a	n/a
Burgan Bank	533	7.0	3746	-1.4	14.2	35	6.8	0.94	20.4	13.3
Oman										
National Bank of Oman	258	107.3	1825	19.9	14.1	44	23.2	2.43	17.6	n/a
Oman International Bank	217	1.2	1782	15.9	12.2	34	15.8	1.91	15.8	10.6
Commercial Bank of Oman	183	71.6	1522	76.6	12.0	31	21.6	2.1	n/a	n/a
Bank Muscat	139	77.2	1714	6.9	8.09	34	31.2	1.98	14.7	4.85
Oman Arab Bank	83	20.1	680	-3.3	12.2	21	27.8	3.11	16.4	5.5
Qatar										
Qatar National Bank	874	9.7	5354	6.5	16.3	116	13.9	2.17	5.7	3.4
Commercial Bank of Qatar	132	12.2	1205	20.8	10.9	24	19.2	1.99	13.1	2.99

Table 4.2 (continued)

Name of top five banks in each of the GCC countries	Strength $USm	%Δ	Size $USm	%Δ	CAR %	Profits $USm	ROC %	ROA %	BIS %	NPL %
Doha Bank	108	16.3	1249	10.3	8.6	22	22.0	1.76	17.3	4.8
Qatar Islamic Bank*	80	13.4	1028	10.9	7.7	16	21.5	1.56	n/a	n/a
Al-Ahli Bank of Qatar	64	21.4	652	17.4	9.9	16	27.8	2.51	n/a	n/a
Saudi Arabia										
National Commercial Bank	2144	3.1	24815	7.5	8.6	284	13.4	1.14	n/a	n/a
Riyad Bank	2071	2.7	16200	4.9	12.8	276	13.5	1.7	n/a	4.2
Al Rajhi Bank & Inv Corp	1455	5.5	10162	8.3	14.3	388	27.4	3.8	n/a	n/a
Saudi American Bank	1301	6.4	13327	9.4	9.8	317	25.1	3.38	n/a	n/a
United Saudi Bank	847	-0.3	7294	2.7	11.6	163	19.2	2.24	27.9	15.3
United Arab Emirates										
National Bank of Dubai	1004	1.5	6638	5.7	15.1	109	11.0	1.65	n/a	n/a
Abu Dhabi Commerce Bank	779	12.5	5890	16.4	13.2	139	18.8	2.35	17.7	n/a
Emirates Bank International	769	15.2	5368	14.9	14.3	132	18.4	2.46	23.7	3.7
National Bank of Dubai	685	9.1	9566	12.8	7.2	111	16.9	1.16	17.1	9.6
Mashreq Bank	617	16.9	4971	5.5	12.4	145	25.3	2.91	14.4	15.2

Notes:
* Islamic Bank.
All efficiency indicators are calculated from data for December 1998; changes relate to December 1997. Bank strength refers to Tier 1 capital. Size is defined in terms of assets. CAR denotes the capital assets ratio and is used to measure the soundness of the bank. Profits are given here before tax (i.e. pre-tax profits). The ROC denotes the return on capital, measured as profits on average capital, this is used to measure performance. BIS denotes the capital adequacy ratio as calculated using the Bank for International Settlements formula. NPL denotes non-performing loans as a percentage of total loans.

in that, compared with some OECD countries, branches per capita are quite low in the Gulf (Murinde and Ryan, 1999). For example, Belgium, which topped the pre-EU Single Market efficiency measures, had less than half the population per branch (2637) compared with the UAE (6044). The figures for the USA and the UK are 66 and 75 per cent of the UAE total respectively. Arguments that the GCC is overbanked are therefore difficult to accept and appear designed to prevent the entry of more efficient competitors. The evidence on differing levels of efficiency in the sector, presented in Tables 4.1 and 4.2, appear to bear out this contention of a lack of competition.

While less efficient operators are understandably fearful of increased competition, the EU experience suggests however, that this fear is somewhat exaggerated. Within the context of the EU Single Market, the threat of liberalization was the spur for many banks to improve their efficiency levels by way of labour-shedding, reorganization, improved technology and upgrading staff skill. Indeed, pre-integration forecasts of implied labour-shedding, based on simulation models using late 1980s data, not only matched the actual outcomes almost perfectly but also suggested that the implied changes had largely been implemented by the time the barriers to entry were removed in 1992 (see Ryan, 1992). There was also a degree of acquisitions and mergers within countries to rationalize and improve the distribution of branch networks and to avail themselves of some operational economies (Murinde et al., 1999). The lesson would therefore appear to be that, when faced with credible deadlines for competition, the efficiency of existing operators rose and foreign entry was relatively insignificant.

Another popular contention among policy-makers and the trade press is that there is a need to increase minimum capital requirements, aside from the Basle requirements, to encourage larger banks and improve asset quality and scale efficiency. While there has been a general presumption that increasing returns to scale in banking exist, the results of research on the economies of scale hypothesis is rather mixed. More recent research on the EU Single Market suggests that there may be scale economies in the wholesale end of the market, off-balance-sheet activity, full management, investment services and large corporate loans, particularly with respect to smaller banks (see Gardiner and Molyneux, 1997). Note that, while the measures of efficiency in the banking sector used in Tables 4.1 and 4.2 show considerable variation, they do not appear to be correlated with bank size.

Overall, increased competition as a consequence of implementing the GATS ought to remove the variations in efficiency, in line with the EU evidence, and encourage mergers or take-overs where commercial pressures deem it appropriate. Nevertheless, those banks currently identified as efficient have little to fear from market liberalization and, indeed, could reasonably expect to be able to expand and compete, at the very least, in regional markets.

The evidence in Tables 4.1 and 4.2 suggests that the Islamic banks in the GCC are operating at acceptable levels of efficiency in terms of asset quality, capital strength and liquidity levels.[7] The ratings of the Islamic banks are also relatively high compared to the other banks, notwithstanding the fact that these banks rely on investment activities rather than the traditional yardstick of interest rates on loans and deposits. The main effect of GATS for Islamic banks would be to facilitate their expansion to regional markets both within the GCC and abroad, especially in Sudan, Pakistan and Malaysia. Since Iran, where the largest of these banks is located, is not currently a signatory to the GATS, this represents a significant opportunity for Gulf-based banks, especially in the light of the learning-by-doing argument of banking practice.

Commercial Bank Pricing Policy

Interest rates are an important banking sector indicator as they represent the pricing decisions of commercial banking operations. Table 4.3 reports data on nominal and real deposit rates as well as nominal and real loan rates in the GCC countries 1994–97. The real rates are calculated using published inflation data. It is useful to note that there are high spreads in the banking market in most GCC countries; these translate directly into high bank profits to the extent of the number of deposit and loan accounts held. These spreads are consistent with the view that there is a lack of competition in the Gulf banking sector.

The data in Table 4.4 suggest that there is a high rate of liquidity in the Gulf banking sector, and that a considerable portion of these funds is therefore available for investment in the local market. The absolute levels of the real loan and real deposit rates reported in Table 4.3 are low by international standards in spite of the large spread in borrowing and deposit rates. This observation is consistent with the view that the GCC market is very liquid. In addition, the apparently low absolute rates highlighted in Table 4.3 and the high level of liquidity are indicative of a bias towards domestic lending at the expense of an appropriately diversified international portfolio.[8] The reasons for such a bias, even where there is little or no restriction on the movement on capital, were discussed in section 2. It should be emphasized that this bias might be in addition to, or a severe example of, the 'normal' bias associated with the Feldstein–Horioka puzzle commonly observed even in developed Western countries.[9]

This sub-optimal investment diversification may be a concern for any

Table 4.3 The pricing of banking services in the GCC countries: deposit and loan interest rates (%)

GCC country	Year	Lending services			Deposit services		Spread: lending – deposit rate
		Nominal loan rate	Inflation rate	Real loan rate	Nominal time deposit rate	Real deposit rate	
Bahrain	1994	10.8	−3.9	14.7	4.0	7.9	6.8
	1995	11.8	−6.4	18.2	5.7	12.1	6.1
	1996	12.5	2.7	9.8	5.2	2.5	7.3
	1997	12.3	5.2	7.1	5.3	0.1	7.0
Kuwait	1994	7.61	1.1	6.51	5.70	4.6	1.91
	1995	8.37	5.2	3.17	6.53	1.33	1.84
	1996	8.77	4.9	3.87	6.05	1.15	2.72
	1997	8.80	0.4	8.4	5.93	5.53	2.87
Oman	1994	8.57	4.7	3.87	4.34	−0.36	4.23
	1995	9.38	−0.3	9.68	6.53	6.83	2.85
	1996	9.23	6.8	2.43	6.85	0.05	2.38
	1997	9.30	9.2	0.1	7.30	−1.9	2.0
Qatar	1994	9.5	−8.1	17.6	6.0	14.1	3.5
	1995	8.1	−4.9	13.0	4.8	9.7	3.3
	1996	7.2	4.4	2.8	4.1	−0.3	3.1
	1997	n/a	6.3	n/a	n/a	n/a	n/a
Saudi Arabia	1994	n/a	3.4	n/a	n/a	n/a	n/a
	1995	n/a	−0.9	n/a	n/a	n/a	n/a
	1996	n/a	6.8	n/a	n/a	n/a	n/a
	1997	n/a	6.1	n/a	5.79	0.31	n/a
UAE	1994	7.61	4.72	2.89	4.89	0.17	2.72
	1995	7.59	5.24	5.02	5.02	−0.22	2.57
	1996	7.55	3.08	4.47	4.79	1.71	2.76
	1997	7.48	3.01	4.47	3.65	0.64	3.83

Source: Data for nominal loan rates, nominal deposit rates and price indices were obtained from IMF (1998). Inflation rates, real rates and the spread were calculated by the authors.

Table 4.4   Bank performance and efficiency indicators in the UAE

	Bank ratings	Assets quality	Capital strength	Operational efficiency (ROAE)	Liquidity
The National Bank of Abu Dhabi	BBBpi	14.65	7.35	15.51	45.78
The National Bank of Dubai Ltd	Api	n/a	15.77	10.63	n/a
Mashreqbank	BBBpi	n/a	11.20	27.74	59.13
Emirates Bank International PJSC	BBBpi	3.39	13.45	19.03	66.80
Abu Dhabi Commercial Bank	BBBpi	17.96	14.99	17.51	58.24
Commercial Bank International Plc	BB−	−41.38	17.32	30.82	69.90
Dubai Islamic Bank	BB+	30.41	8.03	10.80	76.94
Union National Bank	A−	13.93	12.60	n/a	58.05
Abu Dhabi Investment Co.	A−	5.68	16.26	7.06	35.57
National Bank of Umm Al-Qaiwain	A−2	1.92	25.24	17.29	62.86
United Arab Bank	A−3	12.13	20.88	11.47	69.34
Bank of Sharjah	BB+	30.45	21.41	12.24	60.93
National Bank of Sharjah	B+	−45.80	18.41	20.94	59.00
First Gulf Bank	BB+	46.07	24.35	7.74	45.75
Arabian General	B	−3.49	42.91	5.68	45.76
Arab Emirates Investment Bank	B	n/a	27.48	9.31	9.74
Arab Bank for Investment & Foreign Trade	BBB+	53.87	19.94	16.29	23.42
Commercial Bank of Dubai	A+	n/a	19.40	20.26	62.57
National Bank of Fujairah	BBB+	12.67	20.85	14.27	61.35
Investbank	BB	32.50	16.44	18.13	62.28
Middle East Bank PJSC	B	6.27	25.53	19.40	90.58
National Bank of Ras Al-Khaimah	BBB	35.69	23.25	6.77	48.98

Notes:
Asset quality: estimated using the ratio of loan loss provisions to net internal revenue. A negative value of this ratio indicates that the bank is losing its assets given the level of net internal revenue generated from operations.
Capital strength: measured using the ratio of equity to total assets. Figures denote the ratio of equity to net loans.
Operational efficiency: measured by the return on average equity (ROAE).
Liquidity: measured by the ratio of net loans to total assets. Figures denote the ratio net loans to short-term funding.

country subject to cyclical shocks but, where a high-net-worth country is seeking to diversify in order to compensate for the future decline of a resource-depleting industry such as oil, it is potentially more serious. International evidence suggests that the degree of diversification of lending portfolios is greater, not only where there is freer capital mobility but also where the domestic financial sector is more competitive and where there is a liberal market-access regime leading to an increased international focus. Overall, Table 4.3 suggests that, in the absence of more competition and international exposure, GCC banks are not making the best use of their available funds.

In this context the GATS offers several opportunities for the GCC. First, by increasing market access or even by simply creating the possibility of market access to foreign banks, there is likely to be an increase in the competitiveness of the domestic market and a reduction in the spreads reported in Table 4.3. Second, GATS is likely to result in the further internationalization of the Gulf banking sector, both by domestic and foreign banks, leading to better identification of both foreign investment opportunities and improved portfolio allocation. The likely effects are that the absolute level of savings and deposit rates will rise, although the effects on lending rates and investment are ambiguous. Domestic investment may fall and foreign investment rise, but this will be determined by the market and represents the correct balance between domestic and foreign investment in accordance with the optimal diversification and growth strategy by GCC countries. Third, and perhaps most important from the perspective of the Gulf banking sector, by liberalizing and internationalizing world financial markets, the GATS will increase the GCC's investment opportunities and facilitate its optimal diversification and growth strategy in the light of diminishing oil resources. Given the existing level of distortions internationally, it is difficult to predict the effect of liberalization on world deposit and lending interest rates generally. As a high net lender, however, and in line with the observation that they are very liquid and have low deposit rates, GCC countries are likely to enjoy a higher return on their deposits in the new liberalized environment. The effect on borrowing rates is ambiguous.

4.   CONCLUSION AND CONCLUDING ISSUES

While the data on efficiency levels suggest that liberalization will lead to a large shake-up of the Gulf financial industry, the analysis suggests that banks in the GCC have little to fear, at least in terms of the continuing existence of a locally owned banking sector. It might even be argued that market discipline is more likely to benefit the owners of capital at the expense of labour generally, and low-skilled foreign workers in particular. Although the interests of the bank owners are undoubtedly important in the minds of the Gulf governments, this is not really the key issue. It is the nature of the employment these banks will provide that is the more strategic issue.

As with other sectors in the Gulf generally, the banking sector employs significant numbers of non-local labour, with nationals often employed only in a nominal capacity in management.[10] There is also an implied restriction on the promotion of non-nationals within firms, creating powerful disincentives within the context of banking organizations. These measures are unlikely to survive the increased competition which liberalization under the GATS will bring.

The development of a high-skilled cadre of domestic financial workers, however, is hampered by current fiscal policy. Governments often distribute transfer payments to nationals, based upon age of majority and other non-productive qualifying criteria. In spite of the declared objective of developing certain industries which can provide 'suitable' white-collar professional employment when oil revenues dwindle, there is therefore little incentive for nationals to develop the necessary level of education or the expertise acquired as a result of learning-by-doing under the current system. The real issue for regional governments is therefore not whether to proceed with liberalization under the GATS, but rather whether they should permit banks the freedom to develop their management cadre of overseas workers without discriminatory and educationally ineffective national quotas or to develop competitive home talent by revising social and educational policies within the states themselves.

The evidence from the EU's Single Market is that a firm target date for the removal of restrictions relating to commercial presence results in a rapid improvement in efficiency measures in advance of the deadline. This must be tempered with the evidence on the length of time required to develop the knowledge associated with learning-by-doing. Even if the transfer payment policy were to be immediately revised (which is politically most unlikely), the appropriate time-scale for learning-by-doing is unlikely to be less than five years and more realistically ten (see Ryan, 1990). It is not clear, however, that this window of opportunity exists. The sooner competitor economies respond to the prospect of the GATS, the lower the probability that the Gulf sector can develop sufficiently quickly, in line with government aspirations, before WTO pressure for full liberalization becomes overwhelming. The move towards a regional free trade area in financial services would therefore appear to be a sensible step.

Further problems within the sector are caused by the historical practice of name-based lending and a lack of transparency. There has been a recent trend towards providing appropriate accounts certified by qualified accountants, but the GCC still lags behind developed-country standards in this regard.[11] The absence of certified accounts seriously limits the ability of banks to assess returns and risks on new projects with respect to specific firms and whole sectors of the economy. Hence, lending decisions tend to be dominated by the reputation of the borrower and new entrepreneurs find it difficult to get start-up financing.

Increasing competition, especially from new foreign entrants, is likely to put further pressure on older-style lending policies, leading to more widespread use of auditing and accounting procedures and greater transparency.

A further impediment to trade in financial services which needs to be addressed is the provision of a comprehensive and transparent judicial superstructure for handling disputes, in particular bad loans and bankruptcy. For example, there is a belief that courts in some jurisdictions are unwilling to find against nationals in dispute with foreign banks and there have been instances where central banks have prevented the effective award of damages by limiting foreign exchange transactions. While there are few restrictions on capital flows in the region generally, if the GCC is to emerge as an international banking player, the judicial superstructure needs to pay attention to foreign as well as national interests.

NOTES

1. Before the last set of trade negotiations under the GATT, the focus was on the effect of tariffs, quotas and other non-tariff barriers on trade in goods. However, previous talks had assiduously eschewed some contentious areas where developed countries were at a comparative disadvantage *vis-à-vis* developing countries, most notably textiles and agriculture. In return for concessions in these areas in the Uruguay Round, the developed nations urged the GATT to take a much broader view of trade and, in particular, added to the discussion issues such as TRIPS, TRIMS and GATS.
2. In fact the Agreement does not state this explicitly, although there are various clauses in Article XI which essentially amount to this. Footnote 8 in Article XVI, however, appears to limit some of the obligations normally associated with these modes of supply. In particular, it seems to relieve obligations on signatories regarding the outflow of funds under cross-border supply and commercial presence. Countries also have the right to impose restrictions in times of balance of payments crises and to take appropriate prudential and regulatory measures as they see fit.
3. Some countries have listed non-discriminatory exemptions, regarding licensing and so on, in their schedules which are essentially regulatory in nature.
4. The GATT originally worked on the basis of a general commitment combined with a negative list of exemptions. This approach made the trade restrictions in place transparent and thus allowed the GATT to monitor any attempt to engage in further restrictive

practices. This formed the basis for future negotiations. While, in theory, a positive list and a negative list could be the same, in practice, with a positive list, measures not made explicit are not transparent and there is essentially no means of preventing countries from implementing new restrictive measures.

5. The performance of Islamic banks is complex, given that the traditional interest rate yardstick is not acceptable, discussed by Murinde et al. (1995). Some assessment, however, is conducted below.

6. The 1998 GCC Heads of State Summit agreed, in principle, to allow the right of establishment of Gulf banks in one another's states. This has yet to be implemented.

7. Because Islamic banks are typically quite small in the context of their markets, only three Islamic banks are reported in Tables 4.1 and 4.2; one each from Kuwait and Qatar in Table 4.1 and one from the UAE in Table 4.2. Their reported ratios, however, are not uncharacteristic.

8. Foreign assets of the aggregate banking sector varied between 34 and 47 per cent during the 1990s, while the corresponding figure for liabilities was 15 to 18 per cent.

9. The Feldstein–Horioka puzzle seeks to explain why a country's saving and investment rate are highly correlated.

10. By way of example, 87 per cent of the UAE's banking staff are non-nationals. Where UAE nationals are employed, they are overwhelmingly in the managerial ranks, accounting for 19 per cent of that grade, with only 4.5 per cent in lower grades.

11. The region has suffered periodically from scandals in respect of failures associated with poor accounting practices, of which the BCCI is the most outstanding example. Both Kuwait and Bahrain have had problems in this regard in recent years, as has the UAE generally as a result of the 'Patel' scandal and the problems of the Dubai Islamic Bank. This has led to renewed pressure for greater adherence to International Accounting Standards.

REFERENCES

Gardiner, T. and P. Molyneux (1997), *Credit Institutions and Banking (The European Commission's Single Market Review)*, sub-series 2, vol. 3, Luxembourg: Office for Official Publications of the European Communities.

IMF (1998), *International Financial Statistics*, Washington, DC: IMF.

IMF (1999), *International Financial Statistics*, Washington, DC: IMF.

Klein, L.R. (1998), *Implication of WTO Membership for the Global Economy*, Emirates Lecture 9, Abu Dhabi: The Emirates Center for Strategic Studies and Research.

Lensink, R., N. Hermes and V. Murinde (1998), 'The effect of financial liberalization on capital flight in African economies', *World Development*, **26** (7), 1349–68.

Murinde, V. and J. Kariisa (1997), 'The financial performance of the East African Development Bank: a retrospective analysis', *Accounting, Business and Financial History*, **7** (1), 81–104.

Murinde, V. and C. Ryan (1999), *The Implications of the General Agreement on Trade in Services for the Banking Sector in the United Arab Emirates*, Geneva: UNCTAD.

Murinde, V., K. Naser and R.S.O. Wallace (1995), 'Is it prudent for Islamic banks to make investment decisions without the interest rate instrument?', *Research in Accounting in Emerging Economies*, **3**, 123–48.

Murinde, V., J. Agung and A. Mullineux (1999), 'Convergence of European financial systems: banks or equity markets', in M.M. Fischer and P. Nijkamp (eds), *Spatial Dynamics of European Integration*, Berlin: Springer Verlag, pp. 129–42.

Ryan, C. (1990), 'Trade liberalisation and financial services', *The World Economy*, **13** (3), 349–66.

Ryan, C. (1992), 'The integration of financial services and economic welfare', in L.A Winters (ed.), *Trade Flows and Trade Policy After '1992'*, Cambridge: Cambridge University Press, pp. 92–117.

5. Options for regional integration in Southern Africa

David Evans*

The Southern African Development Coordination Conference (SADCC) and its successor, the Southern African Development Community (SADC), had strong anti-apartheid political orientations. Initially, economic cooperation was based on a sectoral approach. The Windhoek Treaty of 1992 changed the basis of economic cooperation to allow for 'efficiency, economy and competitiveness'. This shift led to the 1996 SADC Protocol on Trade Cooperation for the creation of a free trade area (FTA) which is now almost complete. Successful regional associations usually require a strong political rationale for economic benefits to be realized.[1] It remains to be seen whether or not the original unifying anti-apartheid politics in Southern Africa are strong enough in the post-apartheid era to enable SADC to build the institutions necessary for rules-based economic integration and thus realize the potential economic benefits.

In terms of economic conditions, the SADC countries are an extremely heterogeneous group. This can be seen from Table 5.1, which includes those SADC member countries covered in this study. At the time of the Windhoek Treaty, the GDP per capita ranged roughly 20:1 from richest to poorest. In terms of economic size, the range was nearly 100:1. GDP growth performance in the previous 20 years varied considerably, but some SADC countries had a surprisingly good record of economic management in terms of the average rate of inflation, poverty reduction and human development.[2]

An important characteristic of the SADC region is the historically high level of barriers to trade. While there was a considerable lowering of protection in the region in the 1990s, there are still significant barriers to trade (see Table 5.1, columns 2 and 3). The fall in tariffs reflects the fact that several SADC countries underwent WTO tariff reform or World Bank Structural Adjustment Programmes (SAPs) during the 1990s. Thus, there was an overall fall in average tariffs from 15.1 per cent to 9.3 per cent from the early 1990s to the tariff levels that prevailed roughly at the time of the 1996 SADC Protocol on Trade Cooperation. Although this decline in

Table 5.1   GDP per capita, tariffs and the direction of trade in 12 SADC countries

	GDP per capita $US current 1991–93, avg.	Tariffs, early 1990s: average, %	Tariffs, approx. 1996: average, %	Imports to GDP ratio: 1991–93, %	SADC share imports: 1991–93, %	Exports to GDP ratio: 1991–93, %	SADC share exports: 1991–93, %
Angola	339	11.4	10.8	19.9	13.8	39.6	0.1
Botswana	2651	9.4	11.8	51.8	84.9	51.1	10.5
Lesotho	282	9.4	11.7	163.9	90.4	18.1	45.3
Malawi	204	22.9	20.6	24.5	40.7	23.1	13.3
Mauritius	2418	15.3	22.7	65.4	10.9	56.5	6.3
Mozambique	79	25.5	12.0	73.7	37.2	29.8	6.1
Namibia	1601	9.4	12.6	58.7	89.3	63.9	29.7
South Africa	2985	9.4	5.6	12.9	8.1	19.2	27.0
Swaziland	914	9.4	6.3	94.1	93.9	74.3	53.1
Tanzania	161	24.2	19.0	46.5	2.0	20.6	2.2
Zambia	356	29.7	11.4	34.1	42.0	53.5	2.2
Zimbabwe	502	40.3	15.8	39.2	27.9	30.2	32.5
SADC	1103	15.1	9.3	19.6	26.3	24.1	21.4

Note:
GDP is measured at factor cost. Estimates are from the World Bank (1999). These estimates of GDP differ slightly from earlier estimates used in the model database (see Evans with Cortijo, 1998 appendix 2). The latter were retained in the model for consistency reasons. All other data are from Evans with Cortijo (1998, appendix 2).

average tariffs was relatively large, the height of the tariff protection that prevailed at the time of the Trade Protocol was still substantial, particularly in the Southern Africa Customs Union (SACU) countries, in Mozambique, Tanzania, Zambia and Zimbabwe. Thus, the basis exists for the first steps to be taken towards regional integration around the mutual reduction of trade barriers in terms of economic structure.

Other aspects of economic structure are also shown in Table 5.1. As expected, the smaller countries have a larger GDP-to-trade ratio than the larger ones. The trade statistics show that the SADC shares of imports and exports vary greatly from country to country. An overall picture of the trade flows within SADC can be seen from the last four columns, which show the overall magnitude of the trade flows, with intra-SADC trade being mostly about 20 per cent to 25 per cent of trade with the rest of the world. Thus, the direction of trade, the height of tariffs, the sectoral structure of each economy and the level of per capita GDP interact in a complex way in influencing the effects of the FTA. There have been changes in the tariff structures since the 1996 Trade Protocol and in the economic structures since the earlier part of the 1990s that affect the empirical findings reported here. Nevertheless, these results lend themselves to a broad-brush interpretation of the major options for regional integration in the SADC region.

1. THE INSTITUTIONAL FRAMEWORK FOR REGIONAL INTEGRATION[3]

SADC has committed itself to an ambitious project of regional integration. The completion of this task will cost SADC members a great deal in terms of effort, loss of sovereignty and economic adjustment. Equally, the costs of non-integration, that is the costs of not seizing this historical opportunity for greater regional integration, are potentially high. They lie not only in foregoing all the gains from the agreed FTA but also in a loss of credibility should the agreed FTA fail, sacrificing the opportunity to go further to a full customs union with a common external tariff.

Forms of Regional Integration in Southern Africa

The SADC Trade Protocol, as it stands, embodies a limited ambition, but an FTA requires a rules-based system to succeed. Otherwise, producers, traders and consumers will not be willing to take the FTA seriously. If economic actors in the region are to plan their economic activities to take advantage of the opportunities for linkages across the region, they must know that the commitments are real and irreversible. The conditions for institutional reform that could deliver a workable FTA are demanding and amount to a requirement that interstate economic relations be governed by codes of law rather than political pressures. This process can be seen as a pooling, rather than as a loss, of sovereignty. If this argument is correct, a failure by the SADC to realize the FTA would not just lose the potential benefits of the FTA itself; it would diminish the credibility of commitments made by the region's governments. The SADC would also lose the potential benefits from moving on to establishing a customs union. It may in addition lose the opportunity for regional cooperation while lowering trade barrier discrimination against non-members or 'open regionalism'. The latter is a process of trade barrier reduction towards freer regional trade carried out on the basis of MFN tariff reductions.

Each form of regional integration has a different level of mutual co-operation, from collaboration on infrastructure projects to establishing common laws and policies governing economic life. With the possible exception of open regionalism, the alternative forms of regional integration would require an additional element of supranationality for the SADC, in which member states can gain from the transition to a rules-based economic environment. In each case, estimated costs and benefits of integration have both impact effects and more dynamic consequences that are realized over a longer period of time. Both the impact and dynamic effects are influenced by the global economic environment affecting the access of regional products to world markets, the terms of trade and the growth of the world economy. As Winters (1996) notes, it is an empirical matter whether or not regional trade associations are regionally or globally gainful.

In this context, the central questions addressed here in a regional context are:

- What are the impact effects of the different routes towards regional integration in Southern Africa – an FTA, a customs union or free trade?
- Does trade creation dominate trade diversion under the proposed FTA?
- Is there trade diversion under a customs union that might grow out of the proposed FTA?
- What are the likely revenue effects of the regional integration options?
- What are the likely dynamic consequences of the different forms of regional integration?
- What are the possible terms-of-trade consequences of the different forms of regional integration?

Trade Creation and Trade Diversion

At the heart of the analysis of regional integration is the concept of trade creation and trade diversion. Terms-of-trade effects are also potentially important when regional integration affects the level of exports to the rest of the world. Thus, regional integration through tariff variation has a total effect that is the sum of trade diversion and trade creation less any loss of income through adverse terms-of-trade effects arising from the overall expansion of trade. In essence, trade creation occurs when an economic union leads to the growth of intra-union trade that exploits comparative advantage, that is, when the union members experiencing expanded trade have relatively lower costs than do third-country suppliers. Trade diversion takes place when an economic union leads to an expansion in intra-union trade in which the relative costs are higher than those in competitor countries in the rest of the world, that is, where the expanded intra-union trade is against comparative advantage.

It follows from the above that the static or impact effect of economic union is to improve members' welfare when trade creation outweighs trade diversion. This statement is qualified in three important ways. First, when global rather than regional welfare is taken into account, global welfare may also gain when there is regional trade creation. Similarly, when there is regional trade diversion, global welfare may also lose. Second, a regional trade association may have a positive or negative effect on its terms of trade. However, from a global perspective, this simply redistributes global income. Third, the welfare benefits of a regional customs union are dependent on the height of the common external tariff. A customs union that is predominantly trade-diverting, and therefore welfare-worsening, can be transformed into a gainful and predominantly trade-creating customs union by appropriate choice of the common external tariff towards FT.[4] Finally, regional integration involves possible dynamic benefits, many of which are difficult to quantify. It is here that much of the controversy is generated about the conflict between potential medium-run costs of trade diversion against hoped-for longer-run dynamic benefits. The empirical results reported here focus on the impact effects of the options combined with qualitative and back-of-the-envelope estimates of some possible dynamic effects added in an *ad hoc* manner.

2. REGIONAL INTEGRATION IN SOUTHERN AFRICA: AN OVERVIEW

Three basic options are considered in the empirical part of this chapter. Elaborating a little on the definitions above, they are:

1. *Free trade area* This applies when existing tariff structures applicable to non-member countries or the rest of the world are maintained as the SADC moves towards free trade between member countries. Typically, rules of origin have to be applied to a free trade area (FTA) to prevent importation through the country with the lowest tariff for a particular commodity.
2. *Customs union* The central difference between a customs union and an FTA is that the former has a common external tariff, thus dispensing with the need for rules of origin. As already noted, the higher the

common external tariff, the greater is trade diversion and the greater the chance that the customs union will be welfare-contracting.

3. *Open regionalism* An extreme form of open regionalism is free trade (FT), where each country in the regional association cuts trade barriers against both member and non-member to zero. In practice, open regionalism envisages a bargaining process concentrating initially on coordinated MFN-based trade policy reforms among the key member states.

Application to SADC

It is important to emphasize that the SADC FTA is critically dependent upon the successful operation of the rules of origin. However, the administrative capacity of SADC customs authorities for the enforcement of the rules of origin is likely to be very weak. It is therefore unlikely that the rules of origin will be enforceable. If this observation is correct, then abstracting from internal transport costs, an SADC FTA will operate more or less as a customs union in which the common external tariff is formed by the lowest tariff on each commodity in each of the member states of the proposed FTA. For simplicity this is called the CUmin.

It is perhaps for this reason that, just as ratification of the SADC FTA is about to be completed, moves are being made for a move to an SADC customs union. Thus, there are really two FTAs. The 'intended' FTA is interpreted as if the rules of origin could be strictly enforced without cost. The 'actual' FTA with unenforceable rules of origin will be very much the same as the CUmin that results from the application of the minimum tariff on any item for all member countries as the common external tariff for that item. Internal transport costs will modify this outcome, but the CUmin considered here provides a useful counterfactual to consider. CUmin would in fact have a low external tariff, an obvious advantage for minimizing trade diversion.

In the SADC context, free trade (FT) without coordination or negotiation with trading partners is the logical outcome of a trade policy reform process under World Bank SAPs or under the WTO. It is therefore appropriate to develop an analytical framework within which the impact effects of each of the options discussed can be modelled. This facilitates the analysis of the effects of each form of regional integration on the potential welfare gains and dynamic effects.

3. METHODOLOGY USED IN THE STUDY

The initial work on the impact of the SADC FTA for SADC (Evans, 1997) relies on a partial equilibrium model and weak data set. The data set was greatly improved in Evans with Cortijo (1998) but the earlier partial equilibrium methodology was retained. The additional data requirements for the computable general equilibrium (CGE) version of the model, over and above the partial equilibrium version, are mainly on the demand side and input/output coefficients. While these data are assembled using strong assumptions, the main structural differences between SADC countries are preserved. Thus, it is judged that the extended data set was adequate for a first general equilibrium exploration of SADC integration.

Overall, the CGE model is based on 12 SADC countries and 37 productive sectors for each country. There were nine agricultural sectors, a mining sector, one non-traded service sector and 26 manufacturing and mining sectors. The production and trade data were for 1991–93 averages and the tariff data were for the most recent year available. The database used in partial equilibrium applications is described in Evans with Cortijo (1998).

Some of the key assumptions and structural characteristics built into the general equilibrium model include:

- Armington functions on the import side where the share of imports in total supply of a tradable good is inversely related to the price of imports relative to the price of domestic production. Similarly, imports from within the SADC region and from the rest of the world are treated as imperfectly substitutable and responsive to relative price changes. It is therefore possible to use the Armington functions to construct a composite import commodity, made up of imports from within the SADC and from the rest of the world, and for this composite import to be imperfectly substitutable with import-competing production. The composite importable commodity enters into domestic demand in a straightforward manner.
- Perfectly elastic supply of goods in each sector. Where there is excess capacity, this is likely to be a good approximation. For agriculture, mining and manufacturing sectors operating close to full capacity, the supply response is likely to be exaggerated.
- Full employment of labour, where labour is measured in wage goods. This is achieved by a macro-expenditure adjustment to maintain full employment at the initial constant wage. This is not a good assumption since it is likely, in the SADC economies, that skilled labour is fully employed, but there is likely to be surplus unskilled labour and underemployment in the informal sector.[5]

- A mark-up model of domestic cost formation. The mark-up is on wages and intermediate input costs. The model assumes fixed coefficients in production for labour as well as the more usual assumption of fixed proportions for intermediate inputs.
- Balance of payments equilibrium is maintained via variation of the real exchange rate.
- Government expenditure and investment is held constant while consumer demand and intermediate demand varies through price and income changes.
- A micro-based welfare function is constructed based on an estimate of the consumer surplus change net of estimated intermediate demand less the loss of tariff revenue and the lump sum tax or subsidy required to maintain macroeconomic balance.
- An unsatisfactory attempt was made to estimate SADC price elasticities of demand for exports to the rest of the world. Given the underlying weakness of these data, sensitivity tests are carried out.
- Solution of the model is achieved with a Gauss–Seidel iterative procedure.

4. THE REGIONAL INTEGRATION OPTIONS FOR SOUTHERN AFRICA IN DETAIL

The 'Intended' Free Trade Area

Under the GATT Article XXIV, members are constrained when forming a free trade area, or regional trade agreement (RTA), as to how the external tariffs are set. They must be set on an MFN basis and the external tariffs and other trade regulations shall not be higher than those existing before the RTA. The tariffs of the existing RTA member country tariffs towards rest of the world countries remain as before and intra-RTA tariffs are reduced to zero. The rules of origin are required to back up this arrangement, preventing individual economic agents from importing goods into the country with the lowest rest of the world tariff for that item and transshipping within the RTA without further tariff charges. This RTA is referred to here as the 'intended' FTA.

A Customs Union: Specifying the Common External Tariff

For GATT/WTO members forming a customs union under GATT Article XXIV, the external tariffs must also be set on an MFN basis. Further, the common external tariff must not increase. One way of defining the common external tariff for a customs union would be to choose for each commodity the highest tariff of the member countries, or CUmax. However, this method would fall foul of GATT Article XXIV, whereby the common external tariff should not increase. A second method would be to average the individual tariff items for the member countries, or CUavg. The CUavg would be less likely to fall foul of Article XXIV since there is some ambiguity in the definition of what is an increased tariff. Finally, the common external tariff could be formed by taking, for each traded item, the lowest of the member-country tariffs and applying that as the common external tariff, or CUmin. The CUmin, as defined above, is unambiguously consistent with GATT Article XXIV. Compared with the CUmax and CUavg alternatives, the CUmin is more likely to produce an overall welfare gain and, in practice, the CUmin always produced a positive welfare change. The CUmin was therefore adopted for the customs union experiments carried out.

The 'Actual' Free Trade Area

One of the characteristics of the SADC already noted is that member states have a weak capacity to enforce the rules of origin. Importers will seek to route their imports through the country with the lowest relevant sectoral tariff, with scant regard to formal customs requirements. Thus, the proposed or 'intended' FTA could turn out to operate as if it had a common external tariff chosen on the basis, for each sector, of the lowest sectoral tariff amongst member countries. That is, abstracting from internal transport costs, the 'actual' FTA with unenforceable rules of origin will in fact operate as the CUmin defined above. This is to be compared with the 'intended' FTA as previously defined.

Free Trade: the Limiting Case of Open Regionalism

The hallmark of open regionalism, compared with both the FTA and a customs union, is that the negotiated tariff reductions for each country are all made on an MFN basis. While it may appear that the MFN constraint takes away the incentive for member countries to negotiate tariff reductions, this is not necessarily the case. For example, the MFN constraint creates an incentive for member states to negotiate tariff reductions which maximize the growth of regional trade without 'passing on' benefits to third parties. Within open regionalism, other areas of cooperation may be identified, for example over foreign investment, technology or infrastructure. However, in all of these endeavours, open regionalism is a cooperative arrangement rather than a rules-based community set up under GATT

Article XXIV such as an FTA or customs union. It is also very different from the unilateral trade policy reform carried out in many SADC countries in the 1990s which lowered tariffs towards free trade (FT) under the auspices of World Bank SAPs or the WTO.

5. QUANTIFYING THE OPTIONS

As a first exercise to explore the implications of the open regionalism option, the simple extreme case is explored whereby all intra-SADC and rest of the world tariffs are removed, that is, free trade is applied.

Comparative Static Welfare Effects

When there is net trade creation from freer regional trade, SADC countries will transfer resources from lower-productivity to higher-productivity activities. In the real SADC economies, there is unemployment, particularly surplus unskilled labour, so that the welfare benefits may have a downward bias. The comparative static welfare changes for each of the options for 'large' and 'low' export elasticities are shown in Figure 5.1.

It can be readily seen from Figure 5.1 that the 'low' and 'large' export elasticities assumption does not alter greatly the welfare gain for the

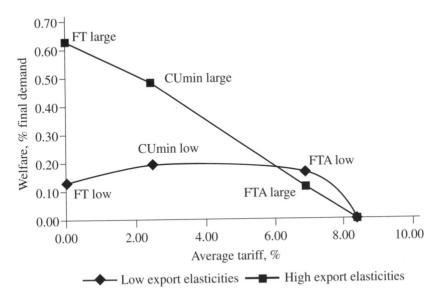

Figure 5.1   Regionalization options compared

'intended' FTA of a little over 0.10 per cent of initial final demand.[6] For CUmin and FT, with large export elasticities, the comparative static gains increase greatly to nearly 0.50 per cent and over 0.60 per cent respectively. However, with 'low' export elasticities, the gains fall dramatically, particularly for FT, to very similar orders of magnitude to the 'intended' FTA. Thus, provided the export elasticities are large, the gains from trade would appear to be much larger for FT compared with the 'intended' FTA. It would therefore appear that the neoclassical presumptions on the regional gains from freer trade that inform both World Bank and WTO thinking are correct.

Trade Creation and Trade Diversion

It is of some interest to explore the implications of the results for trade creation and trade diversion. There are a number of ways in which trade creation and trade diversion can be measured. A simple indirect measure is to see if either the 'intended' FTA or CUmin produces regional welfare gains. The presence of regional welfare gains implies that regional trade creation dominates trade diversion. The regional welfare results shown in Figure 5.1 suggest that trade creation dominates trade diversion, a finding of other studies of regional associations using CGE models (see Robinson and Thierfelder, 1999).

Another way of looking at trade creation and trade diversion is to compare aggregate intra-trade flows under the 'intended' FTA and FT or CUmin and FT. Table 5.2 shows the overall changes in SADC and rest of the world trade. It can be seen that the ranking of the expansion in SADC trade under the regional integration options considered is as expected. These findings appear to confirm the view that a good deal of intra-SADC

Table 5.2   Trade creation and trade diversion: change in trade flows

	% increase, SADC trade	% Increase, ROW trade
FTA large	9.4	−0.7
FTA low	9.2	−0.5
CUmin large	7.2	6.8
CUmin low	7.3	5.2
FT large	6.5	11.7
FT low	6.8	9.1

Note:
Percentage increase in trade calculated as the average change in imports.

trade expansion would take place anyway under FT. This phenomenon is often remarked upon in relation to the East Asian NICs whose intra-regional trade has expanded rapidly, as have their exports to the developed North. In the SADC, the model shows a rise in intra-trade only one-third greater under FTA than under FT. Thus, the aggregate data on estimated intra-trade flow changes for the SADC also appear to confirm the observation that trade creation dominates trade diversion.

A closer examination of trade creation and trade diversion for the SADC as a whole can be made using the seven-sector disaggregation of the changes in employment over the base levels shown in Table 5.3. The results

Table 5.3   SADC employment effects for seven sectors: FTA, CUmin and FT

SADC	Base L	FTA L %	CUmin L %	FT L %
Agriculture	7420	−0.14	−0.07	−0.07
Mining	1130	−0.19	1.68	3.22
Food, tobacco & beverages	556	−0.44	−0.21	0.01
Textiles	254	0.70	−8.59	−9.58
Clothing	251	0.81	−3.41	−4.31
Other manufacturing	1468	0.11	0.51	−0.17
Services	8821	−0.05	0.01	−0.09
Total	19902	−0.07	−0.05	−0.07

Notes:
Large export elasticities; L − Labour units employed, '000s'. Table 5.3 is aggregated from Table 5A.1.

for the SADC FTA suggest that there is trade creation in the aggregate manufacturing sectors. On the other hand, there is trade diversion for agriculture and services. The amount of trade diversion falls dramatically under CUmin. This finding is confirmed by the regression analysis based on the full 37 sectors reported in Table 5.4.

Table 5.4 reports two regressions in which the change in sectoral GDP under FT compared with the initial sectoral GDP is used as the independent variable and the changes in GDP under the FTA and CUmin respectively are used as the dependent variables. In both cases, there is a positive and statistically significant relationship between the change in GDP under the FTA and the CUmin compared with that under FT, although the FTA regression is much weaker than for the CUmin. Thus, taking the sectoral GDP changes from base to FT as the indicator of SADC comparative

Table 5.4   Trade creation and trade diversion: regression estimates

A					
Dependent variable:		dGDP (FTA)			
Independent variable:		dGDP (FT)			
R-square	0.09				
Adjusted R-square	0.08		Estimate	S. E.	*t*-statistic
Standard error	0.65	Intercept	−0.03	0.03	−0.94
Observations	444	Coefficient	0.08	0.01	6.41
B					
Dependent variable:		dGDP (CUmin)			
Independent variable:		dGDP (FT)			
R-square	0.91				
Adjusted R-square	0.91		Estimate	S. E.	*t*-statistic
Standard error	0.55	Intercept	0.00	0.03	0.02
Observations	444	Coefficient	0.69	0.01	65.36

Data source: Full results for 37 sectors.

advantage, the estimated FTA and the CUmin change in GDP move towards FT. Similar results are obtained using the change in employment rather than the change in GDP as the indicator of sectoral change. The implication is that, under the CUmin, most of the increased SADC trade is trade-creating, whereas, under the FTA, the net trade-creation is much weaker.

Revenue Implications

Recall the macro-assumption used in the calculation of the impact effects of the options whereby a macro-expenditure adjustment is made to maintain full employment measured in wage units at the initial constant wage. Since government expenditure and investment are held constant, this is equivalent to a lump sum tax to offset any decline in tariff revenue. While it is unrealistic to assume that any tariff revenue loss can be made up without efficiency loss, it is useful to examine the magnitude of the customs revenue losses and their share of estimated government expenditure, shown in Table 5.5.

The first point to note about Table 5.5 is the large variation in the percentage loss of tariff revenue and government revenue under the FTA and CUmin options. In the case of FT, by definition, all tariff revenue is lost. Second, the total impact on SADC government revenue of tariff losses is relatively small because the small effects in South Africa enter into the

Table 5.5   Revenue response under FTA, CUmin and FT

	Base	FTA		CUmin		FT	
	CR	CR %	GR %	CR %	GR %	CR %	GR %
Angola	196	−17.4	−3.7	−54.8	−11.7	−100	−21.3
Botswana	39	−21.1	−4.1	−76.3	−14.6	−100	−19.2
Lesotho	23	−56.4	−31.4	−83.5	−46.4	−100	−55.6
Malawi	100	−45.0	−9.9	−87.2	−19.2	−100	−22.0
Mauritius	364	−10.5	−4.5	−82.6	−35.2	−100	−42.6
Mozambique	117	−50.9	−10.8	−83.2	−17.7	−100	−21.3
Namibia	17	−4.4	−1.5	−61.1	−20.3	−100	−33.3
South Africa	775	−11.3	−0.4	−48.1	−1.6	−100	−3.3
Swaziland	3	−13.8	−7.7	−54.1	−30.1	−100	−55.6
Tanzania	212	−2.7	−0.5	−73.1	−12.6	−100	−17.3
Zambia	98	−49.2	−10.5	−82.0	−17.5	−100	−21.3
Zimbabwe	274	−34.4	−6.5	−83.9	−15.9	−100	−19.0
Total	2218	−19.6	−1.4	−67.3	−5.0	−100	−7.4

Notes:
Large export elasticities. $US million average 1991–93 for financial variables. Lump sum tax adjusted to maintain internal balances or labour market equilibrium.

SADC with a large GDP weight. However, several individual countries have government revenue losses of 10 per cent or more under the FTA. These losses are even higher under the CUmin and FT. When regional partners are poor and where alternative tax instruments, such as income tax or value-added tax, are not well developed, there is a strong case for transitional arrangements to deal with the customs revenue impact of regional integration on some member governments.

Dynamic Effects

In straightforward welfare terms, the analysis so far suggests that to aim for regional free trade (FT) is the best option, tempered only by the transitional difficulties in some SADC member states in replacing lost customs revenue. The question therefore arises as to whether there are excluded factors that may drive reasonable policy-makers to adopt either the FTA or the CUmin in preference to FT. Consider the potential dynamic effects.[7] These can be divided into two types:

1. *Scale economies and productivity effects*   Within SADC, there are widespread opportunities for reaping scale economies outside traditional

heavy industry, including the better use of infrastructure. When combined with productivity effects from trade creation and increased inducements for networking, this effect is likely to be very large. Typically, these effects are associated with increased intra-trade.

2. *Reinvestment of initial gains*   SADC economies have traditionally had low rates of investment and utilization of existing investment. If some of the excess capacity that exists in the region is taken up and when a substantial part of the gains from freer trade are reinvested, faster growth can be expected. These gains are particularly likely to be realized when wider measures affecting the investment environment, such as greater certainty, are implemented.

It is difficult to estimate the size of the dynamic gains without explicit modelling of these effects, especially since the options considered here have different implications for the size and composition of intra-SADC trade, including different capital requirements of output expansion. However, very rough orders of magnitude of these effects range from four to six times the impact effects.

Taking the lower estimate, the total welfare effects could be of the orders of magnitude shown in Table 5.6. The very approximate measures of dynamic gains shown in Table 5.6 are assumed to operate in a multiplica-

Table 5.6   Static and dynamic effects of regional integration, large export elasticities

	% Final Demand
FTA	0.4%
CUmin	2.0%
FT	2.5%

Source: Evans with Cortijo (1998).

tive rather than additive manner on the original welfare gains. They reflect a mix of impact effects, once-and-for-all dynamic changes and dynamic benefits that continue into the future and should be treated with great caution. In particular, the CUmin and FT imply a very different sectoral mix of output so that the assumption of multiplicative dynamic benefits may not be a good one. It is not clear that the very approximate estimates of the dynamic benefits for the FTA would carry over to the CUmin or FT. Nevertheless, the measures suggest that the potential benefits of regional integration in SADC are large indeed.

The full model results together with the sectoral impact effects of large export elasticities on the structural variables are given in the Appendix, in Tables 5A.1 and 5A.2 respectively.

The Impact of Deep Integration

Regional economic integration can add to the process of multilateral liberalization when there is a commitment to a deeper form of integration going beyond just the WTO framework. The idea of 'deep integration', developed by Lawrence (1996), offers a simple but powerful insight into the relationship between pure trade liberalization and policy coordination. Thus, the initial trade liberalization alone under the FTA may bring small benefits. However, as already noted, the 'intended' FTA is unlikely to succeed because of unenforceable rules of origin. For credibility, the FTA needs to move on quickly to something like the CUmin. Without a progression from the FTA, there will be unenforceable rules of origin at the core of the regional cooperation arrangement. Once credibility has been restored, for example with a CUmin, the benefits of specialization, investment and growth effects will fully appear. A question therefore arises, would it be possible to go from a regional arrangement, such as CUmin, and realize the even greater welfare benefits, as under FT? Since deep integration is not implied by the FT option, this option may not be as attractive as it appears from the orders of magnitude of gains relative to CUmin shown in Table 5.4.

Potential Terms-of-trade Effects

In addition to the exclusion of the benefits from deep integration in the FT option, the attractions of FT are tempered by potential terms of trade costs, noted by Kaplinsky (1998) for the East Asian case. Kaplinsky finds that the newer East Asian NICs suffered terms-of-trade problems compared with the older NICs. This suggests that the older East Asian NICs were better able to offset any terms-of-trade problems in particular product lines by constantly upgrading products for niche marketing. In the SADC context, the effects on welfare of low export elasticities are much greater for FT than for CUmin. Put the other way around, a CUmin with deep integration would be less likely to face adverse terms-of-trade effects than FT. It would also have a greater potential capacity to assist SADC exporters to upgrade their products constantly to counter adverse terms-of-trade pressures.

6. CONCLUDING REMARKS

Any assessment of conclusions based directly on the evidence from the
SADC CGE model should be interpreted in the light of the preliminary
nature of this modelling exercise and any key data deficiencies that have an
important bearing on policy choices. With all the qualifications and cau-
tionary remarks, the key conclusions from this chapter are:

- There are important regional welfare benefits, both static and
  dynamic, to be gained from the SADC FTA, were this to be implemented as intended.
- It is unlikely that the 'intended' FTA can be implemented because of
  unenforceable rules of origin. Thus, regional integration according to
  the 'actual' FTA will end up being like the CUmin.
- There is substantial trade diversion associated with the 'intended'
  FTA, although trade creation dominates. The CUmin has very little
  trade diversion.
- CUmin offers many advantages for the SADC. Both static and
  dynamic welfare gains would be dramatically increased. In particular, the opportunities for long-run gains from a rules-based system
  with deep integration are likely to increase greatly.
- FT appears to offer some advantages in terms of welfare gains compared with CUmin. However, FT may miss the benefits of deep integration and it may not be as effective in providing firms with an
  enabling environment that may assist in offsetting potentially adverse
  terms-of-trade effects.
- There is scope for further research into the impact effects of the
  options for regional integration when the full employment assumption is dropped and more up-to-date data are used. Such modelling
  work will be greatly assisted by the forthcoming availability of the
  Global Trade Analysis Project (GTAP) data set for 1997 for further
  CGE modelling of regional integration in Southern Africa.
- There is much scope for complementary work with sector case studies
  and on institutional aspects of regional integration. Such work can
  only complement both case studies and political-economy research
  on micro- and institutional aspects of the path toward regional
  integration.

The weakest part of the above analysis is its lack of attention to historical
and political factors (see, for example, Clapham, 1996). It is widely held
that the glue that binds successful regional integration must start from
strong mutual political interest and it must also deliver substantial

economic benefits. The history of economic integration in developing countries is littered with cases where the political preconditions apparently held. However, the external tariffs were often set so high that trade diversion dominated and the customs union or FTA fell apart because the few winners and many losers from trade diversion were all too apparent.[8]

Economic analysis of regional associations in Southern Africa has now reached the point where powerful insights can be gained on the regional and global costs and benefits of different forms of regional integration. If the political glue is strong enough, the trick is to find that height of external tariff that is consistent with regional and global economic interests while providing a context for regional institution building for rules-based deep integration in a customs union. Unfortunately, almost all of the new-wave regional associations are FTAs. These associations generally have little political glue to hold them together and their institutional structure is correspondingly weak. The privileged and beneficial access of developing countries to the EU in the past under the Lomé Convention has been transformed into FTAs by its successor, the Cotonou Agreement. The lesson from the SADC is that a low external tariff customs union with political and institutional support could provide an alternative model for deep regional integration.

NOTES

*   This chapter was first presented as a paper at the September Forum 1998, Trade and Industrial Policy Secretariat (TIPS), Johannesburg. It has also appeared with the same title as IDS Working Paper No. 94, 2000. A number of people have provided assistance and advice for the series of projects that have yielded the background research. From the IDS, these people include Raphie Kaplinsky, Henry Lucas, Hans Singer, Marie-Jo Cortijo and Adrian Wood. At the University of Sussex, Oxford University and Lusaka, Peter Holmes, David Vines and Peter O'Brien respectively have given continuing support to this work. John Black and others at the September 1999 Conference of the UK International Economics Study Group were also helpful in sharpening the argument. Gerhard Kuhne, Gena Krasnik and Gerrit van Wyck from the Industrial Development Corporation of South Africa assisted in the creation of much of the database upon which this study was based. I thank them all but implicate none.

1.   See for example Page (2000, introduction).
2.   For an extended discussion of this point using data from the pre-apartheid period 1970–92, see Evans (1997, appendix 1).
3.   The argument in the first part of this section is elaborated in Evans et al. (1999).
4.   As noted by Kemp and Wan (1976), it is always possible to define a customs union for which trade creation dominates trade diversion.
5.   Some insights into the demand for skilled labour in the impact calculations can be gained from a comparison of wage units employed and estimated employment changes. See Evans (2000).
6.   The higher gain for the 'low' elasticities comes about because under FTA, exports to the rest of the world decline a little. In this case, the terms of trade are slightly better with

'low' compared to 'large' export elasticities, the opposite to what happens for either CUmin or FT.
7.   This section draws heavily on the arguments developed in Evans with Cortijo (1998).
8.   See also Schiff (2000).

REFERENCES

Clapham, C. (1996), *Africa and the International System: the Politics of State Survival*, Cambridge: Cambridge University Press.

Evans, H.D. (1997), 'Study of the Impact of the Removal of Tariffs for the Free Trade Area of the Southern African Development Community (SADC)', Commonwealth Secretariat Occasional Paper No. 5, London: Commonwealth Secretariat. Based on a report prepared for the SADC Industry and Trade Co-ordination Division (SITCD), with the Assistance of the Commonwealth Secretariat, 1996.

Evans, H.D. with M.-J. Cortijo (1998), *The Regional Trade Model of Southern Africa: New Data and Results*, Final Report to the IDC and the DTI, Pretoria.

Evans, H.D., P. Holmes and I. Mandaza (1999), 'The Costs of Non integration in SADC', *Southern Africa Political Economy Society*, Harare, Zimbabwe.

Evans, H.D. (2000), 'Regional integration and industrialisation in Southern Africa', in M. Tribe et al. (eds), *Industrial Development and Policy in Africa: Issues of De-industrialisation and Development Strategy*, Cheltenham, UK and Northampton, USA: Edward Elgar.

Kaplinsky, R. (1998), ' "If you want to get somewhere else, you must run twice as fast as that!" ': the roots of the East Asian Crisis', paper presented to the East Asia Crisis Workshop, IDS.

Kemp, M. and H. Wan (1976), 'An elementary proposition concerning the formation of customs unions', *Journal of International Economics*, **6**, 95–7.

Lawrence, R.Z. (1996), *Regionalism, Multilateralism and Deeper Integration*, Washington, DC: Brookings Institution.

Page, S. (ed.) (2000), *Regions and Development: Politics, Security and Economics*, London: Frank Cass.

Robinson, S. and K. Thierfelder (1999), 'Trade liberalization and regional integration: the search for large numbers', Trade and Macroeconomics Division Working Paper No. 34, International Food Policy Research Institute, Washington, DC.

Schiff, M. (2000), 'Multilateral trade liberalization, political disintegration and the choice of FTAs versus customs unions', World Bank Development Research Department Working Paper 2350, Washington, DC.

Winters, L.A. (1996), 'Regionalism Versus Multilateralism', World Bank Policy Research Working Paper No. 1687, Washington, DC.

World Bank (1999), *World Bank Economic Indicators, 1989*, Washington, DC: World Bank.

APPENDIX

Table 5A.1 Welfare effects, FTA, CUmin and FT

Countries	Base			FTA			CUmin			FT		
	Tariffs %		Final demand	Welfare gain	ToT	% change SADC	Welfare gain	ToT	% change SADC	Welfare gain	ToT	% change SADC
	SADC	ROW	FD	% FD	Pe/Pm	imports	% FD	Pe/Pm	imports	% FD	Pe/Pm	imports
Angola	10.1	10.8	6974	0.13	0.999	20.19	1.26	0.999	13.13	2.08	0.998	9.45
Botswana	0.5	11.8	3386	−0.15	1.001	0.16	0.59	1.007	−0.60	1.29	1.012	−0.55
Lesotho	1.5	11.7	1279	0.39	0.999	0.41	0.41	0.999	−0.31	0.41	1.002	−0.59
Malawi	21.8	20.6	1886	2.83	0.999	22.72	6.09	0.996	17.46	6.84	0.996	16.40
Mauritius	24.5	22.7	2525	0.32	1.004	25.02	0.67	0.985	21.16	0.30	0.981	20.07
Mozambique	19.5	12.0	1589	0.83	0.989	18.96	1.79	0.979	17.01	2.19	0.976	16.27
Namibia	0.1	12.6	1959	−0.03	1.000	0.08	0.64	1.005	−0.40	1.16	1.009	−0.45
South Africa	6.5	5.6	108822	0.01	1.001	20.83	0.08	0.995	16.09	0.13	0.989	14.19
Swaziland	0.1	6.3	1035	0.38	1.003	0.31	0.33	1.004	0.80	0.44	1.007	1.00
Tanzania	21.9	19.0	3315	0.07	1.000	33.62	2.00	0.981	26.80	2.27	0.975	19.19
Zambia	14.0	11.4	1898	−1.67	0.998	18.82	5.96	0.999	18.39	8.26	0.999	17.77
Zimbabwe	18.8	15.8	4240	1.91	0.979	32.47	2.68	0.957	24.76	2.58	0.956	23.01
SADC	5.7	9.3	138909	0.11	0.999	9.36	0.48	0.994	7.20	0.63	0.991	6.50

Notes:

Large export elasticities.

$USm average 1991–93 for financial variables.

Imports and exports valued fob.

Tariffs import-weighted, most recent year.

Lump sum tax adjusted to maintain internal balances, or labour market equilibrium.

ToT: Terms of Trade; Pe: export prices; Pm: import prices.

Table 5A.2 *Seven-sector impact effects on structural variables, large export elasticities*

		share %	%	%		Base levels						FTA %		
		MS	ES	tS	tR	SM	MS	MR	ES	ER	L	SM	MS	MR
Ang.	Agric.	24	0	4	9	1872	9	30	0	17	3192	0	4	0
	Mining	0	0	10	20	4198	0	3	0	3354	213	0	17	0
	F,T&B.	39	3	4	12	270	174	267	2	66	36	0	8	-4
	Text.	34	0	30	29	89	32	62	0	0	13	-10	74	-20
	Cloth.	26	0	35	28	77	10	28	0	0	8	-5	95	-13
	O. man.	2	1	17	9	683	28	1194	1	223	65	0	16	0
	Serv.	50	50	0	0	4782	0	0	0	0	723	0	0	0
	Tot, av.	14	0	10	11	11971	253	1583	3	3660	4250	0	20	-2
Bots.	Agric.	81	57	0	4	201	99	23	17	13	6	0	0	0
	Mining	93	0	0	1	143	6	0	5	1210	8	0	0	0
	F,T&B.	80	40	0	30	137	183	46	102	155	6	0	0	0
	Text.	84	22	2	44	14	66	13	13	44	4	-2	2	-4
	Cloth.	98	0	7	73	0	30	1	0	0	0	0	2	-15
	O. man.	86	27	0	6	130	1096	179	43	117	14	0	0	0
	Serv.	46	50	0	0	3187	0	0	0	0	188	0	3	0
	Tot, av.	85	10	1	12	3812	1480	262	180	1539	227	0	0	0
Les.	Agric.	83	98	0	1	112	81	17	13	0	577	0	0	-1
	Mining	81	0	0	0	1	11	3	0	0	6	-1	-1	-1
	F,T&B.	88	31	0	18	259	133	18	21	46	2	0	0	0
	Text.	97	62	13	49	10	89	3	7	4	7	-13	6	-28
	Cloth.	100	0	1	75	0	62	0	0	0	0	0	0	-4
	O. man.	91	52	0	11	42	473	49	6	5	3	-1	0	0
	Serv.	50	50	0	0	764	0	0	0	0	247	0	0	0
	Tot, av.	90	45	1	12	1188	849	90	47	57	843	0	0	-1
Mal.	Agric.	44	7	18	5	451	9	12	26	366	330	-1	23	-1
	Mining	62	0	6	9	0	1	0	0	0	1	0	2	-2
	F,T&B.	90	34	21	21	385	37	4	4	8	44	-2	19	-4
	Text.	60	100	39	35	53	16	11	14	0	8	-18	85	-27
	Cloth.	81	98	40	40	19	2	1	2	0	4	-8	88	-24
	O. man.	34	48	20	21	222	128	253	13	14	23	-2	13	-3
	Serv.	50	50	0	0	1912	0	0	0	0	201	0	-1	-1
	Tot, av.	41	13	22	21	3042	193	281	60	388	610	-1	23	-4
Mau.	Agric.	13	1	11	6	27	8	56	3	381	44	0	15	0
	Mining	100	11	15	14	3	4	0	0	0	0	1	9	1
	F,T&B.	23	2	17	16	134	47	158	1	46	13	-3	18	1
	Text.	4	16	18	4	70	15	372	75	392	5	0	51	1
	Cloth.	2	0	71	74	209	0	12	0	302	70	1	251	9

on base			CUmin % on base						FT % on base					
ES	ER	L	SM	MS	MR	ES	ER	L	SM	MS	MR	ES	ER	L
44	−1	−0.1	0	4	0	40	−6	−0.3	0	4	0	38	−8	−0.6
0	0	0.2	0	18	29	0	2	0.5	−1	18	28	0	3	0.9
1	2	0.0	−1	4	0	−5	16	0.8	−2	0	4	−5	22	0.6
0	22	−9.8	−26	48	24	0	58	−25.6	−29	44	31	0	64	−28.7
0	17	−5.5	−12	82	13	0	43	−11.5	−21	72	48	0	46	−21.5
22	1	0.2	−1	10	2	13	5	−1.4	−3	8	4	12	7	−3.7
0	−1	−0.1	0	0	0	−1	−9	−0.3	−1	−1	−1	−1	−15	−0.5
9	1	−0.1	−1	13	3	2	2	−0.4	−1	9	6	2	3	−0.7
3	−3	−0.1	−1	1	2	1	−5	−0.8	−1	1	4	0	−6	−1.4
7	−2	−1.7	0	1	1	8	−2	−1.9	0	2	1	8	−2	−1.7
10	−1	2.4	0	−3	18	9	2	3.3	−1	−3	20	8	5	3.9
43	5	10.6	−11	−10	75	26	33	23.0	−12	−11	82	22	37	25.0
0	0	0.0	0	0	110	0	0	0.0	0	−1	139	0	0	0.0
16	0	2.0	0	0	2	12	3	2.9	−1	0	5	11	6	3.3
0	−1	−0.1	0	3	0	0	−1	−0.2	0	3	0	0	0	−0.2
13	−1	0.2	0	−1	9	10	0	0.5	0	−1	11	9	0	0.5
0	3	−0.3	0	1	−1	−1	11	−0.5	−1	1	−2	−2	14	−0.6
0	0	−0.8	−1	−1	−1	0	0	−0.9	−1	−1	−1	0	0	−1.0
−1	−5	−0.9	0	−1	9	−1	2	−0.1	0	−2	12	−1	5	0.2
48	40	18.6	−16	4	63	20	56	10.9	−16	3	71	14	60	9.5
0	0	0.0	0	1	125	0	0	0.0	0	1	155	0	0	0.0
6	−9	0.2	−1	−1	8	7	−3	0.6	−1	−1	13	6	−1	0.7
−1	−10	−0.3	0	0	0	0	−4	−0.3	0	0	0	0	−1	−0.3
8	2	−0.2	0	0	8	3	6	−0.3	−1	−1	12	2	9	−0.5
17	0	−0.3	−2	23	4	16	5	0.8	−2	23	3	14	6	1.2
0	0	0.0	0	0	0	0	0	0.0	0	−1	0	0	0	0.0
23	−5	−1.5	−3	19	26	21	−6	−2.8	−3	19	28	20	−6	−3.0
139	21	15.5	−28	71	42	113	40	2.2	−29	69	51	108	42	−0.2
209	37	12.1	−9	80	34	204	61	10.9	−10	79	70	202	64	9.8
14	28	2.1	−4	7	5	16	63	2.7	−5	6	7	16	69	2.4
1	7	−0.3	−1	−3	−3	2	21	−1.2	−1	−4	−4	2	25	−1.4
52	1	0.0	−2	17	6	46	7	0.1	−3	16	9	43	8	0.1
43	−2	−1.5	0	14	2	42	17	11.5	−1	13	3	41	19	12.7
−1	−8	0.7	5	11	11	1	9	4.9	5	12	11	−1	6	5.1
19	−9	−4.1	−13	17	15	14	−22	−10.2	−15	17	18	12	−26	−11.8
138	−1	18.2	11	55	1	109	23	33.7	4	46	5	105	31	37.6
157	−12	−7.0	−7	243	196	140	−26	−18.3	−9	237	234	132	−24	−17.8

Table 5A.2 (continued)

		share % MS	ES	%tS	%tR	Base levels SM	MS	MR	ES	ER	L	FTA % SM	MS	MR
Mau.	O. man.	11	4	31	33	223	98	819	6	165	19	0	24	1
(*cont.*)	Serv.	50	50	0	0	2929	0	0	0	0	136	2	5	5
	Tot, av.	11	6	25	23	3595	173	1417	86	1287	287	1	25	1
Moz.	Agric.	28	4	12	4	642	31	79	7	154	8	−1	14	−2
	Mining	78	1	3	3	3	2	1	0	1	3	−2	4	−3
	F,T&B.	71	5	26	15	274	119	49	2	30	25	−7	22	−6
	Text.	22	68	32	29	97	9	33	4	2	8	−4	87	−10
	Cloth.	77	75	35	35	60	6	2	1	0	3	−8	92	−16
	O. man.	28	4	14	12	189	128	334	5	114	22	−1	8	−1
	Serv.	50	50	0	0	665	0	0	0	0	31	0	−1	0
	Tot, av.	37	6	19	12	1930	295	498	19	301	100	−2	19	−2
Nam.	Agric.	93	88	1	6	190	59	5	173	24	195	0	0	−1
	Mining	45	1	0	0	99	8	10	7	522	15	0	0	0
	F,T&B.	82	33	0	17	105	197	43	153	311	4	0	0	0
	Text.	92	94	0	37	17	51	5	24	1	13	0	0	−1
	Cloth.	93	0	0	75	0	44	3	0	0	0	0	0	−1
	O. man.	92	34	0	7	77	719	64	34	67	6	0	0	0
	Serv.	50	50	0	0	2368	0	0	0	0	171	0	0	0
	Tot, av.	89	30	0	13	2855	1079	130	391	925	405	0	0	0
RSA	Agric.	44	29	3	2	7825	302	384	352	847	876	0	5	−1
	Mining	1	1	2	0	7918	23	1533	86	6639	668	0	6	0
	F,T&B.	52	96	1	12	15706	377	345	936	34	242	0	1	0
	Text.	20	55	24	32	1239	153	629	331	272	90	−6	89	−8
	Cloth.	41	72	76	67	1191	18	27	161	64	121	−3	240	−5
	O. man.	2	34	4	5	47399	232	9561	3575	6841	1040	0	11	0
	Serv.	63	50	0	0	119109	0	0	0	0	4831	0	10	0
	Tot, av.	8	27	6	6	200308	1105	12479	5441	14698	7869	0	21	0
Swaz.	Agric.	90	88	0	1	188	68	8	27	4	23	0	0	0
	Mining	89	76	0	1	15	6	1	5	2	1	0	0	0
	F,T&B.	99	47	0	17	307	128	1	201	226	8	0	0	0
	Text.	99	77	0	46	17	59	0	31	9	2	−3	1	−1
	Cloth.	99	0	0	72	0	7	0	0	0	0	0	0	−1
	O. man.	92	56	0	7	196	460	38	61	47	6	0	0	0
	Serv.	50	50	0	0	742	0	0	0	0	52	0	0	0
	Tot, av.	92	53	0	6	1465	728	47	325	288	93	0	0	0
Tanz.	Agric.	9	1	10	25	2059	1	13	3	284	1818	0	15	0
	Mining	3	0	18	17	26	0	10	0	1	106	0	9	0

on base			CUmin % on base						FT % on base					
ES	ER	L	SM	MS	MR	ES	ER	L	SM	MS	MR	ES	ER	L
8	6	0.7	−6	18	16	8	53	5.1	−8	18	18	6	54	3.2
2	−14	1.8	4	9	10	1	−26	4.0	4	10	11	1	−33	4.2
123	−4	−0.9	2	21	13	98	12	−0.4	2	20	16	94	15	−0.1
30	6	0.4	−1	13	0	28	8	0.2	−1	13	0	27	10	0.3
0	6	−0.8	−1	3	−1	−1	21	2.1	−1	3	−2	−1	27	3.3
11	8	−3.5	−7	21	4	8	16	−3.1	−8	20	7	7	18	−3.2
150	14	2.4	−15	64	37	126	53	−7.9	−17	60	44	121	60	−9.7
229	16	−2.5	−7	79	29	230	58	−0.6	−8	77	68	229	65	−1.3
8	18	3.3	−2	7	3	7	42	7.4	−3	6	5	7	49	8.6
1	12	0.1	0	−1	−1	2	21	0.3	0	−1	−1	2	25	0.3
63	11	0.0	−2	17	5	57	22	0.3	−3	16	7	55	26	0.4
0	0	0.1	0	0	3	0	4	0.2	0	0	4	−1	6	−0.1
0	0	−0.3	0	1	0	−1	0	−0.1	0	1	0	−2	0	0.0
0	0	0.3	−2	−1	14	0	5	2.1	−3	−2	21	−1	7	3.0
−1	1	−0.5	−5	−3	68	−33	17	−20.7	−7	−3	76	−40	20	−24.7
0	0	0.0	0	−7	121	0	0	0.0	0	−9	149	0	0	0.0
3	0	0.2	0	0	3	1	3	0.7	0	0	5	0	5	0.9
0	0	0.1	0	0	0	0	0	0.1	0	0	0	0	−1	0.1
1	0	0.1	0	0	11	−2	2	−0.5	0	0	16	−3	3	−0.8
2	−1	−0.1	0	5	−4	3	6	0.7	0	4	−3	3	12	1.1
2	−1	−0.4	0	7	0	2	4	2.0	0	6	−1	2	9	4.2
5	1	0.2	0	1	11	3	7	0.0	0	0	21	3	13	−0.2
19	2	−0.5	−37	55	66	13	23	−19.3	−42	50	76	12	29	−21.5
10	2	−1.6	−6	229	157	6	21	−3.8	−7	225	202	5	27	−4.5
5	−1	0.2	−1	13	3	3	5	0.3	−2	10	10	3	10	−0.2
0	−1	0.0	0	8	−1	1	4	0.0	0	7	−2	1	9	−0.1
5	−1	0.0	0	16	6	4	5	0.0	−1	14	12	4	10	0.0
0	−4	−0.1	0	1	−1	0	1	0.1	0	1	−1	−1	4	0.0
0	−3	−0.1	1	1	1	1	5	1.0	1	1	0	1	9	1.3
5	−3	−0.7	0	1	12	5	4	1.8	0	1	44	3	8	3.0
2	−4	−0.1	−7	3	90	−35	1	−20.9	−8	3	99	−42	4	−24.4
0	0	0.0	0	0	125	0	0	0.0	0	0	157	0	0	0.0
0	−4	−0.7	0	1	2	0	1	0.2	0	1	5	−4	4	−0.5
0	−2	0.1	1	0	0	1	6	0.6	1	0	0	1	10	0.7
4	−3	−0.1	0	1	3	−1	3	0.0	0	1	6	−3	7	0.0
3	0	0.0	0	12	35	−1	4	−0.4	0	12	36	−1	8	−0.5
2	0	0.0	1	9	8	3	13	1.1	1	9	8	3	17	1.4

Table 5A.2 (continued)

		share %	%	%	%	Base levels						FTA %		
		MS	ES	tS	tR	SM	MS	MR	ES	ER	L	SM	MS	MR
Tanz.	F,T&B.	9	4	30	25	26	10	98	3	83	70	0	47	−4
(*cont.*)	Text.	2	1	37	16	41	1	71	0	33	58	−1	93	−1
	Cloth.	0	0	26	14	4	0	25	0	1	5	1	81	0
	O. man.	1	6	14	19	181	9	871	5	80	66	0	15	0
	Serv.	50	50	0	0	1475	0	0	0	0	1472	0	0	0
	Tot, av.	2	2	22	19	3812	22	1088	11	481	3596	0	34	0
Zam.	Agric.	29	23	6	5	459	14	33	10	33	41	0	8	−1
	Mining	65	0	11	11	204	19	11	1	1123	60	−1	9	−1
	F,T&B.	90	69	19	8	439	44	5	2	1	62	−2	27	−2
	Text.	57	8	18	20	71	19	14	1	13	19	−11	51	−12
	Cloth.	90	58	25	25	82	3	0	1	1	21	−3	80	−5
	O. man.	37	23	13	12	553	231	393	12	40	94	−3	12	−3
	Serv.	50	50	0	0	1856	0	0	0	0	83	0	0	0
	Tot, av.	42	2	14	11	3662	331	456	27	1210	380	−1	19	−3
Zim.	Agric.	19	13	21	22	721	22	96	73	474	310	−1	25	0
	Mining	76	18	5	6	333	35	11	14	62	50	−1	1	−1
	F,T&B.	36	53	22	19	869	20	37	42	37	42	−1	40	0
	Text.	52	64	31	30	210	38	36	48	27	25	−18	114	−14
	Cloth.	41	59	93	92	53	1	1	18	13	20	−4	232	5
	O. man.	25	47	18	15	1170	342	1004	217	241	110	−5	15	−3
	Serv.	50	50	0	0	2446	0	0	0	0	684	−1	−3	0
	Tot, av.	28	32	19	16	5801	459	1184	410	854	1241	−2	32	−3

Notes:
$USm average 1991–93 for financial variables; '000' for employment; Imports and exports valued fob; tariffs average applied tariffs in % import weights.
Key: MS: Imports from SADC; ES: Exports to SADC; tS base tariffs on imports from SADC; tR base tariffs from ROW; SM: Import competing production; MR: Imports from the ROW; ER: Exports to the ROW; L: Labour employed; Ang.: Angola; Bots.: Botswana; Les.: Lesotho; Mal.: Malawi; Mau.: Mauritius; Moz.: Mozambique; Nam.: Namibia; RSA: Republic of South Africa; Swaz.: Swaziland; Tanz.: Tanzania; Zam.: Zambia; Zim.: Zimbabwe; F,T&B.: Food, tobacco and beverages.

on base			CUmin % on base						FT % on base					
ES	ER	L	SM	MS	MR	ES	ER	L	SM	MS	MR	ES	ER	L
7	0	0.0	−11	42	3	−10	8	4.2	−12	28	6	−9	12	7.3
130	1	0.6	−11	74	10	120	31	8.5	−15	66	13	122	42	11.0
0	2	0.8	19	79	−2	0	48	24.9	−9	41	7	0	72	6.1
26	1	0.6	0	7	6	24	61	5.6	−1	5	8	24	69	4.3
0	0	0.0	0	1	1	−1	−10	0.4	0	1	1	−1	−9	0.4
18	0	0.0	0	27	6	11	16	0.3	0	19	8	11	21	0.4
24	3	0.4	0	8	2	22	12	0.3	0	9	2	21	12	0.1
1	3	2.6	0	9	9	0	6	5.2	0	9	8	0	8	6.5
20	2	−1.6	−3	31	18	6	−16	−2.1	−3	32	25	4	−20	−2.2
128	2	−6.9	−20	53	36	89	−16	−17.8	−22	53	48	82	−18	−20.1
235	4	0.5	−2	78	26	224	10	1.3	−2	74	65	224	22	2.0
16	3	−1.9	−2	10	4	9	18	−1.9	−3	10	8	6	16	−2.8
9	5	−0.1	0	0	0	6	−21	−0.3	0	0	0	5	−24	−0.3
34	3	−0.6	−1	18	5	26	6	−0.8	−2	18	9	24	8	−1.0
17	−3	−1.3	−3	21	16	17	15	0.5	−3	22	16	16	22	1.8
11	−7	−1.8	−1	0	3	14	8	0.9	−1	0	2	13	14	1.7
30	−7	−0.2	−2	33	34	34	13	−0.2	−2	33	41	33	17	−0.4
97	−7	1.9	−31	101	82	84	3	−8.7	−33	101	95	80	7	−10.5
222	−15	43.7	−7	230	196	210	−16	39.1	−8	231	231	206	−14	38.0
18	−4	−0.4	−8	10	7	19	13	−0.6	−10	10	12	17	18	−1.6
4	−10	−0.9	−1	−5	−1	5	−2	−0.8	−1	−5	−1	5	3	−0.8
37	−4	−0.2	−4	25	11	36	13	0.1	−4	23	16	34	19	0.3

PART II

Competition

6. Trade and competition in the new WTO Round

Peter Holmes

This chapter is concerned with the origins of the 'trade and competition' debate. This is not, in fact, a 'new' issue for the world trading system but one which, for reasons explained below, has been a preoccupation for more than 50 years. Studies and policy experience show that there are important cross-border issues in practice. It is argued, however, that while the case for some form of multilateral rules in principle is clear, it is not at all evident what this should be in detail. Positions differ, with the EU seeking a clear WTO involvement and the USA less keen, and with divisions among developing countries. One of the strongest arguments is that WTO rules already do cover some aspects of competition policy and there is a multiplicity of bilateral systems; there is, however, a need to clarify this aspect of trade law. Examination of the EU's recent proposals shows that it has responded significantly to the criticism that it was only interested in forcing other countries to use EU-type rules to ensure market access for its firms. There still remains, however, reluctance on the part of many WTO members to initiate actual negotiations with a commitment to produce an agreement.

1. THE BACKGROUND TO THE TRADE AND COMPETITION DEBATE[1]

The topic of 'trade and competition policy' was put on the WTO agenda by the Singapore Ministerial Meeting in 1996 and a decision was taken to set up a working group to consider this interface. The Working Group is not a negotiating forum but its work is influencing the attitudes of WTO members in favour of such negotiations.

In the *Wealth of Nations*, Adam Smith denounced the monopolistic power of the East India Company which, he argued, hurt both India and the UK. Smith thus presciently drew attention to the significance of international anti-competitive behaviour in the service sector and to the symbiotic role of private and public actors (Smith, 1776/1976, vol. II, pp. 87–103).

In the first half of the twentieth century, international cartels had a high profile and the 1947 Havana Charter of the abortive International Trade Organization (ITO) contained a requirement on members to police international restrictive behaviour:

> Article 46 (1). Each Member shall take appropriate measures and shall co-operate with the Organization to prevent, on the part of private or public commercial enterprises, business practices affecting international trade which restrain competition, limit access to markets, or foster monopolistic control, whenever such practices have harmful effects on the expansion of production or trade and interfere with the achievement of any of the other objectives set forth in Article 1. (ITO, 1947)

The Havana Charter would thus have required its members to act against anti-competitive behaviour affecting trade but contained no general obligation to adopt a competition law. The ITO as an organization would have been called upon to investigate any complaints not resolved by consultation and make recommendations for action in a report. It appears that it was envisaged that failure to comply would have been dealt with by the standard procedures laid down in the Charter which, interestingly, were less judicial than the WTO procedures. The Havana Charter also allowed for intergovernmental cooperation. It also provided a specific means in Article 51 for dealing with disputes in the services sector, although this involved reference to existing international bodies in the sector which might well not have been sympathetic to competition considerations. It has been suggested that the Havana Charter framework would indeed make a great deal of sense today (Mathis, 2000); however, the WTO is not the ITO and the more judicial nature of its dispute settlement procedure raises problems.

The current debate has moved a long way from the Havana Charter in many respects, but it is quite striking that the aims of 1947 seem quite sensible today, for example that of preventing private business practices nullifying the benefits from the removal of governmental barriers to trade. Perhaps the most striking difference is the fact that current debates distinguish less sharply between domestic and international business and the discussion concerns how far the (non-)application of general competition law may affect trade.

2.   WHY COMPETITION POLICY IS AN INTERNATIONAL ISSUE

The wording of the Havana Charter makes it quite clear that its framers did, in fact, believe that practices of private firms could affect trade. Taking the wording of Article 46(1), it seems almost self-evident that it would be desirable for governments to act as the Charter would have required. It is hard to imagine an international agreement on trade making the specific exclusion: 'There is no obligation on Members to take appropriate measures or to co-operate with the Organization to prevent, on the part of private or public commercial enterprises, business practices affecting international trade which restrain competition . . .'.

It is hard to reconstruct how far the rejection of this Chapter of the Havana Charter had to do with a principled view that these aims were undesirable rather than only scaling back the ITO to just the GATT. Work continued at the GATT and the OECD on restrictive business practices and also at UNCTAD, on suitable principles for domestic competition policy in developing economies.

Presented in these terms, it is hard see why any country would object to an agreement along the lines of the Charter. Before discussing the reasons for such objections, it is worth briefly outlining why anti-competitive practices in one jurisdiction and policy towards them may have spillover effects in the global economy (admirably reviewed in WTO, 1997).

The heart of the problem is that anti-competitive behaviour can have cross-border effects but national competition authorities have as their objectives only the interests of their jurisdiction. The EU and the USA both take into account in their decisions actions taken elsewhere affecting their economies, but not actions affecting only foreign markets. And behaviour in one market can, of course, affect welfare in another. A dominant firm or cartel may use its market power in one market to leverage its position in another, for example by predatory behaviour. Aside from crude price-fixing behaviour in the form of export cartels, mergers can easily have cross-border effects. It is not unusual for competition laws specifically to exclude sectors of activity where foreigners may be the main victims of anti-competitive practice. Shipping conferences have traditionally been exempted, and many jurisdictions exempt export cartels, either explicitly or implicitly, by providing only for acting against cartels with internal effects.[2] Dominant positions or anti-competitive agreements may directly restrict imports. Licensing by owners of intellectual property rights (IPRs) in one market may have anti-competitive effects in another. In addition, there are genuine global cartels which may operate from cyberspace or, more mundanely, be located in a 'competition haven'. International mergers pose problems not foreseen in 1947. Two firms may merge in a home market where there is plenty of competition, but they may also have subsidiaries in markets where the new combined entity has a dominant position.

It should be noted that many exporting countries, notably Hong Kong (China), have argued that the interface of trade and competition policy

should also be construed as covering governmental trade policy instruments such as safeguards, especially VERs, and, above all, anti-dumping,
which both directly and indirectly reduce competition in the importer's
market. It is, however, sadly 'a red herring' to suppose that a WTO competition policy agreement might end up replacing anti-dumping laws with
competition policy. There are a very few instances in which anti-dumping
actions operate in the place of effective cross-border competition rules (see
Belderbos and Holmes, 1995) but there is ample evidence to show that the
aims of anti-dumping policies are not to prevent predatory monopolistic
dumping (see Sykes, 1998).[3]

In all these cases, it is unlikely that governments in the affected countries
alone will be able to obtain the evidence needed to pursue infringers, even
if they have effective laws. Indeed, government policies of action or inac-
tion can aggravate these tendencies. It was alleged, but subsequently not
proven, that the Japanese government deliberately used competition law in
such a way as to favour Fuji Film over Kodak in the Japanese market.
(Slightly) more convincingly, failure to apply competition law to the consumer electronics sector in Japan created excess domestic profits that allowed
a form of predatory behaviour in the USA.[4]

The capacity of competition authorities to assess all the factors in cross-
border mergers adequately may well be limited, even if there is no problem
of willingness. The increasing number of international mergers and strategic alliances where the authorities are forced to rely on whatever information the parties supply clearly raises the question of the need for enhanced
cooperation.

3. THE CASE FOR AN INTERNATIONAL COMPETITION AGREEMENT

Three reasons for wanting some form of international competition agreement can be identified: international anti-trust; market access concerns;
and transactions costs.

The distinction between international anti-trust and market access concerns is not always clear, however, but it is important. In the early years of
the establishment of the EU, only (West) Germany had a vigorous domestic competition policy. The Treaty of Rome put in place a form of supranational competition policy which gave the European Commission powers
to intervene directly and control anti-competitive behaviour by firms which
could distort trade between member states, thus addressing the problem
identified in the Havana Charter. The Treaty went further than the Charter
in giving the executive the authority to act, not merely to report and recom-

mend, but the jurisdiction of the Commission was strictly limited to practices affecting cross-border trade. The EU did not create an internal competition regime for its members. Market access was the driving force and the avoidance of distortions to trade is the prime goal. The rights of consumers are not totally neglected and, of course, the mercantilist and welfare economics goals can be reconciled by ensuring symmetry of market access for all suppliers.

EU competition policy concerns, however, are sometimes presented solely in terms of the rights of one group of suppliers to enter a market. The EU's Europe Agreements with its partners in Central and Eastern Europe (CEE) are designed to ensure that the same provisions as are in the Treaty of Rome governing private anti-competitive market access barriers also apply to trade between the EU and its CEE partners (see below). The Agreements are symmetrical in that abuses on either side affecting trade are illegal, but the fact remains that only the EU has the power to ensure that its firms get the 'level playing field' that they seek. The Agreements do not formally require partner countries to adopt a purely domestic competition law, but it is clear that it would be hard to achieve the stated aim without having one. The ban on trade-distorting practices does not require national law to be effective if, of course, there is a supranational authority – as exists within the EU.

Similar considerations were present in the US Structural Impediments Initiative (SII), where accusations arose about the protection allegedly given to Japanese *keiretsu* groups by the way in which Japanese competition law was enforced or not.

Market access considerations lead to a focus on the absence of effective competition policy in importing countries, leading to a lower volume of exports by other parties. Obviously, such an emphasis will ultimately benefit consumers but, if there is a cartel and the foreign firms are allowed to join it, their complaints may ease off!

International anti-trust concerns are somewhat different. Here the main preoccupation is the effect on consumer welfare of agreements or dominant firms which may charge excessive prices for exports. The remedy is likely to be different since the cross-border effect is now that of failure of the home jurisdiction to act against anti-competitive behaviour, including mergers and export cartels.

The third consideration for advocating some form of agreement is that, with globalization, the transactions costs of allowing each national jurisdiction to deal separately, for example with international mergers, is becoming intolerable. The conflict over the Boeing–McDonnell-Douglas (MDD) mergers was a classic example; the EU was minded to declare illegal a merger approved by the USA without last-minute concessions by

Boeing. And, as noted above, national or regional authorities in many cases simply lack access to vital information.

The Case for Competition Policy in the WTO

There is a powerful case for some form of international agreement on the regulation of competition and competition policy in the world economy, and the WTO seems a natural place to agree it. Unlike the Havana Charter, however, there is no suggestion of an active role for the WTO as an organization. Rather, the debate is about whether the obligations of member states should include that of having a competition policy incorporating the international dimension.

The case that, in a globalized economy, the regulation of competition cannot simply be a national matter appears overwhelming. In the face of the arguments, it is sometimes surprising how much opposition there is to the starting of negotiations on trade and competition. On close examination, however, the sceptics have a powerful case that must be answered before any agreement is possible. Even apart from the intellectual case, the fact is that the US authorities are deeply sceptical of the value of any WTO agreement on competition. The US position is that there are very serious international cartel problems out there, but a WTO agreement is not the solution.

To establish the case for international competition under the WTO it is necessary to pose a kind of 'subsidiarity test' (Rollo and Winters, 2000):

1. Are there significant cross-border competition issues in practice?
2. Do current national or EU regimes deal adequately with these?
3. If not, could currently envisaged non-WTO cooperation arrangements provide a solution?
4. If not, is the reason for this a revealed political preference not to address them?
5. Or, is there an assurance paradox that can be solved by binding agreement?
6. If so, would some form of WTO regime have benefits greater than costs?
7. If so, what form?

The cross-border dimension of competition policy is argued to justify its appearance on the WTO agenda (Maskus, 2000). There are sceptics, however, notably spokespersons for the Clinton Administration – above all former Assistant Attorney General Joel Klein – who, while acknowledging that there is a big problem and that it is not yet adequately addressed, insisted that voluntary intergovernmental cooperation can solve it; a WTO regime would be at best worthless. They argue that there is not enough common agreement on core principles. The discussion here comes to a different conclusion.

The Need for an International Competition Agreement: Evidence

In the early 1990s, some economists argued that it would be enough to remove state-imposed barriers to entry – the classic Chicago critique of anti-trust. The European Commission has always argued, however, that its continuing competition activity, even after the completion of the Single Market programme, proves that just getting rid of border and other regulatory barriers is not enough.

Meanwhile in the later 1990s, the US Department of Justice under Assistant Attorney General Joel Klein became extremely active investigating and prosecuting cartels in vitamins, steel and animal feeds *inter alia*. It uncovered evidence on a massive scale of global violations and became seriously concerned to find the right response. The Citric Acid and Lysine cartels involved global markets of around $US2 billion in the late 1990s. The Department of Justice set up an International Competition Policy Advisory Committee (ICPAC) which reported recently (ICPAC, 2000).

A survey of the evidence on international cartels for ICPAC took as a key starting-point for its work the fact that, by definition, illegal cartels are secretive and are almost certainly underestimated (Evenett and Suslow, 2000). Nevertheless, it found that they existed on a large scale and that, contrary to simplistic industrial economics, they did not break down rapidly. Their estimate of the mean duration of cartels was four to eight years, but they found some that had lasted for decades. Cartels were found to raise prices by anything between 10 and 60 per cent. It was, however, harder to get convincing evidence of a negative impact on the quantity of US exports.

Another study comments:

> The enforcement record of the 1990s has demonstrated that international private cartels are neither relics of the past nor do they always fall quickly under the weight of their own incentive problems. Of a sample of forty cartels prosecuted by the US and the EU in the 1990s, twenty-four cartels lasted at least four years. And for the twenty of the cartels in this sample where sales data are available, the annual worldwide sales in the affected products exceeded $30 billion. (Evenett et al., 2001)

There is no shortage of figures on international merger activity; international mergers in 1999 were estimated at $US3.4 trillion. The costs of multijurisdictional filings are clearly substantial but there is less powerful evidence that they are unnecessarily burdensome (see Whish and Wood, 1994).

Do Current National or EU Competition Regimes Deal Adequately with these Problems?

The paradox of the US position is that the Department of Justice has been drawing attention both to the scale of the problem and to the effectiveness of its actions. In the late 1990s, for example, some UK officials privately – not publicly, as this would depart from the collective EU stance – doubted the significance for British exporters of private barriers to entry from a market access point of view. Meanwhile, the USA has been loudly signalling its successes in finding and prosecuting cartels. One aim of this is quite simply to scare wrong-doers into informing. The new US policy involves very generous leniency to the first firm which reveals details of a cartel, combined with huge fines and personal imprisonment for executives (including non-US ones setting foot in the USA) for those that do not confess. Fines can be up to $US500 million per firm – Hoffmann-Laroche in the Vitamins Case. In fact, there is no resource problem for the international activities of the Anti-Trust Division since it generates more revenue from fines than the cost of its operations.

Nevertheless, there is powerful evidence that cartels are not being adequately policed. There are numerous bilateral agreements between the major industrial countries, most famously the EU–US Agreement providing for 'positive comity'. Roughly speaking, this allows jurisdictions to request that others take action under their own laws when the requesting party's interests are affected. The European Commission regards positive comity as important but the ICPAC Report (2000) and Janow (2000) show its weaknesses. There is no obligation to exchange confidential information – in fact there is no obligation to do anything – merely a right of request. The requested jurisdiction can only act on matters which would be illegal under its own laws. There are numerous international cases where no assistance was in fact supplied across the Atlantic in spite of the existing agreements (Waller, 2000). The USA has, for some time, sought to replace the cooperation agreements with 'Multilateral Legal Assistance Treaties' (MLATs). Obligations under an MLAT are much stronger than in the EU–US Agreement: there is no MLAT with the EU. A German–US MLAT exists and a US–Australian Agreement on anti-trust enforcement allows for exchange of confidential information.

Mergers are not covered by the EU–US Agreement and the Boeing–MDD mergers revealed the risks of different views. Nevertheless, the inevitable inconveniences arising from the existence of overlapping jurisdictions seems likely to persist (Whish and Wood, 1994). The costs are manageable and the differing objectives of different jurisdictions cannot easily be reconciled with compulsory common procedures. There is extensive day-to-day cooperation on some matters. It is reported that the European Commission's DG Competition and the US Authorities routinely manage to agree on common definitions of the relevant market where both are looking at the same case (Janow, 2000).

Conflicts, however, cannot be ruled out. It is far too early to assess the implications of the 2001 GE–Honeywell affair where the EU blocked a merger approved in the USA. Commissioner Monti downplayed its significance and said that it showed the need for further cooperation: 'The GE–Honeywell is a rare case where the transatlantic competition authorities have disagreed. I am determined to strengthen our bilateral cooperation in the future to try and reduce this risk further' (Commission of the European Communities, 2001a). The European Commission also pointed out that this is only the fifteenth case that it has actually ever vetoed. Although both the US Department of Justice and the Commission claimed to be deciding solely on the basis of the impact on competition *per se*, US critics argue that the EU's decision was based on a desire to protect Airbus while the EU argues it was solely interested in the impact on consumers of GE's control of a broad portfolio of aerospace activities (see *Financial Times*, 2001). There is anecdotal evidence that the EU may have suspected that GE was losing interest in the hastily proposed merger and so thought it could get away with showing regulatory muscle at low cost. But the GE–Honeywell case raises systemic issues.

Would Currently Envisaged non-WTO Cooperation Arrangements Provide a Solution?

As noted above, the US position is that MLATs or other bilateral agreements are what is needed. US officials repeatedly insist on the lack of common rules across jurisdictions that would make any WTO rules unsustainable. They insist on the need for more cooperation but stress that it must be voluntary. In spite of the existence of an MLAT between the USA and Canada, however, the Canadians have not yet changed their law to allow the exchange of confidential information. The USA has passed an International Antitrust Enforcement Act which provides a framework for bilateral cooperation but the US–Australian Agreement is the only one in existence.

The weakness of the ICPAC Report is that it effectively criticizes the existing framework for cooperation but its concluding call for more of the same, that is, voluntary bilateralism, seems off the mark. This leads to the conclusion that there is a need for stronger cooperation and that existing voluntary mechanisms are not delivering.

Is there a Revealed Political Preference not to Address these Problems?

If there is such a revealed preference, it provides a *prima facie* case for a binding international regime. If, however, things are as they are because this is what the key actors and interests want, there will be no progress. Industry in the EU is very strongly opposed to any agreements that would oblige the EU to give confidential information to the US Authorities. Certain business spokespersons regularly argue very articulately at conferences that EU firms, not necessarily of course the ones whose executives are making the case, have had to notify the Commission about concerted practices that can be given exemption from Article 81 (*ex* Article 85) if notified but which constitute illegal behaviour *per se* in the USA where criminal imprisonment penalties are possible. The response of their academic audience is generally that this problem could be solved by the cessation of illegal activity in the USA.

It is clear, however, that there is principled opposition to certain of the potential elements in a WTO Agreement. The USA recently proposed at the OECD a code on the treatment of hard-core cartels. This is not antagonistic to the eventual adoption of such a code by the WTO, but the proposed OECD Agreement would only have enjoined members to act against cartels which were already illegal under their existing laws. That is, the recommendation did not include a commitment to police export cartels. Even the EU, desirous as it is to see enhanced cooperation, is not willing at the time of writing to include a commitment to police the anti-competitive behaviour of its firms in export markets.

It is worth noting that there has been quite strong political reticence from the competition policy community itself. Discussions at the OECD revealed that the Trade Committee and the Competition Committee had very different approaches. In particular, competition specialists do not want trade people taking over their 'turf'. Indeed, it is possible at conferences to sense the commonality of competition officials with each other and their distrust of their own trade colleagues who, they suspect, are seeking to take over the hallowed competition system for dirty mercantilist reasons which they could not avoid being contaminated with. The discussion often focuses on vertical restraints, where aggressive arguments by trade officials usually demand that exclusive distribution systems be allowed and parallel imports be banned. As argued below, however, the market access emphasis of the discussions has eased off somewhat.

Is there an Assurance Paradox that can be Solved by Binding Agreement?

It is clear that, even if there is maximum goodwill, international anti-trust enforcement is, in large part, a public good. Any country that offers to take other countries' interests into account without an assurance that they will do the same does risk incurring a cost. But is it the case that everyone is likely to be willing to adopt effective anti-trust enforcement if others agree to do the same? At the recent WTO conference for African trade and competition officials in Cape Town, the most common reply of delegates, off the record, as to why competition policy was developing slowly in Africa was 'lack of political will'. If a government is uninterested in anti-trust or, indeed, positively welcomes the pay-offs local monopolists can offer, then the fact that others are indeed offering to act will not be of interest. If the European Commission is persuaded that business people risk unfair imprisonment in the USA, they will not be persuaded to change this view if the USA offers to jail its own businessmen too.

The fact that there are real differences of opinion does not mean that agreement is impossible, but it helps to explain why there isn't one as yet.

Can a WTO Regime be Devised with Benefits Greater than Costs for All?

It is clear from the discussions taking place that the original idea of an international agency reporting on and eventually policing international competition issues is not even to be discussed. Proposals were developed in this direction (see Scherer, 1994, 1998), including the so-called Draft International Anti-Trust Code (DIAC) of Fikentscher and Immenga (1995), but were resolutely stopped after a debate at the OECD. The DIAC proposal received an echo in Singh and Dhumale (1999), who were otherwise very sceptical of norms being imposed on developing countries.[5] The EU is arguing (see below) for an obligation on WTO members to have their own competition law and for the creation of stronger modalities for cooperation, not for a global equivalent of its Competition Directorate. The big difference between the ITO and the WTO is that the former would have had a political executive able to carry out investigations and make recommendations although it had no provision for a judicial arm. Purely legal disputes would have been submitted to the International Court of Justice in The Hague, while the WTO has a judicial arm but no executive. Bringing in the WTO means bringing in the Dispute Settlement Body (DSB).

The US position is different. It has been argued that the international competition issue should be split into two (Fox, 1999).[6] There should be a general obligation under the WTO to have a competition law that ensures market access is not unreasonably impaired. Other matters should be left to other forums. Her views are summarized here:

> Eleanor Fox thus proposed the following rule, very narrowly focused at this point of intersection of trade and competition: nations should agree that in their economy there should be no unreasonable market-blocking restraint of trade. They should be able to implement that rule as they choose in their own law. Nations that have mature competition law have such rules now. Nations that do not have competition law yet could do what they like as long as they prevent unreasonable market-blocking restraints of trade. Cartels with a boycott against foreign products are perhaps the prime example; monopolistic anti-competitive exclusion and anti-competitive vertical restraints that are not justified by efficiencies are also potential blocks to market access. Countries would adopt the principle into their law and agree to enforce the law. (OECD, 1999a)[7]

US official opinion would not go this far (see below). Many analysts argue that there are such substantial differences in philosophy between jurisdictions (and between trade and competition officials) that any substantive rules on competition law, for example those on vertical agreements the EU has sought to impose on its Europe Agreements partners, would risk forcing one option in a domain where opinions are divided and even risk efficiency considerations in vertical restraint being subordinated to market access ones (for example Marsden, 2000).

The fact is, however, that as discussions have proceeded at the WTO and the OECD there has been a clarification of what is commonly agreed and what is not. There is a consensus that non-discrimination and transparency are key components in a core that anyone must respect. As will be seen below, it is hard to argue that the current general obligations under the GATT and the WTO in these domains exempt competition law. What remains to be agreed, therefore, is not whether these principles should be made to apply, but how.

While the EU could, in 1995, be said to have seriously sought to achieve convergence on substantive as well as procedural issues at the WTO, its aims are now much more modest. It is unimaginable that the EU would propose that all countries adopt a WTO competition code that was so specific that it ruled out any of the existing provisions of US law.

The Position of the Developing Countries

If a WTO Agreement obliged all of its members to have a competition law of some kind, then clearly the main impact of such a provision would be on those countries that do not have a competition law. These are mostly developing countries, but there is an additional category of Asian countries, led by Hong Kong (China), which argue that their own open trade policies are sufficient to guarantee fully competitive markets. There are also certain less vocal Asian states that think competition policy is a Western fad.[8] China is less opposed to a competition agreement than Hong Kong (China) but would probably agree in insisting that anti-dumping action by industrial countries is even more important to them. Historically, India has been in favour of multilateral competition disciplines but, at the time of writing, is arguing that the time is not ripe for negotiations. At the same time, research undertaken in India by the Consumer Unity & Trust Society (CUTS) Institute in Jaipur strengthens the case for a positive link between competition policy and development.[9]

The question needs to be asked as to why developing countries should need a WTO Competition Code to adopt domestic laws they could adopt anyway. The tally of countries with competition laws shows that the number is increasing every year. Competition policy is spreading in sub-Saharan Africa and there is a growing interest in the need for vigorous competition policy to assist the transition from economies dominated by parastatals. The COMESA regional grouping has recently been paying a great deal of attention to this, with the Zambian experience being widely discussed (see UNCTAD, 2000). South Africa has been in the vanguard of promoting the use of competition policy as a means of achieving both economic and social ends, to make industry more competitive in export markets and to deconcentrate power. Very little opposition to the desirability of the widespread replacement of regulation by competition law was expressed at the recent WTO conference for African trade and competition officials in Cape Town. The South African Trade and Industry Minister spoke of the central role that the interaction of trade and competition was having in the transformation of their economy but, as the then South African Competition Commissioner Alistair Ruiters told the OECD in 1999, it is still not clear to many developing countries what role the WTO has to play in this (OECD, 1999a). Ruiters argued that developing countries had a common interest in protecting their consumers from monopolies and cartels but that, before any agreement could be signed, major technical assistance would be needed to allow the full implications to be assessed.

There is indeed evidence that developing countries are likely to be victims of anti-competitive practices. A study for the World Bank looks at the involvement in developing countries of the major international cartels investigated by the Department of Justice (Levenstein and Suslow, 2001). It shows a very significant impact and, of course, a very limited ability to respond. It is fairly clear that anti-competitive practices regarding distribution can be pernicious, but they are very little documented. An interesting case was recently examined by the CUTS Institute, however: the Indian subsidiary of Unilever (Hindustan Lever) was found to be abusing its control of the distribution system in neighbouring Bhutan (see Mehta, 2000). In this case, the Bhutani Authorities were able to take effective action by insisting that Hindustan Lever also allow a second distributor to carry their products.

It is natural to suppose that the absence of domestic competition is a key factor in retarding development. It would be convenient if convincing evidence could be found that there was a clear line of causation from competition policy to more competition to faster growth. In a cross-sectional study of developing countries, the existence of a competition law was found to be associated with more effective competition although a liberal import regime was the most important factor (Hoekman et al., 2001). A comprehensive survey by Tybout (2000), however, found that there was very little empirical evidence on the link between competition and growth and what there was was at best ambiguous.

Again, the question may be asked as to why there cannot be technical assistance and voluntary adoption of laws. There is even a development-friendly 'model law' developed by UNCTAD which can be adopted voluntarily. There is an interesting parallel in the basic telecommunications field where negotiators produced a 'reference paper' which lays down regulatory and competition principles which countries could sign up to as they wished. No country had to do so but the USA, in particular, was waiting for a 'critical mass' to sign up before opening its markets. Clearly, there is some sense in which pro-free market politicians can use external WTO pressure to secure extra influence. Most of the gains from the adoption of a competition law would indeed accrue to those who adopt it. Although there are clearly spillover benefits to the rest of the world when a country makes its home markets more competitive, the free-rider problem is not the heart of the matter.[10] It is not clear that there would be major benefits from the adoption of competition laws beyond what countries would, on mature reflection, wish to have.

On the other hand, better international cooperation in anti-trust is a positive attraction for developing countries. 'Positive comity' would not go very far, however, as EU–US experience shows. A real commitment to sharing information and expertise where cartels are discovered in industrial countries could be a major benefit and one which could only be taken up by a country that had a competition law.

What is crucial is that any international agreement should not limit the scope of developing countries to apply competition law. One of the most sensitive issues is that of the potential abuse of patents. The Uruguay Round included an obligation on all WTO members to have or to phase in an IPR law. As noted below, this provides a right for host and importing

countries to control these by competition law, although there is no obligation for home countries to assist in this. A key point in the next WTO trade
round will be to ensure that there is no erosion of developing-country rights
here but, perhaps, a strengthening of them.

4.　THE CURRENT LEGAL POSITION ON
　　INTERNATIONAL COMPETITION POLICY

Curiously enough, a detailed examination of the current state of trade law
leads to the somewhat paradoxical case that one of the most powerful
reasons for wishing to see an agreement at the WTO on competition policy
is that competition rules are indeed covered already but in a haphazard and
unclear way. Unless there is negotiation over what the obligations really
mean, there is a risk of a messy process where the DSB may be asked to
define the rules in costly litigation, as in the 'notorious' Kodak–Fuji case.

In fact, discussions continued after 1947 on restrictive business practices
at the GATT and the OECD from the 1950s onwards. The work at the
OECD has both produced proposals for agreement and served to highlight
the differences between the major jurisdictions and between trade and competition officials. A number of recommendations emerged from the GATT
and the OECD from the 1960s to the 1990s, but with no legal force. In 1960,
a GATT Working Group recommended a very loose form of words to
suggest that Contracting Parties should recognize the potential of restrictive business practices to affect trade flows, but the Contracting Parties
declined to act.

The GATT Article III on National Treatment

Although the GATT 1947 made no explicit reference to private conduct,
there is no reason to suppose that the general provisions on domestic regulations exempt competition law. The original GATT does contain some
provisions that could be invoked in a case where a country applies its competition law in a manner that discriminates against importers (OECD,
1999b). Article III, calling for 'national treatment', contains a general ban
on any domestic rule or application of regulation in a manner that discriminates against imported products.

The wording of Article III indicates that it was most obviously designed
to deal with discriminatory taxation and basic quantitative restrictions,
but the text refers to 'all laws, regulations and requirements affecting their
internal sale, offering for sale, purchase, transportation, distribution or
use'. The result is that, if it could be shown that the way a country operates

its competition policy could be said to discriminate against imports or in some manner implicitly violate a GATT or WTO commitment, then this becomes potentially actionable. The WTO Appellate Body, in its 1996 ruling on Japan – Taxes on Alcoholic Beverages case, stated firmly that 'The Article III national treatment obligation is a general prohibition on the use of internal taxes and other internal regulatory measures so as to afford protection to domestic production' (WTO, 1996).

With the introduction of the new WTO system of binding dispute settlement in 1994, it does now matter whether the wording of the GATT and WTO Agreements can be stretched to cover competition issues. The OECD study (1999b, p. 7) argues that Article III could be used in this context and, as will be seen below, there is nothing in the Kodak–Fuji Decision to indicate otherwise. It must be remembered that Article III only covers discrimination by nationality of goods not firms, and its equivalent in the GATS only refers to what has been scheduled.

The GATT Article XIII and the WTO Kodak–Fuji Case

Another element in the GATT is Article XXIII, the so-called 'non-violation article'. Article XXIII was for long an obscure and, until the 1990s, ignored article. It provided for dispute settlement in cases where it is alleged that a GATT signatory has introduced new laws or measures which, while not explicitly forbidden by the rules, nevertheless act so as to 'nullify or impair' elements of the trade liberalization they agreed to in their GATT commitments.

The article came into prominence in the Kodak–Fuji case[11] where the USA (that is, Kodak) alleged that the Japanese government had applied its fair trade laws – mainly but not wholly competition laws – in such a way as to allow Fuji to exclude Kodak from certain distribution methods, essentially by not allowing Kodak to use the wholesalers Fuji controlled. The US government brought an action against Japan alleging that discrimination against US film imports existed and had been facilitated by a number of Japanese government measures, some by MITI, some emanating from the Japan Fair Trade Commission.

In its decision, the WTO Panel appears to have to adopted a fairly wide but strictly legalistic interpretation of the GATT text (WTO, 1998). They acknowledge that some of the US allegations would have amounted to a breach of Article XXIII had they actually obstructed trade even though the alleged actions by Japan were not explicitly outlawed in other articles of the GATT but they found, as a matter of fact, that there was no discrimination against the USA.

It is hard to read a direct message from the Kodak–Fuji case, strictly

USA versus Japan, about GATT and competition law. Most of the measures that the USA complained about were regulations that would not normally be considered part of competition law in that they dealt with rules governing large-scale retail outlets, measures with an industrial policy aim and some measures restricting the kinds of promotion schemes permitted. Since the case was not subject to an appeal, it must be assumed that this result is now the accepted law, but its implications are not obvious. A curiosity of this case is the stress placed by the USA on Article XXIII.

Many people have concluded, rightly or wrongly, that the Kodak–Fuji case shows that it is hard to use Article XXIII in competition cases. A senior EU official recently argued that: 'The Kodak–Fuji case came to naught for the simple reason that the GATT and the WTO do not contain the basic minimum legal provisions that allow a Member to pursue a case of private anti-competitive practices under the WTO itself' (Carl, 2001).

In fact, the WTO Panel made it clear that, while there had to be some government involvement, WTO rules did allow what appeared to be a private action to be challenged if state action were alleged to be behind it. 'These past GATT cases demonstrate that the fact that an action is taken by private parties does not rule out the possibility that it may be deemed to be governmental if there is sufficient government involvement with it' (WTO, 1998, para 10.1).

The simplest reading of the Kodak–Fuji case is that it was decided on the facts. The decision concludes: 'We find that the US has not demonstrated that the three categories of 'measures' *in combination* nullify or impair benefits accruing to the US within the meaning of Article XXIII:1(b)' (WTO, 1998, para. 10.2).

The US stress on Article XXIII is hard to understand. It is not clear how Japan could have been doing what the USA alleged without some discrimination against US products. In this case, there would have been a violation of Article III and the US case would have been easier to prove.[12] It is interesting to note that the EU, in its third-party submission in the Kodak–Fuji case, argued that the heart of the matter was a violation of Article III:4 as a result of measures designed to make life easier for domestic producers and which led to Fuji's alleged exclusionary behaviour. Its submission concludes: 'Therefore, the EC sees no reason to enter into any development of the non-violation claims raised by the US' (WTO, 1998, para. 8.26, p. 360).

The real lesson of the Kodak–Fuji case is that it is still not known what practices would, in fact, be struck down by a WTO Panel; what rules, for example, governing market entry by foreign-owned firms would be construed as discrimination against imported goods.

Other GATT Competition Provisions

The weakness of the dispute settlement system of the GATT before the Uruguay Round may well have led policy-makers to underestimate the scope for litigation under its provisions. Before 1994, GATT Contracting Parties could refuse to accept a Panel Decision given against them. Contracting Parties could therefore operate their competition rules in whatever way they wished, free of the fear that a GATT Panel would declare their practice illegal. This assurance is no longer available. There are other provisions in the original GATT which, when combined with the teeth given to them by the WTO dispute settlement procedures, could be invoked in a competition case.

One interesting provision is the recent Agreement on Safeguards (Article XIX), the wording of which would explicitly outlaw industry-to-industry VER agreements. The problem here is that such arrangements are, in many cases, already illegal under national competition laws, but the authorities often choose not to act (see Frazer and Holmes, 1995) and there is room for a stronger obligation to do so.

GATT Article XVII authorizes Contracting Parties to maintain state trading enterprises (STEs), even monopolies, so long as they do not discriminate between home and foreign goods in their purchases and sales. Article II requires that any trading monopolies authorized by the state must not restrict sales of imports in a manner inconsistent with tariff commitments. The GATT, dealing with goods itself, cannot require a state to open its services sector to foreign competition, except where a specific offer to do so has been made under the GATS.

Interestingly, the GATS does, in fact, incorporate a form of words recommended by a 1960s Working Group for adoption with respect to trade in goods. Articles 8 and 9 of the GATS lay down in very general terms an obligation that is not far removed from an old friend, Article 46(1) of the Havana Charter. Article 8 requires that, where a country has agreed to open up part of a service sector to trade, a supplier which retains a monopoly in a related market must not 'abuse its monopoly' when dealing in the unprotected market. Further, Article 9 says: 'Members recognise that certain business practices of goods suppliers may restrain competition and thereby restrict trade in services. Each Member shall, at the request of any other Member, enter into consultations with a view to eliminating such practices.'

In the field of telecommunications, the GATS text is somewhat more specific and provides more detailed grounds for action in the event that a firm supplying a service, not subject to foreign competition under the GATS schedule of its government, leverages its market power into a supposedly open market segment. The GATS telecoms negotiations in fact continued after the end of the Uruguay Round as coverage of liberalization was extended to basic voice telecommunications. In order to implement the commitments in the GATS to prevent foreclosure by dominant suppliers, a 'Reference Paper' was agreed in 1997 which spelled out in more detail what these obligations entailed, including cost-based access of new operators to incumbents' networks.

Most commentators (including Holmes et al., 1996) see this as a first, but sector-specific, set of competition rules for the international system but one in which many key concepts have not been precisely defined. Hoekman et al. (1998), however, argue that it is actually an agreement on regulatory principles, not competition rules, the distinction being that they see regulation as being sector-specific and that laying down *ex ante* behaviour rules while competition law operates *ex post* is generic. Moreover, the immediate aim is indeed access for excluded service suppliers; there are no rules on how consumers must be treated. The inference drawn, however, is the same as that by the present author, namely that, if there were to be a proliferation of sector-specific regulatory regimes agreed internationally, there would come a point where there would need to be some form of consolidation. Indeed it is a characteristic of liberalization that there is a tendency for sector-specific regulations to evolve into competition base regimes. In markets, especially those services in which the true ideal of contestability can never be hoped to be realized, it is inevitable that negotiations about regulatory barriers will turn into negotiations about 'competition' regimes.

The other WTO Agreement that makes specific reference to competition policy is the TRIPs Agreement, which requires all WTO members to adopt patent and copyright laws along the lines of developed countries, albeit with transition periods for developing countries. Critics of the TRIPs Agreement argue that it gave considerable extra market power, in particular, to pharmaceutical and agro-chemical firms without imposing restraints on potential abuses. The TRIPs Agreement, however, specifically refers to competition policy. It allows countries to take steps, such as compulsory licensing, when they can show that an anti-competitive abuse has occurred. It provides an incentive to have a competition law by making compulsory licensing easier when this route is used. It allows the host countries of multinational enterprises and importers to act in this way but it does not oblige home countries to require their firms to behave in pro-competitive ways in foreign markets. No explicit mechanisms were established to deal with the information problems that might arise.

A key issue that has arisen is the treatment of parallel imports, vertical restraints and the international exhaustion of IPRs. Some industrialized countries have argued that WTO rules should prevent countries from allowing unlimited parallel imports. The issue is basically whether a supplier of

IPR-protected goods which lawfully sold them in one country should be able to prevent those goods being sold on into another market where prices may be different. IPR holders frequently assign sole selling rights to their own subsidiaries or agencies, country by country, in a manner that permits international price discrimination, and do not license export sales. Competition law may invalidate such conditions. For example, any product sold in one part of the EU by a manufacturer to a wholesaler anywhere in the EU may be sold again anywhere else in the EU, but firms have the right to prevent the import into the EU of their branded or otherwise IPR-protected goods that have previously been sold outside the EU. Many consumer groups believe this to be abusive, but some economists argue that it permits efficient price discrimination.

This issue is at the heart of the current dispute between South Africa and 39 pharmaceutical firms. The 1997 Medicines Act, currently being challenged, would allow the South African Authorities to import products legally sold by the manufacturers at lower prices elsewhere, bypassing the official distribution channels. At first, the US government backed the pharmaceutical firms, but it has since acknowledged that Article 6 of the TRIPs Agreement allows member states to adopt their own policies on parallel imports (Maskus and Lahouel, 2000). This is a different issue from authorizing the sale in South Africa of products without a licence (for example in India). The TRIPs Agreement provides for the issuing of compulsory licences under a number of conditions, one of which is that a due-process competition investigation has found an abuse.

5. THE EVOLUTION OF EU AND US ATTITUDES TOWARDS NEGOTIATIONS ON AN INTERNATIONAL COMPETITION POLICY

The positions of the key players have changed in interesting ways in recent years. The USA was, at first, very interested in this area, then less so, but reversed its position again in mid 2001. The EU is, and has consistently been, favourable to the idea of multilateral trade and competition negotiations. This section describes the evolution of their respective positions as of early summer 2001. The concluding section updates the picture somewhat.

The EU Position

The EU has made a point of incorporating into nearly all of its recent preferential trade agreements provisions, for example Article 63 of the EU–Poland Association Agreement, that declare:

1. The following are incompatible with the proper functioning of the Agreement
   in so far as they may affect trade between the Community and Poland:
   (i) all agreements between undertakings, decisions by associations of undertakings and concerted practices between undertakings which have as their
   object or effect the prevention, restriction or distortion of competition;
   (ii) abuse by one or more undertakings of a dominant position in the territories of the Community or of Poland as a whole or in a substantial part
   thereof; . . . (Commission of the European Communities, 1993)

The Agreement declares that the meaning of these terms shall be that
used in the EU under what are now Articles 81 and 82 (*ex* 85 and 86 of
Treaty of Rome). The full wording of this and equivalent Agreements has
been widely seen as dictation by the EU of what form of domestic competition policy the CEE countries should have. In fact, the wording of the
Agreement technically leaves the associate countries free to achieve this end
by their own means but the political relationship with the EU means that
it can make such demands, largely due to the carrot and stick of membership.

The EU–South Africa Free Trade Agreement contains similar but not
identical provisions. Article 35 states:

The following are incompatible with the proper functioning of this Agreement,
in so far as they may affect trade between the Community and South Africa:
(a) agreements and concerted practices between firms in horizontal relationships, decisions by associations of firms, and agreements between firms in vertical relationships, which have the effect of substantially preventing or lessening
competition in the territory of the Community or of South Africa, unless the
firms can demonstrate that the anti-competitive effects are outweighed by pro-
competitive ones;
(b) abuse by one or more firms of market power in the territory of the
Community or of South Africa as a whole or in a substantial part thereof.
(Commission of the European Communities, 1999)

The EU does not, however, spell out the detailed competition policy criteria to be used by South Africa as it does for the CEE countries but it does
contain a 'comity' provision – Article 38.

1. The Parties agree that, whenever the Commission or the South African
Competition Authority has reason to believe that anti-competitive practices,
defined under Article 35, are taking place within the territory of the other
authority and are substantially affecting important interests of the Parties, it
may request the other Party's competition authority to take appropriate re-
medial action in terms of that authority's rules governing competition.

As noted above, this does not actually require or empower either party
to do anything it might not otherwise do: the operative term is 'may

request'. The EU–Mexico Free Trade Agreement contains equivalent provisions (Commission of the European Communities, 2000, Article 39 and Annexe XV).

The EU is thus creating a web of bilateral agreements, including those with the USA, and the USA is doing the same. The difference is that the EU is arguing that it is inadequate and inefficient to have so many overlapping and possibly inconsistent agreements. The USA argues that, given the different interests and capacities of different parties, such an approach is inevitable.

So what does the EU want? A recent statement by a spokesperson from DG Trade makes it clear that the Commission would like to see a generalization of the provisions it has been putting into its trade agreements. The bilateral agreements of the form referred to above are only feasible if a state has a competition law. So the EU is seeking to make this a condition of WTO membership, as is the establishment of an intellectual property law.

> What we are proposing is to introduce, into the WTO, provisions that require its Members to adopt certain minimum standards and core principles as it relates to their domestic competition laws and regulations and to respect certain requirements of international co-operation between competition authorities. The establishment of a domestic competition policy and a competition authority with sufficient enforcement powers remain the basis, in the absence of which a country would not be able to address anti-competitive practices of a domestic or international character. What we are aiming at is therefore, somewhat similar to what we did in the TRIPs Agreement, namely the establishment of a certain number of basic principles for inclusion in domestic laws. (Carl, 2001)

The EU is thus asking for more in a WTO Agreement than was provided in the Havana Charter and more than is actually specified in its trade agreements because it wants to, if not harmonize, then at least 'approximate' elements of domestic law.

> More specifically, we suggest that WTO negotiations should focus on three key issues:
> 1. core principles of domestic competition law and policy;
> 2. co-operation between competition authorities, including both specific cases and more general co-operation and exchange of information; and
> 3. technical assistance and capacity-building for the reinforcement of competition institutions in developing countries. (Carl, 2001)

The EU's recent propositions, however, have stressed that they do not wish to impose excessive requirements on developing countries. In a Communication of 29 June 2001, the EU suggested that:

Individual developing countries may, however, wish to reserve their judgement on the costs and benefits of such an agreement. In this connection, a possible option to explore could be to provide for the possibility for developing countries to decide, at the conclusion of negotiations, whether they wish to subscribe to the competition agreement. (Commission of the European Communities, 2001b)

The Commission argues strongly that the adoption of common core principles, to include non-discrimination and transparency, should not conflict with other development objectives. The Commission also suggests, however, that if countries do want to exclude sectors from competition rules they should be free to do so, subject only to the proviso that exclusions must be transparent, that is, predictable for economic actors. This model is perhaps similar to some elements in the GATS. The EU places great stress on the benefits of a common framework for cooperation which they argue would be helped by some agreement on common principles. They stress, however, that the obligation to undertake cooperation will be 'voluntary' in that the strict obligation will be to consider requests, not to act on them. This gets around the problem of onerous procedural obligations on developing countries, but it leaves open the complaint that the EU can also refuse assistance to them even though one of the EU's aims is said to be that: 'Co-operation provisions would therefore include responding to the longstanding developing country concerns about the importance of assistance by "home" competition authorities in those cases in which foreign firms may be engaged in anti-competitive practices with an impact on developing country markets' (Commission of the European Communities, 2001b).

One solution to this is that the obligation to offer cooperation could be asymmetrical. Here, there is also a possible parallel with GATS, where countries may decline to open up sectors, but the commitments made must be extended to all countries on an MFN basis whether or not they scheduled this. The EU has also proposed that there should be no role for dispute settlement regarding individual cases, but critics complain that it is not clear what dispute settlement would cover under the EU plan.

The US Position

The USA, however, was resolutely opposed to any of this. Under the Clinton Administration, they argued strongly for greater bilateral and voluntary cooperation outside the WTO. During his term in office, Assistant Attorney General Joel Klein stressed the international dimension of competition policy but argued against a WTO role, for example in a hard-hitting speech to an OECD conference where he responded to a plea by Sir Leon Brittan for such a role (OECD, 1999a).

The ICPAC Report, published in April 2000 and commissioned by Klein, highlights the global dimension of anti-trust and the weaknesses of existing arrangements but it firmly argues against WTO involvement.

> At this juncture, the majority of the Advisory Committee believes that the WTO as a forum for review of private restraints is not appropriate. Given the possible risks, and the lack of international consensus on the content or appropriateness of rules or dispute settlement in this area, this Advisory Committee believes that the WTO should not develop new competition rules under its umbrella.
>
> Indeed, the Advisory Committee recommends that the US explore the scope for collaborations among interested governments and international organizations to create a new venue where government officials, as well as private firms, non-governmental organizations (NGOs), and others can exchange ideas and work toward common solutions of competition law and policy problems. The Advisory Committee calls this the Global Competition Initiative. (ICPAC, 2000)

Most economists with a disinclination for harmonization will have an instinctive sympathy for the US position but there is nevertheless an inconsistency in it: the voluntary approach is not delivering. The EU has not rejected the US proposal for a non-WTO forum and is to participate in a 'Global Competition Forum', launched by the OECD, to include up to 25 non-members, beginning in October 2001 (OECD, 2001).

Intellectual property rights are a thorny issue in this. Hoekman and Holmes (1999) argue that there is a need to be very wary of reopening the TRIPs issue because the powerful forces that brought the TRIPs Agreement are still here. They argue further that the most sensible approach to 'exhaustion' is to allow countries to choose their own parallel import regime by omitting any mention of rule in this area. The problem is that any attempt to go further and to be explicit risks awakening the lobbies that at first succeeded in getting the Clinton Administration on the drug companies' side against South Africa. They would want to tighten as much as possible the scope for allowing parallel imports and issuing compulsory licences. This echoes the fear of those competition officials who see policy on vertical restraints dictated by mercantilist export interests (for example Marsden, 2000). However, the political climate has changed since Seattle. The danger of a bad agreement affecting control of IPRs has greatly receded. 'Civil society' has woken up to this issue and the EU has been forced to make access to medication a key plank of its public stance while, at the Uruguay Round, it was much more driven by the interests of pharmaceutical producers (Maskus, 2000).[13]

6. CONCLUSIONS: COMPETITION POLICY AND THE NEW WTO ROUND

Going into the new WTO Round, the EU is still battling for the inclusion of trade and competition. It has an increasing number of countries on its side, probably including South Africa – which does not, however, want to be seen to be dictating to other developing countries. The EU will clearly have to make concessions to attain its goal and is ready to be flexible on opt-outs or phase-ins for developing countries that do not have the inclination or the capability to introduce a competition law. It is going to have to consider seriously going beyond its present offer on export cartels and it will probably have to make concessions on other topics – in particular anti-dumping in this context.

There is perhaps a deal that would interest developing countries under which those countries that agree to have a competition law obtain significant additional rights, above all in terms of cooperation. This is more likely to involve *forums* for discussion and exchange of information than an attempt to address the really sensitive matters such as multijurisdictional review of mergers. No country is going to bind itself to give up the right to review cases, but there are things that can usefully be done even here, for example initially, even on voluntarily agreeing on ways to define relevant markets and so on. Developing countries are slowly losing their scepticism about the EU's proposal but all are not yet convinced that the time is right to negotiate. India, historically a *demandeur* in this area and a potential beneficiary, is still resisting the idea of formal negotiations following Doha.

The USA changed its position sharply, however, after an agreement between Robert Zoellick and the EU's Pascal Lamy in July 2001. US spokespersons insist that they cannot see any way to make WTO rules that would not be justiciable; that is to say, enforceable before the Dispute Settlement Body. If this is so, it is impossible to prevent reviews of individual cases occurring, which they reject. The EU responds that no individual cases should retried by the DSB but that patterns of enforcement could be challenged. Ironically this was precisely what the USA tried to show in the Kodak–Fuji case. There is, however, something that the EU can offer the USA, namely enhanced anti-trust enforcement cooperation under which the EU would have to be ready to exchange confidential information with the USA. However, it is unclear whether this issue is such a priority for the Bush Administration.

In short, the Seattle débâcle was a blessing for the trade and competition agenda. There are, as has been argued here, genuine cross-border issues at stake that are not adequately handled at present. Some form of plurilateral agreement is probably the best target for the time being. However, the EU will not find it easy to secure an agreement that will please both the USA and some sceptical developing countries.[14]

NOTES

1. For a review of the issues as seen at the outset of the WTO discussion, see WTO (1997).
2. Some US experts believe that repealing the US Webb–Pomerene Act, which allows export cartels, would have no effect as any adverse effects only affecting foreigners are legal anyway in the USA – or indeed anywhere else.
3. Hoekman (1998) shows how anti-dumping and competition issues are quite differently treated in regional trade agreements (RTAs).
4. See Scherer (2000) ch. 27 and, for the company perspectives, see
   http://home.fujifilm.com/info/wto/ and
   http://www.kodak.com/country/US/en/corp/pressReleases/pr 19971205–01.shtml.
5. 'The best solution would be the establishment of an international competition authority, having proper representation of the South in its governance and not dominated by the North' (Singh and Dhumale, 1999).
6. Professor Fox was a member of ICPAC.
7. For a full review see OECD (1999b).
8. At the OECD conference of July 1999, the transcript records no interventions by Thailand or Malaysia, although frequent and dissimilar interventions from China and Hong Kong. Intriguingly, the record shows that, at this conference, there were three 'Chinas' – the PRC, Hong Kong China and Chinese Taipei (Taiwan) all cheerfully debating.
9. See CUTS (no date, 2001) and the documentation on the *7-Up* project, CUTS (no date).
10. One senior EU official, when asked privately what developing countries had to gain from what the EU was at that time proposing, said 'more competition in their export markets'.
11. Technically, 'Japan – Measures Affecting Consumer Photographic Film and Paper, Complaint by the US' (see WTO, 1998).
12. In fact, the WTO Panel noted that three allegations of violation of Article III were made in a way that rendered them procedurally invalid (WTO, 1998, p. 467).
13. A US study from the mid-1990s, using the drug firms' own data, actually shows that, far from suffering losses due to inadequate IPR protection, US pharmaceutical companies in the early 1990s were earning profits well in excess of the market average, even using their own cost data and allowing generously for risk (see Scherer, 2000, ch. 23).
14. The major players have modified their position just enough to allow a subtle compromise to be reached at Doha. The EU introduced additional flexibility into its proposals and both the United States and developing country opponents of Trade and Competition negotiations have agreed in principle that negotiations in this area will start after the 'next' ministerial meeting.

REFERENCES

Belderbos, R. and P. Holmes (1995), 'The economics of Matsushita revisited', *Anti-Trust Bulletin*, **40**, Winter, 825–57.
Carl, M.P. (2001), 'Towards basic rules on trade-related competition policy', speech by Director General, DG Trade, Brussels, 2 March, http://europa.eu.int/comm/trade/speeches_articles/sp_mpc01.htm
Commission of the European Communities (1993), *EU–Polish Association Agreement*, http://158.169.50.70/eur-lex/en/lif/dat/1993/en_293A1231_18.html

Commission of the European Communities (1999), *EU–South Africa Free Trade Agreement*, http://europa.eu.int/comm/trade/bilateral/saf.htm

Commission of the European Communities (2000), *EU–Mexico Free Trade Agreement*, http://europa.eu.int/comm/trade/bilateral/mexico/fta.htm

Commission of the European Communities (2001a), DG Competition, press release, 3 July, http://europa.eu.int/rapid/start/cgi/guesten.ksh?p_action.gettxt = gt&doc = IP/ol/939/0/RAPID&lg = EN

Commission of the European Communities (2001b), *Draft Communication from the EC and its Member States: a WTO Competition Agreement and Development*, Brussels, 29 June.

CUTS (Consumer Unity and Trust Society) (no date), http://www.cuts.org/7up-project.htm

CUTS (no date), *Competition Policy in Developing Countries*, http://www.cuts.org/

CUTS (2001), *Contours of a National Competition Policy: a Development Perspective 2001*, http://www.cuts.org/

Evenett, S.J. and V.Y. Suslow (2000), 'Preconditions on private restraints on market access and international cartels', *Journal of International Economic Law*, **3** (4), 593–631.

Evenett, S.J., M. Levenstein and V.Y. Suslow (2001), 'International cartel enforcement: lessons from the 1990s', *World Economy*, **24** (9), 1221–45.

Fikentscher, W. and U. Immenga (eds) (1995), *Draft International Antitrust Code*, Baden-Baden: Nomos Verlag.

Financial Times (2001), 'Monti's block makes waves across Atlantic', 3 July.

Fox, E. (1999), 'Competition law and the Millennium Round', *Journal of International Economic Law*, **2** (4), 665–79.

Frazer, T. and P. Holmes (1995), 'Self-restraint: cars, complaints and the Commission', *European Public Law*, **1** (1), 85–95.

Hoekman, B. (1998), 'Preferential trade agreements', in R.Z. Lawrence (ed.), *Brookings Trade Forum*, Washington, DC: Brookings Institution, pp. 299–320.

Hoekman, B. and P. Holmes (1999), 'Competition policy, developing countries and the WTO', *World Economy*, **22** (6), 875–94.

Hoekman, B., P. Low and P. Mavroidis (1998), 'Regulation, competition policy and market access negotiations: lessons from the telecommunications sector', in E. Hope (ed.), *Competition and Trade Policies*, London: Routledge, pp. 115–40.

Hoekman B., H.L. Kee and M. Olereaga (2001), 'Markups under domestic and foreign entry', World Bank, background paper for *World Development Report 2001*.

Holmes, P., J. Kempton and F. McGowan (1996), 'International competition policy and telecommunications: lessons from the EU and prospects for the WTO', *Telecommunications Policy*, **20** (10), 755–67.

ICPAC (International Competition Policy Advisory Committee) (2000), *Final Report*, http://www.usdoj.gov/atr/icpac/finalreport.htm

ITO (International Trade Organization) (1947), *The Havana Charter*, http://www.globefield.com/havana.htm#CHAPTERV.

Janow, M. (2000), 'Transatlantic co-operation on competition policy', in S. Evenett, A. Lehmann and B. Steil (eds), *Antitrust Goes Global: What Future for Transatlantic Co-operation?*, Washington, DC: Brookings Institution, pp. 29–56.

Levenstein, M. and V.Y. Suslow (2001), 'Private international cartels and their effect on developing countries', World Bank, background Paper for *World Development Report 2001*.

Marsden, P. (2000), 'The divide on verticals', in S. Evenett, A. Lehmann and B. Steil (eds), *Antitrust Goes Global: What Future for Transatlantic Co-operation?*, Washington, DC: Brookings Institution, pp. 117–38.

Maskus, K.E. (2000), 'Regulatory standards in the WTO: comparing intellectual property rights with competition policy, environmental protection and core labor standards', Washington, DC: World Bank, http://www1.worldbank.org/wbiep/trade/TradePolicy.html#TRIPS

Maskus, K.E. and M. Lehouel (2000), 'Competition policy and intellectual property rights in developing countries', *World Economy*, **23** (4), 595–611.

Mathis, J. (2000), 'Towards a positive agenda for multilateral negotiations on competition policy: interests of developing countries', in UNCTAD, *Competition Policy, Trade and Development in the Common Market for Eastern and Southern Africa (COMESA)*, UNCTAD Series on Issues in Competition Law and Policy 01/07/00, Geneva: UNCTAD, pp. 99–102.

Mehta, P. (2000), 'Taming Unilever in Bhutan', Jaipur: CUTS Institute.

OECD (1999a), 'Aide-memoire of the discussion at the Conference on Trade & Competition', 29–30 June, http://www.oecd.org/daf/clp/trade_competition/conference/aideme-e.pdf

OECD (1999b), *Competition Elements in International Trade Agreements*, http://www.olis.oecd.org/olis/1998doc.nsf/linkto/com-td-daffe-clp(98)26-final

OECD (2001), *Global Competition Forum*, http://www.oecd.org/daf/clp/global_forum.htm

Rollo, J. and L.A. Winters (2000), 'Subsidiarity and governance challenges for the WTO: environmental and labour standards', *World Economy*, **23** (4), 561–76.

Scherer, F.M. (1994), *Competition Policies for an Integrated World Economy*, Washington, DC: Brookings Institution.

Scherer, F.M. (1998), 'International trade and competition policy', in E. Hope (ed.), *Competition and Trade Policies*, London: Routledge, pp. 13–30.

Scherer, F.M. (2000), *Competition Policy, Domestic and International*, Cheltenham, UK and Northampton, USA: Edward Elgar.

Singh, A. and R. Dhumale (1999), 'Competition policy, development and developing countries, http://www.southcentre.org/publications/competition/toc.htm* TopOfPage (symbol)

Smith, A. (1776/1976), *The Wealth of Nations*, Chicago: University of Chicago Press.

Sykes, A.O. (1998), 'Anti-trust and anti-dumping: what problems does each address?', in R.Z. Lawrence (ed.), *Brookings Trade Forum*, Washington, DC: Brookings Institution, pp. 1–43.

Tybout, J. (2000), 'Manufacturing firms in developing countries: how well do they do, and why?,' *Journal of Economic Literature*, **38** (March), pp. 11–44.

UNCTAD (2000), *Competition Policy, Trade and Development in the Common Market for Eastern and Southern Africa (COMESA)*, UNCTAD Series on Issues in Competition Law and Policy 01/07/00, Geneva: UNCTAD.

Waller, S.W. (2000), 'Anti-cartel co-operation', in S. Evenett, A. Lehmann and B. Steil (eds), *Antitrust Goes Global: What Future for Transatlantic Co-operation?*, Washington, DC: Brookings Institution, pp. 98–116.

Whish, R. and D. Wood (1994), *Merger Cases in the Real World: a Study of Merger Control*, Paris: OECD.

WTO (1996), *Japan – Taxes on Alcoholic Beverages, Report of the Appellate Body*, 4 October, http://www.wto.org/english/tratop_e/dispu_e/distab_e.htm

WTO (1997), *Annual Report*, Geneva: WTO.

WTO (1998), *Japan – Measures Affecting Consumer Photographic Film and Paper, Report of the Panel*, 31 March, http://www.wto.org/english/tratop_e/dispu_e/ distab_e.htm

7. New rules for international investment: the case for a multilateral agreement on investment (MAI) at the WTO[1]

Alan M. Rugman

One of the emerging economic (and political) issues for the forthcoming WTO Millennium Round is the liberalization of investment. Today, multinational enterprises (MNEs) dominate world trade and investment. Over half of the world's trade and over 80 per cent of the foreign direct investment (FDI) is undertaken by MNEs based in the G-8 countries, namely the USA, Japan and the large Western European countries (Rugman, 2000; UNCTAD, 2001). While tariffs and many non-tariff barriers to trade have been negotiated away in seven successive rounds of the GATT, the issue of investment liberalization on a multilateral basis has largely been ignored. Only in the NAFTA is investment a central part of a regional trade agreement. As a result, the investment provisions of NAFTA are argued to be a model for a multilateral agreement on investment (MAI).[2]

Unfortunately, the discussions to approve an MAI at the OECD between 1995 and 1998 ended in failure. Yet the design and adoption of a clear set of multilateral investment rules should be a priority for the WTO. The first half of this chapter presents a framework for an MAI at the WTO. The nature and content of the MAI is outlined and the difference between shallow and deep integration as well as the role of MNEs is explained. The experience with the MAI at the OECD is used to illustrate the negative side effects of non-governmental organizations (NGOs) in the MAI process.

1. THE POLITICAL NATURE OF THE MAI

The life of the MAI at the OECD can be benchmarked between the Halifax, Nova Scotia G-7 Summit of 1995 and the Birmingham, UK G-7 Summit of 1998.[3] In June 1995 at Halifax, the final communiqué endorsed the negotiation of a set of multilateral rules for investment (the MAI) at the

OECD. Almost concurrently, ministers and delegates at the OECD launched technical and substantive discussions, hoping to conclude the MAI within two years, by April 1997.[4] Failure to conclude the agenda at that date led to a one-year extension but, by April 1998, it was clear that final agreement on the MAI was still far off, so a pause in negotiations of six months was accepted. Without a deadline to force agreement, such a pause (which can lead into an indefinite period) signalled the political failure of the MAI.[5]

The substantive issues of the MAI were not taken up at the WTO as the proposed Millennium Round of multilateral trade negotiations failed to set an agenda at the Seattle Meeting in November 1999, partly owing to NGO opposition. The final GATT round of negotiations, the Uruguay Round, itself took seven years to complete, so the immediate prospects for an MAI at the WTO are not great. It will be even more difficult to generate a consensus at the WTO as there are now some 140 members, as opposed to the 30 members of the OECD. About 90 per cent of all the world's stock of FDI is undertaken by the OECD member states, the rich developed countries from Western Europe, North America and Asia. The economic logic of the OECD as the forum for discussion of rules for FDI remains strong even if the political logic of formal involvement of all parties, including developing countries, through the WTO is of increasing relevance. It has become obvious, however, that the real reason for the defeat of the MAI has little to do with which of the OECD or WTO is the better forum but rather is a result of the negative role of NGOs as critics of international trade agreements (discussed below).

2. A FRAMEWORK FOR THE MAI

This section develops a simple analytical framework for an MAI. The idea of economic efficiency and globalization, as made operational by the activities of MNEs, is shown on the vertical axis of Figure 7.1. A movement up the axis results in a greater degree of 'globalization', yielding a useful dichotomy between low and high degrees of economic integration. With low globalization, there are local small and medium-sized enterprises (SMEs). With high globalization, there are MNEs. Globalization is defined here only in economic terms although there is a growing literature that defines it in sociological terms as a process of convergence towards a commonality of economic, political and cultural functions (Giddens, 1999).

The concept of sovereignty and the independence of the nation state is illustrated on the horizontal axis. Towards the right of the axis, there is, conceptually, a high degree of sovereignty where the regime passes its own

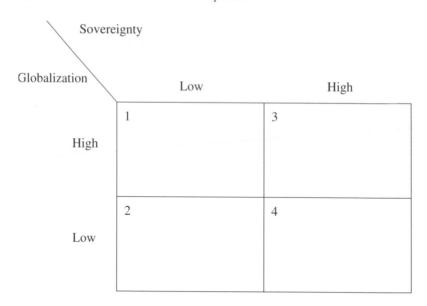

*Figure 7.1   The globalization and sovereignty analysis of investment
regimes*

laws and regulations and has enforcement ability. To the left, there is low
sovereignty, meaning, in this context, that the regime has given up some of
its power to others – either to firms or to other states in a multinational
system. The matrix is a variant of Bartlett and Ghoshal (1989) and is also
explored in Rugman (1996, 1997). The matrix yields four cases:

- *Quadrant 1* This is where triad-based MNEs might prefer to
  operate, without regulation – an economics-based quadrant of pure
  globalization. Here, an MAI would yield transparent and liberal
  rules for MNEs, with special rights in areas such as intellectual property and rules for dispute settlement.
- *Quadrant 2* Where SMEs operate, mainly domestic non-traded
  issues arise and there is little need for an MAI. A strong MAI could
  have efficiency-enhanced effects, however, even for SMEs, where they
  are involved in trade and investment clusters and networks.
- *Quadrant 3* This is the ideal quadrant for the MAI. It allows MNEs
  to be efficient yet affords key aspects of sovereignty, by way of sectoral exemptions from the national treatment principle and other
  non-conforming measures. It is also where the NAFTA investment
  rules-based system operates (Rugman, 1994). Quadrant 3 presents
  the biggest challenge for the MAI, and its success will be determined

largely by the ability of negotiators to make inroads in this quadrant. The biggest challenges and gains are located here, where globalization and sovereignty pressures conflict.

- *Quadrant 4*   This is a high sovereignty and nationalist view of the MAI, in which regulation of MNEs is advocated on distributional grounds and performance requirements are enacted by screening agencies. For a critical analysis of such investment reviews and the economic costs of regulation of FDI, see Rugman (1980, 1996) and Safarian (1993). Here an international accord, such as the MAI, is required to replace individual-country regulations which distort trade and investment patterns.

The matrix is a simple device to capture key elements of the public policy debate about market access issues, FDI and deep integration. It helps to demonstrate that the essence of the MAI is to link economic and political issues. The MAI could improve efficiency in all four quadrants since the international economy is now at the stage of needing integrated rules for integrated MNE production.

3.   THE MAI AT THE OECD

The structure of the MAI at the OECD, as revealed in draft texts of the Canadian government, follows that of NAFTA and is built upon the following platform:

- The principle of *national treatment*, with lists of exempted sectors;
- *Transparency*, that is, all regulations on investment are identified, as are all exemptions to the principle of national treatment;
- *Dispute settlement mechanisms*, to permit individual investors (and companies) to appeal against government regulations and bureaucratic controls;
- A movement towards *harmonization* of regulations although, in the areas of competition and tax policy, not much progress can be expected in the MAI (and none was achieved in NAFTA).

In the draft MAI, all of these four areas are addressed and a reading of the draft reveals that the structure of the MAI is based upon NAFTA's investment provisions, as was predictable. The aim of the MAI is to make domestic markets internationally contestable by providing a basic set of rules for FDI, to which all member countries sign up. The OECD is the correct venue to negotiate the MAI as over 90 per cent of all the world's FDI is conducted by MNEs based in its member states. There is some opposition to the MAI in a few developing countries but, as the WTO had failed to move on investment issues, there was no practical alternative to the OECD in the 1990s as a venue for the MAI. In the future, the WTO could start to deal with investment issues since contemporary economic integration is driven by the MNEs engaging in FDI.

Another reason for the MAI being started at the OECD was that it built upon several existing OECD investment instruments, including a code of conduct for MNEs from 1975 (see Safarian, 1993). The OECD has worked for the last quarter of a century to establish a binding set of legal rules for foreign investment and to ensure market access for investment according to the principle of national treatment. Expert opinion agrees that developing countries would benefit from an MAI as it would encourage long-term investment and support sustainable development (Fitzgerald, 1998). This study does not find support for the concern that developing countries would lose economic sovereignty because of an MAI. Nor was there any question of an MAI leading to lower environmental and labour standards, as argued by NGOs.

4.   THE MAI AND NAFTA

The draft MAI is similar to the NAFTA investment regime in all substantive respects and even in most procedural detail. Its critics have misunderstood the technical details of the MAI, as they did the Canada–US Free Trade Agreement (FTA) and NAFTA. For example, they claim that there are tighter mechanisms for 'standstill' and 'rollback'. Here, 'standstill' means that countries cannot impose any new regulations to restrict investment, while 'rollback' means that countries agree to a timetable to reduce existing regulations on investment. These are technical and legal terms intended to make the MAI function effectively. These process-related issues do not add to the economic or political substance of the MAI in any way when compared to NAFTA. There are similar provisions in NAFTA. There is, in fact, a large overlap in the technical and legal procedures of the proposed MAI and the existing NAFTA. In turn, there was a very strong overlap between the investment provisions of NAFTA and those of the 1987 Canada–US FTA.

One issue seized upon by NGOs in their opposition to the OECD's MAI is the first NAFTA-based investor-state appeal case brought by US-owned Ethyl Corporation. Ethyl were the sole manufacturers in Canada of MMT, a petrol additive, that was banned by the Canadian government in 1997. Although this was the only case in the four years of NAFTA, NGOs used it as a stick to batter the MAI in 1997/8. They generalized the specifics of this case to claim that foreign investors could use the expropriation provision of an MAI to claim compensation for loss of business when an environmental regulation is passed. They argued that any harm to any foreign-owned property or product would qualify for MAI protection. All of this is misconceived. All an MAI, based on NAFTA, could do would be to apply the principle of national treatment. Sovereign environmental regulations can be adopted by countries, before or after an MAI, without the MAI making any difference. All that the MAI could require is that foreign-owned firms be treated in the same way as domestic firms in the face of new legislation. The issue of eminent domain, the power of a sovereign country to regulate, and 'taking' of laws is a matter for legal interpretations and can differ between regimes.[6] The MAI, however, cannot confer more power in law on a foreign-owned firm; all it can do is make a foreign firm equal to a domestic firm in law.

This interpretation is confirmed in a paper by the world's leading expert on Chapter 11 cases, Toronto trade lawyer Julie Soloway. She states that the NGO 'concerns over the expropriation provisions of NAFTA are unfounded' (Soloway, 2002). The judicial standard applied by the NAFTA dispute settlement tribunals in the three pioneering cases (Metalclad, Pope & Talbot and S.D. Myers) is a conservative approach to expropriation. The tribunals defer to the sovereignty of members' governments to regulate economic and environmental activities within their borders. Much the same conclusion is reached in a separate analysis of the cases by US lawyer Sandford Gaines (2002).

5.   THE POWER OF NGOs

The NGOs are a new and powerful actor on the stage of international business. In the 1997 to 1998 period, NGOs assumed a more effective role than previously observed, leading to the defeat of the MAI. Prominent in orchestrating the NGOs was Canada's Council of Canadians, chaired by economic nationalist Maude Barlow. In a clever campaign of unsubstantiated half-truths, exhibited in the Clarke and Barlow propaganda booklet on the MAI (Clarke and Barlow, 1997), the Council filled the websites of NGOs with anti-MAI hysteria which was influential with the media.

With the US and Canadian governments treating the MAI on a technical rather than political level, and ministers being poorly briefed by second-rate trade bureaucrats, there was little political will to counter the gross distortion of the MAI offered by unelected and unaccountable NGOs. In addition, business leaders were unwilling to speak out on the advantages of the

MAI, leaving its defence to a handful of industry association spokespeople. Finally, the academic world, with a few exceptions, had not researched the issue – this being especially true of economists who have no parallel theory of free trade to apply to liberalization of investment. Consequently almost no one was available or willing to debate publicly the substantive issues of the MAI while engaged in their full-time professional duties. The absence of informed government, business and academic commentary left the media open to the distorted propaganda of unrepresentative NGOs.

The success of the NGOs in defeating the MAI builds upon less spectacular but consistent progress in the capture of the environmental agenda of international organizations. The first notable success of environmental NGOs, mostly US and Canadian, occurred in NAFTA when the first Clinton Administration in 1993 inserted two side agreements after NAFTA had been successfully negotiated over the 1990–92 period by the first Bush Administration. These side agreements set up an environmental body, the CEC (in Montreal), and a labour standards one (in Dallas).[7]

The UNCED Rio Summit reflected the agenda of environmental NGOs, leading to an unbalanced agreement with sets of commitments on which the governments were unable to deliver. In spite of these lessons, the Kyoto Summit in December 1997 resulted in standards for reduction of greenhouse gas emissions that, again, most countries could not meet, notably Canada and the USA. Indeed, implementation of the Kyoto Protocol was delayed as only the EU had the political will to ratify it, whereas the USA, Canada and many other countries did not. In Canada's case, this is due to the federal nature of the country, where the provinces have power to control natural resources. Thus Alberta, as the largest energy-producing province, will need to agree to implement Kyoto in order for the government of Canada to implement the Treaty.

6. ANALYSIS OF THE NGOs' ROLE IN THE MAI

This brief description of recent events portrays a gulf between the environmental and self-serving agendas of the NGOs and the economic reality of global business. What analysis can be used to explain this dichotomy? Two theories are considered. First, there is a traditional divide between the redistributional/equity concerns of NGOs and the economic/efficiency drivers of business. Democratic governments in Western economies have been able to balance these dual concerns when they assign different weights to these goals in their political platforms, giving voters the ultimate say in the direction to be followed. Recently, this has not worked as NGOs are operating outside of democratic political representation.

There are hundreds of NGOs, the vast majority of which are unelected special interest groups. Most seek to regulate some aspect of business activity and seek legislation by government to achieve their goals. These laws are usually protectionist since the easiest targets are foreign firms, that is, MNEs. Thus many NGOs have a nationalist agenda. Such unrepresentative, and politically biased, behaviour is undertaken by many North American and European NGOs. Whereas the labour movement and business groups are linked directly to political parties and have their agendas directly voted upon in elections, most NGOs are scared to face the voters, with the exception of the Greens. Yet their unrepresentative views gain vastly disproportionate influence in the media.

Complementary to the undemocratic nature of NGOs, especially in their biased understanding of international trade and investment, is a second failure. This is an intellectual failure of academic theory in which the twin basic paradigms of economics and polities are found wanting as explanations of today's global economy and the nature of FDI. In economics, the traditional efficiency-based neoclassical paradigm, with its associated theory of comparative advantage and the overall country gains from free trade, is unsuitable as an explanation of FDI. In spite of the efforts by international business writers over the last 30 years to develop a modern theory of the MNE, most economists are unable to take on board this explanation of the reasons for FDI (Rugman, 1996). As a consequence, the GATT and WTO have developed institutional frameworks to deal with the 'shallow' integration of tariff cuts but have failed to deal with the 'deep' integration of FDI.

Related to the out-of-date economics paradigm of free trade is the political science focus on the nation state. In spite of minor modifications to nation state paradigms, for example, to incorporate sub-national units in decision-making, there is a limited buy-in to the alternative International Political Economy (IPE) viewpoint, first popularized by Susan Strange (1987). Indeed, there is another unfortunate parallel between economics and political science in that both sets of work on the role and power of the MNE have failed to change the out-of-date thinking of the majority of academics, in spite of the abundant evidence of the relevance of MNEs to the global economic and political systems of today. The NGOs have slipped into this vacuum with their simplistic view of MNEs as big, bad and ugly. Based on prejudice rather than evidence, the NGO thinking is now more influential with government in North America and Europe than is the more scientific, and thereby more qualified, work of serious academic scholars working on MNEs (Ostry, 1997, 2001).

The issue here is one of process. There is an 'administrative heritage' of ideas. Today's media are poorly trained in economics, politics and international business. Those few who have any training are usually victims of the out-of-date paradigms of traditional economics and political science which cannot explain FDI and the MNEs. The MBAs of business schools now exposed to the new thinking on MNEs are in business rather than the media. The professional intermediaries, such as management consultants, have a focus on their business or government clients rather than the media, and their very skills of confidential advice and in-house retraining make them poor advocates in comparison to the pessimistic and opinionated NGOs. Finally, the civil service is basically useless in dealing publicly with NGOs, as bureaucrats attempt to support and influence ministers rather than entering into the public forum. The institutional failure of academics, consultants and bureaucrats to prepare a credible case for the MAI, and to be able to debate it publicly, leaves the field open to NGOs.

Although the NGOs can be credited with the defeat of the MAI at the OECD, the real reason for its failure lies elsewhere. Even with the high-profile activities of NGOs in 1997 and 1998, the MAI would probably still have been concluded at the OECD if one country, the USA of course, had got its act together. The right of the US Congress to pass trade laws and the corresponding lack of power of the President (Clinton) to negotiate international trade and investment treaties was the real explanation for the delay of the MAI. The failure by President Clinton to obtain 'fast-track' negotiating authority from Congress in Autumn 1997, for a free trade area of the Americas (FTAA) but also for a future round of the WTO and for an MAI, was the single most important reason for the failure of the MAI. The NGOs were able to step into this vacuum, and steal the agenda. A priority for the Administration of George W. Bush is to obtain trade negotiating authority from Congress for the 2001 WTO, FTAA, and so on.

Without the full commitment of the USA to champion a trade or investment agreement, there is little hope of success, as is demonstrated by the failed MAI process. In a future MAI, all countries will again be lobbied by various producer groups to exempt certain sectors from national treatment (for example cultural industries for Canada and France). To broker an international agreement, the full participation of the USA is vital as it is still the only country powerful enough to pull along other countries rife with internal dissent and sectional interests. Perhaps President Bush can assemble a coalition to advance new free trade and investment liberalization initiatives.

7.   NAFTA AND THE MAI

There is already a type of MAI in effect. This is NAFTA, whose investment provisions were used as a model for the OECD draft MAI. What, then, are the investment provisions of NAFTA? The investment provisions of the

Canada–US FTA, as signed on 1 January 1988, are the basis of the 1993 NAFTA investment provisions and the draft OECD MAI. For example, both the Canada–US FTA and NAFTA incorporate the key principle of national treatment, that is, equal access for foreign investors but according to local rules. Both the FTA and NAFTA also have exemptions from national treatment for important sectors, including the big five of health care, education, social services, cultural industries and transportation.[8]

Any MAI would be negotiated along the same lines; countries can readily agree to the national treatment principle but will always disagree over the number and type of exempted sectors. It is clear that governments will continue to insist on exemptions for the five service sectors, especially culture, but that the logic of the Canada–US FTA/NAFTA will be used as a model for the MAI. The underlying structure of the Canada–US FTA, NAFTA and MAI can be understood as a clever balance between the pressures of globalization (national treatment) and the need for sovereignty (exempted sectors), as illustrated in Figure 7.1.

The current challenge in international trade negotiations, somewhat paradoxically, is to negotiate investment rules rather than trade rules. This is because, through seven GATT rounds and important bilateral agreements, such as the Canada–US FTA, the best known barriers to trade, in the form of tariffs, have already been reduced to a trivial hurdle, even when calculating effective rates of protection – which take into account the value added and labour component of the protected good.

Today, the majority of international business is not undertaken through trade in goods but through services and investments. Over 70 per cent of North Americans and Western Europeans work in the service sector and only 30 per cent in manufacturing. So the new agenda for international agreements is to negotiate rules for trade in services and for international investment (Ostry, 1997, 2001). The 'shallow' integration, achieved by reducing tariff barriers to trade in goods, is being replaced by 'deep' integration, through FDI, trade in services and the international networks of MNEs (Brewer and Young, 1998).

Graham (2000) explodes the myth that anti-global activists defeated the MAI. Using careful analysis and 'insider' information as a closely involved and well-informed expert on US foreign direct investment policy-making, Graham concludes that the draft OECD MAI was a very weak document. In fact, the investment liberalization being negotiated was so weak that the US business community stopped supporting it long before anti-global activists started to protest against it in Paris. There was also a lack of leadership by the US government as well as tepid support in the EU and eventually hostility to the MAI by the French government of Lionel Jospin dependent upon left-wing 'green' support in his political coalition.

Graham (2000) is an objective discussion of environmental issues in trade and investment agreements. He has useful insights on the environmental provisions of NAFTA, especially the important initial Chapter 11 investor–state case on MMT. Trade and interprovincial trade in MMT was banned by the Canadian Minister of the Environment, Sheila Copps, on the grounds that it was an environmental and health hazard. The US-owned Canadian producer of MMT, Ethyl Corporation, used the Chapter 11 provisions to win a settlement from the Canadian government for denial of its business. The Canadian anti-global activists claim that this case demonstrates that MNEs could overturn the environmental decisions of host-country governments. The draft OECD text of the MAI had a similar provision to NAFTA Chapter 11, so that the anti-global activists claimed that the MAI was a charter of rights for MNEs to overturn the sovereign domain of governments – that the MAI was a 'NAFTA on steroids'.

Graham probably attaches too much importance to the MMT case, which was a purely technical application of Chapter 11, incited by trade lawyers hungry for business, and has no long-term policy relevance. The Canadian Minister apparently ignored the advice of her bureaucrats in banning the trade in MMT since NAFTA rules apply as soon as trade-related measures are introduced. Instead, Copps should have banned the production of MMT on the grounds of environmental hazard, an internal matter subject to Canadian law. Several subsequent NAFTA Chapter 11 cases have been resolved on technical grounds, with no loss of sovereignty to host nations in their environmental policies (Soloway, 2002).

Perhaps what the MMT case really illustrates is the 'dialogue of the deaf' taking place between trade experts and activists. The latter used the MMT case in a general assault on the MAI and subsequent international trade and investment liberalization initiatives at the WTO and G-7 summits. Graham argues that, as a consequence, the environmental NGOs especially have missed the boat (Graham, 2000). Trade negotiators were open and willing to incorporate environmental concerns into the MAI but violent opposition to it has now closed the window for cooperation between NGOs and governments.

This view is probably accurate and any more Genoas will probably permanently alienate the general public from the anti-capitalist agenda of the more extreme anti-global activists. A small and over-publicized section of the NGO movement is apparently opposed to any reforms of the global governance mechanisms and they continue to protest violently against MNEs. Eventually, the more serious NGOs must dissociate themselves from these violent activists in order to push forward a more sensible co-operative reformist agenda for civil society.

8. CONCLUSIONS

In general, because investment has a long-term time horizon, business people need to be assured that political risk is low. New and capricious investment regulations deter FDI and thereby reduce global economic efficiency. The worst excesses of protectionist economic nationalism advocated by NGOs can be offset through the investment provisions of an MAI. The WTO is a suitable forum for such an agreement on trade and investment rules affecting MNEs. Even the failed MAI at the OECD was a good news story. All of the substantive concerns raised by NGOs were being dealt with in those negotiations for an MAI, which followed the NAFTA model. The NAFTA is such an advanced trade and investment pact, because it incorporates the environmental and labour issues of the civil society, that it would also be relevant for an MAI at the WTO.

An MAI will help to open up markets in the world economy by providing clear and transparent rules for international investment and the associated business activities of MNEs. Such an MAI would incorporate the environmental and labour concerns of the more responsible and serious NGOs. Yet it would never satisfy the anti-global activists, whose blanket opposition to global capitalism is potentially leading to public alienation from the overall agenda of the civil society.

NOTES

1. A previous version of this chapter was presented as a paper at the IESG Annual Conference, University of Birmingham, September 1999.
2. For further discussion of the relationship between NAFTA and the MAI and the argument that the MAI could be based on the investment provisions of NAFTA, see Gestrin and Rugman (1996), Rugman and Gestrin (1996) and Rugman (1997). For discussion of the investment process of NAFTA, see Rugman (1994).
3. At a pre-summit conference in Halifax Nova Scotia in May 1995, several academic papers expressed the need for an MAI. These included those subsequently published by Rugman and D'Cruz (1997) and by Winham and Grant (1997). Other important contributions at that time include Brewer and Young (1995) and Smith (1995).
4. In mid-1994, the OECD organized a conference on trade, investment, competition and technology policies to develop a 'New Trade Agenda' with more of a focus on the issues of 'deep integration' (that is, investment-related) rather than the traditional 'shallow integration' of tariff cuts. Following this, the OECD organized a series of Trade Committee sessions at which several important papers were prepared which laid out a policy for the MAI. The most important of these were subsequently published by Gestrin and Rugman (1996), Lawrence (1996) and Graham (1996).
5. This is recognized by other commentators, such as Schwanen (1998).
6. The MMT case is discussed by Rugman et al. (1999) and Soloway (1999).
7. For discussion of the political process in the US at the time of approval of NAFTA, see Liebler (1994).
8. For details, see Rugman (1994, 2000).

REFERENCES

Bartlett, C. and S. Ghoshal (1989), *Managing Across Borders: the Transnational Solution*, Boston, MA: Harvard Business School Press.
Brewer, T.L. and S. Young (1995), 'The multilateral agenda for foreign direct investment: problems, principles and priorities for negotiation at the OECD and WTO', *World Competition*, **18** (4), 67–83.
Brewer, T.L. and S. Young (1998), *Multilateral Investment Rules and Multinational Enterprises*, Oxford: Oxford University Press.
Clarke, T. and M. Barlow (1997), *MAI: the Multilateral Agreement on Investment and the Threat to Canadian Sovereignty*, Toronto: Stoddart.
Fitzgerald, E.V.K. (1998), *The Development Implications of the Multilateral Agreement on Investment*. Study for the UK Department for International Development (DfID), Oxford: Queen Elizabeth House.
Gaines, S.E. (2002), 'The masked ball of NAFTA Chapter 11', in J. Kirton and V. Maclaren (eds), *Linking Trade, Environment and Social Cohesion: NAFTA Experiences, Global Challenges*, Aldershot: Ashgate.
Gestrin, M. and A.M. Rugman (1996), 'The NAFTA investment provisions: prototype for multilateral investment rules', in P. Sauvé and A.B. Zampetti (eds), *Market Access after the Uruguay Round: Investment, Competition and Technology Perspectives*, Paris: OECD, pp. 63–78.
Giddens, A. (1999), *Runaway World*, London: Profile Books.
Graham, E.M. (1996), 'Investment and the new multilateral trade context', in P. Sauvé and A.B. Zampetti (eds), *Market Access after the Uruguay Round: Investment, Competition and Technology Perspectives*, Paris: OECD, pp. 35–62.
Graham, E.M. (2000), *Fighting the Wrong Enemy: Antiglobal Activists and Multinational Enterprises*, Washington, DC: Institute for International Economics.
Lawrence, R.Z. (1996), 'Towards globally contestable markets', in P. Sauvé and A.B. Zampetti (eds), *Market Access after the Uruguay Round: Investment, Competition and Technology Perspectives*, Paris: OECD, pp. 25–34.
Liebler, S.W. (1994), 'The politics of NAFTA', in A.M. Rugman (ed.), *Foreign Investment and NAFTA*, Columbia, SC: University of South Carolina Press, pp. 27–46.
Ostry, S. (1997), *The Post-Cold War Trading System: Who's on First?*, Chicago, IL: University of Chicago Press.
Ostry, S. (2001), 'The multilateral trading system', in A.M. Rugman and T. Brewer (eds), *The Oxford Handbook of International Business*, Oxford: Oxford University Press, pp. 232–58.
Rugman, A.M. (1980), *Multinationals in Canada: Theory, Performance and Economic Impact*, Boston, MA: Martinus Nijhoff/Kluwer.
Rugman, A.M. (ed.) (1994), *Foreign Investment and NAFTA*, Columbia, SC: University of South Carolina Press.
Rugman, A.M. (1996), *Multinational Enterprises and Trade Policy*, Cheltenham, UK and Brookfield, USA: Edward Elgar.
Rugman, A.M. (1997), 'New rules for multinational investment', *The International Executive*, **39** (1), 21–33.
Rugman, A.M. (2000), *The End of Globalization*, London: Random House.
Rugman, A.M. and J. D'Cruz (1997), 'Strategies of multinational enterprises and governments: the theory of the flagship firm', in G. Boyd and A.M. Rugman

(eds), *Euro-Pacific Investment and Trade: Strategies and Structural Inter-dependencies*, Cheltenham, UK and Lyme, USA: Edward Elgar, pp. 37–68.

Rugman, A.M. and M. Gestrin (1996), 'A conceptual framework for a Multilateral Agreement in Investment: learning from the NAFTA', in P. Sauvé and D. Schwanen (eds), *Investment Rules for the Global Economy*, Toronto: C.D. Howe Institute, pp. 147–75.

Rugman, A.M., J. Kirton and J.A. Soloway (1999), *Environmental Regulations and Corporate Strategy: the NAFTA Experience,* Oxford: Oxford University Press.

Safarian, A. (ed.) (1993), *Multinational Enterprises and Public Policy*, Cheltenham, UK and Brookfield, USA: Edward Elgar.

Schwanen, D. (1998), 'Chilling out: the MAI is on ice but global investment is hot', C.D. Howe Commentary, No. 109 (June), Toronto: C.D. Howe Institute.

Smith, A. (1995), 'The Development of a Multilateral Agreement on Investment at the OECD: a preview', in C.J. Green and T.L. Brewer (eds), *Investment Issues in Asia and the Pacific Rim*, New York: Oceana, pp. 101–12.

Soloway, J.A. (1999), 'Environmental trade barriers under NAFTA: the MMT fuel additives controversy', *Minnesota Journal of Global Trade*, **8** (1) (Winter), 55–95.

Soloway, J.A. (2002), 'Expropriation under NAFTA Chapter 11: the phantom menace', in J. Kirton and V. Maclaren (eds), *Linking Trade, Environment and Social Cohesion: NAFTA Experiences, Global Challenges*, Aldershot: Ashgate.

Strange, S. (1987), *States and Markets: an Introduction to International Political Economy*, London: Pinter.

UNCTAD (2001), *World Investment Report 2000*, Geneva: UNCTAD.

Winham, G. and H.A. Grant (1997), 'Designing institutions for global economic co-operation: investment and the WTO', paper for Halifax Pre-G7 Summit Conference, May, in G. Boyd and A.M. Rugman (eds), *Euro-Pacific Investment and Trade: Strategies and Structural Interdependencies*, Cheltenham, UK and Lyme, USA: Edward Elgar, pp. 248–72.

8. Trade liberalization and state aid in the European Union

David Collie

In contrast to most other trade blocs, such as the North American Free Trade Area (NAFTA), the European Union (EU) has supranational regulations on subsidies or state aid.[1] In return for this supranational regulation of state aid, the member states of the EU have relinquished their right to use countervailing duties against the subsidies given by other member states, as permitted by Article IV of the GATT. Article 87(1) of the EC Treaty states that: 'Any aid granted by a Member State or through state resources in any form whatsoever which distorts or threatens to distort competition by favouring certain undertakings or the production of certain goods shall, in so far as it affects trade between Member States, be incompatible with the common market.' Although this appears to be a strong prohibition of state aid, Article 87(2) lists a number of exceptions that are always compatible with the common market while Article 87(3) lists a number of exceptions that may be exempted by the European Commission.[2]

Responsibility for the implementation of the regulations on state aid in the EC Treaty lies with the Directorate-General for Competition Policy of the European Commission (DG-IV). Under Article 88(3) of the EC Treaty, member states are required to notify DG-IV of any proposed state aid so that they can determine whether it qualifies for exemption. However, DG-IV raises no objection in 80–90 per cent of cases and only reaches negative final decisions in 1–5 per cent of cases. Recently, DG-IV has started to publish annual reports on state aid in the EU. Table 8.1 shows state aid as a percentage of value-added, for the EU12/EU15 from 1993 to 1997 and for individual member states for 1993–95 and 1995–97. Although state aid has fallen over this period, its level in the EU still seems quite high. With the completion of the Single Market in 1992, DG-IV has argued that there is greater need to control state aid in order to create a 'level playing field'.

Since the formation of the GATT in 1947, barriers to international trade have steadily been reduced. The completion of the Uruguay Round has resulted in the average trade-weighted tariff of the EU falling from 6.9 per

Table 8.1 *State aid to the manufacturing sector as a percentage of value-added*

	1993	1994	1995	1996	1997
EU12	3.8	3.5	3.2	2.9	2.6
EU15	N/A	N/A	3.1	2.8	2.5

	1993–95	1995–97
Austria	N/A	1.5
Belgium	2.5	2.4
Denmark	2.7	3.0
Germany	4.4	3.1
Greece	5.2	5.6
Spain	2.1	3.0
Finland	N/A	1.6
France	2.1	2.0
Ireland	2.4	2.2
Italy	6.1	5.3
Luxembourg	2.2	2.3
Netherlands	1.1	1.2
Portugal	2.7	2.8
Sweden	N/A	1.0
United Kingdom	0.8	0.9
EU12	3.5	2.9
EU15	N/A	2.8

Source: Commission of the European Communities (1999a).

cent in 1988 to 3.5 per cent in 1998. This has led, inevitably, to an increase in market penetration of imports in the EU market. It seems reasonable to conjecture that an increase in import penetration might affect the incentive of the member states of the EU to give state aid and that of the European Commission to control it. In the absence of international trade, when all EU member states give state aid to their firms, the result will often be a prisoners' dilemma situation where they all lose and their welfare can be increased by the European Commission prohibiting state aid. With international trade, state aid can be used by member states as a strategic trade policy against foreign firms rather than as a beggar-my-neighbour policy against firms in other EU member states. In this case, it is not clear that there is as strong an economic rationale for the prohibition of state aid by the European Commission. The objectives of this chapter are to assess how trade liberalization affects the incentive for EU member states to give state aid and to assess how it affects the economic rationale for the prohibition of state aid by the European Commission.

There has been little formal economic analysis of the EU's state aid policy until several recent articles: Besley and Seabright (1999); Nicolaides and Sanoussi (1999); the collection of articles in Commission of the European Communities (1999b); and, the most relevant for this chapter, Collie (1999, 2000a). A common misconception in the economic analysis of state aid is to argue, by analogy with the Brander and Spencer (1985) model of profit-shifting export subsidies, that member states giving state aid will lead to a prisoners' dilemma situation.[3] In fact, when lump sum taxation is feasible, EU member states giving state aid leads to a Pareto-efficient outcome when products are homogeneous and the member states are assumed to be symmetric, as Collie (2000a) shows in a Cournot oligopoly model.[4] However, Collie goes on to show that the outcome when member states give state aid becomes a prisoners' dilemma situation when taxation is distortionary so that the opportunity cost of government revenue exceeds unity. There always exists a range of values for the opportunity cost of government revenue where the member states give state aid but where its prohibition would increase the welfare of all member states. This model is extended by Collie (1999) to consider differentiated rather than homogeneous products and Bertrand oligopoly in addition to Cournot oligopoly. Most significantly, EU member states will not gain from the prohibition of state aid when the products are sufficiently differentiated, as state aid given by one member state will have little effect on firms producing differentiated products in other member states.

In this chapter, the model of Collie (2000a) is extended in a different direction by the introduction of foreign firms into the analysis. As in Collie (1999, 2000a), a production subsidy is used as a proxy for all types of state aid. There are three main results. First, it is shown that the Nash equilibrium subsidy will be positive, provided that the opportunity cost of government revenue is less than a critical value, and that this critical value is increasing in the number of foreign firms. Second, when the number of foreign firms is less than the number of EU firms, it is shown that there exists a range of values for the opportunity cost of government revenue where the Nash equilibrium subsidy is positive and where the prohibition of subsidies will increase the welfare of all EU member states. Third, when the number of foreign firms is greater than the number of EU firms, it is shown that the welfare of all EU member states would be reduced if subsidies were prohibited. The practical relevance of these results is assessed by computing some numerical results for the critical values of opportunity cost and comparing them with empirical estimates.

1. THE BASIC MODEL OF STATE AID

The basic model is similar to that in Collie (2000a) except that imports from outside the EU are included in the partial equilibrium analysis of state aid. The EU Single Market is modelled as an integrated market consisting of M identical countries with no barriers to trade or arbitrage between the member states. In each country, there is a single oligopolistic firm representing the manufacturing sector that produces a homogeneous product for sale in the EU. All firms in the EU are assumed to be symmetric with identical and constant marginal cost c. The ith firm in the EU receives a production subsidy s_i per unit of output, a proxy for all types of state aid, and produces output x_i for sale in the Single Market. The EU is supplied with imports by F foreign firms, that are assumed to be symmetric with identical and constant marginal cost c, and each firm exports output y to the Single Market.[5] For simplicity, it is assumed that the EU does not impose a tariff on imports from the foreign country and that the foreign countries do not subsidize their firms. Trade liberalization (or globalization) is represented by an increase in the number of foreign firms supplying the EU market. All member states of the EU are assumed to be the same size with demand in each given by the linear inverse demand function: $P = \alpha - \beta q$, where q is consumption of the homogeneous good in the member state while $\alpha > c$ and $\beta > 0$. Hence, the aggregate inverse demand function for the Single Market is:

$$P = \alpha - \frac{\beta}{M} Q$$

where
$$Q = \Sigma_{i=1}^{M} x_i + Fy \tag{8.1}$$

Technically speaking, the model is a two-stage game where each EU member state sets its subsidy to maximize its national welfare at the first stage and then the firms compete as Cournot oligopolists at the second stage. As usual, the game is solved by backward induction to obtain the subgame perfect Nash equilibrium.

The first step is to solve the second stage of the game, where the firms compete as Cournot oligopolists, given the production subsidies set by the member states of the EU. In the second stage of the game, the profits of the ith EU firm and a typical foreign firm are:

$$\pi_{1i} = (P - c + s_i)x_i \qquad \pi_2 = (P - c)y \tag{8.2}$$

At a Cournot equilibrium, the M firms in the EU and the F foreign firms independently and simultaneously set their outputs to maximize their profits, given the subsidies set by the EU member states. With linear demand functions, each firm's profit function is concave in its own output so that the second-order conditions for profit maximization will be satisfied. Also, the Cournot equilibrium will be unique and the reaction functions of the firms will be downward sloping so outputs are strategic substitutes. Assuming an interior solution, where the outputs of all firms are positive, the first-order conditions for the unique Cournot equilibrium are:

$$\frac{\partial \pi_i}{\partial x_i} = P + x_i P' - c + s_i = 0 \quad i = 1, \ldots, M$$

$$\frac{\partial \pi_2}{\partial y} = P + y P' - c = 0 \tag{8.3}$$

Noting that $P' = -\beta/M$ from (8.1), these first-order conditions can be solved for the Cournot equilibrium outputs:

$$x_i = M \frac{\alpha - c + (M + F)s_i - \Sigma_{j \neq i} s_j}{(M + F + 1)\beta}$$

$$y = M \frac{\alpha - c - s_i - \Sigma_{j \neq i} s_j}{(M + F + 1)\beta} \tag{8.4}$$

The Cournot equilibrium output of a firm is increasing in the subsidy given by its own government and decreasing in the subsidies given by other governments. Substituting these outputs into the demand function (8.1) yields the Cournot equilibrium price:

$$P = \frac{\alpha + (M + F)c - s_i - \Sigma_{j \neq i} s_j}{M + F + 1} \tag{8.5}$$

All subsidies have the effect of reducing the market price. If all of the EU member states give a common subsidy, then, with symmetry, all EU firms will produce the same output and all foreign firms will produce the same output. These symmetric Cournot equilibrium outputs and market price are:

$$x = M \frac{\alpha - c + (F + 1)s}{(M + F + 1)\beta}, \quad y = M \frac{\alpha - c - Ms}{(M + F + 1)\beta},$$

$$P = \frac{\alpha + (M + F)c - Ms}{M + F + 1} \tag{8.6}$$

An increase in the common subsidy increases the output of the EU firms, reduces the output of the foreign firms and reduces the market price. These results are used later to analyse the effects of a uniform reduction in subsidies and the multilateral prohibition of subsidies.

2. THE OUTCOME WITH STATE AID

Having derived the Cournot equilibrium of the second stage of the game in section 1, the next step is to solve the first stage of the game for the Nash equilibrium subsidies. It seems reasonable to assume that each member state in the EU maximizes its own national welfare and attaches zero weight to the welfare of other member states. Hence, the welfare of each EU member state is given by its consumer surplus plus the profits of the domestic firms less the cost of the production subsidy. Since the production subsidy is financed by distortionary taxation, the opportunity cost of government revenue will exceed unity (as in Neary, 1994 and Collie, 2000a). Therefore, the cost of the production subsidy will include the deadweight loss imposed by the distortionary taxation used to finance the subsidy. Thus, the welfare of the ith EU member state is:

$$W_i = \int_0^q (\alpha - \beta z)dz - Pq + \pi_{1i} - \lambda s_i x_i = \frac{\beta}{2}q^2 + (P - c)x_i - (\lambda - 1)s_i x_i \quad (8.7)$$

where $\lambda \geq 1$ is the opportunity cost of government revenue; $\lambda = 1$ if lump sum taxes are feasible. The first term on the right-hand side is consumer surplus, the second is producer surplus and the third is the deadweight loss from distortionary taxation.

At the first stage of the game, the EU member states set their production subsidies to maximize their national welfare, realizing that the firms will behave as Cournot oligopolists in the second stage of the game. Thus, the first-order conditions for the Nash equilibrium in production subsidies are:

$$\frac{\partial W_i}{\partial s_i} = (x_i - q)\frac{\partial P}{\partial s_i} + (P - c)\frac{\partial x_i}{\partial s_i} - (\lambda - 1)\left(s_i \frac{\partial x_i}{\partial s_i} + x_i\right) = 0$$

$$i = 1, \ldots, M \quad (8.8)$$

The first term is the terms-of-trade effect, which is positive if the member state is a net importer and negative if it is a net exporter, since the subsidy reduces the market price. The second term is the profit-shifting effect, which is positive if price exceeds marginal cost since the subsidy increases the output of the domestic firm. The third term is the distortionary taxation effect, which is negative since the financing of the subsidy incurs a deadweight loss.

Since all EU member states are assumed to be identical, there will be a symmetric Nash equilibrium where they all give identical production subsidies, $s_i = s^N$, and all firms in the EU produce the same output. As foreign firms export to the EU, all member states will be net importers, so that the terms-of-trade effect of the production subsidy will be positive. Using (8.4) and (8.5) to solve (8.8) for the symmetric Nash equilibrium subsidy yields:

$$s^N = \frac{(2M+1)(M+F) - \lambda M(M+F+1)}{M\Delta}(\alpha - c) \qquad (8.9)$$

where $\Delta \equiv (M+2F+1)(M+F+1)\lambda - 2(M+F)(F+1) - 1 > 0$. When lump sum taxes are feasible, $\lambda = 1$, the Nash equilibrium subsidy is unambiguously positive as both the terms-of-trade effect and the profit-shifting effect are positive while the distortionary taxation effect vanishes. By differentiating (8.9), the Nash equilibrium subsidy can be shown to be decreasing in the opportunity cost of government revenue:

$$\frac{\partial s^N}{\partial \lambda} = \frac{-(M+F+1)(2M+2F+1)(M^2+MF+F)}{M\Delta^2}(\alpha - c) < 0 \quad (8.10)$$

An increase in the opportunity cost of government revenue obviously reduces the incentive for EU member states to use subsidies, thereby leading to a reduction in the Nash equilibrium subsidy. Thus, with distortionary taxation, the Nash equilibrium subsidy will be positive only if the opportunity cost of government revenue is less than the unique critical value λ^S, which is defined by setting the numerator of (8.9) equal to zero.[6] This yields:

$$\lambda^S = 1 + \frac{M^2 + MF + F}{M(M+F+1)} = 2 + \frac{F-M}{M(M+F+1)} > 1 \qquad (8.11)$$

With no foreign firms, $F = 0$, this expression reduces to the same expression as in Collie (2000a) for the case when demand is linear, and is always less than two. With foreign firms, $F > 0$, the critical value of opportunity cost is greater than one and is greater than two if the number of foreign firms exceeds the number of EU firms. Differentiating (8.11) with respect to the number of firms/countries yields:

$$\frac{\partial \lambda^S}{\partial M} = \frac{(M-F)^2 - F(2F+1)}{M^2(M+F+1)^2} \quad \frac{\partial \lambda^S}{\partial F} = \frac{2M+1}{M(M+F+1)^2} > 0 \quad (8.12)$$

The effect of an increase in the number of EU firms/member states has an ambiguous effect on the critical value of opportunity cost. If the number of EU firms/member states is sufficiently larger than the number of foreign firms, however, then this effect will be positive. An increase in the number of foreign firms has an unambiguously positive effect on the critical value of opportunity cost. As the number of foreign firms increases, imports increase in all EU member states so that the positive terms-of-trade effect of the subsidy is strengthened. Hence, the incentive for EU member states to use a subsidy to improve their terms of trade is increased and so the critical value of opportunity cost required to make the Nash equilibrium subsidy equal to zero will be higher. This leads to the following proposition:

Proposition 1. The Nash equilibrium subsidy is positive if the opportunity cost of government revenue is less than the critical value λ^S. This critical value of opportunity cost is increasing in the number of foreign firms.

As in Collie (2000a), the Nash equilibrium subsidy will be positive if the opportunity cost of government revenue is sufficiently low. Trade liberalization, an increase in the number of foreign firms, strengthens the incentive for the EU member states to use subsidies as a means of improving the terms of trade. In effect, subsidies are being used as a substitute for a tariff.

3. THE OUTCOME WHEN STATE AID IS PROHIBITED

Having derived the Nash equilibrium in subsidies, the next step is to analyse the welfare effect of a uniform reduction in subsidies by all of the EU member states and then to consider the welfare effect of the multilateral prohibition of subsidies. Since all EU member states are assumed to be identical, they will all set the same subsidy and have the same level of welfare in the Nash equilibrium. Thus, as this symmetry will be maintained if there is a uniform reduction in subsidies by all EU member states, the welfare of each member state can be considered to be a function of this common subsidy when looking at a uniform reduction in subsidies or the multilateral prohibition of subsidies. Since the welfare of all EU member states is identical, the aggregate welfare effect on the customs union can be assessed by looking at the welfare of any one EU member state. The welfare effect on any EU member state of a uniform reduction in subsidies can be assessed by differentiating with respect to the common subsidy, which yields:

$$\frac{\partial W}{\partial s} = -(q-x)\frac{\partial P}{\partial s} + (P-c)\frac{\partial x}{\partial s} - (\lambda - 1)\left(x + s\frac{\partial x}{\partial s}\right) \qquad (8.13)$$

The first term is the terms of trade effect, the second is the profit-shifting effect and the third is the distortionary taxation effect. Since all EU member states are net importers, $q > x$, the terms-of-trade effect is positive. When lump sum taxes are feasible, $\lambda = 1$, the distortionary taxation effect vanishes, leaving the terms-of-trade effect and the profit-shifting effect, both of which are positive. Then, an increase in the uniform subsidy increases the welfare of all the EU member states by improving their terms of trade and shifting profits to their firms. This implies that welfare in the symmetric Nash equilibrium in subsidies is higher than welfare when subsidies are prohibited if lump sum taxes are feasible. Thus, the Nash equilibrium in subsidies is not a prisoners' dilemma type of outcome for the EU member states in this case.

Consider a small multilateral reduction in subsidies starting from the Nash equilibrium subsidy. To evaluate the derivative (8.13) at the Nash equilibrium in subsidies, the first-order condition for the Nash equilibrium (8.8) is used together with comparative static results derived from (8.6), which yields:

$$\frac{\partial W^N}{\partial s} = \frac{1}{(M+F)}\left[\frac{M^2+MF-F-1}{M+F+1}(q-x)-(M-1)(\lambda-1)x\right] \quad (8.14)$$

The first term in square brackets is positive while the second is negative if taxation is distortionary, $\lambda > 1$. Hence, this derivative will be positive (negative) if the opportunity cost of government revenue is less (greater) than the critical value obtained by setting the term in square brackets equal to zero:

$$\lambda^N \equiv 1 + \frac{q-x}{x}\frac{M^2+MF-F-1}{(M-1)(M+F+1)} \geq 1 \quad (8.15)$$

When the opportunity cost of government revenue is greater (less) than the critical value, $\lambda > (<)\lambda^N$, the distortionary taxation effect will outweigh the oligopolistic distortion effect so that a uniform reduction in subsidies will increase (reduce) the welfare of all EU member states. When $\lambda = \lambda^N$, the derivative (8.14) is equal to zero so that the joint welfare of the EU member states is maximized and the outcome is Pareto efficient. This leads to the following proposition:

Proposition 2. A uniform reduction in subsidies by all EU member states, evaluated at the Nash equilibrium in subsidies, will increase (reduce) the welfare of all countries if the opportunity cost of government revenue is greater (less) than $\lambda > (<)\lambda^N$.

This shows that a uniform reduction in subsidies, evaluated at the Nash equilibrium, may increase the welfare of all EU member states, but it does not show that the multilateral prohibition of subsidies may yield higher welfare for all EU member states than the Nash equilibrium in subsidies. To demonstrate that the multilateral prohibition of subsidies may be beneficial, Figure 8.1 shows the welfare of an EU member state when subsidies

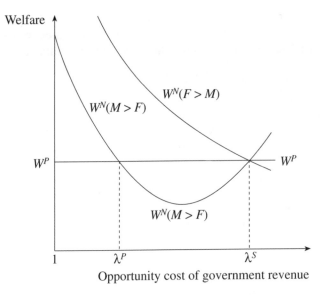

Figure 8.1 Welfare comparison of Nash equilibrium with prohibition of subsidies

are prohibited, W^P, and in the Nash equilibrium, W^N, as functions of the opportunity cost of government revenue. When subsidies are prohibited, welfare is clearly independent of the opportunity cost of government revenue since, with no subsidy to finance, there is no deadweight loss from distortionary taxation. It is shown above that welfare in the Nash equilibrium will be higher than welfare when subsidies are prohibited, $W^N > W^P$, if lump sum taxes are feasible, $\lambda = 1$. On the other hand, when opportunity cost is equal to the critical value, $\lambda = \lambda^S$, the Nash equilibrium subsidy is equal to zero, so welfare is clearly the same in the Nash equilibrium as when subsidies are prohibited.

To determine the relative positions of the two curves for values of opportunity cost between one and λ^S, consider the slope of welfare in the Nash equilibrium. This is obtained by differentiating (8.7) with respect to opportunity cost and evaluating at the Nash equilibrium:

$$\frac{dW^N}{d\lambda} = \frac{\partial W^N}{\partial s}\frac{ds^N}{d\lambda} + \frac{\partial W^N}{\partial \lambda} = \frac{\partial W^N}{\partial s}\frac{ds^N}{d\lambda} - s^N x^N \tag{8.16}$$

At the critical value of opportunity cost, $\lambda = \lambda^S$, the Nash equilibrium subsidy is zero so the second term vanishes. Since EU and foreign firms are assumed to have identical costs, they will all produce the same quantity when the Nash equilibrium subsidy is equal to zero, $x = y$. By equating demand and supply, $Mq = Mx + Fy = (M + F)x$, it can be shown that $q - x = Nx/M$. Substituting this expression together with the critical value of opportunity cost from (8.11) into (8.14) allows (8.16) to be evaluated:

$$\frac{dW^N}{d\lambda} = \frac{(M-1)(F-M)x^N}{(M+F+1)M} \frac{ds^N}{\partial\lambda} \qquad (8.17)$$

Since $ds^N/d\lambda$ is negative, from (8.10), this derivative will be positive if the number of EU firms is larger than the number of foreign firms, $M > F$. If welfare in the Nash equilibrium is positively sloped at the critical value of opportunity cost, $\lambda = \lambda^S$, then it must be 'U'-shaped, as shown in Figure 8.1. Hence, there must be some value of opportunity cost, λ^P, greater than one but less than the critical value of opportunity cost, λ^S, where welfare in the Nash equilibrium is equal to welfare when subsidies are prohibited, $W^N(\lambda^P) = W^P$. Thus, for values of opportunity cost in the range (λ^P, λ^S), the welfare of all EU member states is higher when subsidies are prohibited than in the Nash equilibrium. This leads to the following proposition:

Proposition 3. When the number of foreign firms is lower than the number of EU firms, $F < M$, there exists a range of values for the opportunity cost of government revenue, $\lambda^P > \lambda > \lambda^S$, where the Nash equilibrium subsidy is positive and the welfare of all EU member states would be higher if subsidies were prohibited than in the Nash equilibrium in subsidies.

As in Collie (2000a), where there are no foreign firms, $F = 0$, there exists a range of values for opportunity cost where the Nash equilibrium subsidy will be positive and where the prohibition of subsidies would increase the welfare of all EU member states. Hence, this model explains why EU member states wish to give state aid to their firms and why the EU attempts to prohibit state aid.

When the number of EU firms is smaller than the number of foreign firms, $M < F$, it follows from (8.17) that $\partial W^N/\partial\lambda$ is negative at the critical value of opportunity cost, $\lambda = \lambda^S$. From Proposition 2, it follows that $\lambda^S < \lambda^N$ so $\partial W^N/\partial s$ is positive for all values of opportunity cost between one and the critical value λ^S. Hence, both the first and second terms in (8.16) will be negative so that welfare in the Nash equilibrium will be negatively sloped for all values of opportunity cost between one and the critical value λ^S. Therefore, as shown in Figure 8.1, welfare in the Nash equilibrium will be higher than welfare when subsidies are prohibited for all values of opportunity cost where the Nash equilibrium subsidy is positive, $1 < \lambda < \lambda^S$. This leads to the following proposition:

Proposition 4. When the number of foreign firms is larger than the number of EU firms $F > M$, the welfare of all EU member states would be lower if sub-

sidies were prohibited than in the Nash equilibrium in subsidies whenever the Nash equilibrium subsidy is positive, $1 < \lambda < \lambda^S$.

In contrast to Collie (2000a), when the number of foreign firms is sufficiently large, the prohibition of subsidies will reduce the welfare of all EU member states. The explanation is that, with many foreign firms, the subsidy improves the terms of trade of the EU and shifts profits from foreign firms to EU firms rather than shifting profits between EU firms (and member states). Basically, the subsidies are being used mainly as a strategic trade policy against foreign firms rather than as a beggar-my-neighbour policy against other EU firms. For this reason, the welfare of all EU member states would be reduced if subsidies were prohibited. This suggests that increased import penetration of the EU market as a result of trade liberalization would reduce the incentive for the EU to prohibit state aid. In fact, in recent years, the EU seems to be attempting to enforce its prohibition of state aid more forcefully.

The result in Proposition 4 is qualitatively similar to a result in Collie (1999), where there are no foreign firms but products are differentiated. If products are sufficiently differentiated, all EU member states will lose from the multilateral prohibition of subsidies. This is because the negative effect of subsidies on other countries will be weakened when products are sufficiently differentiated.

4. NUMERICAL CALCULATIONS OF THE CRITICAL VALUES OF OPPORTUNITY COST

The practical relevance of these propositions can be assessed by calculating the critical values of opportunity cost for various parameter values and then comparing these critical values with empirical estimates of the opportunity cost of government revenue. Based upon the review of empirical estimates in Snow and Warren (1996), it seems reasonable to argue that plausible values for the opportunity cost of government revenue are in the range from 1.2 to 1.4, and this range of values should be borne in mind. The critical value of opportunity cost λ^S comes from (8.11) while λ^P is obtained by choosing the appropriate solution of the equation $W^N(\lambda^P) = W^P$, which can be solved explicitly using the Mathematica computer program, but this solution is not presented as it is somewhat messy. These critical values of opportunity cost only depend upon the number of EU firms/member states and the number of foreign firms so they can be plotted for a given number of foreign firms or EU firms. Note that the Nash equilibrium subsidy is positive, and prohibiting subsidies would increase the welfare of all EU member states if the opportunity cost of government revenue were $\lambda^P < \lambda < \lambda^S$.

Consider the case when there are no foreign firms, as in Collie (1999, 2000a). Figure 8.2 shows the critical values of opportunity cost as functions

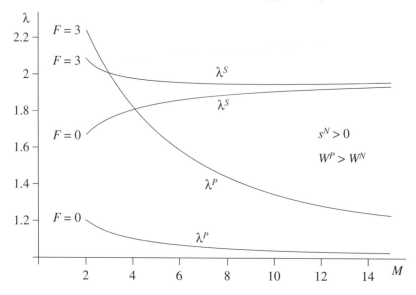

Figure 8.2   Critical values of opportunity cost versus the number of EU firms

of the number of EU firms/member states. In this case, there is a wide range of values for opportunity cost where the Nash equilibrium subsidy is positive and where the prohibition of subsidies would increase the welfare of all EU member states, and this range includes the plausible estimates of opportunity cost. With no foreign firms, there seems to be a strong argument for the prohibition of state aid by the EU. With three foreign firms, $F = 3$, both critical values of opportunity cost shift upwards in Figure 8.2 with λ^P shifting upwards more than λ^S. Consequently, the range of values for opportunity cost where the Nash equilibrium subsidy is positive and where the prohibition of subsidies would increase the welfare in all EU member states shifts upwards and becomes smaller. The argument for prohibition of state aid is weakened by the presence of foreign firms as it requires values of opportunity cost that are at the higher end of plausible estimates.

The effect of an increase in the number of foreign firms on the critical values of opportunity cost when the number of EU firms/member states is

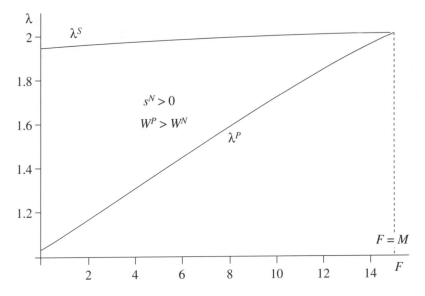

Figure 8.3 Critical values of opportunity cost versus the number of foreign firms

fixed at 15 is illustrated in Figure 8.3. With no foreign firms, there is a wide range of values for opportunity cost where the Nash equilibrium subsidy is positive and where the prohibition of subsidies would increase the welfare of all EU member states. As the number of foreign firms increases from zero, both critical values of opportunity cost increase with λ^P, increasing much more rapidly than λ^S, so that the range of values for opportunity cost shrinks very quickly. When the number of foreign firms is equal to the number of EU firms, the two critical values of opportunity cost are equal, $\lambda^S = \lambda^P$. If the number of foreign firms is larger than the number of EU firms, then no range of values for opportunity cost exists where the Nash equilibrium is positive and the prohibition of subsidies would increase the welfare of all EU member states, as shown in Proposition 4. With a signifi-cant number of firms, the argument for the prohibition of state aid becomes fairly weak as it requires an implausibly large value for the opportunity cost of government revenue.

5.   CONCLUSIONS

This chapter analyses the effects of trade liberalization on the incentives for EU member states to give state aid to their firms and the incentive for the

EU to prohibit state aid. First, it is shown that trade liberalization strengthens the incentive for EU member states to give state aid to their firms. When the EU market is supplied by foreign firms, all of the EU member states are net importers, so state aid acts as a strategic trade policy and improves their terms of trade. Second, when there are fewer foreign firms than EU firms, there exists a range of values for opportunity cost where the Nash equilibrium subsidy is positive and where the prohibition of subsidies would increase the welfare of all member states. Prohibiting state aid can increase the welfare of all EU member states by avoiding a prisoners' dilemma situation. Third, when there are more foreign firms than EU firms, the prohibition of subsidies will not increase the welfare of all EU member states. Prohibiting state aid prevents member states from pursuing strategic trade policies, primarily against foreign firms. Hence, it is clear from the results that trade liberalization will increase the incentive for EU member states to give state aid and reduce the incentive for the EU to prohibit state aid.

Since these results have been obtained in a relatively simple and not particularly general model, they should be treated with caution. The most important assumption is probably that EU exports are ignored in the model, either because there are no exports, or EU firms export to segmented foreign markets and exports are not subsidized by state aid. If the world market is treated as one integrated market and state aid is used to subsidize all the output of EU firms, then the EU may be a net exporter or net importer so that the terms-of-trade effect might be ambiguous. Then, the effect of trade liberalization on the incentives for state aid would probably also be ambiguous. The assumption of linear demand probably does not matter, since the results in Collie (2000a) hold for non-linear demand. Ignoring the common external tariff of the EU is probably reasonable since it is now fairly low for most manufactured goods. The assumption that EU and foreign firms have the same marginal cost is made to keep the equations relatively simple and does not significantly affect the results. Clearly, there is a need for further research on this issue before firm conclusions can be drawn about the relationship between trade liberalization and state aid.

As Behboodi (1994) notes, there are three approaches to the general control of subsidies: multilateral regulation through the GATT/WTO; unilateral regulation through the use of countervailing duties; and supranational regulation – of which the EU state aid policy is a unique example. The multilateral approach has not always been very effective, while the unilateral approach risks increased trade conflict. Increasing regionalization suggests that the supranational approach may therefore offer a solution to the problem of controlling subsidies that is both effective and avoids the risk of trade conflicts. Table 8.1, however, suggests that EU state aid policy has not really managed to control subsidies in some member states although its implementation now appears to have been strengthened.

NOTES

1. Behboodi (1994) discusses the different approaches used to control subsidies by the GATT, EU and NAFTA.
2. The regulations on state aid are detailed in Commission of the European Communities (1999c), and explained in Commission of the European Communities (1997).
3. See, for example, Besley and Seabright (1999).
4. A similar model is used by Collie (2000b) to explain the rationale for the GATT/WTO prohibition of export subsidies.
5. Assuming that EU firms and foreign firms have the same marginal cost greatly simplifies the expressions later in the chapter without really affecting the generality of the results.
6. As the Nash equilibrium subsidy is decreasing in the opportunity cost of government revenue (8.10), the critical value of opportunity cost where the Nash equilibrium subsidy is equal to zero will obviously be unique.

REFERENCES

Behboodi, R. (1994), *Industrial Subsidies and Friction in World Trade: Trade Policy or Trade Politics*, London: Routledge.
Besley, T. and P. Seabright (1999), 'The effects and policy implications of state aids to industry: an economic analysis', *Economic Policy*, **14** (28), 14–53.
Brander, J.A. and B.J. Spencer (1985), 'Export subsidies and international market share rivalry', Journal of International Economics, **8** (1/2), 83–100.
Collie, D.R. (1999), 'Prohibiting State Aid in an Integrated Market: Cournot and Bertrand Oligopolies with Differentiated Products', Cardiff Business School Discussion Paper 99–101.
Collie, D.R. (2000a), 'State aid in the European Union: the prohibition of subsidies in an integrated market', *International Journal of Industrial Organization*, **18** (6), 867–84.
Collie, D.R. (2000b), 'A rationale for the WTO prohibition of export subsidies: strategic export subsidies and world welfare', *Open Economies Review*, **11** (3), 229–45.
Commission of the European Communities (1997), *Competition Law in the European Communities, Volume IIB: Explanation of the Rules Applicable to State Aid*, Luxembourg: Office for Official Publications of the European Communities.
Commission of the European Communities (1999a), *Seventh Survey on State Aid in the European Union in the Manufacturing and Certain Other Sectors*, SEC(99)148, Luxembourg: Office for Official Publications of the European Communities.
Commission of the European Communities (1999b), 'State Aid and the Single Market', *European Economy, Reports and Studies, No. 3*, Luxembourg: Office for Official Publications of the European Communities.
Commission of the European Communities (1999c), *Competition Law in the European Communities, Volume IIA: Rules Applicable to State Aid*, Luxembourg: Office for Official Publications of the European Communities.

Neary, J.P. (1994), 'Cost asymmetries in international subsidy games: should governments help winners or losers?', *Journal of International Economics*, **37** (3/4), 197–218.

Nicolaides, P. and B. Sanoussi (1999), 'An appraisal of the state aid rules of the European Community: do they promote efficiency?', *Journal of World Trade*, **33** (2), 97–124.

Snow, A. and R.S. Warren (1996), 'The marginal cost of funds: theory and evidence', *Journal of Public Economics*, **61** (2), 289–305.

9. State trading, agriculture and the WTO

Steve McCorriston and Donald MacLaren

There has been a considerable literature in recent years on the links between competition policies and trade, the obvious implication being that these links should be seen as an important aspect of trade negotiations under the auspices of the WTO. More specifically, while the effects of trade policy instruments in restricting market access to or affecting competition in export markets are well known to trade economists, the anti-competitive practices of firms can have equivalent effects. To take the case of an importing country, the exercise of market power in the domestic market can limit the extent of import competition from foreign firms where the exercise of that market power is not restricted to 'horizontal' activities but also extends to vertical ties and contracts. For example, the use of vertical restraints or vertical integration (or contracts that replicate such an outcome) can foreclose competition between domestic and foreign firms (see, for example, Spencer and Jones, 1991). Horizontal mergers may also limit competition by giving domestic firms greater market share at the expense of foreign competitors (Barros and Cabral, 1994). On the export side, price discrimination or dumping gives foreign firms an 'excess' market share in the domestic market and gives rise to the use of countervailing measures and anti-dumping duties. At a broader level, the exercise of market power over a number of jurisdictions, for example market-sharing agreements involving a limited number of firms that prevent competition between countries, is another area where the link between competition and trade negotiations has been mentioned. While some of these issues, for example price discrimination and anti-dumping, can be directly linked to trade policy issues, there is a broader range of anti-competitive practices that directly refer to the application of competition policies in promoting market access and fostering competition in export markets. Hence, there is a direct link between competition policies and trade (see for example, Hoekman 1997; Graham and Richardson, 1997; WTO, 1997). Whether, or to what extent, the link between competition policies and trade negotiations in the WTO will materialize is open to question, given the complexity of identifying the extent of anti-competitive practices and how they may affect trade as well as the different perception and aims of competition policy that apply across WTO member countries (discussed in Chapter 6).

While the literature on trade and competition focuses predominantly on private firms, little has been made of the existence and practices of state trading enterprises (STEs). This is the subject of this chapter, with particular attention given to STEs that arise in the agricultural sector. As discussed below, this is the sector where STEs, as covered by GATT rules, are most prevalent. Specifically, the aim of this chapter is to consider the STE issue in the context of the forthcoming negotiations on agricultural trade. The emphasis is on the ways in which STEs are deemed to be anti-competitive and how their practices may affect both domestic and world markets. Although STEs arise in both exporting and importing countries, the former have been the focus of WTO submissions by supporters of STE reform. Moreover, there has been a history of trade disputes involving trading partners where STEs have been a specific issue. Sections 1 and 2 define what is meant by an STE and examine the incidence of STEs throughout the world economy with reference to their use in the agricultural sector. Sections 3 and 4 consider the anti-competitive practices of STEs and issues arising from the existence of STEs in Australia and Canada which are discussed in greater detail. In particular, the focus is on the recent debate in Australia about the desirability of STEs and the recent anti-dumping investigations in the USA involving the practices of the Canadian Wheat Board, an STE that is likely to come under scrutiny in the forthcoming negotiations. The current status of WTO Rules with respect to the existence of STEs is considered in section 5 and conclusions are drawn in section 6.

1.   WHAT ARE STATE TRADING ENTERPRISES?

The use of the word 'state' need not necessarily refer to ownership. The WTO definition of an STE is: 'Governmental and non-governmental enterprises, including marketing boards, which have been granted exclusive or special rights or privileges, including statutory or constitutional powers, in the exercise of which they influence through their purchases or sales the level or direction of imports or exports' (WTO, 1994, p. 25).

Close reading of this definition shows that it is not ownership *per se* that matters but the extent to which an enterprise, even if it is a private organization, has been bestowed exclusive or special rights by government. This is an important distinction since, while in practice many STEs are 'state-owned', some well-known STEs are not. For example, the Canadian Wheat Board (CWB) is an STE that is formally owned by the state. The Australian

Wheat Board (AWB), however, has recently been deregulated and is formally under the ownership of shareholders but is nevertheless deemed to be an STE because the Australian government has given it exclusive rights to export wheat to foreign markets. Thus, while the nature of ownership differs in each case, both Wheat Boards are regarded in the WTO (GATT Article XVII) under the same umbrella. The nature of the exclusive rights of the AWB makes it 'equivalent', in a legal if not an economic sense, to the CWB.

The second aspect worthy of note in the WTO definition is the likely concerns that arise from the existence of STEs, specifically those relating to the way in which exclusive rights distort trade. These rights give rise to a number of issues including: the creation of a dominant position that results in the exercise of monopoly and/or monopsony power; in the exercise of monopoly/monopsony power, the STE can discriminate among trading partners and affect the terms of trade; and there may be other advantages available to the STE that would not be available to private competitors on an equivalent basis. With regard to the former two issues, much of the debate on STEs in the context of the WTO comes down to the creation and use of 'single-desk' status. The single desk can take a variety of forms: for example, in the case of the CWB, the Board is responsible for all domestic procurement of wheat and barley produced in the Prairie Provinces. It is also responsible for all exports and a large proportion of domestic sales. Hence, Canada as a major producer and exporter of wheat may benefit from the exercise of this 'single-desk' STE in that it creates or aids the exercise of market power in both domestic and foreign markets. The AWB has single-desk status as far as exports are concerned, but it has to compete with private traders with respect to procurement for domestic sales. It is this single-desk characteristic of many STEs which is the basis for the concerns of many countries in the WTO negotiations.

With regard to the 'other advantages' available to STEs, there is a worry that their ties with government may distort competition in that such ties are not available to private traders. For example, subsidies for storage, transportation and so on may be of concern. Perhaps more of an issue is governments' underwriting of the financial obligations of the STE to producers should adverse market conditions arise, an advantage that would not be available on equal terms to the private sector. More generally, there is a perception that the budget constraint for the STE is softer than it is for the private sector.

As can be seen from this discussion, the concerns about STEs arise not necessarily from ownership but from exclusive rights. It is the nature of these exclusive rights that gives rise to worries about their impact on competition. Although two cases where STEs arise have been mentioned, the concerns about competition relate to the agricultural aspects of the WTO negotiations more generally since STEs arise predominately in the agricultural sector.

2.   THE INCIDENCE OF STATE TRADING ENTERPRISES

Although STEs can arise in any sector of the economy, it is important at the outset to distinguish between STEs involving trade in goods and those involving trade in services for two reasons. First, the issues involving STEs are arguably different in that, in the services sector, access to networks, rights of establishment and so on are competition issues that are specific to that sector and would not apply to trade in goods. Further, trade in goods is covered by long-established GATT statutes and rules, while trade in services is dealt with by the GATS.[1] In terms of STEs covered by the GATT, it should be noted that STEs involved in trade in goods are particularly prevalent in the agricultural sector in both developed and developing countries. In their recent submissions of their preliminary negotiating agendas to the WTO, many countries have put STEs as one of the main issues to be dealt with. Paradoxically, therefore, although agricultural trade is not often linked with the trade and competition issue, this is the area in the forthcoming negotiations where issues of anti-competitive practices and their impact on export competition and market access will most probably be discussed.

The range of STEs covers both exporters and importers, developed and developing countries, countries where agricultural policy intervention has been relatively high and countries where policy intervention has been relatively low. Of the more than 150 STEs that have been notified to the WTO in recent years, around 70 per cent occur in agriculture. Table 9.1 lists some key examples of STEs among current WTO member states that are likely to be key players in the forthcoming WTO negotiations.

On the export side, three countries are listed where the use of STEs is a key characteristic of managing their exports. There are three interesting features about the exporting countries listed. First, the relevant STE, in most cases, accounts for almost all of the country's exports of a particular commodity. For example, the Australian and Canadian Wheat Boards account for all of the exports of wheat from these countries. This characteristic is also true for exports of sugar from Australia and dairy products from New Zealand. Second, these countries are major exporters of those products to world markets; Canada and Australia together account for 30 per cent of world wheat exports while New Zealand accounts for around 7 per cent of world cheese exports and around 15 per cent of world

Table 9.1   Examples of STEs among current WTO members

Exporting country	Examples of STEs	Commodities covered	Share of country's exports (%)[a]
Canada	Canadian Wheat Board	Wheat	100
		Barley	100
Australia	Australian Wheat Board	Wheat	100
	Australian Barley Board	Barley	38
	Queensland Sugar Corporation	Sugar	100
New Zealand	New Zealand Dairy Board	Skimmed Milk Powder	100
		Cheese	100

Importing country			Share of country's imports (%)[a]
Japan	Food Agency	Rice	99
		Wheat	99
		Barley	99
South Korea	Ministry of Agriculture and Forestry	Rice	100
		Barley	100
	Livestock Products Marketing Organization	Meat	61

Note:
[a] The data on trade shares relate to the year the notification was made to the WTO.
Source: WTO notifications of STEs.

skimmed milk exports. Third, all three countries are commonly characterized as countries where the extent of government intervention in agriculture, as measured by the producer subsidy equivalent (PSE), has been
relatively low.[2] This is shown in Table 9.2.

As can be seen from Table 9.2, those countries that are characterized by
the presence of an STE typically record low values for their PSEs. For
example, for Australia and Canada, the levels of percentage PSE for wheat,
at 10 and 9 per cent respectively, are well below the OECD average of 42
per cent. Similarly New Zealand, although characterized by a wide range
of STEs, has very low levels of government intervention as recorded by the
PSE measure. Moreover, all three countries were major participants in the

Table 9.2 *Producer subsidy equivalent (PSE) measures for selected countries, 1997–99 (%)*

Country	Overall	Wheat	Sugar	Dairy	Rice
Australia	7	10	4	21	5
Canada	17	9	n.c. [a]	57	n.c.
New Zealand	2	0	n.c.	0	n.c.
USA	20	37	56	54	17
EU	44	53	51	54	23
Japan	61	88	64	78	83
Korea	65	n.c.	n.c.	67	77
OECD	36	42	48	54	76

Note:
[a] n.c. means not calculated.

Source: OECD (2000, Table III, various).

Uruguay Round where, as members of the Cairns Group, they argued for substantial liberalization of agricultural protection and the end of export subsidies. On the other hand, exporting countries that do not record the presence of STEs, such as the EU, have typically had higher levels of government support for agriculture. The accusation that STEs distort trade and hence should be dealt with in the forthcoming negotiations, suggests that other WTO members see STEs in some way as being a substitute for more explicit forms of government intervention that have not been dealt with thus far.

In the case Japan and Korea, two major importers of agricultural commodities, STEs account for a major proportion of imports into each country. In fact, the Japan Food Agency accounts for all imports of grains and rice. Similarly, the Ministry of Agriculture and Forestry in Korea accounts for all imports of rice and barley. In contrast to the export example, however, these countries have high levels of government intervention in agriculture and have typically played a role in trade negotiations as opponents of broad-based reform of agricultural trade policy. As shown in Table 9.2, the measures of government support for Japan and Korea show PSE levels well in excess of the OECD average for all of the commodities covered in the table. The most obvious cause for concern with regard to the next stage of negotiations is that, even if market access could be extended by traditional methods of increasing import quotas and reducing subsidies, the extent of liberalization will be limited by the fact that STEs will retain their dominant position. This will stifle the extent to which liberalization will arise in practice.

There are of course many other examples of STEs that arise in agriculture; the five countries reported in Table 9.1 only provide some indication of the STE issue arising among exporting and importing countries and among countries that are key players in the next round of negotiations. Many other examples could be mentioned, including the USA which, in the past, has reported the Commodity Credit Corporation as an STE. The STE issue also extends beyond current WTO members, with many acceding countries being characterized by the presence of STEs as the main way in which they conduct agricultural trade. Particularly notable in this regard are China and Russia on the import side and Ukraine on the export side. Clearly, the incidence of STEs is likely to rise when these countries become full members of the WTO and, in the case of China, this has been an issue in their WTO accession negotiations.

3.   THE IMPACT OF STEs ON COMPETITION: THE AUSTRALIAN WHEAT BOARD

Table 9.1 gives some indication why state trading is a competition issue. In many cases, STEs account for all of a country's exports or imports. Associated with this dominant position in trade, although not transparent from the data, is that STEs often account for all of the domestic procurement of agricultural products and they can dominate sales in the domestic market. This monopoly status over the supply of exports and, in some cases, domestic procurement and sales to domestic consumers is referred to as single-desk trading. This has become the particular focus of participants in the next round of WTO negotiations who have the desire to see STEs deregulated or at least brought under stricter controls. In the following two sections, some competition issues arising with respect to single-desk trading of exporting-country STEs are explored in more detail. The particular emphasis is on recent issues affecting the Australian and Canadian Wheat Boards. As will become apparent, in spite of some commonality, the issues have been different in each case.

Australia has a long history of state trading in the agricultural sector dating back to the early interwar period.[3] The most cited justifications for the creation of STEs have been the depression of agricultural prices in the 1920s, the free-riding problem that reduces the effectiveness of cooperatives in controlling supply, and the offsetting of the high levels of protection given to the manufacturing sector. Although this led to the creation of several marketing boards, it was not until 1939 that the AWB was established, with monopoly power being granted for both domestic and export sales. The single-desk status given to the AWB was further aided by the

Australian government's underwriting of its activities, first in guaranteeing producer prices and, later on, the Board's borrowings. As far as wheat producers were concerned, the price they received was a pooled price, being a combination of prices attained in domestic and export markets during a given marketing year.

Although the activities of the AWB have been amended periodically, perhaps the two most notable changes to have occurred thus far have been the loss of its monopoly in the domestic market in 1989 and its privatization in 1999. There were two important aspects of these changes to its exclusive rights and to the privatization of the AWB. First, the AWB no longer had monopoly rights in the sales of wheat in the domestic market although it retained its single-desk status as far as export sales were concerned. Second, when state ownership ended, the AWB became a grower-owned organization with a view to its shares becoming tradable and the company being listed on the Australian Stock Exchange. This change of ownership is important because, although the AWB has been privatized, as far as the WTO definition of an STE is concerned, the monopoly rights over wheat exports mean that it is still regarded as an STE.

The recent trend towards deregulation across many sectors in Australia has given rise to a debate on the future of STEs and with it the future of the AWB. As part of the National Competition Policy Initiative, all agricultural marketing arrangements are being reviewed. For wheat, a report was submitted to the Commonwealth Government in December 2000 on the future of the Wheat Board's export monopoly (NCP-WMA Review Committee, 2000). After reviewing the arguments for and against the single export desk, the Committee made eight recommendations, of which only Recommendation 6 is directly relevant for the purposes of this chapter. In essence, the Committee recommended that

> the 'single desk' be retained until the scheduled review in 2004 by the Wheat Export Authority (WEA) of the AWBI's [Australian Wheat Board (International)] operation of the 'single desk'. However, the main purpose and implementation of this scheduled review should be changed so that it provides one final opportunity for a compelling case to be compiled that the 'single desk' delivers a net benefit to the Australian community. (p. 8)

The Committee went on to recommend that, should such evidence not be forthcoming, the single desk should be discontinued and, even if a case could be made, that a further National Competition Policy review should be undertaken in 2010.

In brief, the supporters of the AWB essentially base their argument on the belief that the Board exerts market power to the benefit of domestic producers. These arguments can be summarized with reference to Figure

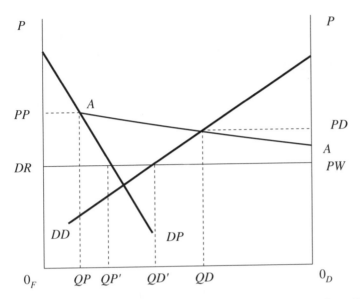

Figure 9.1   The single-desk activities of the Australian Wheat Board

9.1. The markets in which the AWB competes are segmented between 'premium' markets in Asia, with a relatively inelastic demand *DP*, and a rest-of-the-world demand curve *DR*. The main characteristic of the latter is that, in the figure, it is more (perfectly) elastic, given product substitutability, the large number of competing countries and so on. In between, there is a domestic demand curve *DD* that is more elastic than *DP* but less so than *DR*. Although the AWB no longer has monopoly status as far as the domestic market is concerned, given that it still accounts for a large share of domestic procurement (around 80 per cent), it will affect the domestic market so, for the sake of presentation, it is assumed that the AWB manages domestic sales too. On the assumption that these three markets can be segmented, the single-desk status of the AWB allows it to control sales to each of these markets so as to maximize its overall returns. Specifically, it price-discriminates in each market, charging *PP* in the premium market, *PD* in the domestic market and *PW* in the world market. The price received by producers is a price pooled across these three markets and is given by the curve *AA*.

The advantages of single-desk trading to Australian wheat growers are readily apparent from Figure 9.1. They attain a higher price than they would otherwise have received in the absence of the AWB through the restriction of sales to the 'premium' and domestic markets; and their share of the world market also increases. There is, of course, a downside; domestic users of wheat have to pay higher prices, given that the supply to the domestic market is restricted in order to maximize returns over the three market segments, even if this is no longer a consequence of AWB's practice of having single-desk status as far as domestic sales are concerned.

Figure 9.1 captures the essence of the domestic debate in Australia about the impact of the AWB. For its supporters, the AWB exerts market power that would not be available if its single-desk status were withdrawn. Those against a continuation of the Board's exclusive rights argue that market power in world markets is ephemeral, owing to the large number of competitors and, even if 'premium' markets exist, the benefits of extracting high prices could be attained by some other scheme, such as the export licensing of private firms.[4] The opponents of the AWB also argue that the domestic impact is also relevant. For example, Watson (1999) notes: 'Consciously or unconsciously, astute grain growers support the single desk because of market power on the Australian market not the world market, as their rhetoric would have it' (p. 436). The report from the National Competition Council had to weigh up these alternative perceptions of the merits or otherwise for the continuation of the single-desk status of the AWB. Despite receiving more than 3300 submissions, the Committee appears to have found no compelling evidence to support one side of the argument or the other.

Before closing on the AWB case, it is worth noting that the single-desk issue is not just a domestic concern; it is also a concern for other exporting countries and this, in turn, causes it to be a source for negotiation in the WTO. First, note that the level of sales to the rest of the world has increased. Specifically, with the activities of the single desk, $0_F QP$ goes to the 'premium' market and $0_D QD$ is sold on the domestic market with $QPQD$ sold on the rest-of-the-world market. This is more than if the AWB did not exist since, in the absence of the single desk and with no market segmentation, the level of export sales to the world market would be $QP'QD'$. Therefore, the activities of the single desk increase Australia's share of the world market at the expense of the USA and other grain-exporting countries. Second, it has been noted above that the measured level of government support to Australian farmers has been relatively low. The single-desk activities of the AWB, however, raise returns above the market level even though these do not arise from direct or indirect government transfers as commonly measured by the PSE. As such, the single desk is equivalent to an export subsidy even though it is not treated as one.

4. THE IMPACT OF STEs ON COMPETITION: THE CANADIAN WHEAT BOARD

Many of the issues outlined with respect to the AWB also apply to the CWB. As with the AWB, the CWB has its origins in the interwar period when concerns about food supplies, the public-good benefits of creating a state marketing organization and the coordination of grain supplies to the UK were prevalent. The present CWB was created in 1935.[5] It also has single-desk status and consequently accounts for all Canada's wheat exports and also all its barley exports. Moreover, the CWB has a more dominant position than the AWB with respect to domestic procurement, accounting for all the supplies of wheat and barley that are produced in the Prairie Provinces. Unlike the AWB, however, the CWB also controls the domestic market; the returns to farmers are therefore a pooled price, the price being some combination of the domestic and export prices. Assuming that the CWB can segment markets, it can price-discriminate and raise overall earnings for producers by exerting market power.

Many of the arguments that have recently been presented in Australia about the desirability of the AWB have also been rehearsed in Canada. This debate has spawned some research, albeit relatively limited, on the impact of STEs. On a number of occasions, the CWB has stated that the exercise of market power and its ability to price-discriminate between markets is its principal objective. In terms of research on this issue, Kraft et al. (1996) find that the Board earned significant price premia from wheat export sales, given its single-desk status, that would not have been available if export sales had been characterized by multiple private sellers. Moreover, Schmitz et al. (1997) conclude that the single-desk status of the CWB allowed it to generate substantial rents in world markets, in this case from barley exports. In other words, the benefits of administering sales through a single desk allowed it to exercise market power in foreign markets. In a simulation study, Alston and Gray (1998) provide evidence that the CWB's activities benefit Canadian wheat producers. As such, the arguments in favour of single-desk status relate to the exertion of market power on export markets. The impact of the CWB in exerting market power, however, is disputed. For example, Carter and Loyns (1996) dispute the appropriateness of the methodology used by Schmitz et al. In addition, reflecting Watson's analysis of the AWB (Watson, 1999), they note that: 'the domestic anti-competitive aspects of the Canadian Wheat Board are probably far more important than genuine foreign market power issues' (p. 28).

As a major competitor of the CWB in both the North American and overseas markets, the USA has taken issue with its activities in a number of cases. These have given rise to several trade disputes between the two countries. In an initial inquiry into the CWB, the US General Accounting Office (GAO) accused the CWB, and also the AWB, of being non-competitive sellers due to unfair pricing, price pooling, cost pooling, lack of transparency in pricing and government underwriting of initial payments and export credits. Moreover, following the increase in durum wheat sales into the USA, the US International Trade Commission (USITC) was requested to investigate the 'conditions of competition' between the two countries. The USITC Report published in 1990, however, did not vindicate the complaint against the CWB. Further, a Canada–US Free Trade Agreement (CUSTA) Panel, again at the instigation of the USA, investigated the issue of dumping. In this case, the CUSTA Panel, which reported in 1993, did not rule in favour of the US complaint. The threat of a trade war between the USA and Canada was only averted in 1994 following US threats of prohibitive tariffs on imports of grain from Canada (for a discussion, see Carter and MacLaren, 1997).

The most recent dispute between Canada and the USA relates to an anti-dumping investigation by the US Department of Commerce concerning the dumping of feed grains in the US market, concluded in late 1999. Perhaps the most interesting aspect of this case is the apparent cause of injury faced by US feed producers. As noted in the discussion above, the common assumption of single-desk trading is that it charges a high price in the inelastic demand markets, that is, the domestic or premium markets, while charging a low price on the rest-of-the-world market. Consequently, domestic users of grains would be expected to pay high prices which, if the downstream sector subsequently exported processed grain products, would make them uncompetitive. In October 1998, however, a coalition of US ranchers, Ranchers–Cattlemen Action Legal Fund (R–Calf), petitioned the US Department of Commerce to conduct an inquiry into the alleged subsidies provided to the Canadian cattle industry, the users of grain, owing to the activities of the CWB. This seems at odds with Figure 9.1, which suggests that the Canadian cattle industry would be adversely affected by the activities of the single-desk CWB. This was found in Australia for poultry producers from the AWB's activities (see Watson, 1999, p. 436), although the AWB denied that this effect was important (see AWB (International) Ltd, 2000, pp. 58–61).

In reconciling this apparently strange account of the consequences of the CWB, research by Carter et al. (1998) was used in the evidence provided by R–Calf in their submissions to the investigation. Specifically, Carter et al. argued that the CWB over-provided marketing services, such that it reduced the efficiency in the export of grains from Canada. They apply a Niskanen model of bureaucratic behaviour to the CWB, the key feature of which is that the bureaucracy maximizes its budget (Niskanen, 1967). In their adaptation of the model, Carter et al. assume that the CWB controls the size of its budget by determining its workload and its fee structure in order to maximize revenues in the handling market. Thus, the CWB over-provides marketing services and captures surplus from farmers. Carter et al. provide some empirical evidence to show that the marketing costs of the CWB are significantly higher than in a comparable benchmark market where a single-desk trader does not exist. In turn, this makes the CWB less competitive on world markets, reducing their exports and increasing sup-plies to the domestic market. The lower domestic price therefore lowers input costs for the Canadian cattle sector and so gives them a cost advan-tage in the US market.

Although the anti-dumping investigation did not find cause for injury, the analysis of the CWB in this case is interesting and suggests an outcome different from that suggested in Figure 9.1. Specifically, the dominant market status bestowed on the CWB causes it to be less efficient than a private sector counterpart. By exporting less, it sells more on the domestic market and so effectively subsidizes domestic users rather than taxing them. If these producers subsequently export, the activities of the CWB are equivalent to an upstream subsidy. Either way, the single-desk status has a trade consequence. If it is efficient and markets are segmented, it exports 'too much' and causes concern for other grain exporters. If it is relatively less efficient, it exports 'too little' grain but subsidizes the users of grain and so causes the downstream activities to export more than they would other-wise do. Either way, single-desk STEs affect trade and it is this trade impact that many countries wish to see addressed in the forthcoming WTO nego-tiations on agricultural trade policy.

5.   STATE TRADING ENTERPRISES AND THE WTO

So far, it has been suggested that, in discussing the links between competi-tion and trade, the focus should not be restricted to the activities of private firms. In highlighting the role and incidence of STEs, it has been argued that single-desk STEs in particular are associated with dominant positions in the supply of exports and, in some cases, also with respect to supplies to the domestic market. In principle, if markets are segmented, STEs may be able to exert market power which affects trade in foreign markets. It should be noted, however, that in spite of the recent emphasis on the STE issue, STEs have long been regarded by the GATT/WTO as legitimate players in trade. Moreover, a number of GATT articles refer explicitly to the activities of STEs, with the aim of limiting their impact on trade.

Specifically, Article XVII of the GATT addresses the state trading issue, whereby STEs are subject to the GATT principle of non-discrimination and MFN treatment (Article I) and should act on the basis of 'commercial considerations'. Further, Article II:4 states that, in the case of importing countries, STEs should not maintain mark-ups higher than the tariff levels bound in GATT. Restrictions on the activities of STEs are not limited to Articles I, II and XVII. They are also mentioned in Article III (on national treatment); Article XI (on the elimination of quantitative restrictions); Article XII (on restrictions to safeguard the balance of payments); Article XIII (on the non-discriminatory administration of quantitative restrictions); Article XIV (on exceptions to the rules on non-discrimination); Article XVI (on subsidies); and Article XVIII (regarding government assistance for economic development) in terms of import and export restrictions made effective through STEs. Moreover, some activities of STEs, while in economic terms an apparent cause for concern, are legitimate under the original GATT Articles. For example, the analysis above suggests that the exertion of market power allows single-desk STEs to price-discriminate but such activities are legitimate under GATT rules. An interpretative note to Article XVII states: 'The charging by a state enterprise of different prices for its sale of a product in different markets is not precluded by the provisions of this Article, provided that such different prices are charged for commercial reasons, to meet conditions of supply and demand in export markets' (WTO, 1994, p. 550).

Although STEs are regarded by GATT/WTO statutes as legitimate partners in trade, the fact that they are likely to emerge as a key part of the forthcoming negotiations suggests dissatisfaction with current rules, or at least the application of them, in dealing with STEs. For example, many key players in the negotiations, in their preliminary submission of their negotiating agenda to the WTO, have explicitly highlighted the STE issue. The USA has proposed to 'end exclusive rights to ensure private sector competition in markets controlled by single-desk exporters' (WTO, 2000a). It also proposes dealing with single-desk STEs in importing countries in a similar manner. A submission from Latin American exporters proposes 'to discipline the activities of governmental and non-governmental enterprises and marketing boards which benefit from monopoly import/export rights with a view to avoiding distorting effects on the market' (WTO, 2001). Perhaps most interesting of all is the negotiating stance of the EU. Often targeted for its use of export subsidies, the EU has linked further negotiations on the use and level of such subsidies to the issue of STEs. Specifically, 'that in respect of the operation of STEs, cross-subsidisation, price-pooling and other unfair trade practices in exports be abolished . . . On the condition that all forms of export subsidization are treated on *an equal footing*, the EC stand ready to negotiate further reductions in export subsidies' (WTO, 2000b, emphasis added).

It is notable that many of the leading players in the agricultural trade arena see STEs as a negotiating issue although how the negotiations will proceed is as yet unclear. In line with the discussion above, however, many countries view STEs as trade-distorting.[6] One potential way forward, therefore, is to attempt to measure the trade-distorting effect of STEs explicitly. There is a limited literature on this effect, the general idea being that the activities of STEs are equivalent to the use of standard trade policy instruments, the level of which can then be measured and their reduction negotiated (see, for example, Lloyd, 1982). Dixit and Josling (1997) mention this framework in direct connection with agricultural trade issues. One problem with these earlier contributions, however, is equating the presence of a single-desk STE with a monopoly in an export market for a homogeneous product which is assumed to be perfectly competitive. The consequence of this assumption is that the STE will limit its exports. This does not seem to concur with the concern that STEs export 'too much', contained in the submissions of WTO members who wish the issue of STEs to be addressed. More recently, this issue has been addressed by McCorriston and MacLaren (2001), who show that single-desk STEs which can price-discriminate between markets have an effect that is equivalent to an export subsidy. The level of the subsidy, however, and, in some cases, its sign depend upon the underlying benchmark: specifically, how competitive domestic and export markets are and on the existence of other forms of government intervention, such as price support policy.

6.   CONCLUSIONS

It is argued in this chapter that, in spite of the recent attention given to the link between competition and trade, with the typical emphasis on the behaviour of private firms, arguably the most immediate competition issue in the context of the WTO relates to the activities of STEs. Moreover, since the greatest incidence of STEs arises in agriculture, the issue of the impact of competition on trade is likely to arise in a sector where imperfect competition is seldom seen to be a major issue. As is outlined in the discussion, the focus is principally on the activities of single-desk STEs that can, allegedly, exercise their monopoly power across different markets through price discrimination and consequently raise overall returns to producers. The discussion of the activities of the Australian and Canadian Wheat Boards highlights the different ways in which STEs may affect trade. Although there has been public debate on the desirability of maintaining STEs, particularly in Australia, arguably the most immediate pressure for reform will come via WTO negotiations on agricultural trade, where many of the leading players have put the issue high on their agendas. It is too early to form a view on how far the debate in the WTO will progress, but one possible way forward is to measure the consequences of single-desk STEs directly. Given the relative lack of research on STEs on trade, research in this area is likely to be fruitful and relevant for trade negotiators.

NOTES

1. Mattoo (1998) provides a discussion of GATS and GATT rules for dealing with STEs.
2. The producer subsidy equivalent (PSE) is a measure of government support given to agriculture. Specifically, it is the payment that would be required to compensate farmers for the loss of government support and protection. Unlike other measures of trade protection, it also includes not just border protection but also domestic support such as deficiency payments.
3. An overview of the history and current debate surrounding the AWB can be found in Productivity Commission (2000).
4. In an empirical study, as part of the background for the AWB (International) submission to the NCP Inquiry, Gans and Hirschberg (2000) found that there were price premia; that is, the average export price received by the AWB was US$6.17 above the Pacific Northwest price of wheat on an FOB basis, about 4.35 per cent. The authors found that, using hedonic pricing, 60 per cent of this premium could be explained by transportation costs, seasonality and quality. They concluded that part of the unexplained 40 per cent was the result of AWB's single-desk activities.
5. Carter and Loyns (1996) document the history of the CWB.
6. There are two additional concerns in the agricultural sector that arise from the Uruguay Round Agreement on Agriculture (AoA). The first arises from the introduction of Tariff Rate Quotas and the alleged maladministration of these by importing-country STEs. The second arises because it is felt that exporting-country STEs have the opportunity to circumvent the restrictions placed on the use of export subsidies.

REFERENCES

Alston, J.M. and R. Gray (1998), 'Export subsidies and state trading: theory and application to Canadian wheat', in T. Yildirim, A. Schmitz and W.H. Furtan (eds), *World Agricultural Trade*, Boulder, CO: Westview Press, pp. 281–97.
AWB (Australian Wheat Board) (International) Ltd (2000), 'Review of the Wheat Marketing Act 1989', Submission to the National Competition Inquiry, 17 July.
Barros, P. and L. Cabral (1994), 'Merger policy in open economies', *European Economic Review*, **38** (5), 1041–55.
Carter, C.A. and R.M.A. Loyns (1996), 'The Canadian Wheat Board: its Role in North American Trading', mimeo, University of California, Davis.
Carter, C.A. and D. MacLaren (1997), 'Canada–U.S. Wheat Agreement of 1994', *American Journal of Agricultural Economics*, **79** (3), 703–14.
Carter, C.A., R.M.A. Loyns and D. Berwald (1998), 'Domestic costs of Statutory Marketing Authorities: the case of the Canadian Wheat Board', *American Journal of Agricultural Economics*, **80** (2), 313–24.
Dixit, P. and T. Josling (1997), 'State Trading in Agriculture: an Analytical

Framework', International Agricultural Trade Research Consortium, Working Paper 97–4, University of Minnesota.

Gans, J.S. (with J. Hirschberg) (2000), 'Competition and Single-Desk Selling of Wheat From Australia: an Economic Analysis, Technical Appendix B'. The Melbourne Business School, www.mbs.unimelb.edu.au/jgans/papers/awb.pdf, July.

Graham, E.M. and J.D. Richardson (1997), *Global Competition Policy*, Washington, DC: Institute for International Economics.

Hoekman, B. (1997), 'Competition policy and the world trading system', *World Economy*, **20** (4), 383–406.

Kraft, D.F., W.H. Furtan and E.W. Turchniewicz (1996), *Performance Evaluation of the Canadian Wheat Board*, Report for the Canadian Wheat Board, Winnipeg.

Lloyd, P.J. (1982), 'State trading and the theory of international trade', in M.M. Kostecki (ed.), *State Trading in International Markets*, New York: St Martin's Press, pp. 117–41.

McCorriston, S. and D. MacLaren (2001), 'The trade distorting impact of single-desk State Trading exporters', mimeo, University of Exeter.

Mattoo, A. (1998), 'Dealing with monopolies and State Trading Enterprises: WTO rules for goods and services', in T. Cottier and P.C. Mavroidis (eds), *State Trading in the 21st Century*, Ann Arbor, MI: Michigan University Press.

NCP-WMA Review Committee (2000), *National Competition Policy Review of the Wheat Marketing Act 1989*, Canberra.

Niskanen, W.A. (1967), 'The peculiar economics of bureaucracy', *American Economic Review*, **58** (May), 293–305.

OECD (2000), *Agricultural Policies in OECD Countries: Monitoring and Evaluation 2000*, Paris: OECD.

Productivity Commission (2000), 'Single-Desk Marketing: Assessing the Economic Arguments', Productivity Commission Staff Research Paper, Canberra.

Schmitz, A., R. Gray, T. Schmitz and G. Storey (1997), 'The CWB and Barley Marketing: Price Pooling and Single-Desk Selling', Report for the Canadian Wheat Board, Winnipeg.

Spencer, B.J. and R.W. Jones (1991), 'Vertical foreclosure and international trade policy', *Review of Economic Studies*, **58** (1), 153–70.

Watson, A.S. (1999), 'Grain marketing and national competition policy: reform or reaction?', *The Australian Journal of Agricultural and Resource Economics*, **43** (4), 429–55.

WTO (1994), *The Results of the Uruguay Round of Multilateral Trade Negotiations: The Legal Texts*, Geneva: WTO.

WTO (1997), *Annual Report 1997, Volume I*, Geneva: WTO.

WTO (2000a), 'Proposal for Comprehensive Long-Term Agricultural Trade Reform', Submission from the US, G/AG/NG/W/15, Geneva: WTO, 15 June.

WTO (2000b), 'EC Comprehensive Negotiating Proposal', G/AG/NG/W/90, Geneva: WTO, 14 December.

WTO (2001), 'State Trading Enterprises', Proposal by Argentina, Brazil, Paraguay and Uruguay (MERCOSUR), Chile and Colombia, G/AG/NG/W/104, Geneva: WTP, 23 January.

PART III

The World Trade Organization (WTO)

10. The WTO agenda and the developing countries

Sam Laird*

Since the Third Ministerial Meeting in Seattle in late 1999, members of the World Trade Organization (WTO) have made relatively little progress in resolving the issues that caused the breakdown at that Meeting. Doha set a broad agenda for a comprehensive new round of trade negotiations but developing countries feel that it is first necessary to address outstanding questions of implementation of the Uruguay Round. Divergences are such that it is unlikely that they will be resolved rapidly. Given the important changes that have taken place in trade and related polices in developing countries in the last 10–15 years, it is argued that developing countries have a strong interest in a relatively broad-based agenda provided that they can obtain both assurances that their concerns will be addressed and adequate technical assistance.

1. THE INTERESTS OF THE DEVELOPING COUNTRIES

Trade policy in the developing countries has changed in a major way since the mid-1980s. Under various lending programmes of the World Bank and the IMF, comprehensive macroeconomic and structural reform programmes were introduced across the developing world (Drabek and Laird, 1998). Trade policy reforms were a critical component in the reform packages, with many non-tariff barriers being swept away, tariffs being rationalized and reduced to averages which, with some important exceptions, are generally in the range of 10–20 per cent, and measures being introduced to facilitate trade. There is still more to be done: tariff peaks and escalation, anti-dumping procedures, licensing systems, local content plans and technical barriers are being used to protect certain sectors at the expense of other parts of the host economies. Nevertheless, these policy changes have made developing countries more stable and secure trading partners, stimulating new investment which has helped to achieve productivity gains and

227

enhance international competitiveness. Before the recent crises, the results were evident in a number of Asian and Latin American countries with falling levels of inflation and solid growth in the 1990s.

The Mexican financial crisis of December 1994 and the Asian, Russian and Brazilian crises put the reform programmes to the test. It seems certain, however, that where reforms were introduced, these helped to offset the worst effects of the more recent crises. There have been a few examples of trade policy reversals, notably through the imposition of temporary tariffs, increased vigilance on anti-dumping and special safeguards in the textiles and clothing sector (WTO, 1998a). These are generally within WTO commitments and have to be seen against the backdrop of continuing implementation of new liberalization commitments made in the Uruguay Round. Indeed, it is fair to say that these commitments have helped governments resist pressures for protectionist measures. In addition, the restructuring under the reform programmes has facilitated the recovery.

One reaction to the crises has been to stress the need for greater caution about globalization, and the IMF has been widely criticized for its caution. In terms of trade policy, however, reduced levels of sector-specific protection, a characteristic of earlier import-substitution policies, have helped to correct the previous anti-agricultural anti-export bias associated with such policies. It is also becoming evident that countries which have undertaken reforms are recovering relatively rapidly from the crises. It is also clear that, while there may be room to discuss the level of restraint, fiscal responsibility needs to be a crucial element of the reform agendas. Any expansion to offset the contraction associated with falling import demand has to be consistent with the need to stop inflation running out of control.

Additional efforts, however, may be needed to ensure that political and legal systems send the right signals of credibility and enforceability to the business community at home and abroad (Stiglitz, 1998). Anti-trust laws may need to be reinforced to ensure that open competition can prevail and the benefits of the reforms are passed on to consumers. The functioning of the judicial system in the area of commercial law might also usefully be examined for possible improvements. Support for the programmes among the general public can also be built through greater attention to the social agenda, strengthening social programmes to alleviate the more difficult phases of adaptation to more open economies and to education programmes – the most important investment in a country's own future. The Chilean experience of the 1990s also shows that this switch in emphasis need not mean foregoing rapid growth.

Overall, there has been a profound change in developing-country thinking about trade policy. Macroeconomic policy, rather than trade policy, is being used more effectively to address macroeconomic imbalances, including in the current account. Trade policy is now more open and neutral between sectors. It is also perceived that, in order to attract foreign direct investment (FDI) to achieve productivity gains, there is a need to demonstrate greater stability and credibility in trade regimes. This can be done by locking in the reforms through multilateral commitments: governance is a key idea in the WTO system of rights and obligations. This change in thinking means that many developing countries have a greater interest in applying and being seen to apply a wider range of disciplines in trade and related policies, consistent with the notion of improved governance that is part of the new development paradigm (Stiglitz, 1998).

On the other hand, it would be wrong to suppose that there are no dissenting views, and, even where there is agreement about the broad approach, some countries consider that a more measured pace of reform can avoid political problems that might arise in the case of more rapid change. In addition, a number of developing countries are unwilling to take on new WTO commitments before developed countries have met their commitments to liberalize trade in areas of special interest to them. These include: the application of Special and Differential (S&D) Treatment for developing countries; technical assistance to help developing countries implement the WTO Agreements and to be able to take advantage of the new dispute settlement mechanism (DSM); implementation of the WTO Agreement on Textiles and Clothing; the application of anti-dumping and safeguard measures; and problems of the least-developed countries. They have emphasized the need for a development dimension to future negotiations and, in this, they have also found support from a number of European countries.

It is important to draw a distinction between the negotiating position of the developing countries and their more fundamental economic interests. Clearly, it is to their advantage if their trading partners open their markets for developing-country exports. It is therefore normal for negotiators to take a hard line, saying that they will not make liberalization commitments unless new concessions and full implementation of earlier commitments are forthcoming from their trading partners. If this does not occur, the developing countries may still choose to liberalize but not to bind such commitments in the WTO. The dilemma is that such binding is also seen as providing security for foreign investors and the full benefits of the liberalization may not be achieved without it.

2. IMPLEMENTATION OF THE RESULTS OF THE URUGUAY ROUND

The first WTO Ministerial Meeting in Singapore in December 1996 agreed on reviews and other work on almost the entire range of WTO Agreements. In this respect, some of the more important and sensitive issues of particular interest to the developing countries include the operation of WTO Agreements in the areas of textiles and clothing, dispute settlement, anti-dumping, government procurement, regional trade agreements and technical barriers to trade, which are discussed further in this section. On the whole, the position of developing countries has been that, while developed countries may not have not broken any legal commitments, backloading and the use of other measures have offset the liberalization commitment and have gone against the spirit of the Agreements. On the other hand, a number of developing countries have also been asking for more time or technical assistance to allow them to meet their own commitments.

In looking at the implementation of the results of the Uruguay Round, one question that is frequently posed by developing countries is 'Where is the cheque?' This refers to estimates at the end of the Uruguay Round that the implementation would yield global welfare gains variously estimated to range between US$212 and US$510 billion, while the estimated gains for developing countries range between US$86 and US$122 billion (reviewed in Safadi and Laird, 1996). Since these estimates were cumulative over the implementation period, the gains for any individual developing country in one year could be quite modest. Moreover, these welfare gains are largely proportionate to each country's own liberalization efforts (ibid.). Thus, many developing countries lowered their bound MFN tariffs and increased the binding coverage in the Round. In many cases, however, their applied rates were already lower than the new bound levels, so that little tariff liberalization took place in a number of these countries and they should expect few direct gains as a result. There was also a backloading of liberalization in the textiles and clothing sector, so that the main export gains for many developing countries are expected from liberalization that has yet to take place. On the other hand, the calculations do not capture the positive contribution to trade liberalization made by the increasing application of multilateral disciplines by the developing countries or by their unilateral liberalization in the context of accession to the GATT/WTO. Thus, while the results of the models show substantial gains in welfare, they take little account of the importance of systemic issues.

Textiles and Clothing

Developing countries have raised concerns in the WTO Textiles Monitoring Body about the backloading of the integration process, the large number of safeguard measures in use, more restrictive use of rules of origin, tariff increases, the introduction of specific rates, minimum import-pricing regimes, labelling and certification requirements, the maintenance of balance of payments provisions affecting textiles and clothing, export visa requirements, as well as the double jeopardy arising from the application of anti-dumping measures to products covered by the Agreement. In spite of these concerns, however, the process of integration of the sector into the GATT 1994 is generally continuing as scheduled for completion by 2005. In principle, any further negotiations in this sector would be covered by the general approach to market access negotiations in manufactures (discussed in Chapter 2).

The WTO Dispute Settlement Mechanism

The WTO Dispute Settlement Mechanism (DSM) is one of the main features which distinguishes the WTO from the GATT, unifying the sometimes parallel processes in various GATT committees and strengthening the legal rigour of the system. In particular, this is the case through the new rule that a consensus is required to reject the findings of a panel whereas previously a party to a dispute could block the adoption of a panel report which went against it (reviewed in Hudec, 1999). There has been a large increase in the number of disputes being referred to panels and a large share of such cases also find their way to the new Appellate Body. It has been argued that the increase can be mainly attributed to the increased scope of WTO obligations rather than increased confidence in the new system (ibid.). In effect, the DSM is being used to clarify WTO rules in a way that would otherwise be difficult in the negotiating process. While developing countries are now major users of the DSM, Hudec also shows that their increased use of dispute settlement started before the WTO in the early 1990s. Nevertheless, since the WTO there has been a very substantial increase in cases against developing countries, many by other developing countries. However, the developing countries have also won some important cases against developed countries.

A key problem for developing countries is finding the expertise and resources to pursue a dispute settlement case. To address the problem, a number of developed and developing countries have announced the establishment of an Advisory Centre on WTO Law to provide advice to developing countries in relation to dispute settlement cases. Although complaints have been made by NGOs about certain findings, this is less a criticism of the DSM than the fundamental WTO rules on environment and competition policy. On the other hand, one concern that has emerged from the bananas cases is the use of the existing process to delay implementation of panel findings (see Chapter 11), for example, by changing practices through minor modifications which again have to be challenged, offering compensation or allowing the withdrawal of 'equivalent' concessions, thereby delaying implementation of panel findings. Ways of further streamlining the DSM to accelerate the procedures and enforce results, as well as US proposals to increase the transparency of panel proceedings, are under consideration.

WTO Rules on Anti-dumping

There is no explicit provision for a review of the operation of the WTO rules on anti-dumping although the Agreement on Implementation of Article VI of the GATT 1994 was one of the most contested areas in the Uruguay Round. An attempt to provide for a review in the Seattle draft Ministerial Declaration was resisted by the USA but finally accepted Doha. The Agreement sought to clarify provisions on: the computation of dumping margins; injury determination; the definition of domestic industry; investigation procedures; standards of evidence; and *de minimis* provisions for the termination of cases where the margin of dumping is less than 2 per cent or the market share of particular exporters lies below 3 per cent or, cumulatively, 7 per cent among exporters supplying less than a 3 per cent share. It also required greater transparency in relation to the conduct of anti-dumping procedures. Anti-dumping duties must be terminated after five years unless a new review demonstrates that the removal of duty would probably lead to continuation of dumping and injury. The Agreement did not include any provisions for anti-circumvention measures, but a Ministerial Declaration on Anti-Circumvention recognized the need to develop appropriate rules in this area. Developing countries were to be given special consideration, although there is little indication of such treatment. Indeed, developing countries are more targeted by developed countries than other countries (Miranda et al., 1998); moreover, they are often the target of such actions by other developing countries (Table 10.1). There has also been a resurgence in anti-dumping actions after 1995, particularly among developing countries as users of anti-dumping procedures (Miranda et al., 1998). These problems are argued to relate to the lack of appropriate implementation rather than to the Agreement itself and it is thought that they may be corrected by dispute settlement panels. This increase in the number of cases, however, underlines the risk that gains

Table 10.1 *Anti-dumping investigations by groups of reporting countries and countries investigated, 1987–97*

Reporting country group	Affected country group			
	Developed	Developing	Economies in transition	Total
Developed	570	591	340	1501
Developing	249	216	205	670
Economies in transition	24	0	1	25
Total	843	807	546	2196

Source: Miranda et al. (1998).

achieved through unilateral negotiations and in the market access negotiations may be subverted by anti-dumping actions. Thus, it is to be expected that countries affected will seek a strengthening of the rules to prevent abuse, while users will try to tighten the anti-circumvention rules.

Anti-dumping procedures have evidently become a general form of contingency protection given their increased use when economic conditions are difficult or imports increase following exchange rate appreciations. Some form of legalized backsliding may well be necessary in the WTO system. The revised safeguards provisions, intended to facilitate adjustment to import surges (and countervailing measures), are little used but there is some sign of resurgent voluntary export restraints (VERs) in automobiles, aluminium, and so on, albeit under other guises. Although it has been suggested that anti-dumping be replaced with rules on competition (as within the EU, the European Economic Area, the Canada–Chile FTA and ANZCERTA), the USA would be likely to find this approach unacceptable. Any re-examination of anti-dumping by itself could well be a sterile replay of the Uruguay Round negotiations and it may be useful to look again at the whole area of anti-dumping, countervailing measures and safeguards, including special safeguards under the Agreement on Textiles and Clothing and the Agreement on Agriculture (AoA), as a single package.

The Government Procurement Agreement

This is one of the two plurilateral agreements that are not covered by the Single Undertaking of the Uruguay Round and is essentially concerned

with procedures for the conduct of government procurement. Most developing countries have chosen not to become members other than those that
have been obliged to sign up in the accession process.[1] Under the GATT
and the GATS, purchases by governments are excluded from the national
treatment rules; instead, they fall within the scope of the GPA which covers
MFN treatment and national treatment in goods and services. Goods,
other than those for defence contracting, are covered by negative lists specific to each country, while defence items and entities procuring services are
specifically identified on a positive list. The Agreement does not reduce
market access restrictions but national treatment applies in the areas that
are covered. A number of provisions are intended to foster transparency
(Article IX) and to ensure that technical specifications do not create unnecessary obstacles to trade (Article VI).

Several reasons why developing countries have not acceded to the GPA
have been suggested (Hoekman and Mavroidis, 1997). One is to avoid the
costs of information and contract compliance associated with international
tendering procedures under the GPA. Again, large foreign companies may
be able to use their market power to drive out local firms before hiking their
prices, similar to predatory dumping. Domestic firms may be urging their
governments not to adhere – and corrupt officials may fear losses under
more transparent international tendering.[2] There may also be little pressure
on some countries to adhere to the GPA because their markets are of minor
importance and contracts are often tied to foreign aid. On the other hand,
developing countries may believe that they have little chance of winning
export contracts for which they would be able to tender if they were
members of the Agreement.

Overall, developing countries have a vested interest in obtaining goods
and services at the best prices for fiscal reasons. Signing on to the GPA
could therefore help them resist pressures to pay for higher-priced local
goods and services. It is not clear, however, whether a new negotiation
would go beyond an agreement on increased transparency in national legislation as well as procurement procedures, opportunities, tendering and
qualification, and so on, which many developing countries could be likely
to support. In this regard, considerable preparatory work has been undertaken in the WTO Working Group on Transparency in Government
Procurement.

Regional Trade Agreements

Some countries are seeking clarification of WTO rules on regional trade
agreements (RTAs) which spread rapidly in the 1990s. Although the process
of examination of RTAs has been streamlined since the creation of the

WTO, the examination process is effectively bogged down over certain systemic issues, namely, the meaning of key terms in the WTO provisions. These include the requirement that RTAs cover 'substantially all the trade' (goods) or 'substantial sectoral coverage' (services) and that 'other restrictive regulations of commerce' be eliminated on trade between RTA members while 'other regulations of commerce' not be increased against third countries – and how rules of origin are to be considered in this schema. Any clarification of these terms would have an effect on the examination of specific agreements, so participants in existing RTAs seem unlikely to accept clarifications that would require modifications to their agreements unless these were 'grandfathered'. Such a solution is unlikely to be acceptable to third countries. It is not clear how this impasse will be resolved unless perhaps through a shift in the emphasis towards periodic examinations to monitor developments in RTAs – similar to the Trade Policy Review Mechanism (Laird, 1999a). Any review might usefully look at clarifying preferential rules of origin, which is not covered by existing WTO work programmes.

Technical Barriers to Trade and Phytosanitary Measures

Technical barriers to trade and sanitary and phytosanitary measures have become the focus of a considerable number of trade disputes in the post-Uruguay Round era. The WTO Agreement on Technical Barriers to Trade (TBT) and the Agreement on Sanitary and Phytosanitary Measures (SPS) recognize that countries have the right to introduce measures necessary to protect human, animal and plant life. These measures, however, are not to be applied 'in a manner which would constitute a means of arbitrary or unjustifiable discrimination between WTO Members where the same conditions prevail or as a disguised restriction on trade'. Both Agreements promote the use of international standards, such as those of the ISO and the Codex Alimentarius Commission, and are intended to ensure that measures in these areas do not replace tariffs and other barriers reduced or eliminated in market access negotiations. Measures are to be based on scientific principles and evidence.

The second review of the TBT Agreement in 2000 was based on a work programme agreed at the first review in 1997. The review process could well lead to further negotiations linked to the negotiations in agriculture. Among the issues that have arisen in these areas are the use of growth hormones for beef cattle, genetically modified corn and soya beans, packaging and labelling requirements, requirements that fishing methods do not harm dolphins or sea turtles and regulations that limit the use of tropical timbers (Croome, 1998). Another concern is that the use of mutual recognition agreements between developed countries could effectively increase barriers to imports from third countries, mainly in the developing world.

The developing countries have diverse interests in any revision of these Agreements, but most are concerned about their lack of technical capacity in this area. This affects their ability to participate effectively in negotiations on standards, to meet notification requirements and to discern and meet standards for exports. While many are concerned that standards are being used for the protection of affected industries rather than health and safety reasons, other countries are concerned that disciplines should not be relaxed on the basis of non-scientific arguments (Croome, 1998).

3. THE BUILT-IN AGENDA

The built-in agenda may be considered to include negotiations in agriculture, services and, arguably, certain aspects of intellectual property rights (IPRs) where negotiations were already foreshadowed by the WTO Agreements of 1995.[3] These negotiations were begun in 2000.

Agriculture

The conclusion of the WTO Agreement on Agriculture (AoA) was a major achievement of the Uruguay Round. Some commentators, focusing on large-volume temperate zone commodities, have suggested that the tariffication process led to little increase in market access. It is also important, however, to draw attention to the substantial tariff cuts for a wide variety of fruits, vegetable and tropical products. Moreover, the Agreement brought the agricultural sector under more transparent rules. It also set the stage for future, progressive liberalization of trade in the sector and Article 20 of the Agreement already foreshadowed the start of new negotiations one year before the end of the current implementation period (six years from the start of the WTO in 1995), that is, in 2000. This process is now well under way. Under Article 20, it was agreed to take account of: (a) the experience to that date from implementing the reduction commitments; (b) the effects of the reduction commitments on world trade in agriculture; (c) non-trade concerns, S&D Treatment of developing-country members, the objective to establish a fair and market-oriented agricultural trading system and the other objectives and concerns mentioned in the preamble to this Agreement; and (d) what further commitments are necessary to achieve the long-term objective of 'substantial progressive reductions in support and protection resulting in fundamental reform' (Article 20).

Overall, it has been estimated that a further 40 per cent reduction in tariff protection and reduction of subsidies – the difference between producer prices and domestic market prices – in agriculture would lead to an increase in global welfare of the order of US$70 billion by 2005 (Hertel et al., 1999). The trade effects of the change involve substantial increases in imports by Western Europe, Japan, China, the Middle East, North Africa and India, while exports expand most in North and South America and Australia/ New Zealand, but there are also increases in a number of other newly industrializing countries. Efficiency and income gains are widespread across the developing world although it is estimated that there are net losers among the food importers, especially in North Africa. It also seems likely that there would be gains for the poorer rural communities of the developing world. Thus, developing countries have a keen interest in the agriculture negotiations.

Experience with the implementation of the Uruguay Round commitments has also highlighted a number of technical issues to be taken up in the new negotiations. These relate to aspects of market access, domestic supports and export subsidies, as well as the possible extension of the peace clause, state-trading, environment and sanitary and phytosanitary controls.

Market access
In the area of market access, average developed-country tariffs were to be reduced by an average of 36 per cent over 6 years from their 1986–88 base – 24 per cent over ten years in the case of developing countries – but reductions could be less steep on more sensitive products, provided the reduction was a minimum of 15 per cent on each tariff item. There is also a lack of transparency in about 20 per cent of agricultural tariffs resulting from the conversion of many non-tariff measures into specific rates, mixed or compound rates, as well as the continued use of variable levies and similar measures. Tariff quotas apply to some 1370 sensitive products and their allocation is sometimes used to favour some trading partners; the method of allocation is likely to receive some attention, as is the use of special safeguards which are potentially much more restrictive and selective than GATT Article XIX safeguards. Apart from the depth of tariff cut, the problems of tariff peaks and the dispersion of protection could usefully be addressed by establishing a general ceiling or even using a formula that would produce proportionately greater reductions of higher rates, as in the Swiss formula used for industrial products in the Tokyo Round (Laird, 1999b), although this might be hard for some importers to accept (see note 9, Chapter 2).

Domestic supports
Commitments under the WTO Agreement on domestic supports appear to be working, in concert with domestic budgetary limitations, to have

encouraged greater use of supports de-linked from production and set-aside programmes. It would appear reasonable to advance the process of reductions in the permitted levels of the aggregate measure of support (AMS). Limiting the AMS commitment to more narrowly defined sectors would also help to create a ratcheting-down effect, reducing governmental support in areas where such support continues to be linked to production. Developing countries will want to be mindful of the scope they now have under the 'green box' (permitted subsidies) in the use of certain measures to combat rural poverty, to promote alternatives to illicit crops, and so on. Although the word 'multifunctionality' disappeared from the final version of the Doha declaration, the use of supports for non-economic purposes will be an issue in the new negotiations.

Export subsidies

Members of the Cairns Group of agricultural exporters (Australia, New Zealand, most of Latin America and East Asia) are seeking the elimination of export subsidies, agreed in Doha, but it will be difficult to get the EU to go beyond some reduction commitment. A repeat of the key elements of the Uruguay Round negotiations covering volume and budget commitments in this area can therefore be envisaged. Immediately following the Round, relatively high international prices for grains and oilseeds, and perhaps the implementation of set-aside policies, reduced the use of export subsidies but the decline of such prices have seen a resurgence in their use and tensions are again high in this area.

At the end of the Uruguay Round, concerns were expressed that the removal of subsidies in agriculture would lead to higher food prices and that, in consequence, food-importing countries would experience a deterioration in their terms of trade. There were commitments to maintain adequate levels of food aid and agricultural export credits. These are certain to be issues in the agricultural negotiations.

Services

The inclusion of services negotiations in the built-in agenda was envisaged by Article XIX of the General Agreement on Trade in Services (GATS). As in the case of agriculture, these new negotiations were scheduled to begin 'not later than five years from the date of entry into force of the WTO Agreement . . .', that is, in 2000. These negotiations are now fully engaged and positive progress is being made.

The main area for negotiation will be the widening and deepening of specific commitments on market access and national treatment, although there has been considerable stress on the need for flexibility, particularly for developing countries. Negotiations are also mandated in areas such as MFN exemptions – which were, in principle, to last no longer than ten years – in maritime transport and air transport – both potential extensions of GATS to areas not already covered. The absence of customs tariffs or easily quantifiable NTMs makes it difficult to negotiate on expanded market access through the progressive reduction of intervention in services trade by means of any general negotiating formulas or other model approaches which would promote broad-based liberalization across members, sectors and modes of supply. This is why, beyond discussion of how GATT concepts of MFN and national treatment could be applied to trade in services, the Uruguay Round and subsequent sectoral negotiations focused on intra-sectoral reciprocity (Hoekman and Kostecki, 1995).[4] Nevertheless, approaching the new negotiations, it would appear that there is some interest in a formula approach which would allow for economies of scale, benchmarking and increased clarity of schedules as well as a broader balance of concessions, although it is not yet clear how this would work. One possibility for advancing the negotiations would be to start with the generally more extensive commitments undertaken by countries that have acceded to the WTO since its establishment.

The sectoral approach to the negotiations would appear to have the advantage of encouraging WTO members to make offers to liberalize in order to obtain services at world prices, including in the form of establishment, which are inputs to the production, transport and marketing of their exports. The disadvantage of the sectoral approach, which was used in the Uruguay Round, is the emphasis on reciprocal liberalization in key markets – comparable to the zero-for-zero negotiation in manufactures. Finding such a balance in narrowly defined sectoral negotiations in services proved difficult. Moreover, a number of developing countries, in particular, remained concerned about the perceived effects of opening up to FDI, the principal mode of supply for many services (Hoekman and Kostecki, 1995), and, initially, did not even want services included in the Uruguay Round. As a result, the specific commitments leave most trade in services unbound even where it is already liberalized.

Apart from the negotiations on market access and national treatment, another area for negotiation concerns the ongoing negotiations on GATS rules (for example, safeguards, subsidies and government procurement), disciplines for domestic regulation and Article XXI procedures (modification of schedules). Some developing countries would like to see a general safeguard mechanism for services without which their ability or willingness to make concessions would be limited. The inclusion of such a safeguard mechanism, however, could facilitate making commitments on Mode 4 –

the supply of services through the temporary movement of natural persons – not necessarily a result which they now envisage.

In the Uruguay Round, some developing countries were interested in obtaining commitments which would facilitate the presence of natural persons, but this mode of supply remained largely restricted except for human-capital-intensive segments and movements directly related to commercial presence. If no liberalization occurs in this sector, developing countries may use this as an excuse not to take on new commitments in the services negotiations, since Article XIX:2 of the GATS grants 'appropriate flexibility for individual developing countries for opening fewer sectors, liberalizing fewer types of transactions, progressively extending market access in line with their development situation and, when making access to their markets available to foreign service suppliers, attaching to it conditions aimed at achieving the objectives referred to in Article IV' (of increasing participation of the developing countries in world trade). Thus, in spite of the interest that developing countries have in gaining access to services at world prices, persuading them to lock in any commitments through binding offers will be difficult if they perceive that they are being offered little by way of improved market access for their exports of services and they can use Article XIX:2 to limit their offers. Nevertheless, the experience of the Uruguay Round indicates that there will be pressure on the developing countries to participate with meaningful offers. In addition, making such a commitment gives additional security of access which helps attract foreign investors so that, even without achieving reciprocity in concessions, developing countries should still have an interest in making binding commitments for their own sake.

The failure of the Seattle Meeting could run counter to these pressures for developing countries to make commitments in services. For example, it might have been expected that developing countries would have wished to make offers in services in order to obtain concessions in other areas, such as agriculture or industrial tariffs, especially on textiles and clothing. The absence of a potential trade-off in industrial tariffs could well limit their interest in the services negotiations.

Intellectual Property

The built-in agenda may also be considered to include certain aspects of the WTO Agreement on Trade-Related Aspects of Intellectual Property Rights (TRIPs), which developed rules establishing minimum standards of protection in the areas of copyright, trademarks, geographical indications, industrial design, patents, lay-out designs of integrated circuits and protection of undisclosed information. Specific points covered by the built-in agenda are noted in the 1996 Report of the Council for TRIPs (WTO, 1996). These relate to: geographical indications (Articles 23.4, 24.1 and 24.2 of the TRIPs Agreement); the question of certain exceptions to patentability (Article 27.3(b)); an examination of certain aspects of GATT 1994 provisions on dispute settlement (Article 64.3); and a review of the implementation of the Agreement (Article 71.1). Some of these elements had no specific time-frame for new negotiations except that the review of the provision permitting exceptions in respect of plant and animal patentability was to begin in 1999 and the review of implementation was to begin after January 2000.

Article 24.1 refers to an agreement to enter negotiations aimed at increasing the protection of individual geographical indications under Article 23, of which Article 23.4 refers to negotiations intended to lead to the establishment of a multilateral system of notification and registration of geographical indications for wines. In this regard, it has become evident in WTO discussions that some developing countries have an interest in the protection of traditional names, such as *basmati* and *tequila* (Croome, 1998). The review of Article 27.3(b) of the Agreement concerns the patentability of plants, animals and biotechnological processes but not in respect of micro-organisms, micro-biological processes and non-biological processes for the production of plants or animals. There is a requirement of some form of protection for plant varieties. The question of pharmaceutical patents has recently been the subject of extensive debate at a global level and a key legal confrontation in South Africa, highlighting the dilemma between public health issues and the need to provide incentives for future commercial research.

Regarding the general review of the implementation of the TRIPs Agreement, developing-country experience is still limited since they, and certain economies in transition, were given a five-year transition period – except for the national treatment and MFN commitments – compared to one year for the developed countries, whose legislation has now been reviewed. Least-developed countries have a transition period of 11 years and an even longer period may be allowed. The process of review of the developing countries' legislation started in the WTO in 2000 and is expected to continue for several years. Benefits through increased FDI and technology transfer were expected to accrue to developing countries that have already started to develop and export technology-intensive products and services. For developing countries that have less scope for attracting technology-intensive investments, exporting technology-intensive products and services or whose market size precludes such benefits from protection of intellectual property, however, there could be increased prices for products with a significant intellectual property component (Safadi and Laird,

1996). On the other hand, in the sensitive pharmaceuticals area, only about 9 per cent of drugs have patent protection, hardly any of which are essential drugs. The Doha Decision to facilitate compulsory licensing should increase the availability of cheap drugs to combat AIDS etc.

4.   BEYOND THE BUILT-IN AGENDA

At Doha, WTO members accepted the need to go beyond the built-in agenda covering agriculture and services. In the first instance, it was argued that the inclusion of industrial tariffs would allow cross-sectoral trade-offs in the market access negotiations. It was also argued that there is a need to further elaborate WTO rules in areas which are only partly covered by existing rules, such as investment, competition and environment. These, however, are highly sensitive issues for many countries, not only developing countries. Some countries would also like to see a linkage between trade sanctions and labour standards, but this is likely to remain a divisive issue, as it was at Seattle.

Manufactures

There is a widespread impression that industrial tariffs are now modest and that there is little to be gained from further tariff cuts. This is based on the fact that the trade-weighted average tariffs on industrial goods in the developed countries will be of the order of 3.5 per cent at the end of the implementation of the Uruguay Round. This does not, however, take account of the fact that these low averages conceal high tariff peaks and escalation with stages of processing (Laird, 1999b). Moreover, these high rates, in both developed- and developing-country markets, are often concentrated in products of export interest to the developing countries.

It is important to note that developing-country tariffs affecting imports of manufactures are substantially higher than such tariffs applied in the developed countries. Table 10.2 shows that, on average, developing countries' ('All low and middle-income countries') bound MFN tariffs on industrial products will be some 20 per cent after the implementation of the Uruguay Round, compared with 3.5 per cent in industrial-country ('High-income countries') markets. Moreover, there is a substantial margin between their bound and applied rates. In practice, applied rates may be somewhat lower because of preferences, but there is clearly scope for further liberalization of trade by developing countries in areas of export interest to each other.

Table 10.2   Trade-weighted industrial tariffs in the post-Uruguay Round period

Region	MFN bound	MFN applied	MFN applied, weighted by imports from low- & middle-income countries
High-income economies	3.5	2.5	4.4
All low and middle-income countries	20.0	13.3	13.3
East Asia and Pacific	15.8	12.3	13.6
Eastern Europe	9.5	6.4	6.3
Latin America	31.1	11.7	10.4
North Africa	38.4	26.4	19.7
South Asia	33.7	28.6	38.9
Sub-Saharan Africa	15.8	8.0	7.4

Source: Finger et al. (1996).

It is clear from these data that developing countries have much to gain from the inclusion of manufactures in a new round of negotiations, both in terms of gaining improved access and security of access to each other's (and developed-country) markets and in terms of the welfare gains from their own liberalization. Overall, it has been estimated that a 40 per cent reduction in industrial tariffs would lead to a global welfare gain of some US$70 billion, almost identical to that from a similar reduction in agriculture (Hertel et al., 1999). About half of these gains would accrue to the developing countries from global liberalization in the sector, mostly from their own liberalization (Hertel and Martin, 1999).

One issue of concern to developing countries is the possible erosion of tariff preferences such as those granted under the GSP. On the basis of partial equilibrium comparative static analysis, it is possible to compute putative small net negative effects for FTA members, ACP countries and least-developed countries (Safadi and Laird, 1996). This can lead beneficiaries of preferences, including those under RTAs, to oppose any reduction in MFN rates. This, however, has to be compared with the overall dynamic effects on the world economy through the implementation of the results of multilateral negotiations which are likely to benefit all countries. In such negotiations, developing countries may also be expected to gain from the erosion in intra-industrial country preferences, for example intra-EU trade, EU–EFTA, Canada–US trade, and so on.

A number of complex technical questions to be resolved in relation to tariff negotiations are reviewed in Laird (1999b).

Foreign Direct Investment

FDI (commercial presence) is much less emotive than some years ago but is still viewed with suspicion in a number of developing countries and a few developed countries.[5] Many developing countries are now actively promoting FDI to capture associated technology gains and market access and thus accelerate their own development and integration into the world economy. A number of countries, however, developed and developing, still place great emphasis on being able to impose conditions on inward FDI and the provision of support for investment by domestic firms. This attitude continues to block efforts to adopt a comprehensive framework for international investment, such as a multilateral agreement on investment (MAI) (discussed in Chapter 7). This issue is being studied in the WTO Working Group on Trade and Investment, established at the first WTO Ministerial Meeting in Singapore in December 1996. It is not evident, however, that this issue is ripe for any negotiation that would be the equivalent of bringing an MAI into the WTO. Nevertheless, this issue is now on the WTO agenda, including in the context of the negotiations on trade in services where FDI (commercial presence) is one of the main modes of supply. It also lies behind developing countries' interests, especially their automotive parts industries, in obtaining an extension of the time-period for implementing the Agreement on Trade-Related Investment Measures (TRIMs), which was scheduled to expire at the end of 1999.

Competition Policy

The issue of competition policy is being studied in the WTO Working Group on the Interaction between Trade and Competition Policy, which was also established by the Singapore Ministerial Meeting of the WTO (discussed in depth in Chapter 6). The Working Group has been receiving submissions from governments and other organizations as well as working closely with other organizations on the subject, particularly UNCTAD and the World Bank with which it organized two special symposia on the subject.

In spite of the large amount of work carried out so far, however, a number of developed and developing countries are opposed to negotiations on this issue. The idea of an international framework of competition rules, pressed for by the EU (WTO document WT/WGTCP/W/1) and supported by a number of Latin American countries, would tend to see a multilateral agreement as strengthening the domestic constituency for reform. The

USA (WTO document WT/WGTCP/W/6) and a number of developing countries would support the Study Programme but have expressed some reservations about where this might lead. This was recognized by the Working Group which, in its 1998 Report, recommended that the Group continue the educative work that it has been undertaking pursuant to the Singapore Ministerial Declaration. Negotiations start in 2003.

Some countries have highlighted the linkage between competition policy and WTO rules on anti-dumping. For example, Hong Kong China made a written contribution (WTO document WT/WGTCP/W/50) to the Working Group for such a discussion of the link between WTO provisions for trade remedies and competition and the liberalization of trade. The USA, however, takes a negative view of this proposal, which is probably dead – at least in the short term. Korea, supporting Hong Kong China, noted that the WTO Anti-Dumping Agreement did not make any distinction between monopolistic and non-monopolistic price discrimination; the latter could be of benefit to consumers.

Overall, research suggests that open and functioning competitive markets are the most conducive to economic development (WTO, 1997) and therefore developing countries should be supportive of work which would facilitate the functioning of markets. Different market structures, however, may require different competition or regulatory approaches. Thus, the precise regulatory framework needs to be tailored to each country's institutional capability. For example, if the market appears to be working, then a hands-off approach is indicated: competition, transparency and public pressures avoid the need for rules-based solutions. If formal rules are thought necessary to correct market failure, then there needs to be the political will and judicial institutions to enforce the rules in a transparent and stable manner. In this regard, any eventual agreement on a multilateral framework for competition policy could perhaps take the form of a code of conduct, as for other WTO Agreements, or agreement on a set of core principles that would not require any complex institutional structure where markets are seen to be working. To make the proposition for negotiations more attractive, some proponents have suggested exempting an eventual code on competition from WTO dispute settlement.

The Environment

The WTO Committee on Trade and Environment (CTE) was established in January 1995 with a mandate and terms of reference from the Marrakesh Ministerial Decision on Trade and Environment of 15 April 1994. In brief, these are to identify the relationship between trade measures and environmental measures in order to promote sustainable development. The

Committee is also to make appropriate recommendations on the need for: (i) rules to enhance positive interaction between trade and environmental measures, for the promotion of sustainable development, with special consideration to the needs of developing countries, in particular those of the least-developed; (ii) actions to avoid protectionist trade measures to ensure adherence to effective multilateral disciplines to ensure responsiveness of the multilateral trading system to environmental objectives set out in Agenda 21 and the Rio Declaration, in particular Principle 12; and (iii) surveillance of trade measures used for environmental purposes, of trade-related aspects of environmental measures which have significant trade effects and of effective implementation of the multilateral disciplines governing those measures.

Work in the Committee helped to improve the understanding of the issues and may, in so doing, have helped to lower the temperature of the debate between governments and between NGOs and the WTO (Croome, 1998). Negotiations were agreed in Doha, but while some kind of inter-governmental agreement may be desirable, it is not clear whether this should be in the specialized Multilateral Environment Agreements or in the WTO, which is becoming increasingly charged with new issues beyond its traditional competence. A negotiation could legitimize the use of trade measures applied for environmental reasons but set constraints on their use – as in the case of standards. Otherwise, the DSM may be used to clarify WTO rules, for example the scope of Article XX of GATT 1994, but this would not necessarily tackle the more fundamental problems, especially in relation to production processes.

Trade Facilitation

The notion of establishing some form of legal obligations around a core of simplified trade procedures has been proposed by the EU. This would essentially take the form of giving some teeth to the Kyoto Convention on Customs Administration, administered by the World Customs Organization. It is aimed at cutting red tape and bureaucratic formalities, thus reducing delays and the costs of doing business. A number of countries have introduced simplified clearance systems for exports, for example one-stop shops or single windows for documentation, but less effort has been made on the import side, in spite of the fact that they are often inputs into exports and lower-cost imports can improve the real income of consumers.

The proposal has attracted some support in the business community but it is not clear at this stage what form any Agreement would take. There has already been some work on the subject at the WTO, mainly based on assessing the very extensive work undertaken in other international organizations, such as UNCTAD, the Economic Commission for Europe and the International Chamber of Commerce. This is presumably an area where any agreement would also be most likely to require technical assistance to the developing countries in relation to implementation.

Electronic Commerce

The subject of electronic commerce is relatively new to the WTO, being first raised by the USA at the General Council in February 1998 and then in the Second Ministerial Meeting of the WTO in Geneva the following May. The rapid growth of such trade is essentially taking place outside the traditional framework of rules and the USA is proposing that this trade continue with taxation or regulation. As a result, at the Second Ministerial Meeting, Ministers agreed that the WTO study all trade-related issues relating to global commerce, taking account of the economic financial and development needs of the developing countries, and make recommendations to the following Ministerial Meeting in Seattle.[6] In the meantime, Ministers agreed on a standstill on the imposition of any duties on electronic transmissions, confirmed in Doha.

The focus of WTO discussion is the General Council, which has mandated other bodies to look more closely at the issue. For example, the issue is currently being studied in the WTO Council for Trade in Services since the electronic delivery of services falls within the scope of the GATS. Intellectual property aspects, however, are being examined in the TRIPs Council, and the Committee for Trade and Development is looking at developing countries' interests. A number of developing countries do not wish to foreclose the option of imposing duties on this kind of commerce, whether for revenue or other reasons.[7]

Labour Standards

The issue of any linkage between trade and core labour standards has been raised by the USA and a number of European countries. The highlighting of the issue in Seattle by President Clinton was of concern to many developing-country governments which regard the establishment of any such linkage as intended to restrict imports from low-labour cost sources.[8]

At the Singapore Ministerial Meeting of the WTO in December 1996, WTO Trade Ministers recognized that the International Labour Organization (ILO) was the competent body to set and deal with internationally recognized core labour standards. The Ministers noted that 'economic growth and development [were] fostered by increased trade and further trade liberalization contribute[d] to the promotion of these standards', and rejected the use of labour standards for protectionist purposes. They agreed that 'the comparative advantage of countries, particularly low-wage developing countries, must in no way be put into question'. In addition, at the Singapore Meeting, an agreed Interpretative Note stated that the issue of labour standards was not on the WTO's agenda, that no new work had been organized on the subject in the WTO and that the WTO had no competence in the matter, reaffirmed in Doha.

The exploitation of developing countries' comparative advantage, and hence their development prospects, depends upon their being able to export products which make relatively intensive use of low-wage unskilled labour. The shift to higher wages and better working conditions will come as they move through the development process. If there is insistence on higher wages and better working conditions in the short term, this could lead to lower levels of employment and a lower growth rate in the developing countries. Thus, the genuine humanitarian concerns regarding working conditions in the developing countries need to be balanced against the need to maintain employment levels and support effort to lift longer-term growth rates. Since longer-term growth in developing countries will, in turn, increase demand for imports from the industrial countries, short-term protectionism in the industrial countries can therefore also have long-term negative effects in those countries.

5.   SPECIAL AND DIFFERENTIAL TREATMENT

S&D Treatment for developing countries in the GATT/WTO system has been provided in two distinct ways. First, developed countries are exhorted in the GATT 1947 to increase trade opportunities in products of export interest to developing countries (WTO, 1999) and the GSP is the main way in which this has been granted. Second, there is provision in various WTO rules for the developing countries to take on less onerous obligations than other WTO members.

In the past, the developing countries made few tariff concessions or bindings under these provisions and acceded to few of the GATT plurilateral agreements. The situation changed radically in the Uruguay Round, largely as a result of the changes in thinking about trade liberalization, as noted in section 1. Developing countries also came to the view that the absence of commitments on their part had given them little leverage in seeking liberalization by the developed countries on products in which they had an export interest. In the Uruguay Round, however, the developing countries made a major break with the past in undertaking extensive bindings and reductions of bound (but not applied) rates, as well as acceding to the full range of WTO multilateral Agreements.

Nevertheless, there are still a number of areas where the WTO Agreements allow for S&D Treatment (WTO, 1999). In particular, the provisions aimed at increasing trade opportunities are those under Article XXXVII of the GATT 1994 Enabling Clause for goods, to which are added corresponding provisions in Article IV of the GATS. WTO members are also required to safeguard the interests of developing countries when they are applying technical barriers, including SPS measures, anti-dumping, countervailing or safeguard measures. On the other hand, developing countries also have flexibility in applying rules and disciplines governing the use of trade measures, for example, lesser commitments in tariff commitments, in reducing AMS in agriculture, greater scope for the use of subsidies (including export subsidies) and lesser liberalization of services. In addition, developing countries benefit from longer transitional periods than developed countries in applying many WTO Agreements. Finally, there are a number of provisions for technical assistance to the developing countries. There is, however, a limited WTO regular budget for such purposes. Putting technical assistance on a more secure footing was accepted in Doha.

There are also a number of provisions in favour of the least-developed countries. In the Singapore Ministerial Meeting, Ministers adopted an action plan for these countries. Under the plan, in October 1997, the WTO, in close collaboration with the IMF, ITC, UNCTAD, UNDP and the World Bank, organized a High Level Meeting on Integrated Initiatives for Least-Developed Countries' Trade and Development. The Meeting endorsed an integrated framework for trade-related technical assistance to improve their trade opportunities. As a result, many least-developed countries have made a needs assessment, including a wide range of WTO rules and obligations as well as supply-side constraints. In the current stage, the least-developed countries are organizing trade-related donor meetings to which they invite the development partners of their own choice to review and endorse a multi-year programme covering a portfolio of technical assistance projects. Up until now, however, the response by donors has been disappointing.

At the High Level Meeting, several developed- and developing-country WTO members indicated a number of steps to enhance market access opportunities for the least-developed countries. In this regard, Mike Moore, the Director-General of the WTO, has pushed hard for duty-free access for a range of products from the least-developed countries. The EU and some other developed countries have now implemented tariff-free, quota-free access for these countries on most trade.

6. CONCLUSIONS

The recent history of trade reforms means that the developing countries have an interest in a wider WTO agenda, but many of these countries remain concerned about the implementation of aspects of the Uruguay Round and their capacity to undertake new commitments. This means tackling implementation questions in a meaningful way, ensuring a wider development dimension in new negotiations and guaranteeing adequate technical support to developing countries. Doha goes a long way to meeting these concerns, but development provisions will need to be given substance in the new negotiations.

Developing countries could gain substantially from further liberalization in manufactures, the inclusion of which would also permit cross-sectoral bargaining, but this advantage would be defeated if certain sectors, such as textiles and clothing, were excluded. This broader agenda would also enhance the stake that export-oriented sectors have in pressing for liberalization, changing the political-economy dynamics within countries. For example, expanded opportunities for the export of manufactures may encourage developing countries to liberalize their services sectors further, so producing benefits to both user industries and consumers. Moreover, negotiated reductions of trade barriers on a broader scale can help avoid increasing intersectoral distortions which have negative effects on welfare.

How much further it is possible to move on the newer issues, such as investment, competition and environment, remains to be seen. To some extent, these are governance issues where the multilateral system can deliver a higher degree of commitment and transparency than more limited agreements. There are many points of common interest to developed and developing countries, all the more so as a result of the important changes in trade policy and, perhaps more significantly, the thinking about trade policy seen in developing countries in the last ten years. Policy-makers in groups of countries can build on these changes, on this new vision, and bring their experiences to help develop the multilateral system for the new millennium.

NOTES

*   The views expressed in this chapter are those of the author and do not necessarily represent the views of UNCTAD, the World Trade Organization or its member states. Helpful comments were received from Rolf Adlung, Matthijs Geuze, Costas Michalopoulos and Paul Shanahon. The author also benefited in particular from Croome (1998) and Michalopoulos (1999).

1. The other plurilateral agreement is that on civil aircraft. The agreements on dairy products and meat have been terminated.
2. The GPA prohibits preferences in favour of domestic suppliers. However, a preferential margin of 15 per cent for domestic suppliers is allowed under UNDP and World Bank lending operations which entail purchasing contracts.
3. The inclusion of IPR questions in the built-in agenda is disputed by some delegations, notably Australia.
4. If it were possible to compute a price wedge for specific services, then tariffication (or indirect taxation on foreign providers) could be an option, as in the Uruguay Round agricultural negotiations (Snape, 1994), but this does not appear to be under consideration by members of the WTO.
5. Developed countries such as France and Canada are concerned to preserve cultural exemptions for publishing and broadcasting.
6. Declaration on Electronic Global Commerce, WTO document WT/MIN(98)/DEC/2 of 26 May 1998.
7. An introduction to the topic by the WTO Secretariat has been issued as WTO (1998b). See also http://www.wto.org/wto/ecom/ecom.htm for further information.
8. However, at least some trade unions in developing countries would welcome this linkage which they believe would help strengthen workers' rights.

REFERENCES

Croome, J. (1998), 'The Present Outlook for Trade Negotiations in the World Trade Organization', Policy Research Working Paper No. 1992, Washington, DC: The World Bank.
Drabek, Z. and S. Laird (1998), 'Trade policy developments in emerging markets', *Journal of World Trade*, **32** (5) (October), 241–69.
Finger, J.M., M. Ingco and U. Reincke (1996), *The Uruguay Round: Statistics on Tariff Concessions Given & Received*, Washington, DC: The World Bank.
Hertel, T., K. Anderson, J.F. Francois and W. Martin (1999), 'Agriculture and Non-agricultural Liberalization in the Millennium Round', paper presented at the World Bank/WTO Conference on Agriculture and the New Trade Agenda in the WTO 2000 Negotiations, Geneva, 1–2 October 1999.
Hertel, T. and W. Martin (1999), 'Developing Countries' Interests in Liberalizing Manufactures Trade', paper presented at the World Bank/WTO Conference on Developing Countries and the Millennium Round, Geneva, 19–20 September.
Hoekman, B. and M. Kostecki (1995), *The Political Economy of the World Trading System*, Oxford: Oxford University Press.
Hoekman, B.M. and P.C. Mavroidis (eds) (1997), *Law and Policy in Public Purchasing*, Ann Arbor: University of Michigan Press.
Hudec, R. (1999), 'The new WTO Dispute Settlement Procedure: an overview of the first three years', *Minnesota Journal of Global Trade*, **8** (1), 1–53.
Laird, S. (1999a), 'Regional trade agreements – dangerous liaisons?', *The World Economy*, **22** (9), 1179–200.
Laird, S. (1999b), 'Multilateral approaches to market access negotiations', in M. Rodríguez Mendoza, P. Low and B. Kotschwar (eds), *Trade Rules in the Making*, Washington, DC: Brookings Institution and OAS, pp. 205–34.
Michalopoulos, C. (1999), 'Trade policy and market access issues for developing countries', Development Division, WTO, Geneva.

Miranda, J., R. Torres and M. Ruiz (1998), 'The international use of antidumping: 1987–1997', *Journal of World Trade*, **32** (5), 5–71.

Safadi, R. and S. Laird (1996), 'The Uruguay Round Agreements: impact on developing countries', *World Development*, **24** (7), 1223–42.

Snape, R. (1994), 'Principles in trade in services', in *The New World Trading System: Readings*, Paris: OECD, pp. 197–8.

Stiglitz, J. (1998), 'Towards a New Paradigm for Development: Strategies, Policies and Processes', Raúl Prebisch Lecture, UNCTAD, Geneva (19 October).

UNCTAD (1999), *Handbook of International Trade and Development Statistics 1996, 1997*, New York and Geneva: United Nations.

WTO (1996), *TRIPs*, Report of the Council, IP/C/8, 6 November, WTO: Geneva.

WTO (1997), *Annual Report 1997, Volume 1*, Geneva: WTO.

WTO (1998a), *Annual Report 1998, Volume 1*, Geneva: WTO.

WTO (1998b), *Electronic Commerce and the Role of the WTO*, Geneva: WTO.

WTO (1999), 'Background Document', WTO Development Division, prepared for the High Level Symposium on Trade and Development, Geneva, 17–18 March.

11. The EU–US WTO banana dispute and the evolution of the EU banana trade regime

Robert Read*

The acrimonious banana trade dispute between the European Union (EU) and the USA, which has only recently drawn to a close, was precipitated by the reorganization of the EU banana market to conform to the Single European Act. Successive EU proposals for the creation and implementation of a single market in bananas encountered substantial opposition from many quarters: from consumers within the EU, from producing countries – both preferred and non-preferred – as well as from the major firms involved in the international banana export trade. The EU–US banana trade dispute has its origins in long-standing commitments of EU member states to import bananas from former colonies in Africa, the Caribbean and Latin America and the EU's attempts to accommodate these interests simultaneously with its obligations to internationally agreed rules on the conduct of trade.

The development, course and ultimate resolution of the dispute is highly complex given the multitude of conflicting objectives of the many parties involved and the intricate application of international trade law under the GATT and WTO. This chapter provides an overview of the EU–US banana trade dispute from its origins, the successive legal challenges at the GATT and WTO and its final resolution in July 2001. This requires an understanding of the structure of the international banana economy together with the workings of the initial EU banana regime and the subsequent revised regimes. The penultimate section provides a brief discussion of the interaction between trade liberalization and competition in the EU banana market in the context of the WTO dispute.

1. THE INTERNATIONAL BANANA ECONOMY

The apparently esoteric concern of policy-makers and international institutions, particularly the WTO, with regulatory issues relating to international trade in bananas might seem to the non-specialist to be a rather trivial obsession with an exotic tropical fruit. Trade in bananas, however, is driven by the spatial separation of production in the tropics and consumption in the major industrial markets of North America, Europe and Japan. Bananas are the third most important internationally traded foodstuff by value, with total exports worth $US4.7 billion in 1999, after wheat ($US14.4 billion) and coffee ($US11.2 billion) (FAO, 2000). As such, bananas are a critically important cash crop for many developing countries as well as being a local staple food source.

The international banana economy is distinctly dualistic in its structure in terms of cultivation, technology and distribution networks. The greater part of world trade in bananas is undertaken, directly or indirectly, by a small number of multinational enterprises (MNEs). The three largest MNEs – Chiquita (originally United Fruit Co., later United Brands), Dole (originally Standard Fruit Co., later Castle & Cooke) and Del Monte – currently control some 60 per cent of world trade. Their distribution activities, however, are concentrated in the largest and wealthiest consuming markets so that their international market power is significantly greater than their apparent trade share. All three MNEs are highly vertically integrated, incorporating a chain of control from production, specialized refrigerated shipping and ripening facilities through, in some cases, to retail distribution. This vertical control is facilitated by significant economies of scale in technological inputs into cultivation and shipping in conjunction with the inherent perishability of bananas. Vertical control is a critical source of competitive advantage that enables the MNEs to assure consistent supplies to the main consuming markets of high-quality low-cost brand-differentiated fruit commanding price premia (Read, 1985).

A large number of smaller-scale firms, grower organizations and individual smallholders continue to be involved in export-oriented banana cultivation in parallel to the extensive operations of the MNEs. While these producers cannot supply such large quantities of high-quality fruit on a regular basis, they have been able to compete with the MNEs in many of the principal consuming markets. This has generally been on the basis of lower prices (and margins) for their smaller, less standardized but much wider varietal range of bananas, aided by preferential market access via discriminatory tariffs and quotas and the existence of independent supply chains.

2. THE HISTORICAL ORGANIZATION OF THE EU BANANA MARKET: THE MARK I EU TRADE REGIME

The origins of the historical organization of the banana market in the EU lie in the amalgamation of pre-existing obligations and arrangements of many member states to their former colonies, primarily in Africa and the Caribbean, in the Banana Protocol. This Protocol was subsequently incorporated as a special protocol (No. 5) of the Lomé Convention which formalized trade and aid relations between the EU member states and their former colonies, the African, Caribbean and Pacific (ACP) states. Article 1 of the EU Banana Protocol states that: 'no ACP exporter will be treated less favourably in its traditional European markets than it has been used to in the past'.

Preferential access for banana imports from the ACP countries under the Lomé Convention comprised a zero-rated tariff while imports from third countries, generally referred to as the dollar area, incurred the full Common Commercial Tariff (CCT) of 20 per cent. The specific conditions and application of the Banana Protocol were determined by individual EU member states in accordance with their long-standing obligations to particular ACP states. Member states therefore possessed the right to restrict or even exclude imports of bananas from 'non-traditional' sources even though they were classified as preferred under the Lomé Convention.

Several EU member states were also granted special protective provisions for imports of bananas from their overseas territories (Départements d'Outre Mer – DOMs). Initially, these provisions applied specifically to the French Caribbean DOMs of Guadeloupe and Martinique but, after the EU Accession of Portugal and Spain in 1986, they were extended to include Madeira and the Canary Islands respectively. DOM bananas have been eligible for price support payments under the EU's Common Agricultural Policy (CAP) since 1993.

The nationally determined discriminatory measures in EU member states were as follows. Two-thirds of the French market was reserved for DOM producers (Guadeloupe and Martinique) and the remaining third for CFA franc zone ACP states (Cameroun and Côte d'Ivoire). Only in the event of import prices exceeding a specified threshold were imports from alternative sources permitted, including those from other ACP states. Italy operated a global quota together with import licences, with special provisions reserving market share for imports from Somalia (an ACP member). The UK applied a global import quota but only issued import licences to dollar area supplies when imports from the ACP failed to fulfil the overall quota. Portugal had a derogation to protect its DOM producers in Madeira but permitted additional imports to supplement these supplies. The Spanish market was completely reserved for DOM shipments from the Canary Islands. Before enforced liberalization by the EU, Greece imposed a blanket ban on all banana imports to protect its own (very small) growers in Crete, the only producing area within the EU itself. Finally, under a special Protocol to the 1957 Treaty of Rome, (West) Germany was granted a derogation whereby all imports of bananas, regardless of their source, were permitted to enter its market free of all trade barriers. The complex structure of the EU's original trade regime for banana imports is shown in Table 11.1 using the structural typology of Read (1994a).

Table 11.1   The original Mark I EU banana trade regime

Type I:	Complete free trade in bananas, applied to Germany under a special Protocol of the Treaty of Rome.
Type II:	The standard CCT of 20 per cent for non-preferential bananas, applied to imports of bananas by Belgium, Denmark, Ireland, Luxembourg and the Netherlands.
Type III:	The standard CCT of 20 per cent for non-preferential bananas, applied together with additional specific national administered regimes by France, Italy, the UK, Portugal, Spain and Greece.

Source: Read (1994a).

The preferential structure of the Mark I EU banana trade regime was therefore further complicated by additional discriminatory import measures in some member states, creating a highly complex hierarchical system of preferences favouring specific supply sources implemented at the national level. In segmenting individual national markets, this protectionist regime would appear to have been incompatible with the fundamental objective of free trade within a common market in the EU. This segmentation of the EU market, however, was sanctioned under Article 115 of the Treaty of Rome (now Article 134 of the Treaty of Amsterdam) which permits a derogation from free trade in goods where national markets are subject to strict controls. The derogation for bananas remained in place for 35 years until July 1993.

The segmentation of the EU banana market under the Mark I regime had several consequences. The Article 115 derogation prevented the unrestricted movement of bananas within the EU, giving rise to significant market segmentation in accordance with the differing national import regimes. Table 11.1 reveals that there were eight separate and distinct trade regimes for bananas being applied in just 12 member state markets. Free trade occurred only in the German market and simple tariff protection prevailed in only the five relatively small Type II markets. In the Type III markets, dollar area bananas were effectively denied access to the large French and Spanish markets and greatly restricted in their access to the large UK market.

Market segmentation and restricted market access of this magnitude created sufficient scope for national supply and demand conditions to vary significantly and persistently, with potentially adverse implications for both prices and competition. This mix of national regimes raised prices to consumers above the world level by guaranteeing market shares to preferred suppliers regardless of their relative efficiency, thereby generating quota rents. This resulted in a distinctive pattern of banana imports and distorted the international pattern of production and trade. This pattern was further distorted by the impact of the EU's trade regime on the supply strategies of the MNEs. Chiquita, through its former UK subsidiary Fyffes, restructured its sourcing strategy so as to locate part of its production operations in several preferred ACP countries, notably Belize, Cameroun and Suriname. This strategy improved Chiquita's access to the EU market for bananas, in particular to the French and UK markets, enabling it to capture some of the available quota rents.

The welfare effects of the Mark I EU banana trade regime are analysed in an extensive empirical literature. There is a general consensus that this regime generated significant quota rents for producers in the preferred countries at the expense of EU consumers. There is, however, considerable disagreement as to the magnitude of these effects, determined by the underlying assumptions concerning the nature and impact of liberalization (see in particular, Borrell and Yang, 1990, 1992; Borrell, 1994, 1996; Read, 1994a; McCorriston and Sheldon, 1996; Guyomard et al., 1999).

The legal status of the Mark I EU banana trade regime can be queried under GATT/WTO rules on two counts. First, in granting preferences to the ACP states relative to the dollar area, the EU failed to apply the GATT principle of non-discrimination (Article XIII) under Part IV, the Generalized System of Preferences (GSP), with respect to imports from developing countries. This breach of Article XIII remained unchallenged for the duration of the original banana regime. Second, the derogation under Article 115 of the Treaty of Rome, permitting national market controls, was inconsistent with the spirit of GATT Article XXIV governing regional trade agreements (RTAs), since it was effectively permanent. Again, the status of this derogation remained unchallenged for the duration of the import regime. It could therefore be argued that many of the difficulties encountered in implementing a reformed EU banana regime might have been avoided if the status of the original regime had been subjected to earlier legal challenge.

It is pertinent to note that the European Commission has investigated several cases of alleged anti-competitive behaviour by the MNEs in the EU banana market. In 1978, Chiquita were found guilty of price-discriminating between EU national markets, illegal under Article 86 of the Treaty of Rome (Article 82 of the Treaty of Amsterdam) (Commission of the European Communities, 1978). Again, in 1990, they were found to have breached Article 85(i) (*ex* 81(i)) for attempting to restrict the use of the Fyffes brand name outside the UK and Ireland.

3. THE SINGLE EUROPEAN ACT AND THE MARK II EU BANANA TRADE REGIME

The impetus for the eventual reform of the EU's banana trade regime came from the Single European Act of 1986 which was intended to create a truly integrated market between EU member states effective 1 January 1993. The Single Market legislation made obligatory 'the right of third country imports to circulate freely without restriction' (Commission of the European Communities, 1986), so necessitating the abrogation of the Article 115 derogation for bananas. Further, it required a new and unified EU external trade regime for bananas compatible with the Single Market to be devised, regardless of its welfare implications. The objective of the new regime was to satisfy the legal requirement to establish a single internal market for bananas while simultaneously maintaining the preferential access of imports from the ACP (and DOM) in line with Article 1 of the Banana Protocol. Compatibility with GATT/WTO rules for the conduct for international trade was, at this time, of only secondary importance.

The structure of the single banana market regime, generally referred to as the Common Market Organisation (CMO) for bananas, was subject to lengthy internal negotiations which exposed deep divisions between the EU member states (outlined in Stevens, 1996; Cadot and Webber, 2000). The extensive delays in drafting the necessary legislation meant that the new CMO for bananas, under Council Regulation 404/93 (Commission of the European Communities, 1993), only became effective on 1 July 1993. This required the life of the original regime to be extended for a further six months as a stop-gap measure. Because of the need to be Single Market compatible, the new regime could only distinguish between imports by source and not by destination as well. The key elements of the Mark II regime are summarized in Table 11.2, utilizing a similar typology to that of Table 11.1.

There can be little doubt concerning the protectionist nature of both the Mark I and Mark II EU banana trade regimes. The primary intention of

Table 11.2   The Mark II EU banana trade regime

Type M_I:	Imports from the DOMs, subject to general and specific quotas.
Type M_{II}:	Imports from the ACP, subject to a general 'traditional' quota and specific quotas, all tariff-free.
Type M_{III}:	Dollar area and 'non-traditional' ACP imports, subject to a general quota of 2 million tonnes together with a fixed levy (tariff quota) of 100 ecus (euro) per tonne. Imports over the general quota were subject to a penalty levy of 850 ecus per tonne. Further, the right to import under the general quota was allocated according to licences: 'A' licences for 'traditional' dollar importers (66.5 per cent); 'B' licences for DOM and ACP importers (30 per cent); and 'C' licences for new entrants to the market (3.5 per cent).

the EU was to create a new regime which left unchanged the position of the principal constituent interests, EU consumers and preferred suppliers. The restrictive rules for Type M_{III} imports of dollar area and non-traditional ACP bananas, however, actually improved the relative position of the preferred sources at the expense of all other interest groups. For example, the equivalent *ad valorem* magnitude of the tariff quota on Type M_{III} imports was 21 per cent and 24 per cent, based upon figures for 1991 and 1992 respectively (Read, 1994a), compared with the previous *ad valorem* external tariff of 20 per cent. The *ad valorem* tariff equivalent magnitude of the new punitive penalty levy was 177 per cent and 206 per cent for 1991 and 1992 figures respectively (ibid). The Mark II regime was therefore more protective than the Mark I, a view supported by comparative empirical analysis of the two regimes (Borrell, 1994, 1996; Guyomard et al., 1999).

4.   THE INITIAL LEGAL CHALLENGES TO THE EU BANANA TRADE REGIME

The changes to the EU banana trade regime provoked a succession of legal challenges, both at the international level with respect to contravention of the GATT rules and also from interest groups within the EU. This section begins with the case brought by the German government against the European Commission followed by an outline of the two GATT complaints and the evolution of the EU banana regime in response.

Germany versus the European Commission

The six-month delay in implementing the Mark II banana regime in 1993 was partly a consequence of the German government filing a case against the European Commission in the European Court of Justice after the publication of the detailed proposals. The German government submission came in response to a vote by Deputies in the Bundestag (Lower House) regarding the loss of its national derogation under the Special Protocol and concern about the welfare impact of the Type M_{III} tariff quota on domestic consumers. Although there was little external support elsewhere in the EU for the first complaint, support for the second complaint also came from the Benelux countries. The strongest internal opposition to the Mark II EU banana import regime therefore came from those countries that had previously operated the most liberal import regimes (Types I and II).

The European Court of Justice decision in June 1993 ruled against the German and German/Benelux injunctions, so allowing the Commission to introduce the new banana trade regime on 1 July. The final ruling was published in October 1994. With respect to the removal of the German derogation under the Special Protocol, the Court argued that the EU, through the European Commission, had the sole right to determine external trade policy. The joint complaint by Germany and the Benelux countries was rejected on the grounds that the Type M_{III} tariff quota was not fixed over time and did not cause '*serious and irreparable damage*'.

The First GATT Complaint

The first complaint against the EU banana regime was made to the GATT in February 1993 (before the creation of the WTO) during the final negotiations of the structure of the revised banana regime and before the publication of the EU's proposals. The complaint was the outcome of a Joint Declaration at a Latin American Heads of Government Meeting in Ecuador by the Presidents of seven dollar area exporting countries to the effect that the proposed new banana regime was '*protectionist, discriminatory and restrictive*' (see Sutton, 1997). A formal complaint was made by five Latin American producing countries – Colombia, Costa Rica, Guatemala, Nicaragua and Venezuela – with the support of the USA. The complaint was, in effect, a shot across the bows of the EU in that it could only be considered in the context of the current banana regime, the stop-gap extension of the original Mark I regime (1 January to 30 June 1993). A complaint against the proposed Mark II regime that had yet to be finalized and implemented could not be sustained in that there was no actual contravention of the GATT rules. The first GATT complaint had two distinct elements:

- That the temporary regime and, by implication, the Mark I together with the proposed Mark II regimes, was contrary to GATT Article I.1 on the application of MFN to Special and Differential (S&D) Treatment under the GSP. This was because it incorporated a preferential tariff which discriminated between imports from the ACP states (zero-rated) and other developing countries (liable to the CCT of 20 per cent).
- That the restrictive tariff quotas in the temporary regime and, by implication, the Mark I and the proposed Mark II regimes, was contrary to GATT Article XIII.1 on the use of discriminatory tariff quotas.

The first element of the complaint had potentially wide-reaching ramifications in that it challenged the principle of granting discriminatory preferences to selected developing countries, such as under the Lomé Convention. The EU, however, was permitted to favour the ACP states over other developing countries under the Lomé Convention under what was then an annual derogation from the GATT known as the Lomé Waiver. The EU argued that its banana regime was consistent with GATT rules and other undertakings and that, if found, any inconsistencies were covered by the Lomé Waiver. In its decision, published on 3 June 1993, the GATT Panel found that there was no case to answer regarding the EU's discriminatory preferential tariff since this was fully covered by the Lomé Waiver (GATT, 1993).

The second element of the complaint referred to the use of discriminatory tariff quotas in the Type III national markets of the EU. Article X of the GATT regulations generally requires tariff quotas and penalty levies to be tariffied so as to provide greater transparency, although they may be permissible if applied to all imports. Tariffication, however, would have made explicit the deliberate objective of restricting general market access and discriminating between alternative supply sources via administered regulations in the Type III national markets. The GATT Panel decided with respect to this second element that the Lomé Waiver did not give the EU *carte blanche* in its use of discrimination. The derogation was only considered to apply specifically to tariff discrimination under Article I and not generally to include the use of tariff quotas under Article XIII and that they should therefore be brought into conformity with the GATT rules (GATT, 1993).

The two GATT complaints concerning the EU banana trade regime were subject to GATT disciplines and dispute settlement procedures since the WTO and its constituent agreements had not, as yet, been finalized and did not come into effect until 1 January 1995. The weakness of the GATT dispute settlement procedures and the lack of enforceability of a decision, given the need for unanimity, however, meant that the EU was able to veto the verdict and effectively ignore the adverse ruling. The GATT Panel decision was therefore unenforceable. The EU also argued that it did not need to respond to the adverse GATT Panel ruling on Article XIII because it applied to the temporary regime, which was to be superseded by the Mark II banana regime on 1 July 1993.

The Second GATT Complaint

The GATT complaint by the five Latin American countries was renewed in July 1993 with the belated introduction of the EU's Mark II banana trade regime after the expiry of the temporary regime. The grounds for the second GATT complaint were similar but not identical to those of the first. With regard to the implementation of discriminatory tariff quotas, the Mark II regime formalized their general EU-wide application to Type M_{II} and M_{III} imports in place of the specific national quotas used in the Type III markets under the Mark I and temporary regimes. Further, the Mark II regime introduced new special distribution import licences for M_{III} imports under the general quota. The second GATT complaint argued that these licences were in contravention of Article III.4 on national treatment in that they discriminated against non-EU banana distributors and therefore affected market access, especially given the market dominance of established EU distributors.

The general (EU-wide) tariff quota in the Mark II banana regime applied to all 'non-traditional' imports, regardless of source. It was designed to enable dollar area imports to continue to supply their own 'traditional' markets, so allowing the major banana companies to maintain their pre-existing EU market shares. The tariff quotas, however, were highly restrictive in that they were set in excess of best-ever levels of ACP banana exports to the EU such that they contravened Article XIII on discriminatory tariff quotas. The setting of the tariff quota at 2 million tonnes therefore effectively prevented the MNEs from using dollar area imports to penetrate the newly liberalized Type III national markets. Market penetration could only be achieved, and the punitive levies avoided, by switching the supplies away from the MNEs' 'traditional' markets. The tariff equivalent of imports under the tariff quota was just over 20 per cent but the tariff equivalent of the penalty levy averaged 125 per cent for the ACP and 175 per cent for the dollar area (Read, 1994a).

The special distribution licences were intended to improve the market access and competitiveness of DOM and ACP exporters by linking Type M_{III} imports to the internal distribution system via licence quotas. The licensing system was devised to encourage EU banana distributors to diversify their sources of supply, particularly the taking up of ACP supplies by traditional distributors of dollar area bananas. In addition, the system also encouraged distributors of 'traditional' imports in former Type III markets to penetrate Type I and II markets, previously dominated by the three MNEs. Because the licences were allocated according to the past distribution and marketing activities of the licensees, only 3.5 per cent of the quota was reserved for C licences which were freely available to new entrants to market 'non-traditional' ACP and/or dollar area bananas (see Table 11.2). The licences therefore did not determine the source of supply under the general and specific quotas but rather imposed restrictions on the competitive structure of distribution in the EU market. A draft proposal that licences be used to enforce the parallel marketing of ACP and dollar area bananas was dropped after encountering substantial opposition from the major firms and distributors. The new licensing arrangement had important competitive implications for the market structure under the Mark II banana trade regime because it greatly inhibited the contestable impact of entry by new competitors.

The second GATT Panel announced its decision on 11 February 1994. It found against the EU with respect to the use of the new tariff quotas in contravention of Article XIII because they were excessively restrictive and therefore not allocated broadly according to market share. In addition, the new licensing system was found to contravene Article X on national treatment because it unfairly restricted market access and was not permissible on the grounds that it was covered by the general applicability of the Lomé Waiver (GATT, 1994). Again, the inherent weaknesses of the GATT dispute settlement procedures enabled the EU to veto the adoption of the Panel decision. By this time, however, the Uruguay Round negotiations had, among other things, made significant progress in strengthening the WTO's dispute settlement procedures, with effect from 1 January 1995. Given the adverse second GATT Panel verdict concerning the use of tariff quotas and licences, the Mark II EU banana regime therefore became vulnerable to a complaint being made to the WTO.

The Mark III EU Banana Trade Regime: the Framework Agreement on Bananas

The threat of a further complaint against the Mark II banana regime under the new WTO dispute settlement procedures led the EU to enter into negotiations, brokered by the USA, with four of the original Latin American plaintiffs (excluding Guatemala) in an attempt to head off such a legal challenge. These negotiations took place in the context of the Uruguay Round discussions on market access in the Agreement on Agriculture and resulted in the drawing up of the Framework Agreement on Bananas in early 1994. Under this Agreement, the EU agreed to modify the Mark II banana regime by increasing the Type M_{III} general quota for dollar area and 'non-traditional' ACP imports to 2.2 million tonnes. In addition, the new Mark III regime also incorporated specific national quotas within the general quota for each of the four plaintiffs and permitted them to allocate their own import licences (Commission of the European Communities, 1994). In return, the four plaintiffs agreed to suspend any WTO complaint against the EU's banana regime until December 2002 (*Europe/Caribbean Confidential*, 1994).

The signing of the Framework Agreement and the subsequent withdrawal of the threatened complaint by four of the plaintiffs had two distinct effects. The Mark III EU banana import regime further complicated the original Mark II regime by extending the provisions for restrictive tariff quotas in the general Type M_{III} quota. It also increased the likelihood of a WTO legal challenge under Article XIII from dollar area exporters excluded from the Framework Agreement because it enabled the signatory countries to increase their banana exports to the EU at the expense of other dollar area exporters. While the Framework Agreement weakened the existing legal challenge, Guatemala persisted with its Article XIII complaint supported by the remaining dollar area exporting countries.

On 1 January 1995, an additional quota was created within the Mark III regime to take account of the EU Accession of Austria, Finland and Sweden. This autonomous quota of 353000 tonnes was added to M_{III} imports (dollar area and non-traditional ACP imports) with the same tariff rates applied and with quota allocations to all substantial suppliers.

5.   THE WTO COMPLAINT

The third complaint against the EU's banana trade regime was filed in September 1995 and resubmitted in February 1996 and was the first complaint to subject the EU banana regime to the discipline of WTO procedures, including the new and more effective DSP. The WTO complaint differed significantly from the two GATT complaints in that the USA participated as the lead plaintiff. It was supported by Guatemala, Honduras and Mexico and, after its WTO accession in 1996, Ecuador. The USA was not a direct party to the dispute in that only trade between the dollar area exporting countries and the EU was affected. In addition, the Framework Agreement, and therefore the Mark III regime, had actually been drawn up partly at the behest of the US government as part of the Uruguay Round negotiations.

This significant change in the policy stance of the USA was precipitated by the strategic shortcomings of Chiquita, the leading US banana firm, in dealing with the impact of the Mark II and Mark III EU banana regimes. In anticipating a single EU banana market, Chiquita's European supply strategy had switched towards concentrating on Latin American dollar area imports. In addition, Chiquita disposed of its UK and Ireland subsidiary Fyffes, which possessed ACP-based plantation and contract supply operations in Belize and Suriname (as well as Cameroun). This meant that the implementation of the restrictive tariff quotas for dollar area (Type M_{III}) imports under the Mark II and Mark III banana regimes had an adverse impact on Chiquita's EU market share. Its major competitors such as Dole, however, retained their diversified (dollar area and ACP) supply sources and/or acquired traditional distributors.

Chiquita, together with the Hawaiian Banana Association, filed an application under Section 301 of the US Trade Act in September 1994 alleging that the Mark III EU banana regime was detrimental to their own commercial interests and those of the USA. Chiquita's intensive lobbying, including substantial donations to both the Democratic and Republican Parties, produced a cross-party alliance of support from US Senators and Representatives. This pressure led to a Section 301 investigation of the Mark III regime being launched by US Trade Representative (USTR) Mickey Kantor on 17 October 1994 on the grounds of possible discriminatory treatment of US companies. After a preliminary investigation, USTR Mickey Kantor announced on 9 January 1995 that the structure of the Mark III regime, particularly the licensing system and specific quotas, was adversely affecting US economic interests through its discriminatory treatment of US firms. On 27 September 1995, this view was confirmed by the completed Section 301 investigation when Kantor announced that the USA would file a WTO complaint against the EU with respect to the use of the restrictive tariff quotas and distribution licences. The formal announcement of the US WTO complaint is alleged to have been made less than a day after a donation to the Democratic Party of some $US500000 from the Chairman of Chiquita, Carl Lindner (Chiquita's lobbying activities are outlined in Cadot and Webber, 2000). This initial WTO complaint was resubmitted on 7 February 1996 after Ecuador became an additional party to the dispute on acceding to the WTO.

In a further development, Mickey Kantor announced on 10 January 1996 that both Colombia and Costa Rica, as signatories of the Framework Agreement, had also been found to be harming US interests through the allocation of their EU tariff quotas. In return for not imposing trade sanctions, the USA successfully demanded that these two dollar area exporting countries agree to support them in the WTO case and reallocate some of their EU import licences to Chiquita and Dole.

The WTO banana complaint contained many similar elements to that of the first two GATT complaints but was filed according to the more complex rules of the new Uruguay Round Agreements, including the GATS which provided much greater scope for challenging the legality of the distribution licences. The key elements of the WTO complaint are outlined below.

Tariff issues

That the Mark III EU regime (and by implication the Mark I and II regimes) contravened Article I:1 of the GATT 1994 with regard to non-discrimination and the application of MFN with respect to the use of discriminatory tariffs favouring 'non-traditional' imports from ACP countries (WTO, 1997a, IV.2). Guatemala and Honduras also alleged that the Mark III regime (and by implication the Mark II regime) contravened Article II of the GATT 1994 with regard to the schedule of concessions in that *ad valorem* equivalent duties were, either actually or potentially, higher than the 20 per cent bound *ad valorem* CCT rate (WTO, 1997b, IV.96).

Tariff quota allocation issues

That the Mark III EU regime (and by implication the Mark I and II regimes) contravened Article XIII:1 of GATT 1994 with regard to non-discriminatory quantitative restrictions through the use of discriminatory tariff quotas. Guatemala and Honduras also alleged that it contravened Article I:1 of the GATT 1994 with regard to non-discrimination and the application of MFN with respect to the use of discriminatory tariff quotas favouring the ACP countries.

Import licensing regime issues

That the allocation of special distribution licences under the Mark III (and Mark II) regime and hurricane licences under the Mark III (and Mark II and Mark I) regime contravened the GATT 1994 Articles I, III:4, X:3, XI and XIII; the Agreement on Import Licensing Procedures Articles 1.2, 1.3, 3.2 and 3.5; TRIMs Articles 2 and 5; the Agreement on Agriculture Article 4.2; and GATS Articles II and XVII. More specifically GATT 1994 Article I on non-discrimination and MFN, Article III:4 on national treatment, Article X:3 on the impartial administration of trade regulations, Article XI on the general elimination of quantitative restrictions (included only in the plaintiffs' joint submission) and Article XIII on discriminatory quantitative restrictions (Guatemala, Honduras and Mexico only). The Agreement on Import Licensing Procedures Article 1.2 on conformity with GATT 1994 (Ecuador and Mexico), Article 1.3 on neutrality in the allocation of import licences, Article 3.2 on the non-restrictive effects of non-automatic import licences and Article 3.5 on the administration of non-automatic import licences (Mexico and the USA). TRIMs Article 2 on the consistency of national treatment and quantitative restrictions with GATT 1994 Articles III and XI and TRIMs Article 5 on the notification of TRIMs (Ecuador, Guatemala, Honduras and the USA). The Agreement on Agriculture Article 4.2 on the tariffication of quantitative restrictions (Ecuador only). GATS Article II on non-discrimination and MFN and Article XVII on national treatment (both Articles Ecuador, Mexico and the USA only).

The WTO Complaint and the DSP

It is clear from the details of the complaint that the new Uruguay Round Agreements provided much greater scope for a legal challenge to the special distribution licences in the Mark II/Mark III EU banana regimes at the WTO. In addition, one of the principal developments in the Uruguay Round was the introduction of a more effective fast-track DSP under the auspices of the WTO for resolving international trade disputes from 1 January 1996. The resubmitted WTO complaint against the EU banana regime Mark III therefore fell within the provisions of the new DSP. The DSP imposes a 60-day limit on consultation between the disputing parties, after which they may request the establishment of a dispute panel (for details, see Hoekman and Kostecki, 2001, Box 3.1). The failure of the parties in the banana dispute to agree upon a resolution within this time limit led to the convening of a WTO dispute panel in May 1996.

6. THE WTO PANEL DECISION

The WTO Dispute Panel for bananas published its four reports, one for each of the main plaintiffs (Guatemala and Honduras share a report), on 22 May 1997. Its principal findings are outlined below.

Tariff Issues

The WTO Panel noted that the EU's discriminatory tariff preferences for ACP bananas were inconsistent with GATT 1994 Article I:1 but found that there was no case to answer since its obligations were fully covered by the Lomé Waiver (WTO, 1997a, 7.136). With regard to the Article II complaint by Guatemala and Honduras, the Panel agreed with the second GATT Banana Panel that the EU duties were inconsistent with Article II (WTO, 1997b, 7.138). The Panel, however, decided that this inconsistency was cured by the EU's Uruguay Round Schedule such that the Article II complaint was rejected (WTO, 1997b, 7.141).

Tariff Quota Allocation Issues

The WTO Panel's findings concerning the Article XIII:1 complaint were based upon the successive analysis of points relating to the structure and allocation of the restrictive tariff quotas in the Mark III regime, that is, including the provisions of the Banana Framework Agreement. The EU argued that it operated two separate banana import regimes – one for traditional ACP imports and one for non-traditional imports (from the ACP and third countries), with the former based on tariff preferences and the latter on tariff quotas. It argued that each regime should therefore be analysed separately for consistency with the requirements of Article XIII. The plaintiffs, however, successfully argued that this distinction was contrary to Article XIII:1 and circumvented the non-discrimination provision of Article XIII (WTO, 1997a, 7.82).

The Panel then addressed the EU's obligations under GATT 1994 with respect to the issue of substantial interest regarding the Banana Framework Agreement. The Panel were satisfied on this point since Colombia and Costa Rica were the only GATT Contracting Parties with EU market shares over 10 per cent in the reference period (WTO, 1997a, 7.85). The Panel, however, found against the EU with respect to its allocation of tariff quota shares to WTO members without substantial interest (Nicaragua and Venezuela) under the Banana Framework Agreement but not to others, that is, Guatemala (WTO, 1997a, 7.90). Further, the Panel found against the EU with respect to its failure to allocate a tariff quota to Ecuador under this Agreement after its WTO accession in 1996 (WTO, 1997a, 7.93).

The Panel then considered the obligations of the EU under the Lomé Convention to allocate ACP tariff quota shares on the basis of pre-1991 best-ever exports. The Panel agreed that these tariff quota shares were acceptable under Article XIII:1 and therefore covered by the Lomé Waiver, but that tariff quota shares in excess of best-ever exports were not (WTO, 1997a, 7.110).

The Panel also found that the inclusion of the Banana Framework Agreement tariff quota shares in the Uruguay Round Schedule and the Agreement on Agriculture did not permit the EU to act inconsistently with the requirements of Article XIII (WTO, 1997a, 7.118, 7.127) (see McMahon, 2001). The Panel made no finding on the Article I complaint by Guatemala and Honduras relating to tariff quota shares since it preferred to tackle the issue under Article XIII (WTO, 1997b, 7.130).

Import Licensing Regime Issues

The WTO Panel analysis of the import licensing issues is extensive and complex, covering more than 200 paragraphs of legal arguments in the reports. The Panel found that the EU licensing procedures were subject to the scope of the Agreement on Import Licensing Procedures and that GATT 1994 and Article 2 of TRIMs were applicable (WTO, 1997a, 7.156, 7.163). The Panel investigated four principal elements of the EU licensing procedures: operator categories, activity functions, export certificates and hurricane licences.

Operator categories

This refers to the EU's distinction between importers of Type M_{III} imports in the Mark II and Mark III banana regimes in the allocation of licences according to origin, that is, non-traditional DOM and ACP imports (B licences) and non-traditional dollar area and third-country imports (C licences). As with the second GATT Panel, the WTO Panel found that the allocation of B licences was inconsistent with Article III:4 because it required importers to market DOM and ACP bananas if they wished to be allocated import licences for third-country banana imports (WTO, 1997a, 7.182). For the same reasons, the Panel found that the allocation of B licences in particular was inconsistent with Articles I:1 and X:3, specifically X:3(a), and that the Lomé Waiver did not apply to the EU's use of discretionary licences (WTO, 1997a, 7.204, 7.207, 7.212). In the discussion of the allocation of B licences under GATS, the Panel found that it created less favourable conditions for competition for like service suppliers of the complainants' origins such that it was inconsistent with GATS Articles XVII and II (WTO, 1997a, 7.341, 7.353).

Activity functions

This refers to the EU's allocation of A and B licences to operators according to their activity, that is, primary importers, secondary importers and ripeners. The plaintiffs argued that this required operators to change their pattern of economic activity so as to maximize their licence allocation while the EU countered that it limited the potential for vertical control of the distribution chain. The WTO Panel found that, because the EU treated all operators consistently regardless of category, the regime was consistent with Article III:4 but that the differential allocation of licences for traditional ACP imports was inconsistent with Articles I:1 and X:3(a) and that the Lomé Waiver was not applicable (WTO, 1997a, 7.219, 7.223, 7.226, 7.231). The Panel also found that the effect of the licences was to reallocate market share, so providing less favourable conditions for competition, and was inconsistent with GATS Article XVII (WTO, 1997a, 7.368).

Export certificates

These were required by holders of A and C licences for Type M_{III} imports from Colombia, Costa Rica and Nicaragua (Framework Agreement countries), that is, to be matched with import licences. The Panel found that this was inconsistent with GATT 1994 Article I:1 and GATS Articles XVII and II (WTO, 1997a, 7.231, 7.380, 7.385).

Hurricane licences

The EU has used these licences to facilitate compensatory non-traditional and third-country imports in cases where DOM and traditional ACP supplies have been adversely affected by hurricanes. The Panel found that the EU treated non-traditional and third-country imports less favourably in the allocation of hurricane licences even though their actual impact was beneficial in terms of increasing imports from these sources. The allocation of the licences was therefore inconsistent with GATT 1994 Articles III:4 and I:1 and Article 1.3 of the Agreement on Import Licensing Procedures although the Panel agreed that the Lomé Waiver was applicable to Article I:1 (WTO, 1997b, 7.250, 7.256, 7.259, 7.263). The Panel also found that the allocation of these licences was inconsistent with GATS Articles XVII and II for similar reasons to those of the operator categories and export certificates (WTO, 1997a, 7.393, 7.397).

WTO Panel Conclusions

The WTO Panel therefore found that the EU was in violation of its WTO commitments regarding the allocation of import licences and the use of tariff quotas, including the Framework Agreement on Bananas, but that the preferential tariff treatment of ACP exporting countries was permitted under the Lomé Waiver. The EU was therefore required to reform its banana import regime by January 1999 so as to comply with the WTO Panel decision.

7. THE SUBSEQUENT EVOLUTION OF THE EU BANANA TRADE REGIME

The adverse WTO Panel decision concerning the Mark III banana regime led the EU to engage in stalling tactics by using the appeals process to protest against the Panel's ruling. This was based primarily upon the Panel's interpretation of the Agreement on Agriculture in relation to Article XIII and the Lomé Waiver. The WTO Appellate Body report, published in September 1997, supported the Panel decision in the main and thus rejected the EU's appeal (WTO, 1997c).

The Mark IV EU Banana Trade Regime

After the failure of its appeal, the EU began the process of initiating changes to its banana trade regime in order to ensure compliance with the WTO Panel decision. These changes were published in July 1998 in preparation for the 1 January 1999 deadline (Commission of the European Communities, 1998a). The principal changes are shown in Table 11.3. In

Table 11.3   The Mark IV banana trade regime: revisions to the Mark II and III regimes

Type M_{II}: The general ACP quota set at 875 000 tonnes tariff-free with a preferential tariff for imports above this tariff quota.
Type M_{III}: • The 'non-traditional' GATT-bound tariff quota to remain at 2.2 million tonnes but with a tariff rate of 75 ecus (euro) per tonne. • The tariff rate for 'non-traditional' ACP imports to be reduced to zero. • A new and more transparent licence system granting rights to all importers active in the reference period 1994–96. Pure traders in import licences were excluded from this system (Commission of the European Communities, 1998b).

spite of these changes, there are few substantive differences between the Mark II, Mark III and Mark IV EU banana regimes. The principal changes are the considerable easing of the restrictive licensing conditions, a source of particular concern to both the Dispute Panel and the WTO Appellate Body, and the introduction of an autonomous quota. Very little was changed with respect to the critical issue of the use of restrictive tariff quotas and, as such, the Mark IV regime did not appear to comply with the WTO rules either.

The tariff quota issue was again identified as a problem by the plaintiff countries in August 1998. The EU then sought a Panel decision in December 1998 concerning the WTO compliance of its Mark IV banana trade regime. Ecuador retaliated by requesting the re-establishment of the WTO Panel to determine the legality of the changes to the EU regime. A further complaint was also made by the original plaintiffs (minus Ecuador but including Panama) concerning the EU's revisions to the regime in the light of the original Panel decision. The Panel convened at the request of the EU could not confirm that the revisions were WTO-compliant (WTO, 1999a, 5.1), a decision supported by the Panel for Ecuador (WTO, 1999b, 7.1).

The EU–USA Compensation Dispute

The WTO dispute then moved on to an arbitration panel. This panel found that the Mark IV regime continued to be non-compliant with the WTO rules such that the complainants were entitled to compensation via the nullification or impairment of trade benefits. On 3 March 1999, the USA announced punitive sanctions in the form of 100 per cent tariffs, worth $US520 million, on a targeted range of EU exports, including Scottish cashmere products. The decision of the Arbitration Panel was published on 9 April 1999 and stated that the USA had the right to impose sanctions to the value of $US191.4 million (WTO, 1999c, 8.1). The USA then requested authorization from the WTO for the suspension of trade concessions to the EU to this value. The Arbitration Panel also permitted sanctions by Ecuador against the EU to the value of $US201.6 million (WTO, 2000, paragraph 170), rather less than the $US450 million originally requested, but substantially greater than the annual value of its imports from the EU.

The pre-emptive announcement by the USA concerning its punitive sanctions against the EU resulted in a WTO complaint by the EU concerning the legality of the US action. The Panel found that the USA had, in pre-empting the decision of the Arbitration Panel, violated the GATT rules and the provisions of the dispute settlement procedures.

The Mark V EU Banana Trade Regime: Phases 1 and 2

The findings of the WTO Decision and Arbitration Panels against the EU and the consequent imposition of punitive trade sanctions resulted in the EU agreeing to make a number of changes to its banana import regime. Its immediate response was to consider several alternative means to resolve the dispute and to consult with the interested parties, the main problem being to amend the tariff quota system at the heart of the trade dispute. The details of the proposed Mark V banana regime were published in October 2000 and became effective on 1 July 2001 (Commission of the European Communities, 2001). Its implementation signalled the end of the US WTO complaint. The Mark V banana regime comprises two separate and distinct phases, detailed in Table 11.4.

The Mark V EU banana trade regime is of particular interest because it constitutes a significant change in the policy position of the European Commission concerning the WTO compatibility of its preferred regime. Phase 1 is a temporary continuation of the problematic tariff quota system. The introduction of a simple tariff-based system in Phase 2 in 2006, however, represents a fundamental shift in EU thinking and recognizes that

Table 11.4   The Mark V EU banana trade regime

Phase 1:   A transitional system based upon three separate tariff quotas open to
           imports from all origins to remain in place until 31 December 2005.
           • *A* Quota: A 2.2 million tonnes tariff quota at a rate of 75 euro
             bound in the WTO.
           • *B* Quota: A 53000 tonnes tariff quota at a rate of 75 euro.
           • *C* Quota: An autonomous tariff quota of 50000 tonnes at a rate of
             300 euro.
           Imports from the ACP to be zero-rated. Imports from third countries
           over and above the combined *A* and *B* tariff quotas, without
           adjustment of the *B* quota by the EU for market subject to exceptional
           circumstances, to incur a penalty levy of 300 euro per tonne (subject
           to revision). The tariff quotas to be allocated on a first-come first-
           served basis but in accordance with traditional trade flows and
           managed on a fortnightly or weekly basis to ensure a smooth flow of
           banana imports.

Phase 2:   A tariff-only system with a flat-rate tariff from 1 January 2006. The rate
           to be determined so as to provide *a level of protection and trade as close
           as possible to the system of tariff quotas* in order to maintain market
           balance and avoid losses for suppliers (emphasis added).

Source: Commission of the European Communities (2000).

its banana regime should, in future, be compliant with WTO rules for the
conduct of trade. It is important to note, however, that most of the interested parties in the dispute, and the exporting countries in particular, would
nevertheless actually prefer a managed tariff quota system to a flat-rate
tariff regime (Commission of the European Communities, 1999) in spite of
it not being WTO-compatible. The explanation for this apparently paradoxical preference is that, although the flat-rate tariff in Phase 2 will greatly
simplify the import regime, it will result in the loss of quota rents. Further,
it is also likely to lead to increased intensity of competition in the EU
market with an uncertain outcome for many participants.

8.   COMPETITION ISSUES IN THE EU BANANA MARKET

This discussion of the banana dispute has focused solely on trade policy
analysis and the legality of the EU import regime in the context of the
WTO rules for the conduct of international trade. It is well known,

however, that trade policy changes may have important market structure implications because of the critical interaction between trade, competition and contestability. The competitive effects of the reform of the EU banana market are therefore likely to be very significant in the context of trade liberalization since the market is characterized by oligopoly (see Holmes and Read, 2001).

Trade Reform and Competition in the EU Banana Market

The competition dimensions of the banana trade dispute have generally been overlooked and the remit of the WTO Panel was only to consider the legality of successive EU banana regimes. In the absence of an international agreement on competition, the competitive implications of the Panel decision were irrelevant and could not be considered. The need for the WTO to be able to consider the competitive effects of trade policy, as envisaged in the original 1947 Havana Charter of the ITO, is discussed in Chapter 6. Under current WTO legislation, competition policy remains the responsibility of national governments or supranational RTA bodies.

Several studies of the impact of trade liberalization on the EU banana market eschew a competition dimension by being predicated on free trade and perfectly competitive markets (Borrell and Yang, 1990, 1992; Borrell, 1994; Thagesen and Matthews, 1997; Hermann, 1999; Preville, 1999). A number of other studies recognizes that any welfare gains from liberalization could be substantially reduced by the oligopolistic market structure but do not attempt to assess their magnitude (Read, 1994a; Kersten, 1995; Guyomard et al., 1999).

It is clear, however, that the welfare and efficiency effects of trade policy cannot be treated as separate and distinct from the market structure implications of firm behaviour. Explicit analysis of the effects of trade liberalization on the imperfectly competitive EU banana market tend to focus on the German national market. This is primarily because, as the only Type I market in the Mark I regime, it is regarded as having approximated to free trade and was therefore the most contestable market in the EU (Borrell and Yang, 1990, 1992). Some evidence is found of the exercise of market power in the German market (Deodhar and Sheldon, 1995), although these results are disputed (Hermann and Sexton, 1999).

The implications of high concentration ratios combined with vertical control are analysed using a model of successive oligopoly for the UK banana market (McCorriston and Sheldon, 1996) and for the EU banana market as a whole (McCorriston, 2000). Both studies show that the welfare impact of banana trade reform on individual EU national markets, given imperfect markets with vertical control, is significantly reduced. In fact, the positive welfare effects of greater competitive intensity in the EU market are argued to be greater than the effects of trade liberalization (McCorriston, 2000). A more effective use of competition policy to regulate the EU banana market is argued to permit a much greater degree of trade liberalization and therefore generate substantial welfare gains for consumers without greatly compromising the position of preferred producers (Holmes and Read, 2001). This might certainly be feasible under Phase 2 of the Mark V banana regime.

Trade Reform and Competitive Behaviour in the EU Banana Market

The creation of the EU single market for bananas has affected the structure of competition through the effects of (successive) changes in the trade regime combined with the dynamics of firm interaction. It is possible to analyse these changes from two interrelated perspectives, that of the exporting countries and that of the individual firms active in the market.

The principal alternative sources of supply, the ACP, DOM and dollar area, experienced changes in their relative preferences in all of the EU national markets, most particularly in the former Type III markets of the Mark I regime. Under this regime, the supply positions of the ACP and DOM bananas in the Type III markets were relatively entrenched until 1993 because of the considerable magnitude of their margins of protection. In markets where they faced direct competition from dollar area imports (Type I and II markets), they tended to perform poorly for a variety of reasons (Read, 1994a). The expectation therefore was that many 'traditional' suppliers would be forced out of the market by the rigours of competition with the MNEs. This view was reinforced by the expansion of corporate plantation activities and supply contracts in several ACP states, notably Belize and Suriname but also Cameroun and Côte d'Ivoire, to take advantage of both the 'traditional' and 'non-traditional' ACP tariff quotas in the Mark II regime. The competitive structure of the EU market therefore changed as formerly heavily protected markets were penetrated by both dollar area imports and corporate ACP bananas although the expansion of their market share was inhibited by the restrictive licences and tariff quotas.

Chiquita anticipated that this liberalization would be coupled with the introduction of a general tariff quota. It therefore increased its shipments of dollar area bananas to the EU in the (correct) expectation that the quotas would be based upon retrospective import data, but also disposed of Fyffes and its associated ACP supplies. To achieve its former objective, Chiquita initiated a price war in the EU banana market so as to expand its market share in preparation for the Mark II regime quotas (see Arthur

D. Little International Inc., 1995; Commission of the European Communities, 1995; Cadot and Webber, 2000). This price war soon involved most of the leading suppliers in the EU market. Immediately after the start of the Mark II regime in July 1993, Chiquita initiated a further round of price reductions by 'dumping' bananas in targeted EU markets to enhance its market share and drive out both higher-cost ACP and DOM suppliers and also weaker distributors. Curiously, the EU competition authorities failed to take any action against Chiquita on this count (Holmes and Read, 2001).

A significant consequence of Chiquita's strategic behaviour was the exit from the EU banana market in 1996 of Geest, a UK distributor with an exclusive supply contract with the Windward Islands (see Read, 1994b). Geest's withdrawal was a direct outcome of the declining profitability of its banana operations, because of the prolonged effects of price-cutting by Chiquita in the UK market, and its high-cost ACP supply base in the Windward Islands – Dominica, Grenada, St Lucia and St Vincent (Arthur D. Little International Inc., 1995). Perhaps surprisingly, however, Geest's banana activities were acquired as a going concern by a joint venture between (a now independent) Fyffes and the Windward Island Banana Producers Association (Winban). This venture, successful to date, has been driven by the desire of the Windward Islands to gain greater control over the value-added derived from their dominant export, previously a source of friction with Geest (see Read, 1994b).

In spite of the strategic behaviour of the major banana firms, the market position of many preferred exporting countries has not been severely eroded, although some smaller growers have exited the sector. The resilience of many preferred suppliers has surprised commentators as well as the major banana firms, in particular Chiquita, which regarded the cost structures of the small ACP producers as unviable. Several reasons can be advanced for the continued survival of these smaller suppliers in spite of the increased intensity of competition. On the operational side, improvements include increased productivity, better quality control, more effective marketing and coordinated technical and managerial support from national marketing boards. The weak effect of economies of scale in banana cultivation, as opposed to those in technical inputs and shipping, has permitted the parallel development and coexistence of plantation and smallholder production (Read, 1985) and suggests potential scope for factor reversal. Smallholder banana cultivation, such as in the Windward Islands, is often characterized by inter-cropping with basic foodstuffs and used to generate small amounts of cash (Read, 1994b). Many smallholder producers therefore have a flexible labour input and have been willing to accept reduced margins. Nevertheless, the structure of output in the ACP exporting countries has changed as some smallholders have been squeezed out, therefore improving average productivity as the effective mean size of holdings has risen.

The continued survival of many preferred ACP and DOM banana producers also owes much to the continued generation of rents from the use of tariff quotas by the EU in its successive banana trade regimes. The WTO Panel also found that the import licensing system was itself discriminatory and had an inhibiting effect on the structure of competition in the EU banana market. In this case, the implementation of Phase 2 of the Mark V EU banana import regime may constitute a significantly greater threat to preferred suppliers than the previous regimes. This is because it commits the EU to opening up its market to 'true' competition, in which case there may well be a critical need for stricter enforcement of EU competition policy to regulate strategic behaviour by the major banana firms (Holmes and Read, 2001).

9. CONCLUSIONS: TRADE LIBERALIZATION, COMPETITION AND WELFARE IN THE EU BANANA MARKET

The GATT/WTO EU–US banana trade dispute, while extremely complex, has several important dimensions in terms of the interaction between trade liberalization, competition and welfare. Much of the discussion and analysis of the dispute here has taken place in the context of the WTO rules for the conduct of international trade. The underlying cause of the dispute, however, can be seen to be a battle between preferred ACP exporters and the MNEs over the allocation of quota rents in the EU market. In this respect, both sides can be seen to have lost out since the advent of Phase 2 of the Mark V import regime in 2006 will eliminate these rents through the introduction of a flat-rate tariff. A critical question remains as to whether the MNEs will be able to transform these former quota rents into oligopoly rents through the exercise of their market power. This will depend upon the willingness of the EU competition authorities to regulate the internal banana market effectively.

A particular irony of Phase 2 is that the elimination of quota rents in the EU market is a direct result of the US complaint to the WTO at the behest of the major banana firms. The US complaint was unusual in that it was based upon alleged discriminatory treatment of US firms in the EU market although no US jobs were at risk, exposing the USITC to criticism that it was in hock to corporate interests. The WTO complaint, however, has resulted in a likely reduction of the long-term profitability of Chiquita and

Dole in the EU market with the forthcoming introduction of a flat-rate tariff system. This is most probably contrary to their original desired objective of enhanced market power in a still heavily protected market which was a major source of company profits (Cadot and Webber, 2000).

The discussion of the banana dispute also highlights the interaction between competition and the regulation of international trade. This relates to the role of both the GATT and the WTO as arbiters of trade disputes with competition dimensions and the important distinction between free and fair trade. The WTO currently has no remit to consider the competitive dimensions of a trade dispute in spite of a need for such scope (see Chapter 6), exemplified by the oligopolistic structure of the international banana economy and the EU market.

The issue of free versus fair trade follows directly from the competition aspects of the regulation of international trade. The primary concern of the WTO is to enforce the agreed rules on international trade according to its articles and ruling on the legality of member states' trade regimes. Specific allowance is made for granting preferential market access to developing countries under the GSP in Part IV, subject to Article XIII. The EU has been permitted to discriminate between particular developing countries under the Lomé Waiver, an Article XIII derogation. A critical issue in the WTO banana dispute, however, has been the extent to which discrimination can be permitted under such a derogation. The WTO Panel ruled that the Lomé Waiver could only be applied to discrimination in accordance with the GATT 1994 rules such that tariff quotas, whether generally or specifically discriminatory, and restrictive licences were WTO-incompatible.

The problem for the EU has been that its historical obligations to the ACP, enshrined in the Lomé Convention, resulted in its discriminatory treatment of the dollar area developing countries, the principal supply source of the major US banana firms. The successive EU banana trade regimes, excluding Phase 2 of Mark V, can therefore be seen as attempts to utilize trade policy to achieve domestic competition objectives by hindering market penetration by the major banana firms. Having been found to be WTO-incompatible, this policy will have to be pursued via orthodox competition policy from 2006. The attempt by the EU to achieve multiple policy objectives in its successive banana regimes has been criticized for the priority given to special interests over an efficient and transparent trade policy (Read, 1994a; Wolf, 1999). The advent of Phase 2 of the Mark V regime will greatly improve the efficiency and transparency of the EU banana regime, with benefits for all consumers and some producers. Problems relating to restructuring in some ACP states will then have to be dealt with more directly via aid transfers.

The EU–US banana dispute highlights the improved workings and efficiency of the WTO DSP compared with the procedures under the GATT. Neither the EU nor the USA has emerged from this lengthy dispute particularly well (see Wolf, 1999). The EU has been guilty of dragging its feet and making use of the WTO Disputes and Appeals procedures to draw out the final decision and delay WTO-compliant reform of its successive banana regimes. The US action, at the behest of a corporate lobby and involving no material domestic loss, is questionable, although ultimately, the Panel decision is likely to be a Pyrrhic victory for the US banana firms. Further, the pre-emptive (and illegal) inflated initial US claim for trade sanctions worth $US520 million indicated a degree of contempt for the WTO and its DSP that does not augur well for future disputes. Nevertheless, the conclusion of the banana dispute in July 2001 can be regarded as a success for the WTO and its DSP. The dispute also demonstrates, however, that trade policy alone cannot be used to achieve distributional objectives and that free and fair trade requires a competition dimension (Holmes and Read, 2001).

NOTES

*   The analysis in this chapter has benefited from comments by participants at several conferences, including the Banana Session at the DESG Conference, University of Reading, July 1999 and the 24th Annual IESG Conference, University of Birmingham, September 1999. A shorter and less comprehensive version of this chapter, 'The Anatomy of the EU–US WTO Banana Trade Dispute', has appeared in the *Estey Centre Journal of International Law and Trade Policy* (2001). Particular thanks are owed to Peter Holmes, Michael Joseph, Bill Kerr, Sam Laird, Steve McCorriston, Nick Perdikis, Claudius Preville, Jim Rollo and Alan Swinbank.

REFERENCES

Arthur D. Little International Inc. (1995), *Evaluer les Effets de la Mise en Place de l'O.C.M. Bananes sur la Filière et sur les Sociétés Multinationales*, Paris: Arthur D. Little International Inc.

Borrell, B. (1994), 'EC Bananarama 1993', *World Bank Working Paper, WPS No. 1386*, Washington, DC: World Bank.

Borrell, B. (1996), 'Beyond EU Bananarama III: the story gets worse', Canberra: Centre for International Economics.

Borrell, B. and M. Yang (1990), 'EC Bananarama 1992', *World Bank Working Paper, WPS No. 523*, Washington, DC: World Bank.

Borrell, B. and M. Yang (1992), 'EC Bananarama 1992, the sequel', *World Bank Working Paper, WPS No. 958*, Washington, DC: World Bank.

Cadot, O. and D. Webber (2000), 'Banana splits and banana slips: the European and transatlantic politics of bananas', mimeo.

Commission of the European Communities (1978), *United Brands v Commission*, European Court Report 1987, p. 207.

Commission of the European Communities (1986), *Single European Act.*

Commission of the European Communities (1993), 'Council Regulation 404/93 on the common organisation of the market in bananas', *Official Journal*, No. L47.

Commission of the European Communities (1994), 'Council Regulation 3224/94 on the Framework Agreement on Bananas', *Official Journal*, No. L337/72.

Commission of the European Communities (1995), 'Report on the operation of the banana regime', Brussels.

Commission of the European Communities (1998a), 'Council Regulation 1637/98 on the common organisation of the market in bananas', *Official Journal*, No. L210/28.

Commission of the European Communities (1998b), 'Council Regulation 2362/98 on the common organisation of the market in bananas', *Official Journal*, No. L293/332.

Commission of the European Communities (1999), 'Commission proposes to modify the EU's banana regime', Press Release IB99/828, 10 November.

Commission of the European Communities (2000), 'Commission proposes solution to end banana dispute', http://europe.eu.int/comm/trade/whats_new/ebd. htm, 4 October.

Commission of the European Communities (2001), 'Council Regulation 216/2001 on the common organisation of the market in bananas', *Official Journal*, No. L31/2.

Deodhar, S. and I.M. Sheldon (1995), 'Is foreign trade (im)perfectly competitive?: an analysis of the German market for banana imports', *Journal of Agricultural Economics*, **46** (4), 336–48.

Europe/Caribbean Confidential (1994), 19 April.

FAO (2000), *Trade Yearbook, 1999*, Rome: FAO.

GATT (1993), *Panel Report on 'EEC – Member States' Import Regime for Bananas'*, DS32/R.

GATT (1994), *Panel Report on 'EEC – Import Regime for Bananas'*, DS38/R.

Guyomard, H., C. Laroche and C. Le Mouel (1999), 'An economic assessment of the Common Market Organisation for banana imports', *Agricultural Economics*, **20**, 105–20.

Hermann, R. (1999), 'Economic impacts of the new European banana regime: the case of Germany', *Jahrbücher für Nationalökonomie und Statistik*, **218** (1/2), 63–84.

Hermann, R and R. Sexton (1999), 'Re-distributive implications of a tariff-rate quota policy: how market structure and conduct matter', *Discussion Papers in Agricultural Economics*, No. 52, University of Giessen.

Hoekman, B.M. and M.M. Kostecki (2001), *The Political Economy of the World Trading System: the WTO and Beyond*, 2nd edn, Oxford: Oxford University Press.

Holmes, P. and R. Read (2001), 'Competition policy, agriculture and the WTO', in J. McMahon (ed.), *Trade and Agriculture: Negotiating a New Agreement*, London: Cameron May, pp. 307–48.

Kersten, L. (1995), 'Impacts of the EU banana market regulation on international competition, trade and welfare', *European Review of Agricultural Economics*, **22** (3), 321–35.

McCorriston, S. (2000), 'Market structure issues and the evaluation of the reform of the EU banana regime', *World Economy*, **23** (7), 923–37.

McCorriston, S. and I.M. Sheldon (1996), 'Trade reform in vertically-related markets', *Oxford Economic Papers*, **48** (4), 664–72.

McMahon, J. (2001), 'Clear and present danger? dispute resolution in agriculture', in J. McMahon (ed.), *Trade and Agriculture: Negotiating a New Agreement*, London: Cameron May, pp. 249–76.

Preville, C. (1999), 'How will free trade impact on net global economic welfare: an analysis of the EU's banana market structure', paper presented at the Banana Session of the UK Development Economics Study Group Annual Conference, University of Reading, 9 and 10 July.

Read, R. (1985), 'The banana export industry: oligopoly and barriers to entry', in M.C. Casson (ed.), *Multinationals and World Trade: Vertical Integration and the Division of Labour in World Industries*, London: Allen & Unwin, pp. 317–42.

Read, R. (1994a), 'The EC internal banana market: the issues and the dilemma', *World Economy*, **17** (2), 219–35.

Read, R. (1994b), 'Small-scale banana growers in the Windward Islands: external implications of the Single European Market', in T. Lloyd and O. Morrissey (eds), *Poverty, Inequality and Rural Development: Case Studies in Economic Development, Volume 3*, Basingstoke: Macmillan, pp. 184–207.

Stevens C. (1996), 'EU policy for the banana market: the external impact of internal policies', in H. Wallace and W. Wallace (eds), *Policy-Making in the European Union*, Oxford: Oxford University Press, pp. 325–51.

Sutton, P. (1997), 'The banana regime of the European Union, the Caribbean and Latin America', *Journal of Interamerican Studies and World Affairs*, **30** (2), 5–36.

Thagesen, R. and A. Matthews (1997), 'The EU's common banana regime: an initial evaluation', *Journal of Common Market Studies*, **35** (9), 315–27.

Wolf, M. (1999), 'Going bananas', *Financial Times*, 24 March, p. 18.

WTO (1997a), *European Communities – Regime for the Importation, Sale and Distribution of Bananas, Complaint by the United States, Report of the Panel*, Geneva: WTO, WT/DS27/R/USA.

WTO (1997b), *European Communities – Regime for the Importation, Sale and Distribution of Bananas, Complaint by Guatemala, Report of the Panel*, Geneva: WTO, WT/DS27/R/GTM.

WTO (1997c), *European Communities – Regime for the Importation, Sale and Distribution of Bananas, Report of the Appellate Body*, Geneva: WTO, WT/DS/27/AB/R.

WTO (1999a), *European Communities – Regime for the Importation, Sale and Distribution of Bananas – Recourse to Article 21.5 by the European Communities, Report of the Panel*, Geneva: WTO, WT/DS27/RW/EEC.

WTO (1999b), *European Communities – Regime for the Importation, Sale and Distribution of Bananas – Recourse to Article 21.5 by Ecuador, Report of the Panel*, Geneva: WTO, WT/DS27/RW/ECU.

WTO (1999c), *European Communities – Regime for the Importation, Sale and Distribution of Bananas – Recourse to Arbitration by the European Communities Under Articles 22.6 of the DSU, Decision by the Arbitrators*, Geneva: WTO, WT/DS27/ARB.

WTO (2000), *European Communities – Regime for the Importation, Sale and Distribution of Bananas – Recourse to Arbitration by the European Communities Under Articles 22.6 of the DSU, Decision by the Arbitrators*, Geneva: WTO, WT/DS27/ARB/ECU.

12. The influence of the WTO on patenting activities in China

Derek Bosworth and Deli Yang

The introduction of the Open Door policy in 1979 and subsequent economic reform have necessitated the establishment of an intellectual property system in China. The national objectives of these changes are to encourage capital and technology inflows from foreign countries to boost China's overall economic development. The lack of appropriate intellectual property rights (IPR) protection acts as a barrier to inflows of advanced technology from overseas. The willingness of China to introduce IPR protection reflects a growing recognition of the critical need to gain access to advanced technology to improve domestic competitiveness and promote development (O'Connor and Lowe, 1996). Since 1979, there has been a profound change in the view of IPR protection in China: from a situation of not understanding the concept of intellectual property before 1979 to a country that now operates a system of IPR protection. The WTO has played an important role in this process of change. This chapter outlines the current patent system in China and the rationale for its establishment. In doing so, it focuses on the major role of the WTO.

During the 1980s, China promulgated its first Patent Law, established the Patent Office and created judicial protection for patents. The creation of this triple control system is the consequence of both the internal desire for advanced technology and external pressure from the industrialized countries and international organizations, such as the World Intellectual Property Organization (WIPO) and the WTO. The influence of the WTO is clearly reflected in the development of the patent system and the subsequent dramatic changes in the extent of patenting activity in China, especially in the early 1990s. The next section provides a brief introduction to the Chinese patent system and its evolution followed by an analysis of the reasons for its establishment (section 2). Section 3 describes the amendment of the Patent Law, based on the WTO Trade-Related Aspects of Intellectual Property Rights (TRIPs). A statistical analysis in section 4 demonstrates the impact on patenting activities in China. The final section carries out a comparative study of the gaps between the TRIPs Agreement and the Chinese patent system.

Before going further, it is useful to clarify some of the terminology used here. 'Patenting activity' refers to the application and approval of patents within China, from both Chinese and foreigners, including patents for inventions, utility models and industrial designs. 'Patents' refer to the exclusive rights given to inventors or creators for technological solutions relating to a product or process for a certain period of time. In the case of China, the duration is 20 years from the date of application. Any other people must pay a royalty to the owner for access to the invention or creation. 'Utility models' are the exclusive rights given to inventors or creators for minor technological solutions relating to a product or process for a certain period of time. They are sometimes called petty patents because of their lower degree of inventiveness compared to a patented invention. The duration of protection in China is ten years from the date of application. 'Industrial designs' are the rights given to designers for new patterns and/or colours with artistic features for industrial application. 'Patent flows' refer to the movement of patents into China or *vice versa*. This chapter is concerned only with the analysis of patent inflows of intellectual property into China.

1. THE CURRENT PATENT SYSTEM IN CHINA

China's first Patent Law was only enacted in 1984. Before this, inventions were administered by a reward system; that is, inventors only obtained a lump sum financial incentive from the government and they did not own their inventions and creations. The concept of private ownership was only introduced with the Open Door policy. Two laws currently guide patenting activities in China: the Patent Law and the Patent Implementation Law.

Patent Law in China

The current Patent Law is based on the major amendments to the 1984 and 1992 Patent Law introduced in 2000. Four other laws and regulations relating to patents were also promulgated in the early 1990s,[1] including the Patent Implementation Law. The Patent Law uses the 'first-to-file' patent system.[2] The Patent Law and other patent regulations protect three rights: over inventions, utility models and industrial designs if they are granted patent rights. An invention or a utility model must possess novelty, inventiveness and practical applicability. Novelty means no disclosure to the public and no use of the invention before the date of filing (Article 22, CPR,

1992a). Inventiveness refers to 'prominent substantive features' and 'notable progress' in inventions and 'substantive features and . . . progress' in utility models. Practical applicability is intended to imply that 'the invention or utility model can be made or used and can produce effective results' (Article 22). The duration of protection is 20 years for inventions and ten years for utility models and industrial designs from the date of filing (Article 45). Patent applications by foreigners are treated in accord with international conventions or bilateral agreements between China and the applicants' countries. Moreover, foreign applicants must appoint a patent agency[3] designated by the State Council in China to deal with patent related matters (Article 18).

By and large, China has established an ultra-modern patent system. 'Its parallel adoption of the Patent Co-operation Treaty brings China's patent laws to the front of all nations and helps comprise a system incorporating most of the best features of the "Basic Proposal" that emerged in Geneva' (Wegner, 1996).

Administrative Control of Patents in China

The administrative management for patents in China is shown in Figure 12.1. The responsibility of the administrative organs is to deal with specific patent issues, such as examination and approval of patent applications, interpretation of the law and regulations and supervision of patenting activities and administrative settlement for patent related disputes. Two administrative organizations deal with patent affairs: the Patent Office and the Patent Re-Examination Board (PREB), both established in 1984 directly under the supervision of the State Council.

The Patent Office is responsible for the preliminary examination and approval of patent applications and the interpretation of patent law and regulations. It is also responsible for international patent applications, interpretation and other international patent issues. The PREB, within the Patent Office, is responsible for the re-examination, upon request, of applications which have not been approved. In addition, both organizations can supervise patenting activities, stop any patent infringement or passing off, order for correction in public, impose a fine and request compensation. Fines range from 1000 to 50000 renminbi yuan or 100 to 300 per cent of illegal income (Article 78 of the Patent Implementation Law, CPR, 1992b). Moreover, disputes can be brought to the two organs for administrative settlement.

Several other organizations are also involved in patent administration, including the provincial-level Patent Offices and PREBs and ministerial government organizations. The provincial government organizations are

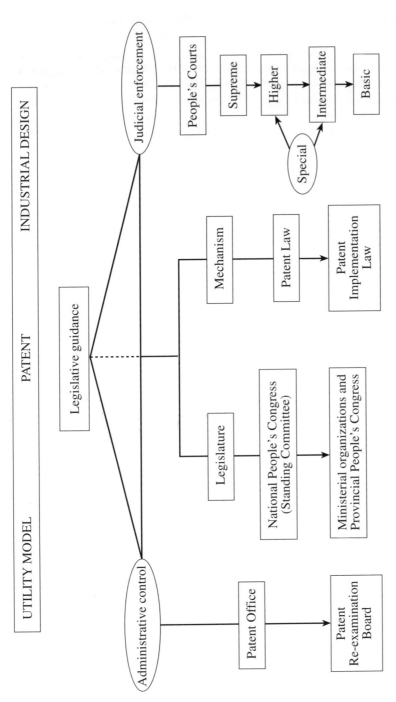

Source: Created based on the author's understanding of the Patent Law and the Patent Implementation Law.

Figure 12.1   The patent system in China

directly controlled by the central Patent Office and PREB and are responsible for supervising provincial patenting activities and dispute administration. Ministerial government organizations also engage in patenting administration associated with products. For instance, the State Drug Administration under the State Council has the Office for Administrative Protection of Pharmaceuticals to manage pharmaceutical products. If patents are related to trading abroad, supervision of protection is undertaken by the Ministry of Foreign Trade and Economic Co-operation (MoFTEC) and Customs.

The administrative control system has, to a great extent, exerted a strong influence on resolving disputes in China. For instance, by 1995, different administrative organizations had received 3248 cases, of which 2847 (88 per cent) had been resolved. In addition, only 6.5 per cent of the cases involved further legal proceedings (Wen, 1996). This can be explained by religious and cultural influence prevailing in China as well as the time and cost, because the judicial route is usually lengthy and expensive. Only in recent years has the legislative and judicial system gradually gained its importance.

Legislative Power in China

China has two tiers of legislative authority, so that both the central government and ministerial and provincial governments have the power to enact laws and regulations. The highest legislative tier is the National People's Congress (NPC), with members elected from different ministerial, provincial and autonomous regions for a term of five years. Its functions include: the amendment of the Constitution and enactment of laws; and supervision of the enforcement of these laws. The NPC functions through the Standing Committee, a permanent body of the NPC, and is responsible for, among other things, the examination of the regulations and rules promulgated by the State Council and the second legislative tier. The State Council is China's highest administrative body and is responsible for drafting legislative bills for submission to the NPC or its Standing Committee.

The second legislative tier comprises the Provincial People's Congresses and their Standing Committees, in provincial, autonomous region and municipality-level government, and the ministerial government under the State Council. These can issue rules and regulations, based on local needs and department requirements, in line with the Constitution and laws made by the first tier. In addition, these rules and regulations must be reported by autonomous region governments to the first tier for approval or by provincial-level governments through local People's Congresses and by the ministerial-level government to the State Council for records.

Judicial Enforcement in China

The function of the Chinese judicial system was only restored in 1979 as part of the policy of reform. The Ministry of Justice, having been abolished in 1959, was re-established to administer the judicial system and legal reform. Its functions are supervision of personnel management, organization of training, allocation of funding to the courts and exchange of legal research with foreign judicial bodies. Judicial enforcement is mainly carried out in People's Courts in a four-tier system, with the Supreme People's Court at the top (see Figure 12.1). The Court is directly responsible to the National People's Congress and its Standing Committee, and has powerful jurisdiction over the lower courts. Below the Supreme People's Court are 33 provincial Higher People's Courts, 381 Intermediate People's Courts in provincially administered cities and almost 3000 Basic-Level People's Courts at the town and county level. In addition, there are 17000 People's Tribunals which provide legal services in remote areas (O'Connor and Lowe, 1996).

Special People's Courts and specialized IPR Protection Divisions dealing with patent disputes were established within the Intermediate and Higher People's Courts in 1993 (Figure 12.1). These courts have jurisdictional power to handle patent issues. When there is no special People's Court or IPR Protection Division, cases are handled in the economic divisions within the courts. Any individual or organization may bring a lawsuit when they believe that their patent rights and interests are being infringed. IPR litigation is first brought to the Intermediate Courts in cities of the provinces in which the alleged infringers reside or where infringement has occurred since most industries are above town and city level. In the event of a contested verdict, further proceedings can be continued in a Higher People's Court, whose verdict is final. The situation, however, is slightly different for companies based in the municipalities (Beijing, Shanghai, Tianjin and Chongqing). A company in Beijing can sue an infringer in the Beijing Higher People's Court with further proceedings in the Supreme People's Court if the result is unsatisfactory. By 1995, there had been some 3052 judicial cases relating to patents, of which 2557 have been resolved (Wen, 1996).

There has been a dramatic change in both the quantity and quality of judicial enforcement since 1979 as Chinese judges and lawyers have gradually gained significance and status with the increasing importance of judicial enforcement. Judges are appointed by the People's Congresses at different levels and serve a five-year term with a maximum of two terms. In 1986, there were only 40000 lawyers in China but this had increased to 70000 by 1994 and the government target was 150000 by 2000. This contrasts greatly with the USA, with an estimated one million lawyers in 2000 (O'Connor and Lowe, 1996) and suggests easier access to legal remedy than in China.

Dispute Settlement in China

Conventional dispute resolution in China is very different to that in the US system. According to the Economic Contracts Involving Foreign Interest Law, foreign enterprises operating in China should abide by Chinese law for contract dispute settlement. Issues not covered by Chinese law should be settled by following international practice. Disputes settlement amongst contracting parties takes the form of consultation, mediation, arbitration and then litigation.

Consultation is intended to seek common ground through meetings of the Boards of Directors so as to find an internal resolution acceptable to all parties. Mediation involves resolution by a third party, which may be a foreign investment administrative institution or association, foreign dispute mediation institution or arbitration institution. Mediation is traditionally practised in China because of its flexibility and simplicity. The Beijing Mediation Centre is the only mediation organ involved in foreign-related matters. Arbitration occurs when parties agree to submit to a non-governmental arbitration institution to find a solution. It is a rigorous quasi-judicial procedure that is also more flexible than litigation, saving time and money. The China International Economic and Trade Arbitration Commission (CIETAC) is a world-famous institution for arbitration. The economic boom since 1978 has seen a dramatic increase in the number of disputes and, by the early 1990s, CIETAC averaged 100 cases per annum (Potter, 1995). Litigation and a reliance on the adjudication of a court is viewed as a last resort. Litigation proceedings tend to be long and adversarial, undermining future cooperation in a way that may be detrimental to the involved parties.

The two preferred means of dispute settlement in China are consultation and mediation, not only because of the traditional cultural desire for harmony but also because of the significance of these methods. Traditionally, the Confucian ethic has emphasized social harmony and cohesiveness, thereby influencing the desire to solve disputes internally rather than by judicial process. Moreover, litigation was historically far more complex, costly and time-consuming than non-legal processes and consequently more unpredictable. Dispute settlement through consultation and mediation is seen as aiding the development of democracy and enhancing the legal system (O'Connor and Lowe, 1996), as well as assisting in repairing the relationship between the disputing parties. In addition, they lead to resolution through compromise rather than adversarial means. Consultation and mediation are also less complex to process and implement than legal action and assist the improvement in the work of the People's Courts (ibid.).

2. THE RATIONALE FOR THE DRAMATIC CHANGE IN CHINESE PATENT PROTECTION

For centuries, China has been thought of as xenophobic. Its relationship with the industrialized countries has been characterized by spectacular changes of imperialism and economic invasion. In recent years, however, the stereotypes have been changing in a more gradual and evolutionary manner because of its open economy. In essence, any exploration of the underlying reasons for the introduction of the patent system is an investigation of the origins of China's Open Door policy. The rapid introduction of the patent protection system can be seen as the natural consequence of a number of influences and developments both within and outside China. This can be partly attributed to China's desire to acquire advanced technology from the industrialized countries and to protect its own indigenous technology. Without proper IPR protection, however, few firms would be willing to transfer their technology to China and the industrialized developed countries, particularly the USA, have pushed for change. Meanwhile, international organizations, such as the WIPO and WTO, have also played an important role in enhancing IPR protection in China.

The Acquisition of Foreign Information and Technology

There is little doubt that the Chinese government recognized the need to gain access to new information and technologies in order to improve China's international competitiveness and, thereby, its rate of growth and development. In spite of the absolute size of both its economy and population, as a developing economy, China was unable to generate sufficiently high-level information and advanced techniques at the rate necessary for development. The lessons of other rapidly developing countries, such as Singapore and Korea, illustrated quite vividly the contribution made by technology transfer, particularly through FDI. The internal pressure for change implied a move not only away from Confucianism but also from Marxist, Leninist and Maoist thought.

In December 1978, the Chinese government introduced a general policy of reform involving opening the economy to the outside world. The encouragement and utilization of foreign investment became both a principal focus of the reform and the main economic objective in China. On 1 July 1979, the Law on Joint Ventures Using Chinese and Foreign Investment was promulgated. The policy, together with this Law, symbolizes the beginning of FDI inflows and the mechanism by which China might gain access to technology, capital and techniques. It was clear, however, that FDI and the transfer of associated information and techniques would not occur without a significant shift in China's historical approach to the protection and exploitation of IPR. Hence, a series of new legislation, dating from 1982, was rapidly introduced.

The Protection of Indigenous Chinese Technology

The export of technology from China is also a result of the Open Door policy. Technology exports began in the 1980s and have been managed formally only since 1986. Although exports are relatively small compared with technology imports, which began in the early 1950s, they have been gaining in importance since the Open Door policy has operated (Figure 12.2). The value of technology imports was $15.9 billion in 1997 while that of exports was only $5.5 billion. However, technology exports have been developing very rapidly.

The increasing importance of technology exports from China has made

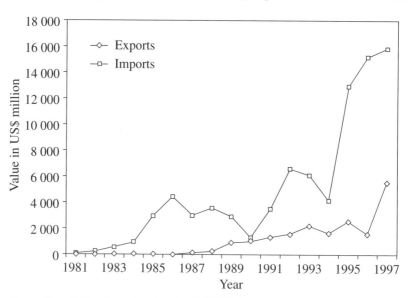

Source: Compiled by the authors based on MOFTEC (1983–98).

Figure 12.2   Chinese technology imports and exports

IPR protection crucial for indigenous technology. Some 70 to 80 per cent of Chinese technology exports were destined for developing countries (Jiang, 1995), most of which have weak IPR protection. At the same time, China has little experience in exporting technology and its laws and regulations provide only general guidance. The significant increase in Chinese exports of technology in recent years suggests that there has been an upsurge in the production of indigenous technology and that new laws and regulations are required to protect the interests of inventors and other IPR holders.

External Pressure from the Industrialized Countries

China's concern with IPR has, to some extent, been promoted by international pressure, especially from the USA, for greater IPR protection and action against piracy in developing countries. The confrontation between the industrialized countries and the developing world, exemplified by the series of IPR disputes between the USA and China, has led to the signing of a number of bilateral and multilateral agreements (Sherwood, 1990).

It has been argued that China's first encounter with IPR issues of this type occurred when its government was negotiating the Sino-US High Energy Physics Agreement and the Sino-US Trade Agreements with the US in 1979 (Zheng, 1996). Negotiations between the two countries reached stalemate because of differences over IPR protection. The USA argued strongly that IPR protection should be an integral part of any bilateral agreement on science and technology, culture and trade and that, in the absence of adequate protection, its representatives would not be permitted to sign. At the same time, the Chinese were extremely reluctant to sign agreements concerning matters of which they had little or no experience. After this debate with the USA, China began intensive research into the area of IPR protection, described as the first 'IPR fever' (Zheng, 1996).

The USA placed further pressure on China under what has become known as Special 301 under the 1988 Omnibus Trade and Competitiveness Act. The effect was to add grievances about IPR to the existing Section 301 regime (Lin, 1996), which authorizes US Trade Representatives (USTRs) to retaliate against countries that have undertaken unjustifiable, unreasonable or discriminatory trade practices. A Priority Watch List (PWL) of countries was established by the USTR to monitor IPR protection policies, acts and practices, in order to determine whether action under Special 301 was required. In addition, the USA used 'Special Mention', which refers to a list of countries that need to further enhance their IPR protection. Following a decision of the US International Trade Commission (USITC), Section 337 can be used to authorize the US Customs to detain all imported products associated with IPR infringement.

This legislation means that, in effect, any country wanting to establish trade relations with the USA must take account of Sections 301 and 337 or risk a trade war. During the period 1991–95, China was on the PWL twice (Table 12.1). After China became one of the priority countries under

Table 12.1   The USA's priority watch list countries, 1991-94

1991	1992	1993	1994
China	ROC (Taiwan)	Brazil	China
India	India	India	Argentina
Thailand	Thailand	Thailand	India

Source: Sun (1996).

Special 301, China and the USA conducted seven rounds of negotiations regarding IPR protection, known as the second period of 'IPR fever'. This created a major shock-wave in China, with IPR issues gaining high levels of publicity. In 1992, the Sino-US Memorandum of Understanding on Intellectual Property Rights was signed, China's Patent Law was amended and the threatened trade war was prevented. In 1994, however, China again became the main PWL country when the USA argued that its copyright protection was inadequate and also pointed to a lack of improvement in IPR protection after the 1992 Agreement. China and the USA again began negotiations with an agreement finally being reached in 1995, resulting in the signing of further bilateral agreements on IPR – the third wave of 'IPR fever'.

While other industrialized countries, especially the EU, have also influenced the improvement of IPR protection in China, their powers of persuasion were much less than those of the USA.[4] This is for a number of reasons: (i) the USA is the world leader in more areas of technology than any other country; (ii) it has the largest domestic market; (iii) it is the largest source of FDI; (iv) it could use (i)–(iii) along with Special 301 to adversely affect any particular economy where it felt IPR protection was inadequate. The USA has, characteristically, been quite adversarial in its threats to use Sections 301 and 337, and this appears to have exerted a strong influence on IPR protection in China.[5] In spite of all that has been discussed about the importance of external influences, it is unlikely that the combined pressure from Western countries alone would have produced the major changes in Chinese IPR protection that have taken place unless they had been pushing on an open door. The Chinese government acceded to Western pressure in order to further its Open Door policy and gain access to Western technologies.

The World Intellectual Property Organization

China joined the Convention Establishing the World Intellectual Property Organization (WIPO) and became a contracting country in 1980. This was the first IPR-related convention China had joined. Since then, it has ratified a series of international conventions and agreements: the Paris Convention for Industrial Property Protection (the Paris Convention) in 1985; the 1989 Treaty on Intellectual Property in Respect of Integrated Circuits; the 1989 Madrid Agreement concerning the International Registration of Marks (the Madrid Agreement); the 1992 Berne Convention for the Protection of Literary and Artistic Works (the Berne Convention); the 1992 Universal Copyright Convention; the 1992 Convention for the Protection of Producers of Phonograms against Unauthorized Duplication of their Phonograms; and the 1994 Patent Cooperation Treaty (PCT). As a consequence, the Patent Office in China has become a receiving office, an international search authority and an international preliminary examining authority of the PCT.

In addition to membership activities, different WIPO conventions have acted as model laws for China. For instance: the Patent Law was based on the Paris Convention; the Trademark Law on the Madrid Convention; and the Copyright Law on the Universal Copyright Convention. The significant influence of the WIPO on Chinese legislation and administration was particularly reflected in the early stages of China establishing IPR protection. China is now not only an active member of WIPO but its laws have remained in line with its different Conventions. The WIPO can be expected to continue to play an important role in harmonizing the IPR system in other countries.

The World Trade Organization

Of parallel importance to the WIPO was the creation of Trade-Related Aspects of Intellectual Property Rights (TRIPs) in the Uruguay Round, incorporated into the WTO (WTO, 1995). Under TRIPs, any country intent on gaining access to world markets must introduce and enforce IPR protection of the same standard as the industrialized countries within five years (ibid.). The WTO has played a crucial role in the improvement of the IPR system in China since the early 1990s. IPR protection has become a central issue since trade and IPR were linked in the Uruguay Round negotiations. China was not a member yet it took an active part in the negotiations and is a signatory to the Final Agreement on TRIPs.

There are three compelling reasons why China was keen to become a member of the WTO (Kwang, 1999):

- Membership will accelerate reform of the state-owned enterprises (SOEs). It also means that China is going to open further to the outside world, leading more foreign companies to invest and bring dynamic competition to the domestic market. It is estimated that FDI could reach $100 billion by 2005. In order to survive in this environment, most SOEs will be forced to reform themselves to be competitive and profitable.
- Membership will compel China to abide by international rules and regulations in trade and economics, such as IPR protection. As a consequence, it will better enhance cooperation and trust between China and other countries.
- Membership will intensify international integration because the WTO safeguards its members' interests, which will certainly assist China in transforming its economy.

The TRIPs Agreement has raised the standard for IPR protection. Therefore, it is not surprising that China amended most of its IPR laws during the TRIPs negotiations. For instance, the Patent Law and the Trademark Law were amended in 1992 and 1993 respectively. In 1993, China promulgated its first Anti-Unfair Competition Law. The first Copyright Law was announced after the TRIPs negotiation commenced. Computer Software Regulations were stipulated in 1991.

3.   THE AMENDMENT OF CHINA'S PATENT LAW BASED UPON TRIPs

The Patent Law in China has a history of less than 20 years. China promulgated its first Patent Law in 1984, based on the Paris Convention of the WIPO, which emphasized the importance of national treatment, priority rights, independence of patents and compulsory licensing. From the late 1980s, the international patent system entered a new phase because of the involvement of the WTO and the negotiation of the TRIPs Agreement. TRIPs has raised the standard of IPR protection, especially in the area of dispute settlement. This posed a need for change in China given that it was very keen to become a WTO member. Thus, in 1992, China made its first amendment of the Patent Law based on the TRIPs negotiations so as to bring domestic law into line with international law (Qiao, 1996).

The four main changes to China's Patent Law, based on TRIPs, are elaborated below. The first major change is the expansion of the protective scope of the Law to cover inventions relating to micro-organisms. TRIPs indicates that 'patents shall be available in any fields of technology' except 'diagnostic, therapeutic and surgical methods for the treatment of humans or animals' and 'plants and animals other than micro-organisms . . .' (TRIPs, Article 27). The amended Patent Law expanded the scope of protection into inventions relating to food, drinks and condiments, chemical substances and medicine, so bringing inventions concerning micro-organisms under protection.

The second amendment is the expansion of patentees' rights. The TRIPs enforces the patentees' rights by preventing third parties from making, using, selling or importing the invented products or products obtained by the patented process (TRIPs, Article 28). This authorizes exclusive import rights to the patentees for their inventions. The amended Patent Law adds this right and stresses that patentees have the right to forbid others from importing related products without their permission. Unauthorized imports constitute patent infringement (Patent Law, Article 11, CPR, 1992a).

The third major change is the extension of the duration of patent protection. The TRIPs stipulates that the term of protection should be at least 20 years for patents and ten years for industrial designs (TRIPs, Articles 26 and 33). China therefore extended its protection from 15 to 20 years for patents and from five years plus three years extension to ten years for industrial designs and utility models (Patent Law, Article 45).

The last major amendment relates to specifying the conditions for compulsory licensing. The Paris Convention does not specify the conditions of compulsory licensing whereas TRIPs provides more precise and comprehensive safeguards in this respect with 12 specific conditions (TRIPs, Article 31). The new Patent Law spells out the conditions for compulsory licensing, including national emergency, difficulties obtaining the rights within a period of time and requirements for a similar but more advanced invention. Further specific stipulations and conditions are included in Article 68 of the Patent Implementation Law, including the extent, period and limit of compulsory licensing. The 12 TRIPs conditions are thus reflected in the Patent Law and the Patent Implementation Law of China.

Apart from these major changes, several minor changes have also been made to be consistent with the TRIPs. In general, the TRIPs has brought more convenience to patentees, including unified requirements for application, approval and protection, and so on. China has replaced the old procedure for objection with a new procedure for revoking. Although China was not as yet a member, the amended law based on the TRIPs demonstrated its desire to be consistent with developments in international patent law.

The Patent Law is summarized in Table 12.2. The headings refer to changes based on the TRIPs. The Chinese government is currently negotiating with the WTO in becoming a contracting party. Only recently, the USA has withdrawn its objection and agreed on China's entry to the WTO.

Table 12.2   Summary of China's Patent Law

Objects	Invention	Utility model	Industrial design
Major Law	Patent Law and its Implementation Law		
First promulgation	1984		
Current version	1992		
Subject(s)	Investor(s), creator(s) and/or consignee(s)		
Requirement	Novelty, inventiveness, and practical applicability		Novelty and applicability
Scope	Products or processes including those in chemical, pharmaceutical, and food and beverage industries		
Application:			
1. Starting date	Filing date		
2. Principle	First to file		
3. Priority application	Within one year	Within six months	
4. Authority	Patent Office (PO)		
Examination and approval		Preliminary examination	
	Substantial examination	No	
Patent holders' rights	1. Make, use and sell related patented products		
	2. Make, use and sell related products by patented method		
	3. Prevent from importing identical products or products made from using the patented method		
	4. Assign the right upon approval from the PO		
	5. License the right with record in the PO		
	6. Right of cessation		
	7. Right to legal protection		
Compulsory licensing	1. National emergency		
	2. Entities or individuals cannot obtain licences in a reasonable period of time		
	3. Exploitation of similar but earlier invention for the purposes of more advanced inventions		
Terms of protection	20 years	10 years	
Infringement solution	Civil procedure, administrative procedure and legal procedure, including injunction, fine, damage compensation, etc.		

Source: Summarized by the authors based on the *Patent Law of the PRC* (1992).

There were other barriers to China's membership of the WTO, however, including tariffs and human rights. For example, the average tariff on imports in most developing countries is 15 per cent but in China it is 23 per cent (Reuvid and Li, 1996).

4. THE DRAMATIC CHANGE IN PATENTING ACTIVITIES IN CHINA

This section examines the evolution of foreign IPR activities in China since the changes in legislation after 1982. The major amendment of the Patent Law in 1992 indicates the important role of the WTO TRIPs Agreement as a model law to enhance Chinese patent legislation. As a consequence of this amendment, Chinese patent activities have also changed dramatically, reflecting the practical effect of the WTO. As noted at the outset, foreign companies seek patent, trademark and other forms of IPR protection as a prerequisite for subsequent licensing activity. Patents are generally linked with innovative industrial activity and are often the subject of technology licensing activities. Further, they are an important source of technical information for China's own R&D activities. Utility models are less widely used although a number of countries such as Japan have used them for many years. They tend to be aimed at more minor innovative activity, hence 'petty patents', and they are intended more as a stimulus to domestic rather than foreign innovators.

There is already some indication in the literature of the importance of IPR flows to China (Qiao, 1996). The following section presents a detailed analysis which utilizes the annual statistical reports of the WIPO to explore the activities of both Chinese residents and foreign-based nationals in terms of patents, designs and utility models. The activities of foreign-based nationals are then broken down in detail by country of origin. Before proceeding, however, it is necessary to note a number of important features of the patent data. First, although all of the countries are signatories to the WIPO Agreement and have broadly similar laws, there are a number of remaining differences – as this discussion makes clear. Second, countries make significantly different use of the different forms of IPR protection. For example, France makes much more extensive use of trademarks, while Germany makes more extensive use of patents. In part, this reflects different industrial structures and areas of creativity across countries. Third, there are some differences in the way in which similar laws are used and interpreted across countries. For example, the Japanese tend to split their inventions into component parts and apply for a separate patent for each part, while the USA tends on balance to have much broader patents.

Trends in Patenting Activity by Chinese Residents and Non-residents

It is useful to begin by reviewing the relative levels of resident and foreign-based (non-resident) patenting activity within China. The comparison reveals important differences between the levels of activity of residents and non-residents across the different areas of patent protection. These differences again reflect the level of inventiveness that is required to obtain protection. The linkages of such differences with inventiveness emerge more clearly with the passage of time and these are unlikely to be visible given the relatively short time period of data available to the present study. The figures presented focus upon application activities in the main, as opposed to grants, since these provide a clearer indication of the growing flows of patents into China.[6]

The growth in patent applications in China is shown Figure 12.3. At the

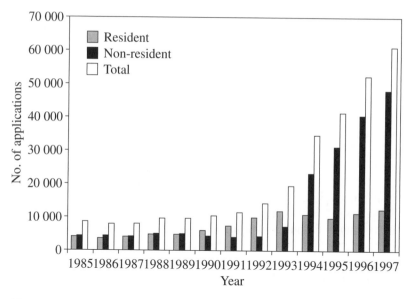

Figure 12.3   Resident versus foreign patent applications filed in China, 1985–97

start of the period, there were roughly equal numbers of domestic and foreign applications. While resident applications grew more quickly than non-resident over the period 1985–92, there was a sudden surge in foreign activity after 1992. This upsurge appears to coincide with China's modification of its patent law in 1992 so as to be compatible with international practice. The net result, however, is that total applications in China from all sources increased exponentially. Whatever the pattern of applications, grants to foreigners exceeded the corresponding grants to residents in every year from 1985 to 1997 inclusive, perhaps indicating the higher quality of non-resident applications. Foreign applications formed around 50 per cent of total applications and grants to non-residents about 61 per cent of total grants.

Figure 12.4 illustrates design activity in China and shows that residents

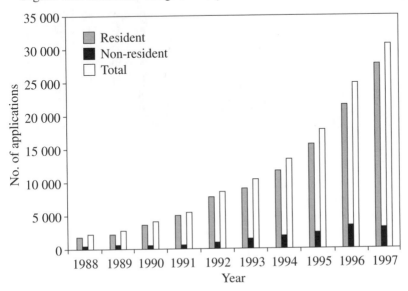

Figure 12.4   Resident versus foreign industrial design applications filed in China, 1988–97

largely dominate design applications and registrations. Nevertheless, the level of foreign activity is not insignificant and there is a major jump in design applications by non-residents between 1992 and 1998. Similar, although smaller, increases in foreign registrations occurred, lagging behind the application figures. The design data are similar to patents in at least one respect, however, in that the ratio of registrations to applications is higher for non-residents; while foreign applications form only 12.2 per cent of total applications, they form just over 18 per cent of total registrations.

Utility models have a lower degree of inventiveness than patents but appear to be important in the early phases of economic development and for domestic rather than foreign inventors.[7] The data confirm that the vast bulk of utility models applied for or deposited in China were by residents rather than by foreigners. In 1995, only 312 out of a total of about 44 000

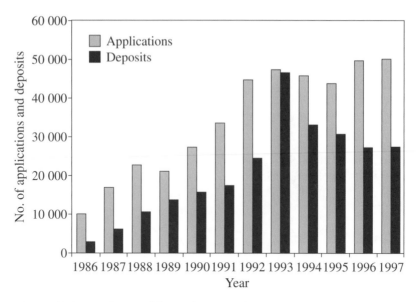

Figure 12.5   Utility models in China: applications and deposits, 1986–97

applications originated from outside China. Figure 12.5 therefore ignores
the domestic versus foreign aspect and provides data on the growth in total
applications and deposits over the period 1986–97. The picture is one of
major growth in the area of minor inventions, rising from just under 10000
applications in 1986 to just under 47000 in 1993, before falling back somewhat to the figure of about 44000 by the end of the period. This suggests a
major growth in lower-level inventive activity by China during the period
following the introduction of the Open Door policy.

The overall growth in IPR in force within China is shown in Figure 12.6,
using the partial data available for patents, designs, and utility models in
force. Given the scarcity of data for patents, after the first few years – where
the figures are known – the cumulative sum of patent grants is used as an
estimate of the stock. This is adjusted proportionally to be consistent with
the 1995 available figure of patents in force. The results show a strong
growth in the patent stock, reaching a total of just under 20000 by the end
of the period, of which around 16000 are of foreign origin. Total designs
in force show a very similar pattern and level to patents, perhaps growing
more weakly earlier in the period but more strongly later. Designs in force
reach just over 20000 by the end of the period but only about 18 per cent
(just under 4000) of these are of foreign origin. Interestingly, utility models
grow much more strongly over this period than either patents or designs.
By the end of the period there are around 80000 utility models in force and

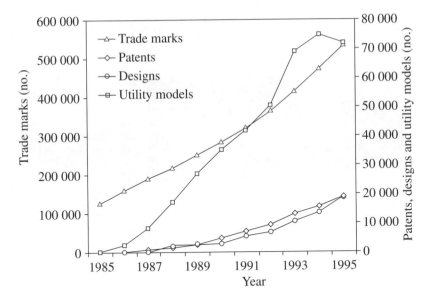

Figure 12.6   *Intellectual property rights (IPRs) in force in China,*
                 1985–95

these are, in number, by far the most important area of IPR activity in
China considered in the present study.

Patenting Activity in China by Country of Origin

The above data demonstrate the rapid growth in patenting activity within
China, with a significant proportion of that activity being undertaken by
non-residents. This section is concerned with the countries involved in
patenting activity within China. Figure 12.7 shows the distribution of
patent flows by country of origin, giving the proportion of the patents
attributable to each country over the period 1985–95. As noted above,
patents tend to be linked with industrial inventions and are often argued to
be associated with more fundamental inventive outputs than utility models
or, indeed, the creative activities that underpin trademarks or designs. It is
perhaps not surprising to find that these flows are dominated by the world's
most important technological players, the USA and Japan. Only Germany
comes close to these two, although the total across the EU is approximately
the same magnitude as the US figure.

     Information about the distribution of design protection by country of
origin is provided in Figure 12.8. Again, it is clear that Japan, the USA and
Germany are the top three ranked countries. Japan's top position reflects

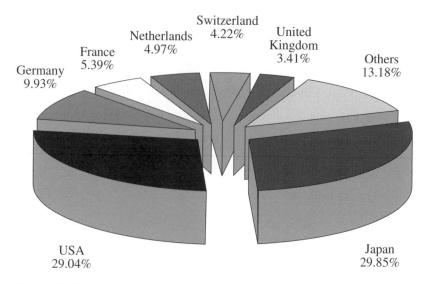

Figure 12.7   Patenting activity in China

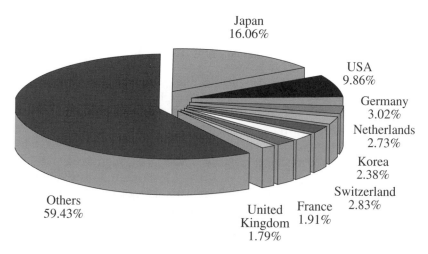

Figure 12.8   Industrial design activity in China

its generally much greater domestic use of design protection than other
countries. Interestingly, Korea appears in the listing with 3 per cent of the
designs registered within China. Designs are generally argued to be associated with a lower degree of inventiveness and, for countries that eventually attain sustained economic development, they are a precursor for

in-house R&D activity, as in the case of Japan. A consequence of this somewhat lower level of creativity is that design activity is again more evenly spread across countries than patenting activity.

5. THE NEED FOR FURTHER INTELLECTUAL PROPERTY RIGHTS PROTECTION IN CHINA

Since the amendment of Patent Law in 1992, the international patent system has developed further. Although the above discussion demonstrates that the WTO has, undoubtedly, been influential in the development of Chinese patent legislation and activities, the amendment was made during the Uruguay negotiations. The WTO negotiations continued until the TRIPs Agreement was signed in 1995. The finalized TRIPs Agreement has improved the draft and thus raises the necessity for China to make further improvement to its patent system. Therefore, it is important to be aware of the gaps between TRIPs and the Patent Law. The major gaps lie in five areas, as outlined below.

Separate Protection for Patents, Utility Models and Industrial Designs

The Patent Law in China protects inventions, utility models and industrial designs but it can be argued that separate protection would be more appropriate for three reasons. First, separate protection is consistent with the TRIPs Agreement which stipulates that members shall be free to meet the obligation for protection through industrial design law or through copyright law (TRIPs, Article 25). Second, both industrial designs and utility models have different features from inventions. This can be seen from the definitions of the three different rights. Utility model is the exclusive right given to inventors or creators for their minor technological solutions relating to a product or a process for a certain period of time. It is also called petty patent because of its lower inventiveness compared to a patent. Industrial design is the right given to designers for their new designs of patterns and/or colours with artistic features for industrial application. Thus, in terms of technological progress, industrial designs and utility models are far behind inventions. Therefore, separate protection can provide more motivation to inventors since inventions represent more advanced technologies. Third, separate protection is beneficial to consumers. When inventions, industrial designs and utility models are granted, they are all called patents. Most consumers in China as well as outside do not understand the differences between them. A product described as having industrial design patent would be assumed to represent significant technological progress. In order not to mislead consumers, therefore, it is also necessary to provide separate protection for the different three rights.

Equal Rights of Proceedings for Three Different Rights Holders

Under the current Patent Law, patents for inventions, industrial designs and utility models have unequal rights for proceedings. The owners of inventions can go to the court for further solution if their inventions are not granted patent rights after re-examination is undertaken by the PREB (Patent Law, Article 43, CPR, 1992b). Owners of industrial designs and utility models, however, have no rights to do so because the re-examination decision of the PREB is final. In order to be equal under the law and motivate creators in these two areas, equal proceedings should be given to the owners of industrial designs and utility models.

Problems of the Two-tier Legislative System

China has, like the USA, a two-tier legislative system. Any provincial and ministerial-level government can implement laws and regulations in addition to the central government. Although second-tier regulations should be in line with the central government laws and regulations, there are no specific stipulations to coordinate related problems. As a result, inconsistency is inevitable. Future amendment needs to stipulate how to prevent such inconsistency.

Legal Enforcement Problems

Legal enforcement is perhaps the most important task relating to IPR in China. This refers not only to better protection of IPR but also organizational coordination and cooperation so as to make IPR enforcement adequate and efficient. One of the important developments of the TRIPs is its requirement for dispute settlement and legal enforcement. The development of the IPR system in China has been revolutionary in that it has taken less than ten years to establish, while the enforcement of IPR will be an evolutionary process because it takes time for the public to realize the need for IPR protection. More importantly, it takes time for different organizations to work harmoniously. There are 23 provinces, five autonomous regions, and four municipalities in the second tier of governmental organizations plus lower-level organizations, all of which form a complicated network. A new IPR environment will gradually form in China if enforcement begins in these organizations while government publicizes the importance of IPR to Chinese society as a whole.

Cooperation and coordination between administrative and judicial organizations at different levels and the same levels need to be enhanced in particular because they are crucial to the enforcement of patent protection in China. An example reveals the problems between an administrative body in China and a pharmaceutical company in the USA. The company sued the Chinese State Drug Administration for not granting protection to its product in China although, based on the Sino-US bilateral Agreement on Patents, administrative protection should have been granted. The case now is being filed in China's Supreme People's Court for settlement (analysed in Yang, 2001).

The Amendment of Ambiguous Articles

The Patent Law in China is basically in line with the stipulations of the Paris Convention and the TRIPs Agreement, but there still exist ambiguous and inconsistent articles. When China promulgated its first Patent Law in 1984, the Paris Convention played the role of a model law. TRIPs introduced new requirements for international patent protection and IPR. Thus, there were amendments to the Patent Law in 1992 based on the TRIPs negotiations. The final TRIPs Agreement, however, signed at the end of 1994, has become the most comprehensive agreement relating to IPR (Gervais, 1998). It sets a higher standard than any other previously signed conventions. Therefore, inconsistency between the Chinese IPR Laws and the TRIPs Agreement is inevitable. The following is not intended to elaborate exhaustively on each inconsistent article in the Chinese laws but to outline one example in the IPR legislation (Yang, 2001).

There is a very controversial stipulation in the Patent Law with regard to unknowing infringement. TRIPs Article 45 stipulates the following:

1. The judicial authorities shall have the authority to order the infringer to pay the right holder damages . . . by an infringer who knowingly, or with reasonable grounds to know, engaged in infringing activity.
2. In appropriate cases, Members may authorize the judicial authorities to order recovery of profits and/or payment of pre-established damages even where the infringer did not knowingly, or with reasonable grounds to know, engage in infringing activity.

Article 45.1 refers to damages; Article 45.2 refers to 'pre-established damages'. In other words, some statutory provisions, for example, in Canadian and US law, allow damage awards regardless of actual loss. 'The judicial authorities shall have the authority' to order compensation only when there is actual or constructive knowledge of infringement. Article 45.2 indicates that relevant authorities may order compensation based on damages and/or profit, but they are not bound to do so.[8]

Article 62.2 of the Chinese Patent Law stands in contrast with regard to unknowing infringement.[9]

> Article 62. None of the following shall be deemed an infringement of the patent right: . . . (2) where any person uses or sells a patented product not knowing that it was made and sold without the authorization of the patentee; . . .

This article actually expresses that there is no infringement if a person does not know that (s)he is using or selling a patented product that was made or sold without authorization. The distinction the article draws between making the product, which is an infringement, and unknowing use or selling, which is not an infringement, seems deliberate. 'The article should not be couched in the language of non-infringement but should rather authorize the grant only of an injunction and perhaps seizure of existing stock.' As a result, this would fully comply with TRIPs. Therefore, the Patent Law in China must be amended to comply fully with TRIPs for the benefit of China's accession to the WTO.

In short, some loopholes remain in China's patent system. Further improvement of the system is necessary to give better protection to patenting activities. Some changes can be made quickly, such as the ambiguous articles, but most of the problems will take time to resolve, such as the problems of organizational coordination and cooperation.

6. CONCLUSIONS AND IMPLICATIONS

This chapter introduces the current Chinese patent system and demonstrates the crucial role of the WTO in the development of the patent system and patenting activities in China. The triple management system in China was only established systematically in the 1980s. The Patent Law and the Implementation Law are the major legislative guidance. The Patent Office is the chief administrative organization dealing with patent-related applications, examinations and even the administrative settlement of disputes. Patent disputes and infringement litigation is undertaken in the People's Courts, such as Intermediate People's Courts and its higher levels. The rapid formation of the patent management system in China is a natural consequence of both internal motivation and external push. Internally, China has a strong desire to acquire sophisticated foreign technologies but, without proper IPR protection, there is little desire to transfer this. At the same time, China also exports its indigenous technology to other countries and these cannot be properly protected without proper guidance. Externally, the leading industrialized countries, especially the USA, have pushed for significant change in IPR protection because of their extensive business in China. Further, international organizations, such as WIPO and the WTO, have played an important role in promoting IPR protection. WIPO strongly influenced the drafting of China's Patent Law in 1984, while the WTO TRIPs Agreement influenced the 1992 Amendment of the Patent Law and patenting activities in China.

The influence of the WTO is mainly reflected in two aspects. First, the WTO TRIPs Agreement is the model for the 1992 Patent Law Amendment. Four major changes are based on articles in the TRIPs, including the expansion of its protective scope, patentees' rights, the extension of the protection period and more specific conditions for compulsory licensing. Second, the statistical evidence indicates that the introduction of the Patent Law in 1984 gave rise to a rapid increase in the flows of patents to China by Western countries. It is also clear that the 1992 Amendment produced a further jump in patent flows. Patent applications reached over 40000 in 1995 and, bearing in mind the lag between application and grant, there were around 20000 patents in force by this time. The bulk of these patents were of foreign origin and will provide a rich base for exploitation, including licensing activity, and a source of technological information for Chinese researchers.

The WTO has influenced both patent law and patenting activities in China and it can be expected to play an even more important role in the future because of China's WTO membership. Further improvement of the patent system is therefore necessary to be consistent with TRIPs. The analysis of the Chinese patent system in the context of TRIPs suggests that five major improvements are crucial. These areas for amendment include separate protection for patents, utility models and industrial designs, separate and equal proceeding rights for the holders of inventions, utility models and industrial designs and changes to ambiguous articles. The remaining two areas, relating to problems of legal enforcement by organizational coordination and cooperation and consistency of the two-tier legislation, will only develop with time since they cannot be improved by regulation. More importantly, they require action by different government organizations and progress in this aspect will represent the biggest future development of the Chinese patent system.

This chapter demonstrates, indirectly, that IPR laws and their enforcement play a crucial role in the process of economic development. Without such laws, the incentive for trade may be severely reduced in so far as the affected product cannot be copied by the importing nation. The potential barriers that the absence of appropriate IPR laws and weak enforcement impose on FDI and technology transfer are even more significant. This chapter shows that the introduction of IPR protection laws in China was a natural corollary of the Open Door policy. This was a very significant development which implies that developing countries need to introduce IPR laws so as to attract foreign capital and provide a safeguard to the owners of technology.

NOTES

1. Other laws and regulations relating to patents are the *Regulation on Patent Commissioning* (April 1991); *The Implementing Regulations for the Patent Law of the People's Republic of China* (December 1992); *Answers Given by the Supreme People's Court to Questions on Hearing of Cases of Patent Dispute* (December 1992); and *The Provisions on the Implementation of Patent Co-operation Treaty in China* (November 1993).
2. First-to-file: the first applicant(s) to file for the same patent should have the priority to acquire the patent right. The first filing date is either the date on which the Patent Office receives the application, if made in person, or the postmark indicating the date of sending, if the application is by mail.
3. Patent agencies refer to 'The service organs that apply for patents or handle other patent-related affairs on behalf of their consignors and within their authorized powers', quoted from Article 3 of *The Regulations on Patent Commissioning* (March 1991).
4. The USA has not only taken the lead in the promotion of IPR protection in the context of developing countries but has also encouraged debate amongst developed countries. This led to some disagreements, particularly with Japan, whose IPR system has significant differences with other developed countries, but also, to some extent, with EU countries. However, the principal points of conflict have been with developing countries, especially with China.
5. The willingness of the USA to invoke Special 301 is itself understandable given the results of a number of surveys regarding the inadequacies of IPR protection in developing countries and their consequences for US companies. Perhaps the most influential survey was by the US International Trade Commission in 1988 which reported on interviews with American MNEs regarding the adequacy of IPR protection outside the USA. The findings suggest that most developing countries had weak IPR protection and MNEs had significant difficulties dealing with IPR issues. The resulting loss was set at a total of US$23.8 billion (Sherwood, 1990). Similar studies have been conducted by individual researchers and organisations (see ibid.).
6. The grant data, or the equivalent for other forms of IPRs such as registrations in the case of trademarks, are affected by the speed of operation of the administrative system but broadly show the same trends. Issues regarding grants are discussed in the text.
7. The authors have separate evidence of the importance of utility models and designs during the early phases of development of Japan, both during the interwar and the early postwar periods.
8. Discussion with Professor D. Vaver from the Oxford Intellectual Property Research Centre at the Manchester School of Management, 17 May 2001.
9. Most Chinese companies are state-owned. How far these companies are required by law to observe patents is a serious problem. The Sino-US MOU appears to track Article 31 of TRIPs allowing state-owned enterprises to use patents on condition of paying reasonable compensation without being subject to injunctions. This issue is too substantial to be directly discussed in this chapter (discussion with Professor D. Vaver from the Oxford Intellectual Property Research Centre at the Manchester School of Management, UMIST, 17 May 2001).

REFERENCES

CPR (China, People's Republic) (1992a), *The Patent Law of the People's Republic of China*, Beijing.

CPR (China, People's Republic) (1992b), *The Implementing Regulations for the Patent Law of the People's Republic of China*, Beijing.

Gervais, D. (1998), *The TRIPs Agreement: Drafting History and Analysis*, London: Sweet & Maxwell.

Jiang, Q. (1995), *International Technology Transfer Law and Practice*, Beijing: Law Publishing.

Kwang, M. (1999), 'China: compelling reasons to join WTO', *The Sunday Times*, 10 October, p. 47.

Lin, L.H. (1996), 'The trend of international intellectual property protection', in P.C.B. Liu and A.Y. Sun (eds), *Intellectual Property Protection in the Asia-Pacific Region: a Comparative Study*, Occasional Papers/Reprints Series in Contemporary Asian Studies, No. 4. (135), pp. 149–52.

O'Connor, B.E. and D.A. Lowe (1996), 'Comparative analysis of intellectual property dispute resolution processes in mainland China, Taiwan and the United States', in P.C.B. Liu and A.Y. Sun (eds), *Intellectual Property Protection in the Asia-Pacific Region: a Comparative Study*, Occasional Papers/Reprints Series in Contemporary Asian Studies. No. 4 (135), pp. 57–132.

Potter, P.B. (1995), *Foreign Business Law in China: Past Progress Future Challenges*, San Francisco: The 1990 Institute.

Qiao, D. (1996), 'On co-ordination between China's Patent Law and the international trend of development', in C. Zheng (ed.), *Intellectual Property Studies*, No. 2, Beijing: Chinese Fang Zheng Publishing House.

Reuvid, J. and Y. Li (eds) (1996), *Doing Business with China*, London: Kogan Page.

Sherwood, R. (1990), *Intellectual Property and Economic Development*, Oxford: Westview Press.

Sun, A.Y. (1996), 'The prospect for a Dispute Settlement Mechanism under the World Trade Organization – international intellectual property and trade disputes: multinational dispute settlement process and the use of unilateral trade sanctions under US Law', in P.C.B. Liu and A.Y. Sun (eds), *Intellectual Property Protection in the Asia-Pacific Region: a Comparative Study*, Occasional Papers/Reprints Series in Contemporary Asian Studies, No. 4 (135), pp. 153–83.

Wegner, H.C. (1996), 'Patent harmonization on the Pacific Rim', in P.C.B. Liu and A.Y. Sun (eds), *Intellectual Property Protection in the Asia-Pacific Region: a Comparative Study*, Occasional Papers/Reprints Series in Contemporary Asian Studies, No. 4 (135), pp. 25–55.

Wen, X. (1996), 'Patent protection in China: present state and future prospect', in C. Zheng (ed.), *Intellectual Property Studies, Volume 2*, Beijing: China Fang Zheng Publishing, pp. 45–64.

WTO (1995), *Trade-Related Aspects of Intellectual Property Rights (TRIPs)*, Geneva: WTO.

Yang, D. (2001), Corporate Intellectual Property Flows from the UK and USA: a Study of Problems, Causes and Solutions, PhD thesis, Manchester School of Management, UMIST.

Zheng, C. (1996), *TRIPs*, Beijing: Law Publishing.

Index